The Wheel of Law

The Wheel of Law

INDIA'S SECULARISM IN COMPARATIVE
CONSTITUTIONAL CONTEXT

Gary Jeffrey Jacobsohn

PRINCETON UNIVERSITY PRESS

PRINCETON AND OXFORD

Copyright © 2003 by Princeton University Press
Published by Princeton University Press, 41 William Street,
Princeton, New Jersey 08540
In the United Kingdom: Princeton University Press,
3 Market Place, Woodstock, Oxfordshire OX20 1SY

All Rights Reserved

Second printing, and first paperback printing, 2005
Paperback ISBN 0-691-12253-9

The Library of Congress has cataloged the cloth edition of this book as follows

Jacobsohn, Gary J., 1946–
The wheel of law : India's secularism in comparative constitutional
context / Gary Jeffrey Jacobsohn.
p. cm.
Includes bibliographical references and index.
ISBN 0-691-09245-1 (cl : alk. paper)
1. Hinduism and state— India.
2. Religion and state—India. I. Title.
KNS2162 .J33 2003
323.44'2'095409045—dc21   2002024301

British Library Cataloging-in-Publication Data is available

This book has been composed in Janson

Printed on acid-free paper. ∞

pup.princeton.edu

Printed in the United States of America

3 5 7 9 10 8 6 4 2

For

Vince Barnett
Dave Booth
Mac Brown
Jim Burns
Fred Greene
Kurt Tauber

CONTENTS

PREFACE

"RELIGION," wrote Jawaharlal Nehru from a prison cell in 1944, "though it has undoubtedly brought comfort to innumerable human beings and stabilized society by its values, has checked the tendency to change and progress inherent in human society."[1] About a century earlier, Alexis de Tocqueville, after traversing the United States to examine its prison system, instead reflected on the place of religion in democracy. "When . . . any religion has struck its roots deep into a democracy, beware that you do not disturb it; but rather watch it carefully, as the most precious bequest of aristocratic ages."[2] For both Nehru and Tocqueville, religion was a restraining influence on changes in civil society, which for the Indian nationalist was a problem and for the French legislator a blessing. Their common devotion to constitutional democracy led them to weigh the political contributions of piety and spirituality quite differently.

This divergence is certainly understandable. As much as the transition to democracy in Tocqueville's America had occurred without a protracted social struggle, in Nehru's India prospects for democracy were directly tied to a transcendence of social divisions entrenched over many centuries as natural and just. If in some democracies religion has been attractive as a potential ally of regime principles, in others it has had a distinctly more adversarial relationship with the democratic way of life.

Religion is most threatening to liberal democracy where it informs national identity or permeates everyday life. In such places the problem of religion is more acute, and the task of securing religious liberty more urgent. How can courts that aspire to defend religious liberty meet such challenges? We have a surer grasp over how religious liberty is protected in societies where religion is fragmented and where its reach into everyday life is relatively shallow. The project of defending religious liberty and secular aspirations in a deeply religious society—India—is the subject of this book.

[1] Jawaharlal Nehru 1997, 511.
[2] Tocqueville 1945, vol. 1.

How do constitutional design and interpretation address this question? I strive for an answer by exploring some striking facets of the Indian experiment in secular governance. Though the book focuses on India and the constitutional dimensions of its commitment to secularism, I hope these pages will contribute more broadly to a spirited discussion within jurisprudential circles that centers on the constitutional essentials of a liberal democratic polity. Accordingly, I have placed the Indian case within a comparative trio that includes the United States and Israel, whose contrasting experiences in secular constitutionalism support an analytical framework that illuminates the complex political interface between spiritual and temporal concerns.

Why the United States and Israel? Through a long scholarly engagement with the constitutional systems in these countries, I have come to appreciate the wisdom in Seymour Martin Lipset's observation that "Nations can be understood only in comparative perspective."[3] Comparing both of these polities clarifies each; adding yet a third country only further enhances the images. But a more compelling reason—certainly more so than my personal interests—lies in the specific analytical perspectives Israel and the United States offer for enriching a comparative study of secularism, targeting India as its principal player.

Religion in Israel, much like in India, presents such a formidable challenge to constitutional forms and aspirations that the failure (or at least extended delay) to codify a formal constitution in the Jewish State stems from the centrality of religious identity in defining the nation's political identity. No similar commitment to religious nationalism has obstructed the development of India's constitution, even if some voices in India continue to deem Israel a model worth emulating. Rather, the strongest religious contender in India's bout with constitutional ideals has always been Nehru's professed fear that ingrained theological beliefs and practices will complicate the movement to embrace democratic justice. India's complex secularism is, at its core, a commitment to major social reconstruction. If this commitment is to be undermined, the source of its undoing will likely be the politics of ethno/religious revivalism, rather than any explicit campaign to defend historically sanctioned social privilege. Viewed comparatively, the model of a nation as a homeland for a particular people may, as in Israel, comport with a genuine secular regard for religious freedom, yet elsewhere, as in India, contradict the essentials of secular aspiration.

The American approach to the Church/State divide recalls its Western roots in assuming that religion can be distilled from the public sphere, though whether they should be maintained separately is still debated. This contrasts sharply with the Indian setting, where, despite a similar call

---

[3] Lipset 1990, xiii.

for State neutrality toward the country's various religions, a profoundly different view prevails on the possibility, let alone the desirability, of relegating the spiritual life to the private realm. Religion pervades both places, but how deeply it penetrates the fabric of daily life has decisive constitutional implications for the two polities. Thus in India, where faith and piety are more directly inscribed in routine social patterns, judges cannot avoid the perilous jurisprudential vortex of theological controversy as conveniently as their American counterparts. The pressures on them to establish which contested practices are essential to the belief structures of religious communities can be, and sometimes are, resisted. But more frequently than American judges, Indian jurists in religion cases are burdened by interpretive responsibilities that exceed their field of expertise. Once again, these alternative perspectives underscore Nehru's caution against religion's regressive tendencies. The American comparison reveals an important constitutional reality: liberal indifference to the substance of religious belief more readily thrives where social conditions are less dictated by religion.

Undoubtedly, including additional examples would appeal to some readers. Were my main objective to test specific hypotheses about secularism and constitutional democracy, a larger field of comparison would be necessary. I hope, however, that even these readers will ultimately value what is essentially an interpretive work that comprehends the "comparative context" of India's secularism. As I have suggested above, only a broader political context illuminates the qualities that distinguish, or at least highlight, the Indian constitutional experience. But this context also incorporates the extended cultural setting that moors a constitutional document or arrangement. Such an attempt to discern a system's constitutional logic from its background social and cultural circumstances embodies the Tocquevillian method. Tocqueville, however, did not explicitly discuss methodology, a void we have since filled through greater self-consciousness about the methods in our social science. Recently, for example, the term *constitutional ethnography* has come to define an approach that relies heavily upon "thick" accounts of actual polities to probe how constitutional systems function.[4] I do not view my work as quite as anthropological as this term suggests, but I have pursued its process in scrutinizing context to develop theoretical possibilities about the trajectory of constitutional design and experience. Above all, I trace the ways in which regimes' founding commitments become encoded in their constitutional schemes and, in turn, inform such fundamental issues as the role of religion in politics and society.

---

[4] The term has been developed by Kim Lane Scheppele, a constitutional scholar at the University of Pennsylvania Law School.

Evidence of these commitments abounds in all the obvious sources: constituent assembly debates, testimonies of key participants in the work of constitutional construction, Supreme Court opinions, and, of course, the official texts themselves. However, understanding how founding principles—idealized abstractions—apply to concrete constitutional scenarios should not depend solely on evidence from the printed page. When Tocqueville arrived in the United States to begin his famous nine-month visit, he immediately noted the strong spirit of religion and its salutary political impact for democratic prospects. This diverged from his experience in France, where religion and freedom were in great tension with one another. "My desire to discover the causes of this phenomenon increased from day to day. In order to satisfy it I questioned the members of all the sects; I sought especially the society of the clergy, who are the depositaries of the different creeds and are especially interested in their duration."[5] From these encounters, he learned that the "peaceful dominion of religion" in the United States was attributable "mainly to the separation of church and state."[6] Intrigued, he continued to troll for the meaning and characteristics of this separation.

Through direct contact with India's constitutional culture, I have sharpened my understanding of that particular nation's secular vision. I have spoken with judges, politicians, scholars, journalists, and academics about many topics, including their involvement in the controversies discussed in these pages. Others have helped me to appreciate more fully the points of contact between the Constitution and the broader political culture. The cab driver in Mumbai, who was "honored" to deliver me to an interview with the leader of the most extreme Hindu nationalist political party in India, worshipfully referred to this leader as "the King of India." The architect in New Delhi, who, while displaying all the worldly characteristics one has come to associate with the burgeoning Indian middle class, allowed me to see how devoted he and his family remained to a traditional discipline of religious practice and belief. Some of the insights inspired by these and other encounters are, admittedly, possible to glean from prose accounts available in many local American libraries; but to satisfy myself of their import for, and relevance to, an interpretive work of constitutional analysis, I relied very heavily on firsthand experience.

The book is divided into two parts. Part 1 presents India's model of secular constitutional design within an analytical framework that incorporates the Israeli and American alternatives. The term *alternatives* may be questioned, since it implies a degree of freedom in the choice of a secular model that may, given my emphasis on the variability of religion's

---

[5] Tocqueville 1945, vol. 1, 319.
[6] Ibid.

penetration into social institutions and practices, be difficult to justify. Whether religion is "thickly" or "thinly" constituted determines the options available to constitution-makers and reformers alike. However, there are always choices to be made, even if they are limited by circumstance. For example, though what I term the *assimilative* model of American secularism may not transfer seamlessly to the Israeli or Indian environments, aspects of American Church/State jurisprudence could benefit places where religion and political experience differ from the United States. Similarly, the American and Israeli cultures may not welcome the wholesale transplantation of India's *ameliorative* model to their respective shores, but each could selectively borrow ideas and approaches from Indian jurists and politicians. Whether such comparative reflection on the diversity of secular experience can spark creative thinking about optimizing the performance of constitutional democracies is by no means certain. But I would like to think it could.

Among the challenges to secularism and constitutional democracy in India, the political ascendance of forces identified with Hindu nationalism has attracted worldwide attention. In part 2 I consider this threat through the lens of several landmark cases in which the Supreme Court became a dramatic venue for the ongoing struggle to legitimize the conflation of Hinduism and Indian nationhood. These cases implicate two controversial pillars of Indian governance—one constitutional (the Center's [Central Government of India] power to dismiss elected governments in the states), the other statutory (the rules for conducting elections)—that expand the argument over Indian secularism to include current questions hotly debated among political and legal theorists. Are there features of a liberal political order so fundamental that they should be protected from ever being nullified by constitutional amendment? Does such a regime's commitment to democratic deliberation require that it ban religious rhetoric, which can be seen to conflict with reasoned discourse, from the public arena?

These questions do not necessarily spring to mind when we first consider secularism in the modern State. Particularly for Americans, a more obvious list would include such matters as prayer in the schools, financial aid to religious institutions, and the display of sectarian symbols on public property. India too confronts issues arising from specific constitutional provisions on religion that I have not addressed in part 2: for example, religious instruction in educational institutions funded by the State, maintenance of religious charities without governmental interference, and legal protection for cows. Had I endeavored to write a comprehensive survey of religion and law in India, these and other issues would warrant greater attention. I focus on dismissing elected governments, using religious appeals in electoral campaigns, and (in part 1) practicing polygamy, because these controversies prove unusually instructive in highlighting, often in surprising ways, the animating principles of Indian secularism. These examples, moreover, each contribute to the evolution of liberal constitutional theory, the primary goal of the comparative enterprise. In the end, Tocqueville's motivation to study the United States best expresses my sentiments about India: "It is not . . . merely to satisfy a curiosity, however legitimate, that I have examined America; my wish has been to find there instruction by which we may ourselves profit."[7]

[7] Ibid., 14.

ACKNOWLEDGMENTS

THE WHEEL OF LAW has taken me many places. At each stop along the way, I encountered generous people who gave direction to an ultimately long and fascinating intellectual journey. Ten years ago, after completing a comparative study of Israeli and American constitutionalism, I turned my sights to India, a country whose unique experience with democracy had always intrigued me but never been my scholarly focus. Confronting the complexity of that country and its constitutional culture was a daunting prospect, which only heightened my appreciation for the advice and assistance I received while developing this book.

A year's residence at the Woodrow Wilson Center for International Scholars was the ideal setting to begin developing many of the thoughts that have found a place in these pages. The Center's staff provided a wonderful environment to encourage the best from its invitees. To perfectly complement this year of splendid isolation (gratefully shared, to be sure, with stimulating colleagues), a Fulbright research fellowship to India allowed me to discover, in the only way one truly can, the disjunction between ideas that looked so promising on paper and the facts on the ground. I am particularly indebted to Rajni Nair of the Fulbright staff in India, who was committed to making my stay in New Delhi as productive as possible. While in India, I had positive affiliations with Jawaharlal Nehru University (JNU) and the Delhi University Law Faculty. JNU's Rajeev Bhargava, Zoya Hasan, and Gurpreet Mahajan were especially helpful in honing my understanding of the Indian political scene. Venkatesh Prasad, a graduate of the law school at Delhi University, was an exemplary research assistant, whose knowledge of the law and passion for its elucidation proved invaluable to me. I am also very grateful for the assistance given me by Gowher Rizvi, head of the Ford Foundation in India, who unsparingly placed the resources of his institution at my disposal.

Gratitude, too, should be extended to those in India, the United States, Israel, and Canada who invited me to present my work at forums whose members invariably offered valuable feedback. The South Asia Seminar at Harvard University and its organizers, Pratap Mehta, Ashutosh Varshney, and Divesh Kapur, deserve special recognition for having asked me to discuss my ideas with them on three separate occasions. These visits gave me hope that I might have something useful to say to an audience possessing vastly more knowledge of my general subject matter than I.

Special thanks to Paul Brass, whose intimate knowledge of Indian politics justified the skepticism in his initial reaction to my project, but whose eventual advice and encouragement were all the more appreciated because it did not come easily. Amelie Rorty, Mark Graber, Mark Tushnet, Russ Muirhead, and Michael MacDonald contributed sharp insights and suggestions in response to different parts of the book. And three Williams College students—Hilary Barraford, Nishant Nayyar, and Andrew Woolf—provided superb assistance in preparing the manuscript. They affirmed for me why teaching at Williams is such a privilege, demonstrating in different ways that learning between student and professor need not be unidirectional.

My deepest gratitude, as always, goes to the Jacobsohn family—to my wife, Beth, and children, Joseph, Matthew, and Vanessa—whose support extended halfway around the world to a place where they had not asked to go. My greatest satisfaction lies not in the fact that they went, but that they are all the better for having done so.

A revised version of some of the material in chapters 2 and 3 appeared in "Three Models of Secular Constitutional Development: India, Israel, and the United States," 10 *Studies in American Political Development* 1 (1996). A section in chapter 8 appeared in an article, "After the Revolution," *Israel Law Review* (2000). Much of chapter 6 appeared in an essay, " 'By the Light of Reason': Corruption, Religious Speech, and Constitutional Essentials," in Nancy Rosenblum, ed., *Obligations of Citizenship and Demands of Faith: Religious Accommodation in Pluralist Democracies* (Princeton: Princeton University Press, 2000). Permission to incorporate this material is gratefully acknowledged.

The Wheel of Law

Chapter One

INTRODUCTION

Ashoka's Wheel

IN 1989 THE United States Supreme Court considered the case of Gregory Johnson, a young man whose fiery protest against the policies of the American government became an occasion for reflection on the symbolic significance of the American flag. The only thing that was certain about Johnson's defiant actions outside the 1984 Republican Convention, however, was that a cloth representation of some aspect of American identity was incinerated in front of a number of passersby, including several who were visibly outraged. Concerning the larger meaning of what was consumed in the flames that leapt from a Dallas, Texas, sidewalk, much was left in doubt.

For some, including Justices William Rehnquist and John Paul Stevens, dissenters in *Texas v Johnson*, the flag was emblematic of American nationhood and national unity; its desecration was therefore actionable regardless of any message Johnson may have intended to communicate through his act. Thus in the ashes that littered the space adjacent to the convening politicians were the collective memories of a people, of sons and daughters lost in war, and of the principles that gave meaning to their sacrifice. But for others, notably Justice William Brennan for the majority, these very principles—especially the "bedrock principle" of governmental tolerance for offensive ideas—could be consumed in flames only if offensiveness were compounded by error, by misconstruing the symbolism of the flag. Properly understood, the American flag represented the political aspirations of a free people, whose forbearance in the face of extreme and offensive provocation was the appropriate response to even the most flamboyant of demonstrations.[1]

---

[1] In the parade of nations that traditionally opens the Olympic games, the United States alone does not permit its flag-bearing athlete to dip the flag when he or she passes the head of state of the host nation. This can easily be taken as a sign of disrespect; so it has become

This disagreement, and the intense emotions accompanying it, may obscure the deeper unity embodied in these alternative symbolic renderings. Both perspectives agree that the flag represents certain principles of American identity that, in turn, constitute the essence of what distinguishes membership in the national community. Indeed, the emotions stimulated by the sentiments of the first are linked to the intellectual content embedded in the second, and are in the end mutually supportive of one another. Thus locating the source of American nationhood in ideas and principles necessitates a substantial reliance on patriotic symbol and ritual; while the principles of republican government have the potential for generating widespread formal support, for most people they are abstractions that may require a more visceral evocation to strengthen political attachment. Where bonds of unity do not flow naturally from such primordial attachments as race, religion, or ethnicity, and are instead an inscribed extension of the human imagination, the national symbol can be interpreted—perhaps should be interpreted—in a way that joins memory and sacrifice to reason and deliberation.[2]

And so the burning of the flag produces two kinds of outrage: first, at the seeming disregard for a shared past that has shaped the lives of all Americans; and second, at a destructive act whose violence stands in apparent repudiation of the "Republic for which it [the flag] stands." The flag's shapes and colors reference national origins with its thirteen stripes, and signify the essential meaning of the nation in the (now) fifty stars. If, as has been often said, the United States was unique in its having been founded on a set of political principles, it is also distinctive in the mutability of the content of its flag. The addition of a new star to denote each alteration of the physical boundaries of the country suggests (in theory at least) that geography, rather than ascription, sets the salient parameters of national identity. In the more recent past, the heightened correlation of physical expansion, multicultural diversity, and inclusion underscores this symbolism. Who one is should matter less than where one lives and ultimately what one comes to affirm.

More important, there is nothing in the design of the flag that would render its desecration offensive to any member of a particular group

---

necessary for American officials to explain that the refusal to participate in the simple gesture is a matter of honoring the republican principles that are represented by the flag. How convincing this is to the head of state who is witness to the display of principle is another matter.

[2] As Michael Frisch has pointed out, "In America, national identity is more political than genetic, and thus the function of civil religion, which gives the country that identity, is extremely important." *New York Times*, December 16, 2000, A17. And as Sheldon Nahmod has observed, "However American civil religion is defined, the American flag is surely one of its most powerful and dramatic national symbols." Nahmod 1991, 537.

within the larger "American" community. Someone, for example, who chose to burn an American flag to express disdain for a religious group would have a very difficult time being understood, unlike Gregory Johnson, whose gesture of defiance was relatively unambiguous in its purpose of calling attention to policies he felt were immoral.[3] In fact, Johnson might even have judged them to be so according to standards derived from the very ideals represented by the American flag, in which case the symbolic meaning of his act would have served a dual intent: the invocation of public philosophy to denounce public policy. On the other hand, if the source of his anger were traceable, say, to his Christian beliefs, then for his message to have been successfully conveyed, a further recourse to words or symbols would have been required.[4]

Of course, the burning of any nation's flag usually means that the flag burner is opposed to something that the nation is doing. But there are other possibilities. The second most incinerated flag among the nations of the world is likely that of Israel; here, however, motive is clouded by the very different character of the national symbol. Is the flag burner protesting Israeli policy on the Palestinian question or expressing ugly sentiments toward the Jewish people? For the skinhead in Chicago or Berlin, the Star of David on the Israeli flag is the only stimulus necessary to precipitate an incendiary act of anti-Semitism. For the Arab demonstrator in Cairo, the scorched flag doubtless reveals an intense hostility for the Zionist entity to the east, which may also include some not very cordial feelings

---

[3] Perhaps one notable exception: The burning of the American flag in some Muslim countries after the destruction of the World Trade Center in New York City can be seen as an expression of solidarity with those who view the United States as the embodiment of the contemporary Christian threat to Islam. Yet here too the act makes at least as much sense as a gesture of rejection directed at modernity and the West, particularly the subversive secular political ideas that these terms represent. As one observer, Scott Appleby, noted, "[The Islamic radicals] would respect the U.S. more if we did not separate God from governance—if we were in fact a Christian state." *Newsweek*, September 24, 2001, 68.

[4] That is not to say that the desecration of the flag is without religious meaning. Indeed, to desecrate is to profane, to violate the sanctity of something (that had been *consecrated*) venerable. The dissenters in *Johnson* can reasonably be seen to have attempted to "sacralize the flag." Underlying their opinions is "the belief that our secular political community requires patriotic symbols much as religious communities require religious symbols." Nahmod 1991, 527. However, the effort to treat the American flag as sacred did not run afoul of the Establishment Clause of the First Amendment, because, as Nahmod has pointed out, it could not be associated with a preference for any particular religion. Ibid., 532. See also, Goldstein 2000. Goldstein argues that, from the beginning, those involved in the flag protection movement "deliberately and systematically sought to create what amounted to a 'cult of the flag' by ideologically transforming it into a sacred object to be treated only in a highly reverential manner." Ibid., 13. In like manner, Michael Welch has noted that "It is precisely Old Glory's venerated status that makes its destruction such a potent form of protest." Welch 2000, 10.

for the Jewish people. And for the Arab in Nazareth, whose minimal contact with Israeli Jews has perhaps disabused him of at least some of the negative stereotypes that typically underlie anti-Semitism, the flames of anger are still directed at the Jewish majority, whose societal privileges are only too *flag*rantly revealed in the chosen symbol of Israeli nationhood.[5]

Unlike its American counterpart, the Israeli flag thus invites viewers to respond to its symbolism in ways that acknowledge the special place of a particular group. One's eye is immediately drawn to the center of the representational pattern, which suggests the centrality of the Jewish people to the meaning of Israeli nationhood. The Declaration of Independence refers to the "self-evident right of the Jewish people to be a nation," and the flag is an unambiguous testament to that commitment. However, a flag can reveal only so much; thus for Israel the prominence to be attached to the religious, rather than ethnic, content of the Jewish people is left open for interpretation. The profound political ramifications of this interpretive question have emerged when the Israeli flag has been burned by ultra-Orthodox Jews in Israel, who view the establishment of a Jewish State prior to the arrival of the Messiah as a grotesque theological travesty. They are so deeply offended by the blasphemous symbolism of the flag that they feel compelled to act in ways that are in turn grossly repulsive to most Israeli Jews, for whom the flag represents the triumphant culmination of the historic Zionist longing for a homeland for the Jewish people.

---

[5] A 1997 law requires that all government-funded schools, including those of the Arab and ultra-Orthodox communities, must fly the Israeli flag. Until very recently the law was ignored, but the decision in 2001 by the education minister to have it enforced provoked an interesting debate about the use of symbols to encourage patriotism among all the citizens of Israel. In response to a member of the Knesset who questioned the wisdom of requiring Arabs and ultra-Orthodox Jews to fly the Israeli flag, another member said: "The flag of the country belongs to everyone, whatever they may think of the government. This value must be internalized by the minorities. . . . In the United States, they've understood this for a long time. There the requirement to fly the flag applies not only to the educational system. Everyone there identifies with the flag, rich and poor, black and white, even if they have ethnic and economic divisions. I would like to see a similar attitude in Israel." To which the first member said: "Of course, I believe that the Arab minority should identify with and show loyalty to the state. The question is one of sensitivity. Building bridges with a minority culture is the sign of a strong country, not a weak one." The second then replied: "We live in a society in which pluralistic differences are valued. This is good, but we must remember and remind others of our common denominator—Zionism. The flag symbolizes Zionism and democracy." *The Jerusalem Report*, July 2, 2001, 56. This dialogue reflects very well the basic tension or contradiction at the core of Israeli nationhood. Thus the Knesset member who defends enforcement of the law looks to the United States for guidance, but he fails to distinguish between the assimilative assumptions prevalent in American citizenship from the visionary ones that prevail in Israel. (This distinction will be developed in detail in subsequent chapters.) When he sees the flag, he thinks of Zionism and democracy without permitting himself to join in his colleague's more empathetic understanding in which the symbolism of the flag bears a message of exclusion as well as unity.

Much of contemporary Israeli politics and constitutional disputation is driven by the uncertainties surrounding the question of Jewish identity. Whereas the absence of any religious symbolism on the American flag comports with the view that questions of faith and piety are to be resolved more properly in private places, the featured presence of the Star of David on the Israeli flag points to the unavoidably public nature of the religious question in Israel.[6] Erecting a "wall of separation" between Church and State will not, one might logically infer, be a very viable option in responding to the inevitable conflict flowing from temporal and spiritual commitments. On the other hand, it does not necessarily follow from this that when such conflicts arise, the spiritual interest will always, or even usually, prevail over the temporal interest. What implications follow from the State's official cognizance of religion, indeed its special recognition of a particular religion, cannot be known in the absence of much more information. That the Kuwaiti flag, like the Israeli, extends pride of place to one religion (in the former case, Islam) suggests only that in both countries, the adherents of the favored religion will in some ways be regarded differently from those who are otherwise affiliated. It provides no information about the substance of the rights and privileges attaching to the differently situated groups.

Another country where religion figures prominently in heated debates over the content of national identity is India. Here the controversy is not over the meaning and implications of the officially designated, preferred status of one of the nation's religious groups, but whether, and if so in what form, such a preference should be instituted. Frequently, this argument leads to soul-searching reflection over the contemporary "crisis of secularism," which turns out not to be a contemporary phenomenon at all but a staple of Indian politics since independence. Nevertheless, with a government in power dominated by a party famous for its critique of mainstream secularism, and with an ominous increase in the recent past of incidents involving appalling acts of communal violence, good reason exists to view the religious problem with a heightened sense of urgency. Perhaps, then, it behooves us to take a close look at the Indian flag.

It is divided horizontally into three broad strands of color, with a wheel in the center of the central white section. Most non-Indians would identify the band of color running across the top of the flag as orange, but to the

---

[6] There had been a debate over the design for the Israeli flag, which ultimately was won by those who favored the adoption of the World Zionist Organization flag as the national flag. The losers in this argument were those who wanted to make a clear distinction between the new State and the pre-State period. This group also wanted a design that would more clearly mark the difference between Jews living inside and outside the State. The blue and white flag matches the colors of the Jewish prayer shawl, and in general the flag is a reflection of the "civil religion in Israel." Liebman and Don-Yehiya 1983, 107.

locals it is saffron. The bottom color is green. In a political climate of communal conflict and consciousness, these colors of the national flag suggest the unfinished business of national integration. Thus the familiar green hue of Islam is separated from the saffron shading that has become emblematic of Hindu revivalism by an expanse of white that can be understood to express the aspiration for peaceful coexistence, if not genuine harmony.

It may be a testament to the power of the obvious identifications evoked by these colors that responsible leaders will seek to disabuse their followers of reflexive investment in readily accessible, but potentially dangerous, symbolism. Jawaharlal Nehru, as he inaugurated the project of constitutionalism in independent India, told the Constituent Assembly: "Some people, having misunderstood its significance, have thought of it [the flag] in communal terms and believe that part of it represents this community or that. But I may say that when this Flag was devised there was no communal significance attached to it."[7] Given Nehru's political proclivities, his preference was that the colors be understood to represent agriculture, revolution, industry, and commerce; but he was enough of a realist to appreciate that in the pliability of symbolic meanings, one could discover a mirror for the transvaluation of national identity. Therefore, the struggle to define the principles of a nation should not be permitted to terminate with the achievement of independence. After all, the fact that the flag had already been freighted with communal significance was a vivid reminder of the fragility of political ascendancy.

Nehru believed that the Constitution had codified the governing principles of the new State, and faithful adherence to them would ensure their secure entrenchment. His voice was one of several at the Constituent Assembly to call attention to the wheel in the center of the flag to explain the substance of the framers' commitment. Whatever significance others might attach to the colors on the flag, the Indian experiment in secular democracy would endure if those responsible for its safekeeping understood and embraced the teaching represented by that wheel. First, however, it would be necessary to distinguish the wheel on the new flag from the one that had appeared on the flag of the preindependence Indian National Congress. The earlier emblem had incorporated an image of Mahatma Gandhi's spinning wheel, or chakra, but Nehru indicates in his speech to the Assembly that the latter-day designers had their sights fixed on a more distant model. "[W]hat type of wheel should we have? Our minds went back to many wheels but notably our famous wheel, which had appeared in many places and which all of us have seen, the one at the top of the Ashoka column and in many other places. That wheel is a

[7] Rao 1966, vol. 1, 500.

symbol of India's ancient culture, it is a symbol of the many things that India had stood for through the ages."[8]

It remained for others to elaborate on what exactly the reproduction of the wheel on the capitol of Emperor Ashoka's Sarnath pillar stood for. The most detailed account came from S. Radhakrishnan, the distinguished philosopher and future president of India.

> The Ashoka's wheel represents to us the wheel of the Law, the wheel of the *Dharma*. Truth can be gained only by the pursuit of the path of *Dharma*, by the practise of virtue. . . . It also tells us that *Dharma* is something which is perpetually moving. . . . There are ever so many institutions, which are marked into our social fabric like caste and untouchability. Unless these things are scrapped, we cannot say that we either seek truth or practise virtue. This wheel, which is a rotating thing, indicates to us that there is death in stagnation. There is life in movement. Our *Dharma* is *Sanatana*, eternal, not in the sense that it is a fixed deposit but in the sense that it is perpetually changing. Its interrupted continuity is the *Sanatana* character. So even with regard to our social conditions it is essential to move forward.[9]

This rendering comports with other views expressed at the Constituent Assembly; for example, that Ashoka's dharma-chakra represented the "balance-wheel of religion that sustains society."[10] Or as one Muslim delegate put it after praising "that great Buddhist Emperor Ashoka," the wheel was "a religious emblem and we cannot dissociate our social life from our religious environments."[11]

From this we can begin to appreciate how the symbolism of the Indian flag conveys a message about the conceptualization of secular democracy that is significantly different from the approaches intimated by the American and Israeli flags. Where religion is emblematically absent in the United States, it is prominently featured on the Indian flag, albeit in a form that is not readily identifiable with narrow sectarian interests. The term *dharma* does not translate very well into English; at the most general level, it refers to beliefs and postulates that, if scrupulously followed, will allow one to lead a moral life.[12] For Hindus, it has had a historic connection to

---

[8] Ibid., 501. Nehru went on to underscore the significance of Ashoka to the national challenge at hand. "For my part, I am exceedingly happy that we have associated with our flag not only this emblem but in a sense the name of Ashoka, one of the most magnificent names in India's history and the world. It is well that at this moment of strife, conflict, and intolerance, our minds should go back towards what India stood for in the ancient days and what, I hope and believe, it has essentially stood for throughout the ages."

[9] Ibid., 504.

[10] Ibid., 495. From the delegate, S. D. Kalkar.

[11] Ibid., 509. From the delegate, Mohammed Saadulla.

[12] The term itself is used in several widely different senses, and is one of the most comprehensive terms in Sanskrit literature. The most frequently employed sense refers to the sum

the caste system, with each caste having its own dharma, that is to say, its own moral code in accordance with which caste members are expected to conduct their lives. As the delegates to the Constituent Assembly knew, the Ashokan conception of dharma separated the phenomenon from its caste and sectarian moorings, retaining much of its spiritual significance, but providing it with an ethical content intended for societal as well as personal transformation. As Romila Thapur has persuasively argued, Ashoka's understanding of dharma makes very clear that it was a concept intended for a secular teaching.[13] That teaching was directed toward the amelioration of social injustices embedded in a status quo of religiously based hierarchy.

It is this Ashokan understanding that I explore in this study, or more specifically, I study its meaning in the context of postindependence Indian constitutional politics. The great challenge in pursuing the elusive goal of Indian secularism is bound up in what is distinctive about the Indian case, namely that critical elements of the social structure are inextricably entwined with religion in a way that renders the possibilities for any meaningful social reform unimaginable without the direct intervention of the State in the spiritual domain. My exploration cannot pretend to be a comprehensive account of secularism in India; as important as the constitutional experience has been, it only provides a limited perspective on the incredibly complex and multifarious problems of spiritual-temporal relations in contemporary India. But within this constitutional focus, I attempt to broaden the perspective by placing the Indian example in a comparative framework. The distinctiveness of the Indian case, represented on the flag by Ashoka's wheel as its symbolic centerpiece, can obviously benefit from comparative reflection on the alternative experiences of other constitutional systems. The American and Israeli flags suggest why these nations— the United States with its tradition of Church/State separation, and Israel with its unambiguous embrace of a particular religious tradition—provide especially rich possibilities for clarifying secular meanings in India.

By placing the Indian case within a comparative constitutional context, I hope also to contribute to some lively contemporary debates within the field of political theory that address the constitutional essentials of a lib-

---

of all the duties that bear upon individuals according to their status (*varna*) and stage of life (*asrama*). It is a concept particularly celebrated in the *Bhagavad Gita*, wherein it is emphatically asserted that "[E]very man has the unique capability of determining all actions by means of the Law of Dharma."

[13] Thapur 1997, 163. Thapur writes of the institution of the *dhamma-mahamattas*, a special cadre of officials installed by Ashoka in the fourteenth year of his reign. They were the people charged with negotiating the practical working of dharma. It was "an attempt made by As'oka to provide some system of social welfare for the lower castes and the less fortunate members of the community." Ibid., 157.

eral democratic polity. American constitutional theorists have increasingly seen the value of comparative reflection to their subject matter. In this they are not alone, for indeed constitutionalism in faraway places seems finally to have come of age among all kinds of scholars of public law. It is entirely possible, of course, that the recent surge of interest in other people's constitutional affairs may turn out to be nothing more than a momentary post-Cold War diversion, in which case comparative constitutional scholarship (especially in the United States) can be expected to return to the relative obscurity that has for many years been its profile within the broader field of public law studies. But even if the interest in constitutional arrangements other than one's own carries beyond the stimulus of current events, the characteristically insular approach toward the examination of American constitutional issues will require persistent attention and resistance lest it reemerge with renewed vigor.[14] To appropriate the famous metaphor from the First Amendment arena that is the concern of this book, it is as if a "wall of separation" has shielded both scholarly and judicial analysis of constitutional issues from the experience of other polities. As a result, too often constitutional debate has been denied the illumination and insights of comparative research.

In chapter 2 I present a conceptual and analytical framework for understanding constitutional arrangements for Church/State relations in liberal democratic polities. Inasmuch as the frame of reference for discussion of constitutional questions pertaining to religion and politics is invariably the American experience, much of the available analysis relies upon conceptual categories (such as accommodation and separation) that portray the array of options confronting constitutional regimes in the form of an unduly narrow spectrum of possibilities.[15] My approach to the conceptual question is based on two critical dimensions: the extent to which religion exists as a constitutive factor in shaping the contours of social life and institutions, and the extent to which the State is identified with any particular religious group. The second of these will be familiar to anyone conversant with contemporary constitutional discourse concerning religion and politics, although a version of it may also be found in an Ashokan edict that reads simply: "You should strive to practice impartiality."[16] Lat-

---

[14] For examples of comparative work that represent excellent exceptions to this characteristic insularity, see Glendon 1987 on abortion and family policy, and Post 1986, 691–742, on the law of defamation.

[15] Thus I believe that even the best theorizing about the role of religion in public life (as, for example, in the work of Michael McConnell and Leonard Levy) can benefit from the refractory insights emerging from the prism of comparative scrutiny.

[16] Ashoka's edicts are inscribed on rocks and pillars that are located in various parts of the Indian subcontinent. They are usually to be found in the proximity of places of religious significance and are a primary source of our knowledge of Ashoka's philosophy and political rule.

ter-day Indian constitutional jurisprudence is emphatic in its endorsement of this principle of equal treatment of religions (*sarva dharma sambhava*); the spokes on a wheel must, after all, be of equal length.

But as an American-Indian contrast quickly reveals, a commitment to impartiality in the relationship between the State and the various religions active within its jurisdiction does not in itself indicate what role public institutions should play in the domain of the spiritual life. Whether desirable or not, in the United States it is at least possible to envision a clear separation of Church and State, in which religion and politics are maintained as distinct areas of human striving, and where the neutrality of equal treatment is broadened to require a hands-off policy for governing the relations between secular and religious institutions. Thus to the extent that religion is either helped or hindered through official action, it must be done inadvertently, the State being obliged to take no cognizance of religion in the course of its activities. As we shall see, such an arrangement is inconceivable in India, where, upon initial analysis, religious and secular life are so pervasively entangled that a posture of official indifference cannot be justified either politically or constitutionally.

That is the case of course in Israel as well, although there the inseparability of the two domains is less the reflection of a thickly constituted religious presence in the social life of the nation than it is a corollary of the politics of ethnoreligious identification. While such identification logically threatens the secular foundation of the State, in practice it has been prevented from destroying it by embracing a religious identity that is relatively restrained in its theological and social ambitions. In sorting these various distinctions out, this chapter highlights three models of secular constitutional development—*assimilative*, *visionary*, and *ameliorative*—that correspond respectively with the American, Israeli, and Indian cases. They are analytical constructs that allow us to better understand the various constitutional options available to nations as they confront the challenges to liberal democratic institutions posed by religion.

These models are given more detailed consideration in chapters 3 and 4, where I examine the assumptions underlying the three approaches. In so doing, it quickly becomes apparent that some of the ideas associated with secular constitutionalism—most notably equality—are featured prominently in each of the separate locales. Readers will not be surprised to learn that such ideas can mean different things in different places, and that their constitutional implementation may produce contrary results. These disparate results are then readily comprehensible in light of the differences in political culture that are evident in a careful consideration of the three cases. But words matter, and, significantly, comparable actors within contrasting systems feel obligated to appeal to the same concept (or at least vocabulary) to justify their arrangements for achieving a goal as important as religious liberty. A secular State may assume a variety of forms, with corresponding sets of constitutional norms and expectations for governing the relationship between public and religious institutions. There are, however, necessary limits to what should be considered acceptable in the way of this governance, so that any blatant, systematic disregard for the fundamental religious liberties of a population or subpopulation, even if executed in the name of equality, should place the nation in question outside the family of secular constitutional regimes. Indeed, categorical exclusion should be predicated precisely on the basis of a failure to comport in fact (rather than rhetoric) with a philosophically coherent and plausible understanding of equality.

India, Israel, and the United States can all legitimately lay claims to recognition as secular constitutional polities. While varying in the degree to which this status is threatened by local circumstances and wavering commitments, they nevertheless display patterns of regard for the practice of religious freedom and for the secular conduct of public business that are for the most part genuine, if imperfectly realized. These patterns reflect the regime-defining attributes of nationhood that are distinctive to each of the cases. In these chapters I consider the ubiquitous problem of polygamy, where the contrasting solutions that have evolved in the three constitutional settings are, if not inevitable, clearly reflective of the dominant strand—assimilative, visionary, or ameliorative—present in the differently configured secular contexts of the respective polities. They can be plausibly defended as reasonable accommodations to the demands of these contexts; so, for example, the differential treatment of religious groups that may be justified in India or Israel will be more difficult to situate comfortably within the assimilative context of constitutional secularism in the United States.

Differential treatment requires special attention in light of its apparent contradiction of the principle of equality. However, in pursuing the ameliorative aspiration of Indian secularism, we will begin to appreciate the complexity of this question. Thus we are introduced in chapter 4 to the challenge posed to secular institutions in India by the revival of Hindu nationalism. To achieve political ascendancy, this movement has appropriated liberal constitutional discourse, which, as applied to problems such as the practice of polygamy, demands that all individuals receive equal treatment under the law (specifically, that India adopt a uniform civil code, which incorporates the very principle of formal equality that would appear to be under assault from the regime of personal laws that provides Hindus and Muslims with disparate legal entitlements). Debate over the desirability of enacting a code has much to contribute to an un-

derstanding of the ameliorative character of Indian secularism. But as
we see in this chapter, the insistence by the Hindu right on immediate
codification has had a significant effect on the shape of the ensuing debate,
often in ways that have produced less than thoughtful responses from
opponents. Nevertheless, the demand, as a featured plank in the political
agenda of those for whom the ameliorative aspiration is of little salience,
and for whom the religious commitments of minorities are of minimal
priority, alerts us to the difficulty in making any easy equation between
secularism and liberal notions of equality.

This lesson is reinforced in chapter 5, in which I examine some of the
constitutional issues flowing from the most devastating political/religious
conflagration on the Indian subcontinent since Partition. The violent dismantling in December 1992 of the Islamic Babri Masjid mosque in the
northern Indian city of Ayodhya precipitated a wave of carnage and destruction that has fundamentally altered the political landscape of the
country. In the immediate aftermath of that event, the Central Government dismissed the elected governments of three states, many of whose
members had supported the activities of the Hindu nationalist perpetrators of the deed. These dismissals were subsequently appealed to the Indian Supreme Court, which, in a landmark decision, upheld the actions
of the Center while also discoursing at length on the subject of secularism
and the Constitution. In so doing, the Court rejected the contention of
the counsel for the three dismissed governments that the only legitimate
grounds for invoking Presidential Rule (the Article 356 dismissal power)
was because of a serious interruption of the democratic *process*. Thus the
justices affirmed that the failure to act in accordance with the substantive
provisions of the Constitution, in this case the commitment to secular
rule, was sufficient to trigger the emergency powers of the Union Government. There was, in other words, no obligation to remain neutral with
regard to critical matters of political orientation and belief. Once again
liberal arguments were placed in the service of illiberal ends; their rejection by the Court served to clarify the essence of the Indian constitutional
commitment to secularism.

As we shall see, the rejection of the process-based logic behind the challenge to the dismissals has implications that extend much further than the
particulars of the case at hand. That the power to remove a duly elected
state government was based loosely on the Guaranty Clause (Article IV,
Section 4) of the American Constitution turns out to be of more than
casual interest, particularly with respect to matters of great interest to
constitutional theorists. For example, the American national government's obligation to guarantee republican governance in the states has
never led to actions analogous to what happened in India. Abolitionists

who had argued that the existence of slavery demanded the invocation of the guarantee provision to reverse the antirepublican policies of the slave-holding states were defeated on the basis of the same sort of claims made by supporters of the dismissed officials in India to counter the secularism-inspired moves of the Indian government. Various explanations can be advanced to account for these differences, including the presence of con-trasting experiences with federalism. But it is in the very different ways in which a constitution is conceptualized, highlighted by the viability in India of the idea of an unconstitutional constitutional amendment, that we find the most compelling explanation for why, in the face of substan-tive challenges to their legitimacy, elected governments in the United States are accorded substantially more deference than elected govern-ments receive in India.

The argument I develop in the constitutional context of the Ayodhya aftermath is that secularism, as a "basic feature" of the Constitution (and therefore unamendable), must be understood within the broader frame-work of the document's commitment to social reconstruction. What some justices referred to in the dismissals case as "positive secularism" helps us to see that the destruction of the mosque by an organized mob of religious zealots involved more than a threat to communal peace and stability; it also threatened to sabotage the Constitution's long-term vision of a truly secular, or socially just, society. Applying a more formalistic American model—which we might call "negative secularism"—fails to capture what is special about the Indian case. Only comparative analysis clarifies this distinctiveness and assesses the clever strategy of religious nationalists in employing familiar categories of liberal constitutionalism to advance a quite illiberal agenda.

Chapters 6 and 7 focus our attention on one of the most vexing and controversial issues of contemporary political theory and constitutional disputation: religious speech in the public forum. Long before John Rawls and other democratic theorists began to reflect on the subject, Emperor Ashoka had this to say in his Rock Edict Number 12:

> [T]he growth of the essentials of Dharma is possible in many ways. But its root lies in restraint in regard to speech, which means that there should be no extolment of one's own sect or disparagement of other sects on inappropriate occasions and that it should be moderate in every case even on appropriate occasions. On the contrary, other sects should be duly honoured in every way on all occasions. . . . If a person acts in this way, he not only promotes his own sect but also benefits other sects. But, if a person acts otherwise, he not only injures his own sect but also harms other sects. Truly, if a person extols his own sect and disparages other sects with a view to glorifying his sect owing

merely to his attachment to it, he injures his own sect very severely by acting in that way. Therefore restraint in regard to speech is commendable, because people should learn and respect the fundamentals of one another's Dharma.[17]

This Ashokan sentiment has been incorporated into modern Indian law in the form of the Representation of the People Act, the foundational 1951 enactment that governs the conduct of Indian elections.[18] Among its many provisions is one that details a number of "corrupt practices," including the inappropriate use of religious speech to advance one's electoral prospects. Much like the Ashokan teaching, it emphasizes moderation and restraint. Candidates for public office must not seek votes on the basis of appeals to their own religion or through the disparagement of others' religions. The impetus behind the law is surely traceable to the gruesome ethnoreligious violence that accompanied the establishment of independent India. But the motivation to minimize religious conflict was also accompanied by a realization that religion was a pervasive and entrenched presence in the social fabric of the nation, so that any law requiring a muting of religious rhetoric in the context of democratic deliberation would doubtless prove to be controversial and litigious.

Just how controversial this law has become is evident from a series of decisions handed down by the Indian Supreme Court in the mid-1990s, known collectively as the *Hindutva Cases*. In deciding these cases, all of which involved questionable campaign activities of prominent politicians on the Hindu right, the Court was being asked to address both the constitutionality of the "corrupt practices" provision of the elections law and the reach of its statutory application. In the end, they upheld the constitutionality of the section while vindicating most of those charged with its violation through a narrow construction of its meaning. In so doing, the justices also addressed core issues of national and religious identity, as well as theoretical questions that are central to debates over the constitutional essentials of political liberalism. Indeed, the philosophical edifice upon which the Court's argument to sustain the law was built is taken essentially from the pages of John Rawls.

In chapter 6 I find the use of Rawlsian public reason-based arguments to sustain the constitutionality of restrictions on religious speech to be notably misplaced in the context of the Indian sociopolitical environment. Without making a judgment on the cogency of such arguments in the assimilative secular setting of the United States, I argue that the effort to

---

[17] Sircar 1957, 50.

[18] There was no direct invocation of the Ashokan edict in the drafting of the legislation, but it is noteworthy that the law's chief architect, Law Minister Ambedkar (also the driving force behind the Constitution), was the Indian figure most closely identified with the ancient emperor. Both were converts to Buddhism, who were committed social reformers.

place religious rhetoric beyond the arena of public disputation requires a rationale more attuned to the ameliorative commitments of the Indian Constitution. Thus to the extent that restrictions are justified, the threat posed by religion to the achievement of substantive aspirations for equality, rather than concerns over the process of democratic deliberation, offers the most compelling justification for limiting appeals to religion in the arena of electoral competition. To be sure, restrictions defended on the basis of content-neutral principles that conform to contemporary depictions of the liberal State may have a strong appeal in elite legal circles in both India and the United States; but the nonneutrality of the Indian State as delineated in the nation's Constitution renders problematic the easy transference of abstract moral reasoning from one constitutional locale to another.

But the story of the *Hindutva Cases*, including their significance to comparative constitutional theory, is not limited to the application of liberal reasoning in the adjudication of the legal issues. In fact, at this point in the progress of the book, the reader may begin to suspect the ulterior motives of anyone who relies heavily on liberal argumentation. Perhaps nowhere are these suspicions better founded than in the case of the author of the *Hindutva Cases*, Supreme Court Justice J. S. Verma. In chapter 7 I pursue the enigma of his central role in the controversial resolution of the "corrupt practices" cases, and in the process seek to illuminate the question of the judiciary's involvement in the campaign to reconstitute the essentials of Indian secularism. The mystery surrounding the Court's judgment has to do with the fact that while the Court upheld the restrictions on religious speech, it did so in a manner that essentially legitimated the core beliefs of the Hindu right on the most fundamental of all questions, the nature of Indian national identity. That Justice Verma's reasoning could find favor with both the liberal legal theorist Ronald Dworkin and the leading theoreticians of Hindu revivalism is vivid testimony to the puzzling quality of the Court's judgment. Through interviews with most of the major players in the complex and multidimensional drama of these cases, I present three alternative narratives of their meaning: first, that the outcome represented a significant victory for liberal principles of equality; second, that it was a triumph of religious and cultural nationalism; and finally, that the animating force behind the decisions was a commitment to precepts of sociological jurisprudence. In the end, however, a fourth story may be necessary to understand the meaning of what happened in these cases, and ultimately what is happening to Indian secularism, namely, a more nuanced and conflicted account that reflects a notably unsuccessful political system in providing the leadership required to clarify the question of Indian national identity. And as we shall see, the failure of judges in this regard is in turn a reflection of this larger political reality.

The challenge to the original secular ideal of a composite culture is not, as illustrated in the *Hindutva Cases*, confined to the fringes of the Indian political system. Nehru's invocation of Ashoka at the Constituent Assembly, to the effect that Indian nationhood consisted of more than the Hindu affiliation of most Indians, resonates less authoritatively than it once did.[19] It therefore comes as no surprise that some of the proponents of Hindu nationalism have found in Israel a political model that merits consideration, if not slavish emulation. A State that serves as an official homeland for the people of a particular religion represents an appealing example for those who see the destiny of their nation entwined in the culture and tradition of the country's dominant religious group. In chapter 8 I look closely at some recent constitutional developments in Israel for the lessons that they hold for Indians who might look to the Israeli example for their own development. I suggest that an enhanced Israeli-like profile for an ascriptive dimension in Church/State relations would very likely undermine the role of the Indian judiciary as an agent of social reform, and with it the larger purposes of Indian secular constitutionalism.

The specific setting for this analysis is the *constitutional revolution* in Israel, the term used to denote the emergence in that country of judicially enforceable rights against the legislative branch of government. It is a development that can be understood as part of a more ambitious effort to reconcile the contradictions in the revolutionary legacy of the Israeli polity. Thus for the jurists who are the driving force behind the effort, judicial review embodies the hope that the universalistic and particularistic strands in Israeli politics and constitutionalism can be rendered harmonious and whole. However, the premature expansion of the judiciary's formal powers before progress in establishing a popular consensus on fundamental issues of nationhood threatens to undermine the Supreme Court as an institution within the broader political system. In applying the lessons of the Israeli experience to India, I speculate on what could happen to the Indian Court's effectiveness as an instrument of ameliorative transformation if it were to become identified with a constitutional revolution in the secular priorities of the State. In the process, it also becomes clear that a Hindu State in India would look very different from a Jewish State in Israel.

But the fundamental differences between polities in how they are constituted with respect to their secular potentials need not obscure the possibilities within these potentials for achieving a degree of convergence in the secular constitutional development of contrasting societies. One of the

---

[19] Ashoka's Rock Edict Number 15 reads: "All men are my children. Just as, in regard to my own children, I desire that they may be provided with all kinds of welfare and happiness in the world and in the next, the same I desire also in regard to all men." Sircar 1957, 56.

hopes for comparative constitutional analysis is that critical engagement across political and cultural boundaries will lead judges, legislators, and others involved in the processes of constitutional change to benefit from the lessons of foreign experience. This hope must always be tempered by a sense of realism concerning the obstacles to constitutional borrowing and transplantation that are embedded in local political and legal cultures. But the benefits of cross-national importation can be experienced in small increments, so that one need not despair in the face of only modest expectations regarding the adaptation of external practice to indigenous circumstances.

In the concluding chapter, I reflect on the adaptive possibilities of two of the constitutionally based models of secularism described in this study—the *ameliorative* and the *assimilative*—by reconsidering what is perhaps the most controversial religion decision (certainly in the free exercise arena) ever handed down by the American Supreme Court. In *Employment Division v Smith*, known widely as the peyote case, the Court created a political firestorm by curtailing the First Amendment's usefulness as a basis for claiming exemptions to laws of general applicability that substantially burden particular religious practices. In my analysis, the subordination of conscience to civic obligation, which is at the heart of the assimilationist reasoning in Justice Scalia's opinion for the Court, flows naturally from the Constitution's secular aspirations. But the uncompromising application of Scalia's logic to the two religiously motivated, peyote-ingesting followers of the Native American Church proves that in law as elsewhere, there can be too much of a good thing. Thus I argue that to challenge the strong presumption in favor of religiously based exemptions is a reasonable thing to do; prioritizing spiritual and temporal affairs in this way furthers the Constitution's role in reinforcing a common American political identity. However, the line between political and social assimilation—the first desirable, the second problematic—is a fine one, which the Court transgressed when it failed to introduce any ameliorative considerations into the mix of its judicially administered prescription for resolving the case. As a result, the decision culminates in a surfeit of liberal formalism that found the justices relying too heavily on the resources of one secular model to maintain the appropriate balance in the constitutional equilibrium between religion and politics.

While I argue in this concluding chapter that a familiarity with the more ameliorative approach of Indian jurisprudence would be useful to decision makers in the United States, the idea behind the analysis of *Smith* is not that comparative constitutional analysis is essential for successful adjudication of these sorts of cases. Rather, it is that the various analytical constructs that assist us in distinguishing alternative contexts for secular constitutional development also reveal complementary approaches to a

more normatively driven model of Church/State relations in liberal democratic polities. The distinctiveness of constitutional regimes will doubtless
persist in the face of the harmonizing effects of liberal globalization and
international law, but increasingly apparent in the rising prominence of
these phenomena are certain common attributes of constitutional organization that transcend national boundaries. Indeed, the "revolutionary"
efforts in Israel to reconcile the visionary aspects of Church/State configuration with a fundamental shift toward more universalistic standards of
constitutional practice present powerful testimony of this trend. As we
shall see, the ameliorative emphasis in Indian secularism highlights for
Americans the importance of substantive equality to the achievement of
religious tolerance, much as the assimilative bent of American secularism
conveys to Indians the salience of liberal democratic ideas in mitigating
the communal obstacles to religious freedom. Each, that is, must be a
contributing factor in the realization of the other's constitutional aspirations. To the extent that this happens, we may come to know how ideal
democratic arrangements for religion and politics might be constituted.

PART ONE

Three Models of Secular Constitutional Design

Chapter Two

NATIONS AND CONSTITUTIONS

Dimensions of Secular Configuration

Two powerful agencies that have done a great deal to
advance social well-being in other countries are not
available to our cause in this country, namely the State
and the Church. Here the State represents an alien
power, which is not well informed on Hindu social
questions and which lacks the propelling force which the
wielders of that power would come under if they were
of the people, and if they shared directly in the
consequences of our social evils and in the adverse
feeling and sense of incongruity they create. . . . In
regard to the Church also, we are at a great
disadvantage. There is nothing amongst us
corresponding to the great and powerful institutions
called the Church in Christian countries. Our
fore-fathers never thought of giving to their religion the
strength of an organised religion.[1]

THESE WORDS were included in an address entitled "The Principles of
Social Reform," delivered in 1897 by G. Subramania Iyer to the Madras
Hindu Social Reform Association. The passage emphasizes four points:
(1) India is at a comparative disadvantage in its capacity to address the
existence of evil in society. (2) Understanding social evil in India requires
familiarity with Hindu society. (3) A government "of the people" would
be *for the people* in the sense that its popular mooring would ensure efforts to counteract entrenched and severe social ills. (4) The Hindu reli-

---

[1] Karunakaran 1965, 195.

gion lacks the organizational structure to mobilize effectively on behalf of social reform and well-being.

Fifty years later an important change had occurred: The State no longer represented an alien power. One hundred years later an important assumption had not as yet been proven: that a democratically constituted State would necessarily be committed to the eradication of social evil.[2] Thus in 1947 the Constituent Assembly of independent India produced the world's longest Constitution, key provisions of which reflected the spirit of social reform that animated many of its framers' endeavors. In the language of a Supreme Court opinion: "The Indian Constitution is first and foremost a social document. The majority of its provisions are either directly aimed at furthering the goals of the socio-economic revolution or attempt to foster this revolution by establishing the conditions necessary for its achievement."[3] But as a new century approached, it was less than clear that this document had contributed much to the alleviation of the massive burdens of social iniquity that had preoccupied Mr. Iyer at the close of the last century. Fittingly, fifty years of independent statehood became an occasion for both celebrating successes in democratic governance and regretting failures in achieving a just social order.

If the State no longer represented an alien power and could therefore, as in other countries, contribute (however inadequately) to the welfare of society, the availability of the Church to the cause of social well-being had not been affected by a similar transformation in its fundamental character. The efforts over the years of Hindu reformers to modify socially regressive religious practices had achieved some measurable positive impact, but Iyer's analysis of the weakness of decentralized and fragmented ecclesiastical power in effecting major change had not lost its relevance. Iyer, however, might have pointed out that the same structural advantage that made the Church in some countries an effective instrument of social reform made it in others a substantial obstruction.[4] Moreover, in India, unlike in many of the Christian countries to which he alluded, the prevalence and perpetuation of social evil were closely connected to a religiously based way of life. If the Hindu forefathers *had* "thought of giving to their religion the strength of an organised religion," then logic suggests that, in contrast with countries where the Church had become a powerful

---

[2] Or as Justice V. R. Krishna Iyer wrote, "The secularizing and socializing influences of the constitutional philosophy, which aims at rendering caste and religious beliefs dysfunctional to social relationships productive of legal consequences, have not as yet produced the liberalising thrust at the grass roots level which they were expected to engender." Iyer 1984, 156.

[3] *Minerva Mills Ltd.* at 1846.

[4] For example, the Church of England, which, particularly in the nineteenth century, used its considerable power to block meaningful reform.

agency fighting social ills beyond its domain, an authoritative religious voice might very well have become a linchpin in a concerted effort to preserve the status quo.

All of this points to the need to place the Indian secular experience within a comparative constitutional context. T. N. Madan has observed that "Secularism in India is a multivocal word: what it means depends upon who uses the word and in what context."[5] Moving from an intrasocietal to an intersocietal context reinforces his insight. Thus the points made in Iyer's speech to the Reform Association, all of which are, as we shall see, central to an understanding of religion and politics in India, require an analytical framework broader than the Indian case to comprehend their significance. Accordingly, this chapter explores the concept and practice of the secular constitution within three nations—India, Israel, and the United States—that are committed, albeit in different ways, to the principle of religious liberty.

The manner in which a polity *constitutes* religion is arguably its most revealing regime-defining choice.[6] These three cases provide an opportunity to consider how contrasting constitutional treatments of religion reflect distinctive patterns of secular foundational commitment. In their unique ways, all three countries emerged from the shadow of British colonialism under circumstances that called attention to the political problems associated with religious diversity. In each instance, the project of nation-building culminated in a constitutional culture within which proposed solutions to the perplexing matrix of issues concerning Church and State make more or less good sense. These solutions are worth investigating for a variety of reasons, including their potential for constitutional transplantation; thus determining which approaches are appropriate for cross-national application requires careful attention to national comparisons and their constitutional implications.[7]

---

[5] Madan 1997, 235.

[6] See, for example, Walker 1994, 504, 510.

[7] At the outset we should be careful in distinguishing between political and constitutional cultures. As we shall see, and as the case of India best illustrates, a constitutional ethos or culture may emerge from a specific political culture expressly in order to modify or transform it. Mark Tushnet uses the term *expressivism* to denote a school of thought in comparative constitutionalism in which constitutions are seen as expressive of a nation's distinctive history and culture. He rightly points out that "[N]ations vary widely in the degree to which their written constitutions are organically connected to the nation's sense of itself." He is also correct in suggesting that the Indian Constitution is in a certain sense a confrontation with a society organized in accordance with principles opposite those embodied in the document. This leads him to conclude that unlike the American constitutional scene, the Indian Constitution (and its interpretation by the courts) tells a much less clear story about who that nation is. Here I would disagree, since the confrontation between constitution and society turns out to be enormously revealing of what is distinctive about Indian politics and

In the cases of India and Israel, these kinds of assessments are frequently made by judges in Church/State cases, with the American experience receiving the lion's share of attention. On the other hand, American judges have paid scant attention to developments elsewhere.[8] This one-directional path of influence is easy to understand in light of the much longer span of American constitutional history. But given the longstanding confusion and controversy in both the judiciary and academic circles regarding the meaning of the First Amendment's religion clauses, the reasons for foreign interest in American precedents might still be somewhat mystifying to a student of the Supreme Court. Indeed, with the possible exception of the Fourteenth Amendment, there is no section of the Constitution whose meaning is more contested. Understandably, then, such a student might well wonder how any sort of consistent and coherent message about Church and State could be getting across to observers abroad.

Viewed from abroad, however, the divisions within the American legal community on constitutional matters pertaining to religion appear relatively inconsequential. Thus Israelis tend to see the American solution as clearly distinguishable from their own (for some to be approximated or even emulated, for others to be avoided), one where, in the words of another foreign observer, Alexis de Tocqueville, "[R]eligion is a distinct sphere, in which the priest is sovereign, but out of which he takes care never to go."[9] In Israel, where religion is so firmly embedded in conceptions of national identity, debates are heard over religion's proper place in the public square, but their juxtaposition with similar debates in the United States only highlights for Israelis the distinctiveness of the critical American *presumption* that religious activity is essentially a private affair. Though in India religion's embeddedness in prevailing notions of national self-understanding proves ambiguous, in marked contrast to the United States it is deeply embedded in the country's social structure, leading Indians to perceive American approaches to Church/State relations as decidedly separatist at their core. Despite a number of serious and influential voices in the United States urging a more "accommodationist"

---

culture. A confrontational constitution can be as *expressive* of a political culture as a document such as the American, which is a more seamless extension of its political environment. Tushnet 1999, 1270–71.

[8] A notable exception was Justice William O. Douglas, who was especially interested in India. Douglas wrote a book (based on his Tagore Lectures) about the Indian constitutional system. Douglas 1956. More important, his reflections on the Indian constitutional approach to Church and State figured prominently in several of his judicial opinions (e.g., *McGowan; Seeger; Sherbert*). Douglas was a sympathetic observer of the Indian experience. At the same time, he used it to highlight some of the distinctive and desirable characteristics of the American approach.

[9] Tocqueville 1945, vol. 2, 28.

position as truer to the nation's ideals, the perception of a characteristically American constitutional segmentation of the spiritual and temporal domains still stands.

Perceptions such as these suggest how the comparative approach accentuates regime differences. While George Fletcher is surely right in insisting that resolving legal disputes is best accomplished by "turn[ing] inward" through reflection upon the legal culture within which a given dispute is located,[10] this sort of effort is not incompatible with an outward turn that looks comparatively to emphasize defining aspects of constitutional identity. This chapter focuses on constitutional policy regarding Church and State, but behind this is a broader engagement with three constitutional cultures. The constitutional provisions that address religious issues need to be examined for the messages they carry concerning distinctive conceptions of national identity that in turn demarcate critical parameters for constitutional adjudication. In this chapter, I introduce a conceptual mapping of the three dominant approaches to the secular constitution embodied in the experiences of India, Israel, and the United States. These models are developed further in the next two chapters, which concentrate on issues within the three constitutional settings that underscore the distinctive—although not mutually exclusive—orientations prevailing in these countries. There I elaborate on the *assimilative* logic behind American Church/State experience and the *visionary* commitments animating Israeli approaches to religious diversity, both of which provide a comparative background for pursuing the *ameliorative* assumptions, aspirations, and implications of Indian constitutional secularism.

THREE CONSTITUTIONAL MODELS: A PRELIMINARY ACCOUNT

In Book IV of Aristotle's *Politics*, the philosopher and father of comparative constitutionalism turns his attention from ideal to actual constitutions: Which is the best constitution practicable for this or that set of circumstances, and what are the best ways of preserving existing constitutions? "[P]olitics has to consider which sort of constitution suits which sort of civic body. The attainment of the best constitution is likely to be impossible for the general run of states; and the good law-giver and the true statesman must therefore have their eyes open not only to what is the absolute best, but also to what is the best in relation to actual conditions."[11] Aristotle refers in this context to a common error, which is to assume that there is only one sort of regime type—for example, democracy or oligarchy—when in fact there are different varieties for each

[10] Fletcher 1993, 737.
[11] Aristotle 1962, 1288b 10.

scheme of constitution. Constitutions vary because of variations in the makeup of the body politic.

Aristotle's point is applicable to the constitutional configuration of secular polities. Here too it is possible (and in a certain sense desirable) to imagine the ideal arrangement for achieving the perfect balance between Church and State, and therewith the maximum protection for both spiritual and temporal concerns. But just as the lawgiver and statesman should be attentive to "actual conditions," so must the student of religion and politics. The analysis of constitutional possibilities for addressing this relationship must be sensitive to the "facts on the ground," especially the manner in which religious life is experienced within any given society and how this experience affects the achievement of historically determined constitutional ends. As Michael Walzer has pointed out, "[T]here are no principles [beyond a basic respect for human rights] that govern all the regimes of toleration or that require us to act in all circumstances, in all times and places, on behalf of a particular set of political or constitutional arrangements."[12] For example, "[W]e [cannot] say that state neutrality and voluntary association, on the model of John Locke's 'Letter on Toleration,' is the only or best way of dealing with religious and ethnic pluralism. It is a very good way, one that is adapted to the experience of Protestant congregations in certain sorts of societies, but its reach beyond that experience and those societies has to be argued, not simply assumed."[13]

Walzer's point can be taken an additional step. Not only is the "one size fits all" option unwise and unrealistic, so too is the expectation that a specific formula for constitutional structuring of the relations between Church and State will or ought to apply uniformly *within* a given polity. Such expectations have been nurtured by our conventional labeling of constitutional approaches to religion and politics. In their generally insightful five-nation comparative study, Stephen V. Monsma and Christo-

---

[12] Walzer 1997, 2–3. Walzer proceeds "to defend . . . a historical and contextual account of toleration and coexistence, one that examines the different forms that these have actually taken and the norms of everyday life appropriate to each." He continues: "It is necessary to look both at the ideal versions of these practical arrangements and at their characteristic, historically documented distortions."

[13] Ibid., 4. A good example of Walzer's point may be found in the Indian practice of State support for public events of a religiously celebratory nature. As Rajeev Dhavan has observed, "This is where Indian secularism is vastly different from American or any other kind of secularism." Rajeev Dhavan, "The Kumbh," *The Hindu*, February 26, 2001. India, he points out, practices a "participatory benign neutrality," rather than a "strict neutrality" of the sort that makes it exceedingly difficult in the United States for public resources to be expended for even small crèche displays at the Christmas season. On the other hand, support for mega events such as the Kumbh (a Hindu ceremonial gathering attended by millions) is accepted as necessary for a healthy secularism in which the infrastructure of religious diversity is kept viable through direct governmental engagement.

pher Soper discuss three contrasting models of Church/State arrangements: strict separation, establishment, and structural pluralism. Among their objectives is the demonstration of the shortcomings of the strict separation model (exemplified by the American experience), which ultimately fails to achieve their basic goal or ideal, governmental neutrality on matters of religion. Thus they criticize American (and Australian) courts' treatment of free exercise rights, because it allegedly discriminates against religious conscience in favor of secular policy, violating the goal of neutrality rightly understood.[14] But reasonable though their specific criticisms may be, their general critique of the judicial subordination of religious conscience to collective goals presumes a virtue of neutrality that may not consistently hold for one society, let alone for all societies. What should be so sacrosanct about strict neutrality between religion and nonreligion in the absence of some overriding principle to which the commitment is connected? In the American case, strict separation should not be viewed as a model, but rather as a doctrine that may in some settings advance the cause of constitutive ends, but which in others may obstruct their attainment. Models of secular constitutional development need to be framed in accordance with these regime-specific ends; they should, as Aristotelian political science teaches, "distinguish the laws which are absolutely best from those which are appropriate to each constitution."[15]

A rough typology can assist in framing the analysis that follows. It requires, however, that we be careful not to identify the secular constitution with *secularization*, meaning, among other things, "the separation of the polity from religion."[16] As Rajeev Bhargava has noted, "[S]ecularism is compatible with the view that the complete secularization of society is neither possible nor desirable."[17] The latter concept denotes a process—usually associated with modernization—in which the various sectors of society are progressively liberated from their domination by religion; but the emphasis on separate spheres unnecessarily obscures the diversity among regimes that aspire to be constitutionally secular. More separation

---

[14] Monsma and Soper 1997, 202.

[15] Aristotle 1962, 1288b 10.

[16] Smith, 1970, 11. There is a substantial literature on secularization. A good sampling may be found in Bruce 1992. In their depiction of the orthodox model, Roy Wallis and Steve Bruce explain the phenomenon as occurring when "[r]eligion becomes privatized and is pushed to the margins and interstices of the social order." Ibid., 11. Or as Peter Berger has described it, "[T]he process by which sectors of society and culture are removed from the domination of religious institutions and symbols." Berger 1969, 107.

[17] Bhargava 1998, 489. A different view has been expressed by another Indian scholar, Achin Vanaik, who sees such a development as quite desirable. "Further secularization means the further decline of religious identity. This is both possible and desirable. Religion should become more privatized and religious affiliation more of an optional choice." Vanaik 1997, 70.

does not in itself mean greater constitutional legitimacy. Also, the secular constitution should be distinguished from secularism as an ideological commitment whose proponents are often hostile toward religion. To be sure, a secular constitution may rest upon an antipathy toward religion, just as it may be premised upon a radical separation of temporal and spiritual spheres. But in the analysis that follows, these assumptions are not intrinsic to the logic of secular constitutional development. In referring to the secular constitution, what is meant is simply this: a polity where there exists a genuine commitment to religious freedom that is manifest in the legal and political safeguards put in place to enforce that commitment.[18]

Two dimensions stand out in considering alternative approaches to the secular constitution. The first is "the consequential dimension of religiosity,"[19] which here connotes more than a subjective determination as to whether religion is deemed important by the people who practice it; it speaks to religion's explanatory power in apprehending the structural configuration of a given society. This dimension is also captured by the anthropological concept of a cultural "way of life," in which a (religious) system of beliefs, symbols, and values becomes ingrained in the basic structure of society and ultimately sets the parameters within which vital societal relations occur. Avishai Margalit and Joseph Raz have employed the term *encompassing group* to highlight a set of characteristics that should qualify a specific collection of people for national self-determination. Such a group will "possess cultural traditions that penetrate beyond a single or a few areas of human life, and display themselves in a whole range of areas, including many which are of great importance for the wellbeing of individuals."[20] They point out that some religious groups, by

---

[18] As Charles Taylor points out, the term *secular* was originally part of the Christian vocabulary, which serves as a useful reminder that liberalism fits most comfortably with certain kinds of religious experience. Taylor et al. 1992, 62. In this regard, Marc Galanter, the leading American student of Indian law, writes of the First Amendment that it is a charter for religion as well as for government. "It is the basis of a regime which is congenial to those religions which favor private and voluntary observance rather than to those which favor official support of observance." Galanter 1989, 249. There is also another kind of separation that should be minimized for our purposes. Harvey Cox's definition of secularization involves, in addition to liberation from "religious and metaphysical tutelage, the turning of [man's] attention away from other worlds and toward this one." Cox 1990, 15. But as Tocqueville suggests, a democratically constituted regime can be undermined by an exclusive focus on this-worldly concerns.

[19] Way and Burt 1983, 654.

[20] Margalit and Raz 1995, 82. See also Rosenblum 2000. Rosenblum uses the term *integralism* to convey a similar idea. "Its defining characteristic is a push for a 'religiously integrated existence.' . . . Integralists want to be able to conduct themselves according to the injunctions of religious law and authority in every sphere of everyday life, and to see their faith mirrored in public life." Ibid., 15.

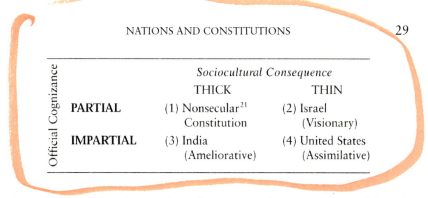

	Sociocultural Consequence	
	THICK	THIN
PARTIAL	(1) Nonsecular[21] Constitution	(2) Israel (Visionary)
IMPARTIAL	(3) India (Ameliorative)	(4) United States (Assimilative)

Official Cognizance

virtue of their rich and pervasive cultures, meet these conditions, although my analysis offers no opinion on the desirability of national self-determination in such instances. Their construction offers an apt basis for distinguishing two senses of religion, *thick* and *thin* (or demanding and modest), the latter referring to a situation where religion bears only tangentially upon the life experiences of most people.

A second dimension refers to the official cognizance of religion, more specifically, the extent to which the State is decisively identified with any particular religious group. The relevant distinction here has less to do with concerns about the public square, that is, the question of governmental support, hostility, or indifference toward religion, than it does with the official favoring of one religion over others for special benefits. Thus in the United States, all separationists and most accommodationists are united (with only trivial exception) in requiring impartiality in the State's dealings with religious groups. Both sides are committed to neutrality among religions but differ over whether there should be neutrality toward religion. While governmental neutrality is thus key to this dimension, the formal identification of a State with a particular religion does not in itself

---

[21] As broad as my working definition of the secular constitution is, it cannot accommodate a regime—I have in mind a country such as Iran—where the State identifies strongly with a religion that is constitutive of society. A recent visitor to the United States from Iran, Mohammad Atrian-far, the head of Teheran's town councils and editor of the daily newspaper *Hamshahri*, remarked: "What surprised me the most when I came to the United States was how many churches there were. I certainly didn't know how religious Americans are." *New York Times*, Week in Review, September 23, 2001, 8. Had he reflected further, he might have noted that being "religious" can mean quite different things from place to place in terms of social and political impact. Indeed, when Tocqueville first arrived in the United States, he had a similar reaction to the Iranian's. "On my arrival in the United States the religious aspect of the country was the first thing that struck my attention; and the longer I stayed there, the more I perceived the great political consequences resulting from this new state of things." Tocqueville 1945, vol. 1, 319. He then went on to comment on the absence of a religious presence in the circles of American government, which led to an observation that causes one to think of contemporary Iran. "Religions intimately united with the governments of the earth have been known to exercise sovereign power founded on terror and faith." Ibid., 321.

remove that State from the category of secular regimes. Sweden (unlike Israel) has had an established Church, but that legal designation hardly disqualifies that country from asserting its secular credentials. Were it to become known as "the Lutheran State," and consistent with that description were it to distinguish in some of its policies and symbols between Lutherans and non-Lutherans, it would violate an essential requirement of liberal constitutionalism, but still admit of the possibility, as the Israeli example will show, of achieving a secular (albeit not unambiguously liberal) constitution.

These two dimensions create quadrants that include three variations on the theme of the secular constitution, each illustrated by one of the countries under consideration.

The lines that separate these four quadrants do not demarcate arenas whose confines are wholly dissimilar from one another. They are meant to be suggestive of orientations toward the secular constitution that are also expressive of salient aspects of national identity. They highlight contrasting emphases, rather than set forth mutually exclusive approaches. Thus in (2), Zionist aspirations for a homeland for the Jewish people frame the debate over Church/State relations, but the predominantly secular orientation of most Israeli Jews tends to dampen whatever theocratic impulse might reside in the founding commitment to ascriptively driven nationalism.[22] In (4), where the Constitution is the paradigmatic case of a governing charter that is central to its people's sense of nationhood, the relative thinness of religion in the United States, conjoined with a constitutional requirement of nonestablishment, encourages the assimilation of a diverse population into a constitutive culture of ideas.[23] And in (3), the constitutional promise of State neutrality toward religious groups is a corollary of the transformational agenda of Indian nationalism, a

---

[22] There is a great temptation to deny Israel the status of a secular regime. See, for example, Tessler 1981, 247. As I will explain, however, one should resist this temptation, even while conceding that Israeli policies discriminate against non-Jews. For another perspective that employs an alternative typology constructed along the dimensions of state establishment and religious participation in electoral politics, see Demarath 2001. One of Demarath's categories is Religious States and Religious Politics, a "stereotypically non-Western" type, under which he places Israel. Ibid., 194–5. Such a placement is defensible (although as Demarath recognizes, controversial), but the absence in this typology of a thickness/thinness dimension may lead one erroneously to locate Israel among a group of non-Western regimes that are hostile or indifferent to the protection of religious liberty.

[23] The thinness of American religiosity is partially explained in theological terms. As Warren A. Nord has observed, "Many Americans believe that believing is enough." Nord 1995, 41. Thus Nord notes that Protestantism made doctrine and belief, rather than good works and religious practices, critical to religion. The contrast with Catholicism, Islam, Judaism, and Hinduism is not without political significance.

principal objective of which is the democratization of a social order inhabited by a thickly constituted religious presence.[24]

The contrast of thickness in India with the relative thinness of religiosity in the United States and Israel is detectable in the influence of the majority religions in these three places on the social practices of adherents of minority religions. For example, it has often been observed that although the caste system in India is uniquely associated with Hinduism, over a long period of time manifestations of its distinctive hierarchical social ordering have become entrenched in other communal settings, most notably among Muslims (most of whom, to be sure, are descendants of converts). As J. Duncan M. Derrett has pointed out, "[I]n an India which is ruled by a Hindu majority the Hindu concept of religion as a *social* identification is accepted virtually by all."[25] There is nothing comparable to this in either of the two other countries. In the United States, Christian influence is discernible in the participation by members of other religions in the traditions of Christmas, but this sort of trivial cultural impact only underscores the relative thinness of American religious practice. In Israel too the religion to which most people belong does not constitute a significant presence in the behavior of nonadherents, although this is at least partly attributable to the nonassimilationist ethos of Judaism.

As the point of departure for a preliminary overview of the secular constitutional logics of India, Israel, and the United States, we go first to Australia, specifically to an important Supreme Court decision from that country.

> There are those who regard religion as consisting principally in a system of beliefs or statement of doctrine. So viewed religion may be either true or false. Others are more inclined to regard religion as prescribing a code of conduct. So viewed a religion may be good or bad. There are others who pay greater attention to religion as involving some prescribed form of ritual or religious observance.[26]

The excerpt appears in a decision that is often favorably cited by judges on the Indian Supreme Court (or one of the state Supreme Courts) to illustrate how religion ought to be viewed from a constitutional vantage point. Occasionally, the citation is conjoined with a reference to two well-known American cases of the late nineteenth century—*Reynolds v United States* and *Davis v Beason*—each addressing the problem of polygamy. In all three cases, considerations of social and political welfare were used to

---

[24] See Dumont 1970, 210; Derrett 1968, 558; Galanter 1984, 17; and De 1976, 105.

[25] Derrett 1968, 558. As a result, although the Muslim and Christian faiths specifically reject the notion of caste, in India both communities recognize caste within themselves.

[26] *Adelaide Co. of Jehovah's Witnesses* at 123.

uphold restrictions on religious freedom, thus demonstrating that respected authority elsewhere could be cited to support similar efforts in India.[27] In addition, the juxtaposition of these cases has enabled the Court to register its preference for the Australian understanding of religion, which, contrary to what the American Court had seemed to be saying in the polygamy cases, does not embrace the distinction between religious opinions and acts done in pursuance of those opinions.

That same Australian opinion speaks contemptuously of "[t]he criminal religions in India,"[28] a phrase one should not expect to find in any judgment of the Indian Supreme Court. What one does find, however, are many references to unattractive behavior associated with these religions, and it is in this regard that the distinctions drawn in the excerpt quoted above merit further consideration. As a belief system, religion may be seen as true or false, which is to say it should rightly be construed as a set of opinions to which one subscribes, and is for that reason arguably of no interest to a liberally constituted government. As a code of conduct, however, valuations of goodness or badness come into play, providing a much weaker rationale for government to maintain its indifference to religious activity. Politically, the ultimate source for the derivation of such valuations are the fundamental principles of a given regime. As Montesquieu observed, "The most true and holy doctrines may be attended with the very worst consequences, when they are not connected with the principles of society; and on the contrary, doctrines the most false may be attended with excellent consequences, when contrived so as to be connected with these principles."[29] Montesquieu's point of course also serves to remind us that beliefs and doctrines (true or false) will have consequences (good or bad), so that distinctions drawn between opinions and conduct are on one level quite meaningless. But on the level of the liberal constitutional playing field, the distinction presumes legitimacy, and Montes-

---

[27] In the Australian case, the Parliament had legislated to restrain the activities of the Jehovah's Witnesses, activities that it felt were prejudicial to the efficient prosecution of the war. The Court upheld these restrictions, while conceding that the religious group had not engaged in any overt hostile acts. For the restrictions to be upheld, it was deemed sufficient that the Witnesses possessed an attitude of noncooperation with the war effort, coupled with beliefs that all governments were "satanic." It is perhaps worth noting that in the same year across the ocean, the Jehovah's Witnesses were faring much better, as the American Supreme Court upheld their right to refrain from participating in a public school flag salute. *West Virginia v Barnett*. The *Reynolds* and *Beason* cases, involving the efforts of the United States to curtail the activities of the Mormons in Utah, are discussed more fully in the next chapter. For a critical account of *Adelaide* that views the decision as sending a message that the Court would not be a strong advocate of religious freedom, see Monsma and Soper 1997, 96–7.

[28] *Adelaide* at 125.

[29] Montesquieu 1966, vol. 2, 38–9.

quieu's argument validates certain imposed limits on freedom of religion in order to prevent religiously based conduct from undermining the constitutive principles of society.

Conduct

This at any rate would seem to be the sort of argument that underlies a key provision of the Indian Constitution. Article 25 provides that "Subject to public order, morality and health . . . all persons are equally entitled to freedom of conscience and the right freely to profess, practise and propagate religion." The second section of the Article goes on to say: "Nothing in this article shall affect the operation of any existing law or prevent the State from making any law—(a) regulating or restricting any economic, financial, political or other secular activity which may be associated with religious practice; (b) providing for social welfare and reform, or the throwing open of Hindu religious institutions of a public character to all classes and sections of Hindus."

With admirable clarity, then, the document guarantees all Indians a broad right to religious freedom, only to declare that this right is subject to substantial possible limitation.[30] Moreover, unlike the other articles in Part III (the "Fundamental Rights" section) of the Constitution, Articles 25 and 26 (providing the freedom to manage religious affairs) begin with a statement of limitations and only then go on to specify the substantive rights that are to be constitutionally guaranteed. It might be an exaggeration to say that this ordering suggests that "[T]he limitations . . . are given the primary place and not the substantive right to which they are appended."[31] But the textual arrangement evinces a clear founding purpose that seeks to reconcile the securing of religious freedoms included in the document with the achievement of social justice.

The debates surrounding the framing of India's Constitution support the most obvious interpretation of this language, that the constitutional undertaking of 1947 had as one of its principal goals the major reform

---

[30] Indeed, the leading authority on law and religion in India, J. Duncan M. Derrett, notes that the Article is "subject to so many qualifications and restrictions that the reader wonders whether the so-called 'fundamental right' was worth asserting in the first place." Derrett 1968, 451. There are additional rights present in this section that relate to religion, such as the freedom of religious institutions to manage their own affairs and the freedom to avoid being taxed for the promotion or maintenance of any particular religion or religious denomination. Part IV of the Constitution—the "Directive Principles of State Policy"—also contains passages implicating religious freedoms, but the articles in this section of the document are essentially hortatory in nature, meaning that they are not justiciable in Court. As will be shown later, this does not mean they are unimportant.

[31] Beg 1979, 36.

of Indian society. Typical of the statements made on this occasion was delegate K. M. Panikar's comment that "If the State considers that certain religious practices require modification by the will of the people, then there must be power for the State to do it."[32] With this, scholarly opinion concurs. One commentator describes the Constitution as "first and foremost a social document,"[33] another as "a charter for the reform of Hinduism."[34] Consistent with these characterizations are statements from the Supreme Court; for example, the observation by a reform-minded jurist that it should "always be remembered that social justice is the main foundation of the democratic way of life enshrined in the provisions of the Indian Constitution."[35] To reformulate this latter proposition in a way that captures the spirit of Montesquieu's insight, we might say that the democratic way of life takes precedence over religious practices; that the conformity of these practices to beliefs that are deemed holy and true is no bar to their proscription because of the bad consequences that flow from their failure to connect with the principles of society.[36]

While this may serve in a preliminary way as an adequate introduction to the secular constitution in India, it also presages difficulties that lie ahead. In a letter published as part of the documentary history of the Constitution's framing, Alladi Krishnaswami Ayyar worried that "[I]f for any reason the Federal Court construes the clause relating to religion and the practice of religion in a wide sense, it may have the effect of invalidating all existing legislation apart from prohibiting such legislation for the future."[37] Were this to happen, the judiciary would be in essence abdicating its prescribed role as "an arm of the social revolution,"[38] leaving the transformational agenda of the constitution-makers for others to pursue. For some, the record of the Court's solicitude for religious practice and autonomy suggests that this abdication has in fact occurred. They refer with disappointment to the "divergence between national aspirations and judicial pronouncements."[39] While this divergence may reflect a failure

---

[32] Government of India Press 1967, vol. 2, 265.

[33] Austin 1966, 50.

[34] Galanter 1989, 247.

[35] Justice Gajendragadkar in *Yagnapurushdasji* at 522.

[36] Note, for example, the concern for the thickness of religion in this debater's comments on Article 44, the section in the Constitution concerning a uniform civil code. "We are at a stage where we must unify and consolidate the nation by every means without interfering with religious practices. If, however, the religious practices in the past have been so construed as to cover *the whole field of life*, we have reached a point where we must . . . say that the matters are not religious, they are purely matters for secular legislation." Quoted in Baird 1981, 423 (emphasis added).

[37] Government of India Press 1967, vol. 2, 143.

[38] Austin 1966, 164.

[39] R. K. Tripathi as quoted in Beg 1979, 49. Gurpreet Mahajan contends that the Court's solicitude has given it the appearance of being a bastion of social conservatism. Her claim,

on the part of some judges to pursue the constitutional path established by founding aspiration, it also reflects an Indian social reality that more or less requires the Supreme Court to reject a narrow view of religion in favor of the Australian model set out in *Adelaide Co. of Jehovah's Witnesses v The Commonwealth*.[40]

Whatever may be the case elsewhere, it would be difficult for an Indian tribunal to do otherwise. Defining religion in the "wide sense" does not occur in a vacuum; it flows from religion-specific characteristics that possess a dynamic and logic of their own. It is one thing to *assert* the priority of the democratic way of life to religious practice, quite another to act accordingly. Consider, for example, that in the same case in which he wrote of the Constitution's enthronement of the democratic way of life, Justice Gajendragadkar described Hinduism as constituting "a way of life and nothing more."[41] While surely there is some exaggeration in this claim ("nothing more"?), to the extent that Hinduism does indeed constitute a "way of life," it renders largely fruitless the task of seeking a narrow definition of religion.[42] It also points to one of the great challenges of

---

contrary to the argument in this chapter, is that this conservatism is consistent with the transcendent emphasis in the Constitution on religious pluralism. "[T]he primacy accorded to religious practice by the Constitution and the Supreme Court has severely limited the modernizing interventions of the Indian State." Mahajan 1998, 72.

[40] In *Ratilal v State of Bombay*, Chief Justice Mukherjea wrote: "A religion is not merely an opinion, doctrine or belief. It has its outward expression in acts as well." *Ratilal* at 392. He elaborated upon this view in *Comm. H.R.E. v Swamiar*: "A religion undoubtedly has its basis in a system of belief or doctrines which are regarded by those who profess that religion as conducive to their spiritual well being, but it would not be correct to say that religion is nothing else but a doctrine or belief. A religion may not only lay down a code of ethical rules for its followers to accept, it might prescribe rituals and observances, ceremonies and modes of worship which are regarded as integral parts of religion, and these forms and observances might extend even to matters of food and dress." Ibid. at 290. Subsequent decisions have confirmed the precedential value of Mukherjea's view. See, for example, *Yulitha Hyde*.

[41] *Yagnapurushdasji* at 513.

[42] This needs to be qualified in a way that incorporates an important insight appearing in Marc Galanter's discussion of caste in India. He maintains that it may make a great difference whether the characterization "religious" is attached to caste groups within a legal context, arguing that actual behavior, and thus real reform, could hinge upon such a determination. Galanter 1989, 141. The Constitution itself provides a negative judgment about caste, but since compliance with constitutional injunctions are rarely automatic, decisions about whether the origins of caste are rooted in religious or racial considerations become relevant to the work of the courts. For an intriguing view of why Hindus often assert to Westerners that caste is a social rather than a religious matter, see Dumont 1970, 25. As a rank amateur in this area, I express no opinion on the question of origins, but feel safe in simply acknowledging the deeply interwoven nature of caste and religion as they have evolved over the centuries. I would note too, in this regard, Donald Smith's observation that it is a relatively recent phenomenon for caste to be repudiated as a Hindu religious value, and that this repudiation has had little effect upon the ordinary Hindu's acceptance

Indian constitutionalism: how to reconcile two ways of life that are in fundamental tension with one another.[43]

Indeed, it is difficult to overstate the extent to which the perception of Hinduism as a way of life has dominated commentary and discourse in both scholarly and judicial venues. "People are aware of God in everything"—a "discovery," according to a 1992 judicial opinion, "that was made in India millennia ago."[44] Thus Bankim Chander Chatterji, regarded by his fellow Bengali writer Nirad C. Chaudhuri as perhaps "the most powerful Indian mind of the nineteenth century," wrote:

> With other peoples, religion is only a part of life; there are things religious, and there are things lay and secular. To the Hindu, his whole life was religion. To other peoples, their relations to God and to the spiritual world are things sharply distinguished from their relations to man and to the temporal world. To the Hindu, his relations to God and his relations to man, his spiritual life and his temporal life are incapable of being so distinguished. They form one compact and harmonious whole, to separate which into component parts is to break the entire fabric. All life to him was religion, and religion never received a name from him, because it never had for him an existence apart from all that had received a name.[45]

Chaudhuri, whose extraordinary life spanned a century, and who was himself a writer of exquisite insight and eloquence, has described in vivid detail how "in his daily life a Hindu is bound hand and foot in regard to all his actions."[46] His account makes it easy to recognize and appreciate the profound tension that penetrates to the core of Indian constitutionalism, where "The State is secular . . . but the people are not."

In warning about the consequences of an expansive judicial definition of religion, it could not have been the future Justice Ayyar's purpose to

---

of the divinely ordained character of the institution. Smith 1970, 35. Robert D. Baird is similarly of the view that caste, for all of the sociological interest it has engendered, is ultimately a phenomenon sanctioned by religion. Baird 1969, 225. And Julius Lipner has observed that "[T]he caste hierarchy . . . is set in a religious context [and] . . . caste is given a sacrosanct status." Lipner 1994, 88.

[43] "[S]ecularism is an ideology which provides a way of life and conduct as against the one provided by religion." Subhash 1988, 140.

[44] *Atheist Society of India* at 318.

[45] Quoted in Chaudhuri 1979, 11–12.

[46] Ibid., 191. The entrenched character of Hinduism in the social fabric of Indian society is a description widely accepted in a variety of literatures. Social theorists: Glock and Stark 1965, 34; Eisenstadt 1968, 34; Loomis and Loomis 1969, 79. India specialists: Weiner 1960, 178; Stern 1993, 24. Indian commentators: Beg 1979, 15; Subhash 1988, 9, 139; Vanaik 1997, 38. And legal scholars: Derrett 1968, 57; Srivastava 1992, 103; Alexandrowicz 1960, 273, 283. All of these perspectives generally share a consensus in highlighting the profound extent to which the religions of India—in particular, Hinduism—are solidly embedded in the existent social structure.

disabuse his fellow constitution-makers of the tension between secular law and nonsecular lives. Thus in another of his remarks at the Constituent Assembly, he said, "[Y]ou can never separate social life from religious life. . . . [I]f there is one thing which has contributed to the merit of the old Hindu system it is the inter-mixture between religion and the social fabric of society. It is a single society."[47] To be sure, the "merit" of the system is a crucial point of contention upon which much of the debate over the secular constitution rests. The late nineteenth-century Indian social reformer K. T. Telang castigated Hinduism for "preach[ing] not the equality of men but their inequality," depicting it in a state of "war against the principles of democracy."[48] The war proved difficult to pursue because it was not simply a clash of ideas, but a contest fought, as it were, in the deep trenches of the social order. Moreover, the fact that other wars—of independence, of culture—were and are being prosecuted concurrently means that the battle lines have not always been sharply drawn.

For example, agreement on the existence of a thickly constituted religious presence has not led to anything close to a consensus on an appropriate response to the difficulties this entails. Thus for some, the secular state is "a vacuous word, a phantom concept,"[49] but a dangerous construct nevertheless for the perverse consequences that its reckless pursuit entails. Others, who agree that traditional religion in India has for most people been manifest in the totality of their lives, welcome for that very reason a Western-oriented secular state that would bring with it a drastic reduction in the scope and sphere of religion.[50] Still others consider an American-like separation of Church and State to be an inadequate response to the problems associated with a pervasive religious presence. For them, "India must give the highest priority to the building of secular counter-institutions in civil society and promoting a more secular popular culture."[51] A secular state is by itself no solution and must be accompanied by the secularization of civil society.

---

[47] Government of India Press 1967, vol. 2, 266.

[48] Quoted in Heimsath 1964, 326.

[49] Madan 1987, 749.

[50] Chatterji 1984, 23.

[51] Vanaik 1997, 54. In this regard consider the argument made by Marty 1969. Marty distinguishes between three approaches to secularization in the West: utter secularity (practiced on the Continent), mere secularity (practiced in England), and controlled secularity (practiced in the United States). Indian critics like Vanaik are essentially advocating a Continental solution, which entails a proactive assault on religion and religious values. Thus in Marty's analysis, utter secularists cannot "let Christendom die a natural death," or "be content to watch its doctrines lose their power." Instead, they "see the Christian syntheses and structures as being the enemy of values and must work to destroy them" by waging "a formal and unrelenting attack on gods and churches and a studied striving to replace them." Ibid., 18, 10. The American embrace of controlled secularity, which seeks the preservation

This debate need not be resolved here; at this juncture it is only necessary to establish as a matter of broad, if not universal, general agreement
a point whose constitutional significance increases when considered in a
comparative context. Within a general framework of sensitivity to the imperatives of group and religious life,[52] the formal commitment of the fundamental law "to constitute India," in the words of the amended Preamble, "into a SOVEREIGN SOCIALIST SECULAR REPUBLIC",[53] represented a
substantial challenge to social, cultural, economic, and political practices
deeply rooted in the soil of an all-encompassing religious tradition. Thus
the observation by Tocqueville that "by the side of every religion is to be
found a political opinion, which is connected with it by affinity,"[54] requires
little elaboration in the Indian context.[55] But his application of the insight
to the United States scene stimulates reflection over important differences
in Indian and American conceptualizations of the secular constitution.

Belief

First, however, it is worth recalling Montesquieu's point about holy doctrines, societal principles, and the consequences that follow from their
consistency or lack thereof. A number of contemporary commentators

---

of religion and religious values in the private sphere, would not be an adequate response to
the problems confronting Indian social and political development. The Modern Schism in
the United States did not divide religious individuals from nonreligious individuals; instead
it split each individual—religion being retained in certain spheres of life, but completely
banished from others. Because of the thickness of religious experience in India, this American solution is, from this perspective, clearly inadequate.

[52] Dhavan 1987, 250.

[53] The politics of this emendation has received a lot of discussion. In particular, as we shall
see in chapter 5, the word *socialist* has complicated the task of construing the significance of
the "secular" commitment. The following interpretation is an appealing attempt to provide
coherence to the language. "The simultaneous addition of the adjective 'socialist' would
indicate that by ensuring respect for all religions the legislature wanted to make clear that
this respect is subject to limits. These limits are imposed by the socialist ideals of freedom
of the community from all forms of exploitation—social, political, and economic—all of
which are secular in nature. In other words, religious ideals are made subservient to secular
ideals." Beg 1979, 16.

[54] Tocqueville 1945, vol. 1, 310.

[55] For a very good elaboration of Tocqueville's point as applied to India, the work of
another French sociologist, Dumont 1970, is an excellent place to go. His principal focus
on the tension between the principle of equality and the principle of hierarchy is one that
has a distinctly Tocquevillian ring to it. The decisive role of religion in this tension was
affirmed in the very important official government report of the Mandal Commission, which
was established in 1979 to investigate the conditions of the socially and educationally backward classes in India. That report indicates clearly that social inequality is deeply rooted in
religious practices, and that the structural reality created by this history cannot be changed
through the routine progress of modernization. See the discussion of the Mandal Commission Report in *Indra Sawhney*.

have followed Tocqueville's well-known defense of religion in a democracy to adumbrate the salutory effects of *in*consistency. The argument relies upon Tocqueville's understanding of religious groups as independent moral and political forces, and consequently their capacity to function as "a bulwark against state authority."[56] As Stephen Carter puts it, "[R]eligion, properly understood, is a very subversive force."[57] In much the same vein, Robert Booth Fowler welcomes religion as "an *alternative* to the liberal order, a *refuge* from our society and its pervasive values."[58] This is not meant as a rejection of those values; subversion, indeed, is to be encouraged in the ultimate interest of those values. Religion's political contribution to a constitutional democracy comes from appreciating it as "[a] source of public virtue outside of government . . . necessary to the ultimate success of the republican experiment."[59]

Carter, Fowler, and McConnell are all scholars who are aligned on the "accommodationist" side of the Church/State debate in the United States. They have worried about the ill effects associated with the secularization of American society. However, the pluralistic arguments they make on behalf of religious liberty are not intellectually bound up with only one side of the debate. In fact, the unstated presumption of their argument for religion as a healthy subversion is more generally associated with the "separationist" advocates on the other side. As part of this presumption, religion in the United States consists of "autonomous intermediate institutions,"[60] which is to say that it constitutes a realm of human experience that is separable from the other realms of a person's life. It is not, as it arguably is for most people in India, a "way of life." There are important voices in India—notably Ashis Nandy and T. N. Madan—who speak of religion as a "bulwark against state authority," but precisely because, in Madan's words, "religion is here constitutive of society,"[61] these voices are the dissonant ones. In the United States, on the other hand, where it makes sense to say (if one is not unduly disturbed by an inelegant redundancy) that the *Constitution* is constitutive of society, the benefits of religion as an alternative to the liberal order *ordained* by that document are, as Tocqueville understood, clearly more evident. Here, unlike in India,

---

[56] Carter 1993, 38.

[57] Ibid., 43.

[58] Fowler 1989, 4.

[59] McConnell 1986, 17.

[60] Carter 1993, 39.

[61] Madan 1983, 12. Madan embraces a Gandhian suspicion of the State, which puts him at odds with mainstream secular opinion in India. "To the extent to which Indian secularism . . . is a state ideology, enshrined in the Constitution in which it is linked to the materialist ideology of socialism, and to the extent to which it has nothing to say about the individual except in terms of his or her rights, it is from the Gandhian perspective a hedonistic ideology, and bound to fail." Madan 1997, 237.

the Constitution is fully consistent with the dominant political culture and is not itself seeking to reconstitute a way of life, which means that Americans can afford (and perhaps welcome) the challenge of alternative ways of life.[62]

Such was certainly the case in *Wisconsin v Yoder*, where the Supreme Court upheld the claim of the Old Order Amish to be exempt from a state's compulsory school-attendance law. The exceptional treatment of this religious group matched its exceptional profile in American society. In Chief Justice Burger's account, "[F]or the Old Order Amish, religion is not simply a matter of theocratic belief. . . . [R]eligion pervades and determines virtually their entire way of life. . . ."[63] Much that has been written about this case rightly focuses on the exemplary law-abiding and self-sufficient ways of the Amish as crucial in explaining the extraordinary deference accorded them by the Court. But however much the Amish demonstrated old-fashioned American virtues, the Court's solicitude should also be seen as a reflection of religion's place in the constitutional order. Thus Burger writes that "A way of life that is odd or even erratic but interferes with no rights or interests of others is not to be condemned because it is different."[64] For most people in the United States, religion is not a way of life; were it otherwise, the rights and interests of others could not so casually be discounted, and the supremacy of the civil law would be dangerously compromised by the kind of accommodation required to adequately acknowledge that reality.

To portray the relative lack of differentiation between religious and secular lives as an essentially aberrant or marginalized phenomenon in American social experience is not to deny the considerable evidence pointing to the religiosity of the American people.[65] A contrast with India will

---

[62] As Achin Vanaik puts it, "In India, a non-denominational State with substantively secularized laws, resting on a secular Constitution, coexists with a civil society where religious influence is pervasive. It is a situation that gives rise to a profound tension." Vanaik 1997, 38.

[63] *Yoder* at 216.

[64] Ibid. at 224.

[65] For example, a March 1994 Gallup Poll found that 59 percent of the American people felt that religion was very important in their lives, and another 29 percent felt it was fairly important. Saad and McAneny 1994, 2–4. This is consistent with the many studies showing, in comparison to many other countries, high attendance rates at formal religious services and high levels of belief in a Supreme Being. In the context of our contemporary "culture wars," figures like these have been cleverly manipulated to show how one side or the other is winning. But to show the relative importance of religion in people's lives is not the same as demonstrating that religion is fundamentally determinative of the social lives of most people. Thus in a comprehensive survey of American religious belief and behavior, Gallup and Castelli conclude: "While religion is highly popular in America, it is to a large extent superficial; it does not change people's lives to the degree one would expect from their level of professed faith." Gallup and Castelli 1989, 21. The special character of religion in the

suggest that this religiosity does not necessarily entail the totalistic commitment of thick religion, but perhaps more tellingly, so will an examination of the distinctive experience of *American* Indians. Indeed, some American Indian languages have no word for religion, because, as Stephen Bates correctly notes, "[T]heir concepts of the holy are fully intertwined with life and culture."[66] As is the case for the Amish, the structure of the social world inhabited by these Americans is fundamentally an extension of their spiritual engagements. As told to a Senate committee by one Barney Old Coyote, "Worship is an integral part of the Indian way of life and culture which cannot be separated from the whole. This oneness of Indian life seems to be the basic difference between the Indian and non-Indian of a dominant society."[67]

Of what relevance is this to the constitutional provisions of the First Amendment? Unlike its Indian counterpart, the American Constitution uses very few words to address issues of very great complexity. Aside from Article VI's proscription of religious tests for holding public office, there are, as far as Church and State are concerned, only the familiar opening words of the Bill of Rights: "Congress shall make no law respecting an establishment of religion, or prohibiting the free exercise thereof." For the impartial reader of the voluminous literature concerning the meaning

---

United States may best be grasped by conjoining this conclusion with another, namely that the American "nation cannot by any stretch of the imagination be described as secular in its core beliefs." Ibid., 90. Indeed, the title of a recent book—*The Diminishing Divide*—conveys the gist of its empirical findings, namely that "Americans have grown increasingly tolerant of closer links between religion and politics." Kohut et al 2000, 123. Again, however, there is very little evidence that this translates into a more thickly constituted religious presence in American life.

[66] Bates 1993, 309. In their study of volitionism and religious liberty, David and Susan Williams describe in detail the many aspects of American Indian religions that are strongly nonvolitionist in character. "This distinguishes them from primarily volitionist religions that dominate the American religious scene, and from the largely volitionist secular legal and philosophical traditions." Williams and Williams 1991, 795. Elsewhere I have described how this more totalistic religiosity is an important factor in the constitutionally anomalous status of Native Americans. Jacobsohn 1993, 18–25. It is interesting, however, that this status does not ensure judicial relief from legal obligations that are challenged because of the burdens they place on the Indian way of life. *Lyng*; *Smith*. On this point see also Gerald Bradley's arguments on separation of Church and State and the Christian tradition. Bradley 1989, 1057, 1086. For those who insist that the lack of differentiation between the secular and the religious is a much more pervasive phenomenon in American life than I have suggested, these cases are not exceptional in what they portray about Indian culture. Thus Justice Brennan's description in his *Lyng* dissent of the interwovenness of religion with the rest of life in the Native American experience has been sharply criticized for its highlighting of the alien features of this phenomenon. Glendon and Yanes 1991, 477, 516.

[67] Quoted in Wunder 1994, 194. In chapter 9 I discuss the case of *Employment Division v Smith*, in which the American Supreme Court ignored this "oneness of Indian life" in ruling against the claim for a constitutionally based exemption to a state statute regulating drug use.

and intentions behind these words, there is likely to be considerable support for Justice White's claim that "[O]ne cannot seriously believe that the history of the First Amendment furnishes unequivocal answers to many of the fundamental issues of church-state relations."[68] Silently acknowledging that for many other issues such answers *can* be provided, White does not proceed to engage the problem of how we go about resolving those fundamental questions that resist clear-cut solutions.

For the resolution of at least some of this latter variety, attempting to establish the relative importance of religion as a "constitutive community" could be quite significant. This effort in turn requires looking at the religious question through the Constitution's broader vision of the meaning of membership in the political community. In an important critique of the liberal view of religion and politics, Michael Sandel has contended that the liberal conception of the person as a free and independent unencumbered self provides inadequate justification for judicial protection of religious liberty. "Protecting religion as a 'life-style,' as one among the values that an independent self may have, may miss the role that religion plays in the lives of those for whom the observance of religious duties is a constitutive end, essential to their good and indispensable to their identity."[69] Alternatively, however, one could say that rather than *missing* this role, the American constitutional solution *recognizes* the potential role of religion as constitutive of individual identity, and *for that reason* guards against the possibility of its subverting the common political identity that inheres in membership in the constitutional community. Thus in the case of the Amish, we might welcome the challenge to the dominant political orthodoxy posed by this "holistic, regulative culture,"[70] and still worry that accommodating the group's constitutive needs creates a disturbing precedent for other constitutive needs: those encountered in creating and maintaining a nation. Mary Ann Glendon and Raul F. Yanes, for example, applaud the outcome in this case. "*Yoder*'s implicit acknowledgment that the religious experience often cannot be separated from the fate of a community—that it may bind the present with the past and the future and play an important role in shaping the character of its members—was an opening to a more capacious approach to free exercise."[71] But the Court's steady closing of this opening, while a disappointment to Glendon and Yanes, may in the end reflect an appreciation of the constitutional weight attaching to the fate of the wider political community. Thus an-

---

[68] *Nyquist.*
[69] Sandel 1993, 493.
[70] Stolzenberg 1993, 636.
[71] Glendon and Yanes 1991, 506.

other take on the problem, one that will be pursued at length in chapters 3 and 8, is that free exercise should not become a passageway to the subordination of national identity to the interests of group identity.

Another group in the United States for whom the observance of religious duties is a constitutive end is composed of followers of Satmar Hasidism, "devoutly religious people who reside in an insular community where religious ritual is scrupulously followed, where Yiddish, rather than English, is frequently spoken, where distinctive dress and appearance are the norm, where television is excluded, and where—in general—children receive their education in private boys' and girls' religious schools rather than in secular public schools."[72] In 1989, the New York legislature passed a law constituting the Village of Kiryas Joel (populated almost exclusively by the Satmars) a separate school district, enabling it to establish a school for handicapped children.[73] The law was invalidated by the Supreme Court in 1994 as being in violation of the Establishment Clause. Most interesting for our immediate purposes is the vigorous dissent of Justice Scalia, who disputed the majority's contention that the law had improperly favored a religion in the making of public policy. It was, he maintained, cultural rather than theological distinctiveness that was the basis of the state's accommodation of the group's needs. "There [was] no evidence . . . of the legislature's desire to favor the Satmar religion, as opposed to meeting distinctive secular needs . . . of citizens who happened to be Satmars."[74]

Scalia's resort to culture as a way of saving the program doubtless embodied a strategic calculation that, under prevailing Establishment Clause criteria, a majority of the Court would surely find that the state's action did not possess the requisite "secular legislative purpose." As part of this calculation, he may have appreciated how difficult it would be to apply such a test in the case of a religion that in fact constituted a way of life for its adherents. He argued that "The neutrality demanded by the Religion Clauses requires the same indulgence towards cultural characteristics that are accompanied by religious belief."[75] He seemed to be in agreement with Sandel's critique of prevailing constitutional wisdom, to the effect that the Court's preferred doctrine rested upon a voluntarist justification of

[72] Brief for the Petitioner in *Grumet* at 3.

[73] The state had been prompted to act by a 1985 Supreme Court decision, *Aguilar v Felton*, which held that public school teachers could not conduct classes on religious school premises. Until that decision, the school district within which the Village of Kiryas Joel was then located had provided special education to disabled Satmar children at a religious school annex in Kiryas Joel.

[74] *Grumet* at 2511.

[75] Ibid. at 2510.

neutrality that was nonneutral in its liberal conception of the person.[76] "It holds that government should be neutral toward religion in order to respect persons as free and independent selves, capable of choosing their religious convictions for themselves."[77] Asking the Court to entertain a broader understanding of religion that incorporated a major cultural component displayed a certain boldness on Scalia's part, not so much for its challenge to judicial precedent as for its departure from a more familiar and less organic American conceptualization of religion. Had he been successful (only Chief Justice Rehnquist and Justice Thomas joined his opinion), he would have put a big dent in one of the basic tenets of separatist constitutional thought in the United States: the requirement that government maintain a posture of strict neutrality between religion and irreligion. It could then have been more forcefully asked whether it was reasonable for government to maintain a position of indifference toward something that is widely perceived as implicating the totality of one's existence—spiritual and temporal.

Ritual

Of course, if the existence of the State itself were at stake, if, that is, its raison d'être made no sense without imagining religion at its core, then the question of a constitutive religious presence is basically irrelevant to the constitutional issue of governmental neutrality. Such is the case in Israel, where, unlike in the United States, religion is more than an influence on national identity (present at the creation but in principle distinguishable from it); it is at the core of that identity. Yet very much like the United States, and in this regard quite different from India, religion does not for the most part function as a regulative culture, in which patterns of deeply ingrained social relations are rooted in religious history and tradition.[78] To be sure, Judaism is a "total religion,"[79] prescribing behavior and practice for all facets of human existence; but most Jews in Israel choose not to place their lives under the regulative jurisdiction of Jewish

---

[76] Involved was the familiar and controversial three-pronged test enunciated in *Lemon*, which required that a law (1) have a secular legislative purpose, (2) not have as its principal or primary effect the advancement or inhibition of religion, and (3) not foster an excessive government entanglement with religion. While criticized repeatedly both on and off the Court, the test still stands—albeit on increasingly wobbly legs.

[77] Sandel 1993, 490.

[78] By this I am referring only to the socioeconomic configuration of the majority Jewish population. Obviously, Jewish-Arab relations are associated with religious differences, and in this sense there surely is a regulative culture decisively at work. I address these issues in detail in the next chapter.

[79] Weissbrod 1983, 190.

law. Socially, then, religion manifests a thin presence in Israeli life as a whole, even if politically it may be viewed as thick; for as Daniel Elazar and Janet Aviad have pointed out, "Judaism is constitutive of Jewish identity even for the unbeliever."[80] The result is a regime in which public support for religion is definitional—an insistence that there be no "government entanglement" in religion has an air of unreality about it—but one in which religious liberty is relatively unconstrained by the burdens of social reconstruction.[81]

This dual commitment, to a public identification with religion and to an official policy of religious freedom for all, reflects the tension that lies at the center of the Israeli experiment in constitutionalism, perhaps most tellingly revealed by the absence of a formal written constitution. While the failure to deliver on the promise of the Declaration of Independence to "a Constitution, to be drawn up by the Constituent Assembly" is a complex multidimensional story, critical to its narration is the difficulty encountered in the effort to reconcile conflicting individualist and communal aspirations. A similar conflict was present at the Indian Constituent Assembly, but as Granville Austin points out, its "members disagreed hardly at all about the ends they sought and only slightly about the means for achieving them."[82] Though communal aspirations would require significant constitutional and, as we shall see, judicial accommodation, a consensus on their necessary subordination (at least for the moment) to liberal, universalist objectives enabled closure on a document.[83] In con-

[80] Elazar and Aviad 1981, 195.

[81] There are, of course, strong, articulate, and passionate voices on behalf of a strict separation of State and religion, but they possess quite limited appeal. Perhaps the most controversial is the late Yeshayahu Leibowitz, whose argument for separation was grounded in an understanding of the thickness of the Jewish religion, the fact that "[T]he regime of the Torah . . . constituted a way of life." Leibowitz 1992, 162. For Geshon Weiler, on the other hand, it is to "escape the yoke of the Torah" that requires Israelis to accept "the principle that the religion of a person must be of no interest to the State." Weiler 1988, 224, 234. For Leibowitz, separation preserves the integrity of Judaism; for Weiler, the integrity of the State.

[82] Austin 1966, xiii.

[83] I emphasize closure in order to highlight the contrast with the Israeli experience. The Knesset's deliberations over the constitutional question concluded with the passage of a compromise proposal, known as the Harari Resolution, that prescribed a process of incremental accumulation of individual chapters—or basic laws—that when terminated will together form the State Constitution. This vaguely worded and much criticized legislation left unclear the status of the basic laws (of which there are presently eleven), just as it was silent as to a timetable for completion of the Constitution. It provided formal commitment (sincere or otherwise) to the principle of a written constitution, while maintaining maximum flexibility in the Knesset's capacity to determine its realization. It was essentially a formula to proceed "with all deliberate speed," although it lacked any method to enforce compliance. It left the State with an evolving constitution that conceivably possesses superior status to ordinary law, but which, predictably, coexists uneasily with the tradition of parliamentary supremacy.

trast, the Israeli failure in this regard is previewed in the opening lines of the Declaration of Independence, which in effect announce that the legitimacy of the State is ultimately rooted in the chronicle of a particular people. "The land of Israel was the birthplace of the Jewish people. Here their spiritual, religious and national identity was formed. Here they achieved independence and created a culture of national and universal significance." Here also they committed themselves, as the next section of the document makes clear, to "precepts of liberty," including the guarantee of "full freedom of conscience, worship, education and culture." And here they quickly discovered that the translation of these sentiments into an enforceable comprehensive legal document was just too formidable a project to accomplish.[84]

With this in mind, we should recall the third religious perspective mentioned in the Australian *Adelaide* opinion. In addition to religion as a system of beliefs, and religion as a code of conduct, "[t]here are others who pay greater attention to religion as involving some prescribed form of ritual or religious observance." Now, of course, ritual and observance are not severable from belief and conduct, and so to focus on them as if they were disturbs our sense of how things actually work. But in the context of the Zionist experiment in Israel, ritual and observance warrant special attention. As many commentators have noted, the Jewish religion played an instrumental role in the survival of the Jewish people during centuries of statelessness.[85] The instinct for survival that developed from this experience was not extinguished with the creation of the Jewish State; rather, it adapted itself to a set of new pressures and responsibilities. It was an adaptation that sought to maximize the integrative potential of the Jewish tradition as the key to developing a strong and vibrant nation.[86] Thus as Charles S. Liebman and Eliezer Don-Yehiya conclude in their

---

[84] It is worth noting that opposition to the adoption of a formal written constitution represented an interesting alliance, consisting on the one hand of extreme secularists such as David Ben-Gurion, and on the other of ultra-Orthodox Jews, who maintained that Israel had no need of *another* constitution, the Torah being a more than adequate fundamental law. Indeed, it was the radically different understandings of the essence of the regime held by these alliance partners that suggests the great dilemma inherent in one of the principal arguments of the document's proponents—that it should serve as a pedagogical device for educating a diverse population in the political principles of the regime. Nevertheless, it is incorrect to suggest that Israel functions without a constitution. With the Declaration of Independence (often appealed to by the Supreme Court), sacrosanct legislation such as the Law of Return (entitling Jews emigrating to Israel automatic citizenship), and the Basic Laws (some of which have been interpreted as entrenched), there is in place the functional equivalent of a formal constitutional document. Much debate, of course, occurs over the question of how well this arrangement actually performs its functions.

[85] See, for example, Birnbaum 1970, 270; Abramov 1976, 328; and Englard 1987, 187.

[86] See Gutmann 1981, 197.

study of Israeli civil religion, for most Israelis, "religious identity is increasingly expressed in the public domain, and its meaning is increasingly associated with public rather than private life."[87]

The famous case of Brother Daniel, the heroic—indeed saintly—Polish Jew who had converted to Catholicism and then applied for citizenship under the terms of the Law of Return, poignantly illustrates what is distinctive about religion in the Israeli political culture. In denying that he was Jewish, the Supreme Court adopted secular reasoning to affirm the common understanding of "the ordinary simple Jew."[88] From this perspective, Brother Daniel, however noble in character, had severed his ties to the Jewish people. "Whether he is religious, non-religious or anti-religious, the Jew living in Israel is bound, willingly or unwillingly, by an umbilical cord to historical Judaism from which he draws its language and its idiom, whose festivals are his own to celebrate, and whose great thinkers and spiritual heroes . . . nourish his national pride."[89] Thus Brother Daniel's fate was sealed in the pages of Jewish history. As Charles Silberman has felicitously observed in another context, "Judaism defines itself not as a voluntary community of faith but as an involuntary community of fate."[90]

From all of this flows the significance of ritual and observance. For a nation that is associated with the fate of a particular people, and yet committed to freedom of worship and conscience, the nonreligious and

[87] Liebman and Don-Yehiya 1989, 3.

[88] *Rufeisen* at 2437. This phrase is reminiscent of language used by the United States Supreme Court in a case that recalls a period in American history when racial qualifications were very much a part of the naturalization process. (Such qualifications were eliminated by the Immigration and Nationality Act of 1952.) The matter at issue concerned the qualifications of a Hindu who, while technically a Caucasian, was not, according to Justice Sutherland, white in the "understanding of the common man." *Thind* at 209. I have discussed the Brother Daniel case at length in another place. Jacobsohn 1993, 63–9. A recent episode in Israel is a vivid reminder of the continuing salience of the issues in that case. It involved the visit to Jerusalem of the Archbishop of Paris, Jean-Marie Cardinal Lustiger, who claimed in his various appearances in Israel to be a Jew. The Cardinal had converted to Christianity as a boy in Europe, a fact that did not in his estimation invalidate his self-identification with the Jewish people. His claim was widely denounced by both Orthodox and secular Jews in Israel, to which he responded: "I am as Jewish as all the other members of my family who were butchered in Auschwitz or in the other camps." *New York Times*, April 4, 1995.

[89] *Rufeisen* at 2438.

[90] Silberman 1985, 70. Silberman's elaboration is not fully consistent with the *Rufeisen* decision, but it speaks to a distinction directly relevant to the distinctions made in this chapter. "[O]ne is a Jew by virtue of one's birth, not one's beliefs or practices. Thus it is that Protestants speak of *joining* a particular church and Catholics of *becoming* a Catholic, whereas Jews speak of *being* Jewish; for Jewishness is an existential fact." Ibid., 72–3. In this regard, it is worth noting the similarities to Hinduism, which like Judaism, is often identified (for all sorts of purposes, good and bad) with the story of a particular nation. More important, Hinduism is also not defined by particular beliefs and practices, a reality

antireligious—who in Israel constitute a clear majority—are, paradoxically, dependent on religion for their political identity. Their stake in sustaining the Jewishness of the State should not be minimized by the absence of an abiding spiritual engagement in their faith. Thus could a distinguished Israeli Supreme Court justice declare in an important case: "There is no Israeli nation separate from the Jewish people."[91] Those accustomed to associating such sentiments with a religious nationalism harboring dangerous extremist ambitions might be surprised to discover that the justice in this case, Shimon Agranat, was a secular Jew widely celebrated for his authorship of landmark libertarian opinions. Another surprise, especially for many secular Jews in the United States, is that the public manifestation of the Zionist commitment is not confined to ritual and symbolism—what might be designated ethnic aspects of Judaism—but also involves matters of religious observance that are prescribed in the Jewish (or halakhic) law.

While there is an obvious political explanation for the official recognition of such religious requirements as kosher food in the military, matrilineal determination of Jewish identity, and bans on public transportation on the Sabbath, the powerful leverage enjoyed by the Orthodox in electoral politics does not entirely account for this phenomenon. Also important is the willingness of the non-Orthodox majority to incorporate parts of Jewish law into the broader legal framework of the polity as a way of encouraging and reinforcing the unity of the Jewish people. To be sure, there is occasionally great resistance to some acts of incorporation when they are perceived as unreasonably burdensome, but most secular Jews in Israel understand the significance of observance to the historical continuity of the Jewish people. They "do not attack religion per se because they define Israel as a Jewish State and this necessarily requires their tacit acceptance of its religious symbols."[92] For the Jewish people "nationalism and religion are inseparably interwoven,"[93] which means that for the non-Orthodox majority, the attraction of halakhic rules (in limited doses) is not theological but instrumental, residing in their capacity to serve the ends of the Jewish State by contributing to a concept of national identity that has at its core certain common strands uniting all members of a distinctive people.[94]

---

even more pronounced in India, where the absence of an official, institutionalized religious hierarchy accentuates the heterogeneity of Hindu doctrine and behavior.

[91] *Tamarin* at 201.

[92] Sharot 1991, 271.

[93] *Rufeisen* at 2447.

[94] Church/State relations in Israel are often characterized with reference to the "status quo," a term referring to a compromise agreement between secular and religious forces that

CONCLUSION

An oft-quoted observation by Montesquieu deserves at least one more go-around. "[Laws] should have relation to the degree of liberty which the constitution will bear; to the religion of their inhabitants, to their inclinations, riches, numbers, commerce, manners, and customs."[95] Further on he wrote, "It is the business of the legislature to follow the spirit of the nation, when it is not contrary to the principles of government; for we do nothing so well as when we act with freedom, and follow the bent of our national genius."[96] As we continue to consider these three models of secular constitutional design, it is important to follow the tenor of these observations. Thus "the spirit of the laws" expresses itself in contrasting constitutional approaches to Church/State relations that reflect, either directly or through designed confrontation, distinctive regime-defining attributes of nationhood. As explored more fully in the next chapter, an *assimilative* model manifests the ultimately decisive role of political principles in the development of the American nation, a *visionary* model seeks to accommodate the particularistic aspirations of Jewish nationalism in Israel within a constitutional framework of liberal democracy, and an

---

goes back to the inception of the State. As a result of the agreement, religious law has been accorded a limited presence in the life of the State. It is easiest to view the arrangement as a standard splitting of the difference, in which both sides settle for as little or as much as they can get away with. This is misleading, however, as it fails to convey a more principled side of the status quo as "one of the unique and prime factors ensuring the Jewish character of the State of Israel." Eliash 1983, 349. The debate over how to characterize this agreement, implicating as it does theological and nationalist dimensions of Judaism, is emblematic of "the crisis of Jewish identity." As Peter Berger aptly puts it: "The Zionist attempt to redefine Jewishness in terms of a *national identity* . . . has the ambivalent character of, on the one hand, reestablishing an objective plausibility structure for Jewish existence while, on the other hand, putting in question the claim of religious Judaism to being the raison d'être of Jewish existence—an ambivalence manifested in the ongoing difficulties between 'church' and state in Israel." Berger 1967, 69–70. For further insight into the intertwining of nationalistic elements and religious practices in Israeli Jewish and political cultures, see Tabory 1981, 280. In general, see Liebman and Don-Yehiya 1989. And for additional insight into the complexity of the relationship between nationalism and religion in Israeli political culture, consider the reaction in Israel to the assassination of Prime Minister Yitzhak Rabin. Secular Jews were especially outraged that Rabin's killer was an Orthodox Jew. For many the slain leader had become "an icon in a new kind of national religion." "Secular Israelis, Too, Have a Faith," *New York Times*, November 19, 1995, sec. 4, 4. Yet despite the backlash against the Orthodox, particularly among young Israelis, a mass movement to get alternative branches of Judaism recognized is unlikely to occur. As the *New York Times* pointed out, "[T]he State itself seems to be enough of an organization to let these young identify themselves as Jews." Ibid.

[95] Montesquieu 1966, vol. 1, 6.
[96] Ibid., 294.

ameliorative model embraces the social reform impulse of Indian nationalism in the context of the nation's deeply rooted religious diversity and stratification.

In each case, "the degree of [religious] liberty which the constitution will bear" reflects, in part, "the religion of the inhabitants," understood in functional rather than theological terms. For the inhabitants of India, the imprint of religion is deeply etched in the patterns of daily life, such that social structure and religious activity are indissolubly linked. For the inhabitants of Israel, religious affiliation is imbued with a political meaning that ultimately determines membership in the larger governing community. And for the inhabitants of the United States, religion is an essentially voluntary activity that pervades the domain of private life, providing active as well as passive support for a shared public theology. In all three countries, religious liberty is a principal, if heavily contextualized, goal of constitutional interpretation, differently provided for in each instance to mirror the sociopolitical conditions of the respective local setting. So Justice Douglas could say of Article 25 of the Indian Constitution, "[I]t may be a desirable provision. But when the Court adds it to our First Amendment, . . . we make a sharp break with the American ideal of religious liberty as enshrined in the First Amendment."[97] To this assertion he could add with confidence that "The First Amendment commands government to have no interest in theology or ritual."[98] Yet perhaps more so than any other modern justice of the Supreme Court, he, as a student of comparative law, understood that the authority behind constitutional commands depends as much upon the nuances of political culture as it does the language of the Constitution or the commitment of its designated interpreters.

However, the comparative perspective's accentuation of distinctive models of constitutional ordering must not be allowed to obscure the shared and overlapping features of contrasting national experiences. Constitutional classifications are usually not sharply isolable, but present themselves along a continuous sequence or range. Whatever utility may be found in our fourfold table will be quickly negated if its typology creates a presumption of categorical exclusivity. Montesquieu's advice to governments, that they should follow "the spirit of the nation" and the "bent of [their] national genius," leaves his advisees with considerable maneuverability; spirit and genius as applied to nations are never unidimensional. Within our models of the secular constitution are internal tensions and

---

[97] *McGowan* at 575–6.

[98] Ibid. at 564. A confidence matched a generation later by his jurisprudential opposite, Justice Scalia, who wrote, "[C]ourts must not presume to determine the place of a particular belief in a religion or the plausibility of a religious claim." *Smith* at 887.

contradictions offering alternative developmental possibilities whose potential is, at least theoretically, to culminate in convergence of the three nations' constitutional experiences.

For example, Israeli judges seeking to advance the more liberal strand of Zionist aspirations may end up shifting the focus of the secular constitution in the direction of an assimilative model. Also, to the extent that the Jewish national movement's historic roots can be traced to rebellion against traditional Judaism,[99] Zionism's political realization through the medium of the Israeli State may be seen to embrace an ameliorative dimension of no small consequence. Similarly, as I will argue in chapter 9, a more concerted effort by American judges to assist minority religions whose religious practices were thought to be threatened by an insensitive majority would provide a more ameliorative tone to the American secular solution. Were this consistently to occur, sentiments expressed in Indian judicial opinions that are generally taken to be emblematic of a distinctive national orientation would become less helpful in demarcating the boundaries between Indian and American Church/State jurisprudence. As one example: "It may sound paradoxical but it is nevertheless true that minorities can be protected not only if they have equality but also, in certain circumstances, differential treatment."[100] Considerably less likely, but nevertheless imaginable, is a United States Supreme Court citing historical precedent for the proposition that the character of the American people has been singularly shaped by a particular religious tradition, and that this experience justifies special official recognition. The result would provide a more visionary slant to the American secular constitution. No longer would an observation such as the following by Justice Brennan serve to distinguish very well the American and Israeli situations: "Under our constitutional scheme, the role of safeguarding our 'religious heritage' and of promoting religious beliefs is reserved as the exclusive prerogative of our Nation's churches, religious institutions, and spiritual leaders."[101]

Table 2.1, then, needs to be supplemented to indicate the spectral as well as typological features of constitutional comparisons.

Perhaps the best way to explain this representation is to point out something that doubtless has by this time occurred to the patient reader, namely that the depiction of nationhood or national identity is not an exact science. It does not, however, detract from the value of such analytical depictions to acknowledge that distinctive attributes of nationhood are neither exhaustive in their descriptive power nor associated exclusively with the particular nations for which they have definitional signifi-

---

[99] See, for example, Cohen-Almagor 1995, 465.
[100] *St. Xavier's College* at 1433.
[101] *Lynch* at 725.

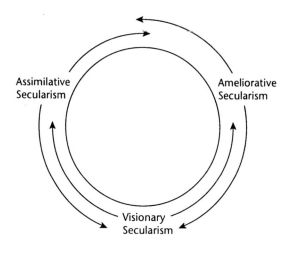

Figure 2.1

cance. Political assimilation, social amelioration, and communal vision provide the animating force behind the respective secular constitutions of the United States, India, and Israel, but in each case these directive principles are also background presences—varying in their prominence—in the two polities where they are not featured. The historical experiences of all three societies are layered in multiple meanings, such that the shaping of national identity remains an ongoing process within which religion's place in the constitutional order is never unalterably fixed. As suggested by the arrows surrounding the circle upon which the constitutional models are located, the distinctiveness of a particular approach to Church/State relations is subject to dilution or obfuscation, as forces within the larger society exert pressures that pull a specific model in one direction or another.

In this context, comparative analysis has much to offer, for unless one subscribes to the view that these forces evade human channeling and control, the constitutional experience of one nation can have a decisive effect on the evolution of constitutional secularism in another.[102] As Michael

---

[102] Here it would be wise to follow the advice of Aristotle, cited at the outset of the chapter. "[P]olitics has to consider which sort of constitution suits which sort of civic body. The attainment of the best constitution is likely to be impossible for the general run of states; and the good law-giver and the true statesman must therefore have their eyes open not only to what is the absolute best, but also to what is the best in relation to actual conditions." As applied to the law-givers in our three countries, they need to understand the limitations imposed on statesmanship by actual conditions, which means in this context remaining sensitive to the constraints that particular dimensions of nationhood place on the achievement of religious liberty. But they need to be aware of more than "what is the best in relation

Walzer has observed in relation to regimes of toleration, "If this or that aspect of an arrangement *there* seems likely to be useful *here*, with suitable modifications, we can work for a reform of that sort, aiming at what is best for us given the groups we value and the individuals we are."[103] Those Americans favorably disposed to a revival of cultural nationalism would do well to explore the implications of ethnorepublicanism or religiorepublicanism in Israel; while others inspired by prospects of ecumenical harmony might wish to consider the tradeoffs spawned by India's legitimation of group rights. For Israelis who wish to pursue with single-minded resolve the logic of their Declaration's liberal aspirations, the American subordination of religion and its attendant denominational neutrality could prove instructive, as could, as we shall soon see, the ambivalent Indian constitutional commitment to a uniform civil code for Israelis contemplating greater religious autonomy in matters of personal status. Finally, Indians determined to place greater distance between the State and activities related to spiritual fulfillment should pause to reflect upon the antiredistributive social implications of the American wall of separation,[104] just as other Indians with their sights set upon a greater separation of another kind—that which divides religious communities—should ponder the politics of religious segmentation practiced in Israel. The results of such reflections may be used in support of change or in justification of the status quo. To whatever purpose they are put, they may help to resolve the issue raised at the outset of a notable contribution to comparative constitutional analysis, *The Federalist*, of "whether societies of men are really capable or not of establishing good government from reflection and choice."[105]

---

to actual conditions" (that is to say, they must be more than vulgar relativists); they must also be open to an evolving nationhood that is guided to some extent by examples of what is better, as well as examples of what is worse.

[103] Walzer 1997, 5.

[104] See Epstein 1990, 391.

[105] Lodge 1888, 3.

Chapter Three

SECULARISM IN CONTEXT

TWO STATEMENTS on the subject of secular principles in India: (1) "[T]he individual should be the unit for policies and laws of the State, and not the religion or caste to which he belongs or the region in which he lives; . . . nothing should be conceded to a religion-based group or organisation which is denied to or not available to a secular group or organisation; . . . nothing should be conceded to a group or organisation of one religion which is denied to or not made available to groups or organisations of other religions."[1] (2) "[S]ecularism, according to our concept, does not mean that religion must be forcibly ousted from all sorts of social relations. Article 44 [The State shall endeavor to secure for the citizens a uniform code throughout the territory of India] cannot be given this meaning as long as religion is playing an active role in most of the other aspects of life."[2] Question: Which of the two comments reveals a stronger commitment to the essentials of secular constitutionalism?

A satisfactory answer would require additional information, but upon initial inspection, the first comment appears more comfortably to comport with liberal constitutional expectations about Church/State relations. Its emphasis on the individual rather than the group, and its expression of neutrality among religions and between religious and nonreligious institutions, suggests greater loyalty to secular constitutional principles than does the second's deference to religiously based differential legal treatment. The answer, of course, is not so straightforwardly simple, as the identities of the two commentators alone point to a larger issue. Arun Shourie, author of statement 1, is perhaps the leading ideologue of the Hindu right, a prolific writer and a BJP (Bharatiya Janata Party)-affiliated member of Parliament. Tahir Mahmood, author of statement 2, is a prominent legal scholar, whose leadership of the National Minorities Commission frequently placed him in opposition to the Central Government's

[1] Shourie 1997a, ix.
[2] Mahmood 1995, 168.

BJP-led government. Each has insisted passionately that he is fighting for a secular India.

Shourie is a fierce advocate for equal treatment of religious groups in India, which, according to his analysis, has consistently been undermined by a policy of appeasement of minorities. "Inflaming minorities," he asserts, "has become lucrative politics."[3] He prefers an American-oriented solution, in which the State takes no formal cognizance of religion.[4] Toward this end, it would be wise to tighten constitutional provisions in order to ensure that the only religiously inspired acts to receive legal protection would be those that were, in John Stuart Mill's sense, genuinely self-regarding. "[I]n every instance the interest of the public, that of the country, must take precedence over the right to religion, just as much as they do over civil rights."[5] Shourie accepts the reality of the thickly constituted character of Indian religious belief and practice, an acceptance that provokes one to ponder whether his fervent declaration concerning the superior claims of public policy over conscientious objection does not in fact amount to a declaration of war against religion. Would not the claims of religion be systematically trumped under his strict separationist scheme?

The answer depends on which claims or, more precisely, which religion's claims? Given the intimacy with which temporal and spiritual realms have been historically entwined in India, the prospect is substantial that important areas of public policy will embody the substance of religious beliefs, *at least those of the majority*. So understood, secularism appears in the form of a radical majoritarianism in the service of an assimilationist agenda, in which those in power have been extended an implicit license to impose the norms and practices of the dominant culture on the rest of the society. In this account, the social reform contemplated in Article 25 refers to the State's constitutional authority to alter the regressive social practices of minority religions. And, as we shall see, the most effective way of realizing these ambitions is to follow the Constitution's directive to implement uniformity in the making and enforcement of law for all the people of India, regardless of their religious affiliation.

For Tahir Mahmood, on the other hand, the liberal presumptions of equal treatment and individual consideration should be qualified by time

---

[3] Interview with the author, New Delhi, November 19, 1998.

[4] In an interview with the author, Shourie used the American model of Church and State to describe his position. But with regard to certain matters, especially involving free exercise questions, his antiexemption views probably reflect a minority perspective within the American political context, and certainly within the academic mainstream. Nevertheless, as we shall see in this chapter, this minority view is quite consonant with the underlying logic of American constitutional secularism. I return to this question in the concluding chapter.

[5] Shourie 1997a, 68.

and circumstance. As a Muslim and a reformer, his sensitivity to both the egregious social inequities within his own community and the malevolent designs of some within the majority Hindu community toward minorities is deeply felt. "In this complex situation, the opinion that Article 44 demands a mechanical application of any single personal law to the entire nation, or that this can be achieved by one stroke of legislative action, ignores the ground realities. . . . A uniform civil code may only emerge, through an evolutionary process, out of the extremely rich composite legal heritage of the Nation, of which all the personal laws are equal constituents."[6]

Shourie considers Mahmood's solicitude for the group interests of minorities to be reflective of the elitist "pseudo-secularism" that passes for enlightened opinion in contemporary India. Mahmood's response is to insist that "If there has been any appeasement in this country it has been of the majority."[7] The polemical tone of this debate need not conceal the importance of the theoretical issues in play here. Nor should the transparency of the political agendas that lie just below the surface of the principled disagreement between these individuals detract from the intriguing conceptual matters that are implicated in their conflicting views. Perhaps of most interest is the question of context. How do we situate arguments of the kind made by Shourie and Mahmood in order to understand their implications for a secular polity? For example, Shourie's arguments have decidedly assimilationist consequences, but their significance for the achievement of secular constitutional goals will vary widely from polity to polity. In the United States, the *political* assimilation that is fostered by the majoritarian subordination of conscience to law might be a good thing; in India, however, its more cultural incarnation penetrates more deeply into the conduct of peoples' lives and could interfere with the constitutionally prescribed goal of social amelioration.

---

[6] Mahmood 1995, 17.

[7] Interview with the author, New Delhi, February 8, 1999. The disagreement is reminiscent of the sharply divergent views expressed on the American Supreme Court by Justices Scalia and O'Connor. In a memorable exchange in one of the Court's most controversial First Amendment cases, Scalia conceded that "[L]eaving accommodation to the political process will place at a relative disadvantage those religious practices not widely engaged in"; but in rejecting a constitutional claim for a religiously based exemption from a general legal obligation, he accepted such a result as an "unavoidable consequence of democratic government," by which he meant, majority rule. *Smith* at 890. O'Connor countered with the assertion that the constitutional guarantee of religious freedom was designed "to protect the rights of those whose religious practices are not shared by the majority and may be viewed with hostility." Ibid. at 902. These opinions receive a more extensive analysis in chapter 9. In both India and the United States, the debate over secularism ultimately turns in large measure on the limits and prerogatives of the majority. The same could be said of Israel, but there the debate is usually framed in terms of the limits and prerogatives of the

This chapter and the next explore the variability of secular constitutional arrangements in light of the three models introduced in the previous chapter. It seeks to join a comparative perspective to a more theoretically driven argument for "contextual secularism." The term appears in the work of Rajeev Bhargava, who, contrary to theorists "who espouse the cause of secularism in order to secure full-blooded autonomy or full participatory democracy or perfect equality," has advanced an alternative rationale geared to the achievement of "a minimalist agenda of decent human existence."[8] At the core of the idea of contextual secularism is the "strategy of principled distance," which, according to Bhargava, means that "[T]he State intervenes or refrains from interfering, depending on which of the two better promotes religious liberty and equality of citizenship."[9] A secular State may consequently assume one of a variety of forms, all of which must comport with the principle of equal dignity for all without necessarily fulfilling a concurrent expectation of equidistance in the government's relations with the religious groups within its jurisdiction.

In Bhargava's account, "Contextual secularism advocates State intervention for the sake of substantive values." Thus a "decent human existence" requires observance of the principle of equal respect; comparative analysis suggests that in addition to this basic, and rather generally stated, minimal requirement, a contextual rendering of Church/State relations should also take into its purview those aspirations that have a connection to the more particular constitutive features of individual polities. With this end in mind, we turn now to our three models of secular constitutional development, considering first the American and Israeli cases.

THE UNITED STATES: ASSIMILATIVE SECULARISM

"The United States of America solves its minority problems, more or less, by trying to make every citizen 100 percent American. They make everyone conform to a certain type. Other countries, with a longer and more complicated past, are not so favorably situated."[10] Nehru of course had his own country in mind when he reflected wistfully on the American solution to the problem of diversity. Unaccustomed as most thoughtful Americans are to viewing their past as uncomplicated, it is worth being

---

minority, specifically the ultra-Orthodox, whose power to impose their will on the secular majority often frames the debate over religious liberty in that country.

[8] Bhargava 1998, 494, 496. For a thoughtful account of religion, the state, and politics that emphasizes the contextual dimension, see Demarath 2001. As Demarath rightly points out, "[A]ny given religion is best understood—perhaps only really understood—in its myriad social and political settings." Ibid., 7.

[9] Ibid., 515.

[10] Nehru 1959, 154.

reminded—in this case by an Indian writing from the darkness of a British prison cell—that in comparison with experience elsewhere, in which problems associated with communal divisions have a way of appearing utterly intractable, the United States, however complex its history, has not been quite so burdened.

Nehru went on appropriately to acknowledge that the history of racial conflict in the United States did not conform to this upbeat account, but as to religion, the solution adverted to in his observation has been as successful as it has been logically consistent with the premises of American nationhood. That is not the same as saying that the solution is or is not fully consistent with the specific intentions of the authors and ratifiers of the First Amendment, only that its broad outlines respect the vision incorporated in the liberal philosophical commitments that informed their work. In the late eighteenth century, "minority problems" had mainly to do with religious differences. The best account of how the new constitutional order addresses these problems will be one that displays the greatest consistency with the larger project of nation-building to which the designers of this order were committed.[11]

It is in this sense that Nehru's allusion to an assimilative solution reveals considerable insight into the nature of the American regime. The effort to "make every citizen 100 percent American" is, rightly understood, a very American thing to do, since being an American consists largely of sharing in those constitutive ideas that define membership in the political community. Assimilation in this context relates exclusively to principles, not to ethnically or religiously derived models of ideal behavior working to achieve social conformity. While these models surely have had a historic association with much of the assimilative experience in the United States, they are not dictated or even encouraged by the logic of the assimilationist assumptions of the American secular constitution. Indeed, the greatest assurance that the protection of diversity for all *religious* beliefs will be taken seriously—including those beliefs that violate the spirit of

---

[11] The novelty and distinctiveness of the project is an oft-told tale that focuses on a set of political principles that together constitute the basis of American national identity. Samuel Huntington, for example, has argued that this identity is understandable only in terms of the political principles of the Declaration of Independence, that Americans have nothing vital in common, no cementing unity, without the amalgam of goals and values that constitute the American Creed. "National identity and political principle [are] inseparable." Huntington 1981, 24. This is the emphasis also of Liah Greenfeld's thoughtful account of American nationalism, with its "essential autonomy from material or 'objective' ethnic and structural factors." Greenfeld 1992, 402. I am in basic agreement with this account, although Rogers Smith is wise to point out that ethnic and cultural factors have historically been important in making sense of American national identity. Smith 1988, 225. I disagree, however, in finding that this historical reality calls into serious doubt the validity of Huntington's creedal understanding of nationhood.

the "self-evident" principles underlying the constitutional agreement—lies in the achievement of *political* assimilation.

A brief examination of the issue of polygamy may make this argument more concrete, while serving as well as a point of comparative reference for India and Israel, which have also had their constitutional battles over this question. In all three countries, restrictions or bannings of a practice seen by many to be morally offensive confronted the judicial system with challenges that illuminate distinctive features of their respective secular constitutions. In the United States, however, this illumination may initially seem dim at best, for in the Supreme Court's rejection of the Mormons' religious-based constitutional claims, its occasional appeal to sectarian and cultural intolerance tends to obscure and confuse the assimilationist logic of its argument.

Thus in *Reynolds v United States*, Chief Justice Waite pointed out that "Polygamy has always been odious among the northern and western nations of Europe, and, until the establishment of the Mormon Church, was almost exclusively a feature of the life of Asiatic and of African people."[12] In *Davis v Beason*, Justice Field found justification for prohibitory legislation against polygamy in "the general consent of the Christian world."[13] And in *Late Corporation of the Church of Jesus Christ of Latter-Day Saints v United States*, Justice Bradley described the practice as "abhorrent to the sentiments and feelings of the civilized world," and opined that "[T]he organization of a community for the spread and practice of polygamy is, in a measure, a return to barbarism."[14] If assimilation is part of the message in these comments, it seems directed toward compelling the Mormons to accept the moral standards of the country's western, Christian majority. Such a message would have echoed (as judicial opinions often do) the sentiments of the general population, whose deep revulsion toward the Mormons and their aberrant ways often expressed itself in a linkage of polygamy with slavery as twin vestiges of a barbaric past.

But the assault on the Mormons may also be viewed, even if not expressly stated in the opinions, as a defense of liberal constitutionalism, and it is in this connection that their peculiar institution became a useful foil for affirming the supremacy of the civil law.[15] It has been pointed

---

[12] *Reynolds* at 164.

[13] *Beason* at 343.

[14] *Late Corporation of the Church of Jesus Christ of Latter-Day Saints et al.*

[15] An 1885 article in the *Salt Lake Tribune* suggested what was ultimately at stake in the combined legislative and judicial attack on polygamy. "The essential principle of Mormonism is not polygamy at all, but the ambition of an ecclesiastical hierarchy to wield sovereignty; to rule the souls and lives of its subjects with absolute authority, unrestrained by any civil power." Van Wagoner 1989, 133. It is in this light that President Hayes's rationale for moving against the Mormons must be seen. "Laws must be enacted which will take from

out, for example, that the early leaders of the Mormon Church rejected Tocqueville's admonition that "religions . . . ought to confine themselves within their own precincts."[16] Marital practices were just one element—albeit the most notorious—in a regulative culture whose domain extended well into the temporal side of human experience. But unlike the Old Order Amish, who could never seriously be accused of harboring theocratic designs, the Mormons made it easy for people to believe that the religion's geographic base in Utah was expected to serve as a home for illegitimate sovereign ambitions. Not so hollow, then, was the claim made in 1888 by Utah's non-Mormon governor that "[The Mormon] priesthood not only rules the Church, it governs the state."[17]

The Supreme Court was well aware that the Mormon challenge was both religious and political. "So here, as a law of the organization of society under the exclusive dominion of the United States, it is provided that plural marriages shall not be allowed. Can a man excuse his practices to the contrary because of his religious belief?"[18] The Court's answer: "To permit this would be to make the professed doctrines of religious belief superior to the law of the land, and in effect to permit every citizen to become a law unto himself. Government could exist only in name under such circumstances."[19] This answer of course could apply with equal force to anyone—Mormon or non-Mormon—who sought immunity from the law on account of religious beliefs. Concerns over whether an individual citizen would be permitted to become a law unto himself or herself naturally escalated to worries of a larger corporate challenge to the supremacy of law, underscoring the wider possible implications of a lax attitude toward law-abidingness. Coupled with the frequent linking of polygamy with slavery in mid-nineteenth-century America and the urgency of protecting national authority against politically concentrated, religiously sanctioned illegal behavior becomes all the more comprehensible.

---

the Mormon Church its temporal power. Mormonism as a sectarian idea is nothing, but as a system of government it is our duty to deal with it as an enemy of our institutions, and its supporters and leaders as criminals." Quoted in Hansen 1981, 144. As Hansen suggests, the close identification of polygamy with the Church as a political force meant that the defeat of one was directly tied to the defeat of the other. It is worth noting in this regard that the treatment of polygamy in American courts has historically been more tolerant than has been the typical approach in many Western countries. As Leon Sheleff has pointed out, this is in large part attributable to the unique legal situation that polygamy created within the Native American community. Sheleff 1995, 253. Unlike the Mormons, the anomalous status of Native American tribes meant that the religions of these tribes posed no threat to the wider political culture.

[16] Hansen 1981, 114.
[17] Van Wagoner 1989, 133.
[18] *Reynolds* at 166.
[19] Ibid. at 167.

If the Court's stance in the polygamy cases is taken to be consistent with the logic of the secular constitution, can one then conclude, as some commentators have done with respect to more recent cases denying constitutional exemptions to religious objectors, that the basic orientation of the approach is antireligious? If not, is it then merely indifferent to religion, an expression of neutrality between religion and irreligion? With respect to the first query, quite the contrary, for while the hostility to Mormonism in the *Reynolds* and *Beason* opinions is scarcely concealed, the broader meaning of the decisions manifests a rather different and more sympathetic sensibility toward religion in general. Even the rigid distinction between belief and practice that figures so prominently in Indian case citations, and that appears increasingly disconnected from contemporary realities associated with the ubiquity of the welfare state, conveys an understanding that the substance of religious opinions is beyond the legitimate reach of the state.[20] "The care of each man's soul," as John Locke argued, "is left entirely to every man's self."[21] Indeed, the formula developed by the Court for protection of speech under the First Amendment—*content neutrality*—arguably has a more appropriate place in the protective arsenal of religious freedom.[22] "The law knows no heresy, and is committed to the support of no dogma, the establishment of no sect."[23] And consistent with this strict neutrality in doctrinal questions of religious faith there is, despite the temptation to avoid restricting religion by defi-

---

[20] On the ubiquity of the welfare state and its implications, see Carter 1993, 133, 138; and McConnell 1992, 692.

[21] Locke 1963, 48.

[22] It may be asked what the Free Exercise Clause contributes to individual freedom that is not covered under the protection of opinions in the speech guarantees of the First Amendment. The answer is not much *if* it is correct to maintain, as the prevailing orthodoxy in these matters has it, that there is no such thing as a false idea as far as the Constitution is concerned, that in the marketplace of ideas all opinions are of equal status and dignity. Walter Berns, however, makes a compelling argument that the Founders drew a principled distinction between religious and political speech, that the very reason for absolute protection of the former means that there must be limits on the latter. Berns 1970, 146. Philip Hamburger too presents compelling historical evidence that religious liberty was considered a unique "inalienable right," immune in a way that speech was not, from governmental restraints based upon the substance of belief. Hamburger 1993, 312. Finally, John Mansfield has written of the Constitution that it embodies a particular philosophy that includes assumptions about human nature, human dignity, and the meaning of life. "It is not neutral in regard to these matters. If 'separation of church and state' requires a constitution that is neutral on these questions, then the United States does not have a constitutional regime of 'separation of church and state.' " Mansfield 1984, 856. From this he properly concludes that certain religious views *are* false under the Constitution. But they are not false as to their *religious* content, merely incompatible, whatever their theological validity, with the political truths underlying the Constitution.

[23] *Watson* at 727.

nitional intervention, a notable absence in the Waite and Field opinions
of any suggestion that polygamy is either nonessential to Mormonism or
untrue to the religion's basic precepts. While not directly at issue here,
one can nevertheless see how, within the framework of liberal constitutionalism, institutional autonomy in matters of belief and theology follows directly from the subordination of spiritual to temporal authority.[24]

It is regrettable that the justices did not elaborate on the theoretical
rationale for this subordination. Thus it is not simply that "Government
could exist only in name" if deference to religious belief required that the
law not be uniformly applied; rather it is that government of a certain
type—one "instituted among men" for the protection of certain unalienable rights—would be in principle untenable. As Philip Hamburger has
shown, this understanding seems to have been accepted even by religious
dissenters in the late eighteenth century, who saw the connection between
rights of exemption for the religiously scrupulous and the creation of unequal civil rights. In the language of the Virginia *Act For Establishing
Religious Freedom*, men's "opinions in matters of religion" shall "in no
wise diminish, enlarge, or affect their civil capacities."[25] The notion that
people formed government to secure their "secular Welfare" was not perceived as antireligious; instead, following Locke, religiously committed
people appreciated that the promotion of their spiritual interests was inseparable from the advancement of their temporal well-being. Michael
McConnell, on the other hand, believes that the assimilation of freedom
of religion into a Lockean philosophical framework denies the singularity
of religion in contemporary life. "Under this view the religion clauses of
the first amendment become an instrument of secularism to be interpreted

---

[24] In a 1976 case, Justice Brennan rightly suggested that civil courts "must accept [ecclesi-
astical] decisions as binding on them, in their application to the religious issues of doctrine
or polity before them." *Serbian Orthodox Diocese* at 709. The key precedent for this important ruling is *Watson v Jones*, which was decided a few years before the *Reynolds* decision. In *Reynolds*, it is interesting to note, the Court alludes to India in raising a rhetorical
question: "[I]f a wife religiously believed it was her duty to burn herself upon the funeral
pile of her dead husband, would it be beyond the power of the civil government to prevent
her carrying her belief into practice?" *Reynolds* at 166. By maintaining the distinction between belief and practice, the Court never puts itself into the position of having to determine
whether the woman's belief is erroneous or misguided. In India, as we shall see, there is a
greater temptation to become judicially involved in the determination of the substantive
merits of the beliefs in question. And this temptation is related to the greater difficulty in
India in separating opinion and practice. The influence of *Reynolds* is obvious in Justice
Scalia's controversial opinion for the Court in *Employment Division v Smith*: "[C]ourts
must not presume to determine the place of a particular belief in a religion or the plausibility
of a religious claim." *Employment Division v Smith* at 887. In chapter 9 I reflect further on
the common assumption that judges must remain completely indifferent to the substance of
theological opinion.

[25] Hamburger 1992, 947.

in secular terms."[26] While perhaps true, this does not mean that a secular interpretation that realizes the goal of equality, understood in terms of Lockean natural rights, is antithetical to the interests of religion. As for denying the singularity of religion, Locke's notion that "[T]he private judgment of any Person concerning a Law ... does not take away the Obligation of that Law"[27] does blur the distinctiveness of religious belief, but more important, it provides a basis for denying government the authority to move against any singular religious belief. His letter, after all, concerned toleration (of religion). As expressed in *Beason*, "However free the exercise of religion may be, it must be subordinate to the criminal laws of the country, passed with reference to actions regarded by general consent as properly the subjects of punitive legislation."[28]

The subordination of religion in this sense does not contradict our recognition of the prominent historical role of religion in the creation and development of the nation. Polemical discourse on Church and State has helped to obscure the connection between secular foundations and spiritual aspirations. The "nonreligious character of its founding principle"[29] provided the "new nation" with much of its distinctive character, but more important, that principle was itself the precondition for a regime of religious liberty. In upholding civil law against the "private judgment" of the Mormons, the Court tacitly acknowledged the secular origins of constitutional authority. Implicitly, too, it affirmed the subordinate position of religious *opinion* to the political *truth* that *constituted* American nationhood. In sharp contrast is McConnell's view that "Even the mighty democratic will of the people is, in principle, subordinate to the commands of God, as heard and understood in the individual conscience."[30] But the logic underlying the Court's judgment suggests that what is "heard and understood in the individual conscience," even if asserted to be divinely inspired, enjoys only the status of opinion, and therefore is in principle subordinate to the commands of law.

McConnell's examination of free exercise bears directly on the nexus between national identity and the secular constitution. "While the government is powerless and incompetent to determine what particular conception of the divine is authoritative, the free exercise clause stands as a recognition that such divine authority may exist and, if it exists, has a rightful claim on the allegiance of believers who happen to be American citizens."[31] Since there can be no serious quarrel with the existence of such

---

[26] McConnell 1990b, 1416.
[27] Locke 1963, 48.
[28] *Beason* at 342–3.
[29] Berns 1970, 20.
[30] McConnell 1990b, 1516.
[31] Ibid.

a claim, the only question McConnell's comment raises has to do with its scope and magnitude. The implication would seem to be that the First Amendment establishes the priority of divine obligation to the obligations of citizenship, for believers "who happen to be American citizens" are clearly not being exhorted to give first consideration to their public secular responsibilities. Tom Paine's declaration—"Our citizenship in the United States is our national character"[32]—will likely not provide convincing justification for them to subordinate their claims of conscience to the public will as expressed in law.

The law in question in the *Beason* case was unusually severe, going so far as to deny the vote to anyone practicing or even advocating polygamy. It was part of a broader legislative design to destroy the political power of the Mormon Church. Its emphasis, however, on the right to franchise, a right that in theory is emblematic of citizenship, makes the point (in an admittedly heavy-handed way) that the pull of divine authority should not be permitted to tear one away from the routine performance of civic responsibilities; that if it does, the price to be exacted will be relinquishment, effectively and symbolically, of one's attachment to the nation. The punitive character of the law and the dubious constitutionality of its transparently targeted attack on a specific religion should not deflect from a central premise of American national identity that is, intended or not, incorporated in its deeper meaning: that bound up in the idea of American citizenship is the bedrock and regime-defining principle of natural equality, according to which, claims grounded in the superior obligation of conscience are not entitled to special consideration.[33] "The voting booth," said a justice of the Supreme Court, "is the temple of American institutions."[34] For the Mormons, who officially abandoned their commit-

---

[32] Quoted in Greenfeld 1992, 426.

[33] Christopher L. Eisgruber and Lawrence G. Sager have in this regard persuasively argued that constitutional solicitude for religious practices should be based upon the vulnerability of religions to discrimination rather than on any unique value ascribed to conscientiously motivated practices rooted in religious belief. Concerns over discrimination might justify constitutional protection, but a claim of constitutional privilege (which extends from the allegedly privileged status of religious beliefs) ought not to override a legitimate governmental interest. "In a liberal democracy, the claim that one particular set of practices or one particular set of commitments ought to be privileged . . . bears a substantial burden of justification." Eisgruber and Sager 1994b, 1260. One should, however, be sensitive to the fact that, as the Williamses have pointed out, nonvolitionist religions (which in the United States are minority religions) will by their very nature pose a greater threat to governmental interests. Thus they remind us that "The Court has . . . arrived at a formally nondiscriminatory position but the etiology of that position is saturated with volitionist bias." Williams and Williams 1991, 846.

[34] Justice Brewer as quoted in Walzer 1992, 59. "If the manyness of America is cultural," Walzer has observed, "its oneness is political." Ibid., 29. By oneness is meant a set of unifying (and universal) precepts into which the diverse strands that contribute to the manyness

ment to plural marriage in response to the *Beason* ruling, this can serve as a summary of the painful lesson learned in their encounter with the American legal system.

If the logic of the secular constitution is not in principle antireligious, is it an expression of neutrality between religion and irreligion? Does it require "a complete and permanent separation of the spheres of religious activity and civil authority by comprehensively forbidding every form of public aid or support for religion"?[35] Does the Establishment Clause, as Kathleen Sullivan has suggested, mandate "official agnosticism"?[36] To queries of this kind categorical response must remain elusive; nevertheless, limited governmental support for religion can be consistent with the advancement of the secular aspirations of American nationhood. Such support is of course not constitutionally required, but may, under carefully circumscribed conditions, be pursued at the discretion of the government. The inquiry, then, into the secular purpose of a given law needs to broach more than one layer of understanding.

The argument presumes the State's posture of official impartiality in its dealings with particular religions. While this neutrality is no longer a matter of serious disputation within legal circles, it is a constitutional requirement that should be seen as an extension of the broader claim being made here about nation-building. In this sense, the framers' permissiveness toward established churches at the state level is arguably in tension with the spirit of the Constitution's underlying principles, which suggest that, as in the case of race (a more notorious example to be sure), constitutional evolution was necessary for the document to work itself pure. The logical conclusion of governmental religious preference would be its use in determining a person's citizenship status, but as Michael Walzer has pointed out, "The United States is a nation of cultural nationalities," and so American "[c]itizenship is separated from every sort of particularism: the state is nationally, ethnically, racially, and religiously neutral."[37] Walzer sees neutrality as vital for immigrant societies such as the United States,[38] but not all immigrant societies—Israel, for example—are so decidedly and profoundly identified with a universalist political creed. It is this latter identification that renders neutrality not only desirable but necessary.

---

of American society come together. Or as Sidney Mead noted: "[A] definitive element of the spiritual core which identifies [the United States] as a nation is the conception of a universal principle which is thought to transcend and include all the national and religious particularities brought to it by the people who come from all the world to be 'Americanized.' " Mead 1975, 63.

[35] Justice Rutledge dissenting in *Everson* at 31.
[36] Sullivan 1992, 206.
[37] Walzer 1992, 9.
[38] Walzer 1994, 70.

This is what is so appealing in Justice O'Connor's much-discussed doctrinal contribution to First Amendment jurisprudence. "The Establishment Clause," she posits, "prohibits government from making adherence to a religion relevant to a person's standing in the political community."[39] "If government is to be neutral in matters of religion . . . [it] cannot endorse the religious practices and beliefs of some citizens without sending a clear message to nonadherents that they are outsiders or less than full members of the political community."[40] Debate over this sort of judicial deference to the sensibilities of outsiders often focuses on the empirical question of whether a particular prayer or religious display actually conveys a message of second-class citizenship. More important, however, is the question of how this deference applies to the content of American identity. For example, in the current debate over multiculturalism, it has been contended against both those who define the nation as little more than a collection of groups, as well as those who define it as the realization of an idea, that "a cultural concept of nationhood," emphasizing the historic connections of the American people to a particular religious tradition, presents the best account of who Americans are as a people.[41] O'Connor's "endorsement test" is a rejection of this concept of nationhood, using religion to establish that full and equal membership in the political community is not to be affected by one's contingent affiliation, that religious identity shall not be permitted to encroach upon the constitutive domain of political identity.[42]

Upon this doctrinal foundation there is an understandable temptation to build to the conclusion that "[T]he Establishment Clause . . . bars 'endorsement' and 'acknowledgment' of religion."[43] After all, if "standing in the political community" captures the essential meaning of American citizenship, and thus underscores the necessity for religion's subordination in the political arena, does it not then require the erection of an impenetrable wall separating Church and State? How, it may be asked, is endorsement of religion in principle any different from the endorsement of any particular religion? If the answer is that the distinction conforms to the intentions of the framers, it will succeed in persuading only those predisposed to accept the mandate of originalist jurisprudence, leaving others to wonder whether such deference is justified under a dramatically reconfigured social and religious environment. And assuming that this jurisprudential battle can be won, along comes someone like Leonard

---

[39] *Lynch* at 687. See also Shklar 1990, 25–62.

[40] *Allegheny County* at 627.

[41] O'Sullivan 1994, 36, 38.

[42] As we shall see in chapter 9, implementation of O'Connor's inclusive ideal can benefit from careful consideration of the Indian emphasis on ameliorative aspects of secularism.

[43] Sullivan 1992, 206.

Levy (ironically an outspoken opponent of a legal philosophy of original intent), making a compelling case that "It was . . . public support on a nonpreferential basis that the establishment clause of the First Amendment sought to forbid."[44] Must we therefore be an expert on the conflicting historical sources to be heard on this issue?

Distinguishing between these two forms of endorsement should neither abandon the quest for historical certainty nor too narrowly restrict the scope of inquiry. We must first pursue the First Amendment implications of the American concept of nationhood—emphasizing its principled foundations—and then assess the significance in the context of the *thinness* of American religiosity. To start, consider the merits of a remark attributed to President Eisenhower: "Our government makes no sense unless it is founded in a deeply felt religious faith, and I don't care what it is."[45] Presumably, Eisenhower was attempting to convey a message along the lines of Tocqueville's admonition that religion is "indispensable to the maintenance of republican institutions," while also displaying a politically astute respect for the great diversity of religious commitment that exists in the United States.[46] His appreciation of the secular benefits of spiritual life might be seen as drawing upon the famous sentiments of the nation's first president, whose farewell address is well known for emphasizing the salutary effects of religion in public life.

But a closer look at the statement reveals a problem if it is taken to mean that the American founding is rooted in a particular religious commitment, since all revealed religions are at their core exclusionary and hence in conflict with the natural right of equality. If, on the other hand, "religious faith" means *religious-like devotion to a set of commonly accepted precepts*, then Eisenhower could have had in mind the Declaration of Independence, which expresses a creed that has appropriately been labeled the "Theology of the Republic."[47] This rendering, however, is also problematic, since the "I don't care" proclamation in the second part of the sentence is in tension with the self-evident truth that lies at the heart of the Declaration. Unlikely as it may be (although mindful of his oft-noted propensity for obfuscation, deliberate or otherwise), let us suppose that what Eisenhower really meant was something like the following: Our

---

[44] Levy 1986, xvi.

[45] Mead 1975, 25.

[46] Tocqueville 1945, vol. 1, 316. Tocqueville's pivotal role in the emergence of the civil religion school is discussed at some length by Sanford Kessler, who sees Tocqueville's intellectual descendants today occupying a middle position in the often heated debate over secularization in contemporary American society. Characterized as "religious fundamentalists," these commentators are quite eclectic in their politics, united only in their shared assumption that religion is crucial in fostering the mores that sustain freedom. Kessler 1994, 5, 14.

[47] Mead 1975, 18.

government makes no sense unless it is understood to rest upon what Chesterton called the "dogmatic and even theological lucidity [of] the Declaration of Independence";[48] and whatever religious beliefs might reinforce the religious-like political truths of that document should be supported by government.

In relation to the assimilative mission of the secular constitution, much of the appeal of this position lies in its functional value, as it exploits the pervasive religiosity of the American people to solidify the consensus underlying the national creed. Over the years, proponents of a *civil religion* have in various ways argued along these lines, agreeing with Benjamin Franklin about "the necessity of a *Publick Religion.*"[49] Dubious over the long-term prospects of the modern liberal state without the legitimating advantages traditionally associated with religion, they have written extensively and controversially about the religious power of American ideals. "The American Way of Life," it is said, "is the operative religion of the American people."[50] The United States is a "Nation with the Soul of a Church," and as such, its reliance upon myth, symbol, and ritual, like that of other churches, is vital to the success of its mission in this world. Accepting the essentially privatized condition of religion in the United States, and yet concerned that this reality will prevent the polity from developing the bonds of unity that a functioning society must have, civil religion theorists hope to nurture and develop what is, in effect, a synthetic religious tradition that draws upon a multitude of sources from within the American political, cultural, and religious experience.[51]

But whatever its functional appeal, drawing upon religious traditions to support the secular purpose of strengthening the bonds of nationhood confronts a potentially fatal objection. How does one go about choosing from among the tenets of religion those that reinforce the political truths of the Declaration of Independence, without engaging in impermissible discrimination, which is to say, endorsement of particular religions? If compatibility with the tenets of the "Theology of the Republic" is a criterion for preferential treatment, then followers of religions whose beliefs and practices are agreeable with egalitarian assumptions about human nature will enjoy a favored status in the eyes of the State. Judges, moreover, will be set up as arbiters of theological doctrine, determining which

---

[48] Quoted in Ibid., 20.

[49] Quoted in Marty 1987, 42.

[50] Herberg 1974, 77.

[51] It is easy to see how the justices of the Supreme Court, guardians of the nation's covenantal document, will naturally be viewed as the carriers of the civil religion. A vast literature in political science is devoted to the sources of the Court's legitimacy, much of it looking into the mystical ways in which the divinity of the Constitution radiates to the advantage of its official interpreters.

religious opinions are, in effect, safe, and which threaten to divert from the goal of political assimilation.[52] The substance of religious beliefs, then, contrary to the results we have seen in applying the Free Exercise Clause, would again enter the purview of the State. As far as the tenets of any given religion are concerned, the law might still know no heresy, but in determining policy in relation to the civil religion, some beliefs would obviously come to be perceived as heretical.

An additional problem in advancing only religious ideas consistent with national ideals is that the salutary subversive role that religion can play in a pervasively liberal society could be discouraged. Perhaps the ideal solution would be to encourage the pluralism of American religious life, so that churches could solidify their standing as sanctuaries *against* the nation (or at least as intermediaries between the State and the individual) while drawing upon many of the beliefs common to most believers in this country—what Franklin called the "essentials of every religion"—to enrich popular understanding of the moral principles that make religious freedom possible. As Christopher L. Eisgruber and Lawrence G. Sager point out, "[P]olicy makers might legitimately take into account the instrumental value of religious institutions as aids to moral development in a democratic society."[53] A delicate balance to be sure—but one that is not in principle unattainable, as is occasionally discernible in the Supreme Court's tortuous maneuvering through the minefield of Church/State litigation. What may appear to the scholar as ad hoc and incoherent is often precisely that, but it is also reflective of the necessarily complex pattern of judicial response to what has been referred to as "the special place of religion in the Constitution."[54] Because the location of this special place is fixed in relation to regime-defining principles, the constitutional law that stems from it should be shaped accordingly.

Those, for example, who might find the Court's guardianship of the public schools against sectarian intrusion inconsistent with its solicitude for the tax-exempt status of religious institutions or its relative tolerance for public displays of religious symbols should consider these results in

---

[52] Consider, for example, how two civil religion legal scholars address the establishment issue. "[T]he preliminary question before the Court in each Establishment Clause case should be whether the questioned practice involves civil or theological religion. If it involves civil religion, it is permissible; if it involves public acknowledgment of or government support for theological religion, then it will be subject to Establishment Clause scrutiny and may be impermissible." Maddigan 1993, 18. A second writes: "When faced with questions arising out of the social context of civil religion, courts must somehow tread a line between the expression of shared and constitutive values on the one hand and impermissible establishment on the other." Mirsky 1986, 1255.

[53] Eisgruber and Sager 1994b, 1267.

[54] Smith 1984.

light of the "delicate balance." While the Court has no business inquiring into the substance of religious belief, it is responsible for determining the conditions under which spiritual and temporal affairs may appropriately intersect. When it excludes *all* religious presence from the public schools, and when it permits *all* religions to benefit from the tax policies of the State, the Court's discretion is limited to specifying criteria and occasions for erecting Jefferson's wall of separation. Informing these determinations is a secular interest in the constitutive principles of the nation, which of course includes doing right by religion. In the case of the schools, it requires a recognition of the unique historic role played by public education in assimilating Americans into a common political culture. As Justice Brennan said in *Abington v Schempp*: "It is implicit in the history and character of American public education that the public schools serve a uniquely *public* function: the training of American citizens in an atmosphere free of parochial, divisive, or separatist influences of any sort—an atmosphere in which children may assimilate a heritage common to all American groups and religions."[55] Or as his jurisprudential adversary, Justice Frankfurter, put it fifteen years earlier: "The public school is at once the symbol of our democracy and the most pervasive means for promoting our common destiny."[56]

Justice Brennan also wrote in a landmark case from New York that "Government may properly include religious institutions among the variety of private, nonprofit groups that receive tax exemptions, for each group contributes to the diversity of association, viewpoint, and enterprise essential to a vigorous, pluralistic society."[57] Brennan, however, went on to justify the ruling by emphasizing how the secular activities of churches benefit the community, thereby underplaying the principal, which is to say religious, mission of these institutions.[58] He was perhaps

---

[55] *Abington* at 241.

[56] *McCollum* at 231.

[57] *Walz* at 689.

[58] Brennan's strategy was consistent with Chief Justice Burger's opinion of the Court, which relied upon the benevolent neutrality of the policy. "The legislative purpose of a property tax exemption is neither the advancement nor the inhibition of religion; it is neither sponsorship nor hostility." Ibid. at 678. In a 1989 case, *Texas Monthly, Inc. v Bullock*, the Court overturned a tax exemption for religious periodicals, with Justice Brennan arguing for the Court that, here, unlike in *Walz*, the exemption was a policy especially designed for the benefit of religion. In *Bob Jones University v United States*, involving the withdrawal of tax relief from a religious school that practiced racial discrimination on the basis of religious belief, the Court upheld the IRS action in a way that clarified the underlying philosophy of the earlier cases. Chief Justice Burger wrote: "[G]overnmental interest [in racial equality] substantially outweighs whatever burden denial of tax benefits places on petitioners' exercise of their religious beliefs." *Bob Jones University* at 604. John Mansfield sees the denial as "necessarily rest[ing] upon a judgment that the religion that preaches racial discrimina-

mindful of Justice Douglas's dissenting opinion, wherein his frequent ally argued that "[S]ectarian causes must remain in the private domain not subject to public control or subsidy."[59] In so doing, he missed the opportunity to articulate the ways in which the community's secular interests might be advanced by the religious activities of religions. "[A]s important as the public schools have been," Robert Bellah has suggested, "the real school of republican virtue in America . . . was the church."[60] The oft-noted paradox in American culture of pervasive secularism and widespread religiosity is not so very difficult to comprehend in light of the mutually reinforcing dynamic that exists between the two conditions. Religion as practiced in most churches, synagogues, and mosques in the United States is generally supportive of the principles upon which the Constitution rests.[61] Where it is not, where religious teachings contradict these principles, the predominant thinness of American religiosity ensures that public support for religion will not become a self-inflicted wound. As a result, judges will not be expected to intervene with regard to the substance of religious opinions. In the American context, being selectively indiscriminate, in the sense of choosing where it is appropriate to support

---

tion in education is false in this respect." Mansfield 1984, 875. He may be right with regard to what the Court intended. If so, what they should have intended is this: Its truth or falsity as religious doctrine is irrelevant to the issue at hand. But in the political arena, it is a mere opinion, which, if incompatible with public policy (and the public philosophy that underlies it), need not benefit from public resources.

[59] *McCollum* at 710.

[60] Bellah 1975, 180.

[61] This phenomenon has historic roots in American political culture. In their study of religion in contemporary American society, Kosmin and Lachman show the connections between late eighteenth-century political ideas concerning the importance of the individual and American denominations of that time. "An interesting aspect of the great diversity of religions in Colonial America was that they all developed a common image of the American nation. This brought about the extraordinary American development of a generalized religion integrating a society even while the nation had many religions. Within American society, the collective religion became America's civil religion, incorporating secular as well as religious values and emphasizing a national purpose." Kosmin and Lachman 1993, 22. This view should be placed within a wider historical perspective. Harold J. Berman, for example, has observed that "Liberal democracy was the first great secular religion in Western history—the first ideology which became divorced from traditional Christianity and at the same time took over from traditional Christianity both its sense of the sacred and some of its major values." Berman 1983, 3, 38. The most discussed and debated attempt to demonstrate the integration of religious and secular ideas and practices in the United States is Max Weber's classic study of the Protestant work ethic and the development of American capitalism. It is not necessary wholeheartedly to embrace Weber's thesis to acknowledge the historical symbiosis between religious and political beliefs. This does not contradict what was said earlier, that religion can also function as a refuge from the values of a liberal order. All of the religious traditions are rich and diverse enough to sustain both supportive and subversive roles.

religion without regard to doctrinal content, is an affordable luxury, both for the pluralism it encourages and the unity of national purpose to which it can contribute.

Looking, then, at the controversial Establishment Clause test introduced by the Court one year after *Walz*, we might say the following. The first prong of the so-called *Lemon test*, that governmental action must have a secular purpose, is, standing alone, quite reasonable. Thus as long as a secular rationale can be legitimately invoked, the provision of non-preferential aid to religion would not under this requirement be proscribed. But in conjunction with the test's second prong, that the primary effect of the action must neither advance nor inhibit religion, there is reason to doubt that framing a secular purpose in terms of facilitating the political assimilation of a diverse population would pass constitutional muster. The primary effect of providing tax relief to churches is by design to advance the interests of religion; in this respect, the majority was surely more disingenuous than the minority. A likely indirect effect of such aid is that religion will be strengthened as a viable source for the legitimation of regime principles, which in the United States is critical to the realization of constitutional and hence national aspirations. Whether governmental support hinders or retards this realization is always an empirical question. Thus the elementary and secondary public school context may reveal, as many of the Court's rulings suggest, that the primary effect of aiding religion through its introduction into a very special environment (i.e., youngsters brought together for a shared learning experience) is to undermine, not support, an acceptable secular purpose. Financial support for parochial schools is more complicated, for the advancement of religious education, while in principle perhaps consistent with a legitimate, if not primary, secular purpose, would have to be considered in light of the possible devastation it might create for the public schools. My purpose here is not to address the particulars of these issues but only to suggest that the appropriate framework for assessing the relevant evidence is one that directs attention to the complex pattern of interaction between religious and national identities. In the end, that means, paraphrasing Jefferson, that for Americans, we are all separationists, we are all accommodationists.

ISRAEL: VISIONARY SECULARISM

[T]his pretended *right of every qualified subject to a share of the honours and profits in the disposal of the supreme magistrate* is altogether groundless and visionary.

Let it be remembered, that . . . it hath been proved at large, that REWARD IS NOT ONE OF THE SANCTIONS OF CIVIL SOCIETY: the only claim which subjects have on the magistrate for *obedience*, being protection.

Now the consequence of this is, that all places of honour and profit, in the magistrate's disposal, are not there in the nature of a TRUST; to be claimed, and equally shared by the subject: but of the nature of a PREROGATIVE; which he may dispose of at pleasure, without being further accountable, than for having such places *ably* supplied.[62]

William Warburton, the author of this formidable prose, was an Englishman whose writings in the 1730s had considerable influence in eighteenth-century American debates over religious liberty. An Anglican defender of an established church, he wrote controversial tracts in which he argued for equal protection for all people to pursue their natural right to religious liberty, while also claiming special privileges for members of the established religion. As Philip Hamburger has shown, supporters of American establishments put Warburton's arguments to effective use in their contest with religious dissenters over the future of Church/State relations in the colonies, and in due course, the new nation. In the end, the Antiestablishment Clause of the First Amendment signaled the eventual triumph of the dissenters' position, a triumph that has come to serve as an appealing model for framers of secular constitutions based on liberal principles.

For many in Israel inspired by the promise of that country's Declaration of Independence to "guarantee full freedom of conscience, worship, education and culture," the American model is eminently worthy of emulation. But it is Warburton's model—or at least a variation thereof—that exemplifies the actual workings of the Israeli secular constitution. The dominant political and legal approach to religion in the preconstitutional period of American history, more so than what has prevailed during most of the subsequent national experience, illuminates the Israeli constitutional solution. The specific facet of the colonial treatment that warrants particular attention is the distinction between *equal protection* and *equal civil rights*, a distinction that is useful in analyzing problems of diversity among religious groups in Israel as well as within the majority Jewish population. A framework for exploring the Israeli experience with *visionary* secularism thus begins with a brief account of the eighteenth-century debate in a place depicted by many at the time as "the new Israel."

Two standards shaped the intellectual contours of the argument over religious liberty. "Equal civil rights was a standard demanding that civil law treat individuals the same [for example, in the allocation of money]— that it not distinguish among individuals on the basis of their religious differences. By comparison, equal protection of the laws was a lesser degree of equality—an equality only of the protection provided by civil law

---

[62] Hamburger 1993, 321.

for natural liberty."[63] *Lesser* in this context does not connote triviality, for indeed religious liberty was widely understood to be the most important of the natural rights for which the safeguards of modern constitutionalism were crafted. Following Locke, eighteenth-century Americans (both dissenters and, increasingly, establishmentarians) shared in a consensus concerning government's need to protect the inalienable right to worship as one pleased. Calculation as much as conviction supported the consensus; thus in the various contests over State neutrality that dominated colonial politics, the equal protection position was used defensively by proponents of established religions to protect their unequal "privileges" against the challenge of the dissenters.

The appeal of Warburton's ideas to the American establishments resided in the ingenuity with which the Anglican balanced toleration and privilege. Advocates of equal civil rights demanded an equality of legal privileges to go along with the equality of natural liberty that the establishments had been willing to extend to them.[64] "With the idea of equal protection, an establishment could provide dissenters an egalitarian reassurance that no one would be subjected to greater legal obligations or 'restraints' than anyone else on account of his or her religion, but an establishment did not thereby promise to share equally or to forgo its privileges, such as state financial support. In short, equal protection required equal obligations and permitted unequal privileges."[65] For Warburton, "honour and profit" were within the "prerogative" of the State, which had the responsibility of delivering "protection" to everyone in the exercise of their religious liberty. This was a solution that worked for a while, only to be superseded by a more inclusive understanding of rights in which the assimilative aspiration of American self-understanding came to be embodied in the Establishment Clause of the First Amendment. Jefferson, in other words, eventually prevailed: The spirit of the secular constitution incorporated his view that the profession of religious opinions by men "shall in no wise diminish, enlarge, or affect their civil capacities."[66]

How does the equal protection argument/defense apply to Israel? There are obvious complications in drawing parallels between eighteenth-century colonial America and contemporary Israel, but the essentials of the comparison are still worth pursuing. One difference in the two situations that need not preoccupy us is that Israel, unlike the colonies, does not

[63] Ibid., 299.

[64] As one dissenter, Samuel Stillman, put it, "The authority by which he [i.e., the 'magistrate'] acts he derives alike from *all the people*, [and] consequently he should exercise that authority *equally* for the benefit of *all*, without any respect to their different religious principles." Quoted in Ibid., 342.

[65] Ibid., 318.

[66] Ibid., 350.

have a legally established religion. In that respect, it also differs from a country like Sweden (at least until very recently), which suggests that the presence of a legally established Church is not a very reliable indication of the functional importance of establishment within a particular country. In a variety of ways—legal and nonlegal—Judaism in Israel enjoys a preferred status over other religions in the country, such that any realistic assessment of its place in Israeli life would have to conclude that it has been effectively established as the nation's favored religion.[67] And essential to this preferred position is another characteristic that distinguishes it from the early American establishments, the ethnic or national attributes of the dominant religion. The equal protection claim voiced by Protestant establishments in the colonies was not used in defense of the prerogatives of *a* people, but of people who happened to share a common faith.

The same Declaration that guarantees full freedom of worship to all its citizens begins by proclaiming Israel as "the birthplace of the Jewish people." "Here their spiritual, religious and national identity was formed." It is within this juxtaposition of individual rights and national self-definition that the distinction between the two forms of equality discussed above becomes quite relevant. The Zionist vision, embodied in the Declaration's assertion of "the right of the Jewish people to national revival in their own country," establishes the constitutional parameters within which Church/State issues are to be addressed. The fact, however, that for most Israelis this religiously informed vision is only minimally imbued with constitutive social significance means that a genuine secular commitment to protect religious liberty is compatible with the nonneutrality of the State in matters associated with religious affiliation.

This compatibility is not entirely unproblematic. There are occasions when policies stemming from the Zionist commitment of the State do impinge on the religious liberty of minorities, but the predominant thinness of religiosity within the Israeli Jewish community prevents *visionary* secularism from becoming an oxymoron.[68] A 1988 Supreme Court case involving the denial of a political party's right to participate in Knesset

---

[67] Donna Arzt has made the useful suggestion that the term *association* be employed to describe the relationship between religion and the State in Israel. Implying something short of *establishment*, it entails regulation of, support for, and recognition (as in imprimatur) of religion. Arzt 1991, 32. Some Israeli scholars have also attempted to demonstrate the preferred position in Israeli practice of European Jews over Middle Eastern Jews, particularly in the 1950s and 1960s when modernization and the consolidation of the State were viewed as critical to the success of the Zionist project. See, for example, Cohen-Almagor 1995; and Smooha 1978.

[68] There have been many empirical studies of Jewish religious commitment in Israel, all of which suggest that for the great majority of Israelis, being Jewish plays an important role in their lives (in different ways) but is not a way of life. Many of these findings are included in Sobel and Beit-Hallahmi 1991.

elections because it denied "the existence of the State of Israel as the state of the Jewish people" speaks directly to these issues.[69] The disqualified party was the Progressive List for Peace (PLP), against which, according to a bare majority of the Court, there was insufficient evidence to justify its removal from the ballot. But there was general agreement that a removal could occur even in the absence of subversive activity; questioning the substantive vision of Israel as the State of the Jewish people could still incur significant political consequences despite the differences among judges on the scope and meaning of that vision. One of the dissenters was Justice Elon, who wrote: "The principle that the State of Israel is the state of the Jewish people is Israel's foundation and mission, and the principle of the equality of rights and obligations of all citizens of the State of Israel is of the State's essence and character. The latter principle comes only to add to the former, not to modify it; [there is nothing in] the principle of the equality of civil rights and obligations to modify the principle that the State of Israel is the state of the Jewish people, *and only the Jewish people.*"[70]

While more emphatically expressed than most judicial pronouncements on the Jewish foundations of the State, these sentiments are nevertheless suggestive of the basic orientation of visionary secularism. Thus the clear distinction between equal citizenship rights and full membership in the political community is discernible also in opinions of judges more secularly inclined than Justice Elon. These equal citizenship rights (analogous to the guarantees of equal protection in the eighteenth century) include religious freedom. This is perhaps not so evident in *Ben Shalom*: Arabs whose religious beliefs require that they live in a land that is not identified with the Jewish people will no doubt experience a denial of equality when they seek, in violation of the law, to support their beliefs with political action. On the other hand, so will the Jews whose denial of the "democratic nature of the state" places them in violation of the same Basic Law as that invoked in *Ben Shalom*.[71] In both cases, the dual aspirations (de-

---

[69] Section 7a to the Basic Law: The Knesset.

[70] Very similar to these views of the observant Justice Elon are the following sentiments of the late secularist Labor Party leader, Yigal Allon. "It is necessary to declare it openly: Israel is a single-nationality Jewish State. The fact that an Arab minority lives within the country does not make it a multinational state. It only requires that the state grant equal citizenship to every citizen of the state, with no differences based on religion, race, or nationality." Quoted in Lustick 1980, 65. There is, however, a sizable and vocal group of Israeli Jews, largely confined to the academic arena, who call into question the continuing relevance of Jewish nationalism. These "post-Zionists" emphasize the obsolescence of Zionism in Israel today while turning a critical eye to the accepted Zionist narrative of Israel's past.

[71] This of course is what happened to Meir Kahane and his anti-Arab Kach list. Unlike the judicial response to the PLP case, the Supreme Court unanimously upheld the removal of Kahane's party from the ballot for the 1988 elections. *Neiman.* Most Jews in Israel found

mocracy in a Jewish State) of the Israeli national commitment (or vision) exert pressure, however indirect, upon religious belief. Rare as this discriminatory result is likely to be, its occurrence is nevertheless a predictable byproduct of the convergence of faith and ethnicity, religious beliefs and national aspirations. In Israeli law, a minimalist conception of the Jewish character of the State prevails, but it is still with much less confidence than in the United States that one can say of the law that "[I]t knows no heresy, and is committed to the support of no dogma." Because the subordination of religion is not a necessary premise of visionary secularism (in the way that it is for an assimilative model), religious opinion is less amenable to judicial protection under the doctrinal aegis of content neutrality.

Direct infringements on free exercise are relatively uncommon in Israel, and as we shall see, at least as likely to be felt by people belonging to the majority community. Much like in India, allegations of legal bias against religion are heard with disproportionate frequency from within the dominant religious group.[72] Consistent with the logic of Justice Elon's comment, minority grievances over religious questions focus less on perceived violations of religious liberty than on inequities associated with the State's distribution of rewards and privileges. They speak most directly to the issue of standing in the political community, and their general target is

---

Kahane's ugly racist attacks on Arabs outrageous and offensive, and had no problem dissociating these views from their understanding of Judaism. But Kahane and his followers insistently maintained that his party's positions were the true expression of the Jewish faith and tradition. For them, in other words, the Basic Law denied them political *and* religious freedom. It should be noted, in this regard, that the Declaration's affirmation of democratic values itself has a specifically religious foundation, as it is "based on the precepts of liberty, justice and peace taught by the Hebrew Prophets." The *Kahane* case warrants comparison to rulings by the Indian Supreme Court that are explored in depth in chapters 6 and 7. On the basis of a stump speech in which the Hindu supremacist Balasaheb K. Thackeray called Muslims "snakes," this leader of the Shiv Sena Party was barred from forthcoming elections, a decision upheld by the Court. At the same time, however, the Court ruled that another politician's pledge to turn Maharashtra into India's "first Hindu state" was not an offense under Indian law. What was forbidden was the conveying of a hostile attitude toward other faiths, not the expression of a politically subversive idea. Thus in both India and Israel you can run afoul of the law by voicing hatred toward communal groups, but in the former, such expression does not implicate one in the illegal larger project of undermining democratic institutions.

[72] In India, however, the complainants tend to be identified with Hindu revivalism, whereas in Israel the people who see themselves as victims tend to be associated with more secular and less nationalistic Jewish loyalties. Apropos this difference, and relevant to my subsequent discussion of personal law in Israel, Varshney has pointed out that Hindu nationalists insist that Muslims assimilate, rather than maintain their distinctiveness. Varshney 1993, 231. In contrast, Jewish religious nationalists are the most adamant of Israelis in opposing any move that might lead to the slightest integration of the Jewish and Muslim communities. These distinctions receive a more extended treatment in chapter 8.

preferential treatment.[73] Implicated are both substantive policies—legal differentiations affecting immigration (the Law of Return), political representation (the Chief Rabbinate of Israel Law), administration of religious endowments, and provision for religious training seminaries—as well as largely symbolic ones—the design of the flag (inspired by items important to the Jewish tradition) and the national anthem (which is also the hymn of the Zionist movement). They amount, in short, to the kinds of policies and privileges that the tolerant establishments in the American colonies defended so vigorously against their dissenting opponents.

But in contrast to the American colonies, the *privileges* at issue in Israel are centrally related to the question of political identity. For this reason their legitimacy will surely prove less vulnerable to erosion than was the case in the United States. It is not that the combination of pecuniary rewards, such as state support of ministers, and philosophical commitments, such as the notion that state-supported Christianity was essential for harmonious social relations, could not help win political skirmishes. But in the long run, a defense of a status quo grounded in considerations increasingly out of sync with revolutionary political ideas could not fall back upon a second line of defense rooted in the primordial instinct of survival. After all, for the American establishments, the enemy was on the other side of a wide sea; that fundamental reality, as well as the fact that establishments and dissenters reversed roles from colony to colony, suggests that the stakes involved in the maintenance of privilege were of insufficient weight to resist the moral and political challenge of the underprivileged.

Scholarly accounts of Israeli political culture rightly emphasize Jewish privileges as an integral component of ethnic or national conflict. For example, Sammy Smooha uses the term *ethnic democracy* to characterize a system "in which the Jewish majority has established institutionalized dominance" over an Arab minority that has been extended political and civil rights to individuals.[74] Similarly, for Yoav Peled, "[T]he dominant strain in Israel's political culture may be termed *ethnorepublicanism*. Jewish ethnicity is a necessary condition for membership in the political community, while the contribution to the process of Jewish national redemption is a measure of one's civic virtue."[75] Implicit in this conceptualization are contrasting notions of citizenship, republican for Jews and liberal for Arabs. "Thus, while Jews and Arabs formally enjoy equal citizenship rights, only Jews can exercise their citizenship as practice, by attending

---

[73] See, in addition to Justice O'Connor's Establishment Clause formulation, the scholarly discussions by Shklar 1990; Karst 1989; and Spinner 1994.

[74] Smooha 1993, 108.

[75] Peled 1992, 435.

to the public good."[76] Peled's portrayal of the Israeli polity as a "two-tiered democracy" mirrors the image evoked by Justice Elon's constitutional assertions in *Ben Shalom*. In essence, the fulfillment of Jewish national aspirations requires the denial of Arab national aspirations, which is another way of saying that non-Jews are effectively excluded from the civil religion of Israel.[77]

Missing from these accounts is an answer to the following question: If, as Elon contends, the principle of equal civil rights does not modify the principle of Israel as the State of the Jewish people, does it also follow that the particularism of the latter principle leaves the universalistic premises of the former principle unmodified? Might it even be the case that under certain circumstances the identification of the State with the fate of a particular people actually strengthens the commitment to equal civil rights, in particular the free exercise of religion? In the case of the Protestant establishments, toleration was a good deal for the dominant religion. "Dissenters sought equal civil rights and were fobbed off with equal protection."[78] Without denying the presence of less cynical motivations in accounting for the Israeli commitment to religious liberty (as there were also in the eighteenth century), surely there is here too a strong element of calculation involved in the official endorsement of the equal protection principle. In addition, it is possible that the strength of the libertarian commitment is reinforced, albeit inadvertently and counterintuitively, by the nationalist impulse in Jewish life in Israel. Thus the pursuit of religious national aspirations—not present in the American case but essential to the Israeli—can, as many orthodox Jews in Israel have, to their dismay, come to realize, weaken and dilute the theological or spiritual content of religious devotion, providing, as an incidental if not unimportant political benefit, a more hospitable environment for exercising religious tolerance toward minorities.[79]

---

[76] Ibid., 432.

[77] Liebman and Don-Yehiya 1989, 48. David Kretzmer suggests that the maintenance of the distinction between rights and privileges is at the root of the otherwise inexplicable Population Registry Law, which requires that all citizens of Israel be registered by "nation." "Registration of 'nation' is irrelevant in determining the rights and obligations of citizens, but it strengthens the dichotomy between the state as the political framework of all its citizens, and the state as the particularistic nation-state of the Jewish people." Kretzmer 1990, 44.

[78] Hamburger 1993, 336.

[79] See in this regard Eric Cohen's comparative analysis of citizenship, nationality, and religion in Israel and Thailand. His study tries to provide an explanation for the Thai polity's failure, in contrast to the mixed success in Israel, in achieving a harmonious solution to its Muslim minority problem. He finds that Judaism, as a political force in Israel, is mediated through the secular ideology of Zionism, leading to an attenuation in the conflict between the State and its Arab minority. Cohen 1989, 68. "[E]ven when symbols originating in Jewish religion were incorporated into the body of the central political symbols of the state,

Israel, like India, operates under a system of personal laws that has its roots in preindependence experience. In Israel, the administration of communal affairs under ecclesiastical authority is traceable to the *millet* system of Ottoman rule. For centuries in the Islamic-dominated Middle East, Jews and other nonassimilating minorities exercised considerable autonomy in maintaining control over the internal affairs of their communities. The establishment of the Jewish State was not accompanied by any effort to uproot the historic patterns of the area, and so deference to the primordial attachments of religion and ethnicity was maintained and institutionalized in the decision-making structure pertaining to questions of personal status. Through the Ministry of Religious Affairs, funding is provided for officially recognized religions to administer the facilities that perpetuate their separate existence. Ethnoreligious groups compete with the State for the right to exercise coercive authority over individuals whom the group views as its members and whom the State recognizes as citizens of one polity.

It is not, however, a zero-sum competition. Thus part of the State's recognition of a common legal citizenship is its accommodation of the group-based nature of membership in the political community.[80] It is in the interests of the State in the pursuit of its visionary aspirations to protect the right of minority communities to freedom *of* religion, although this may leave individuals without adequate freedom *from* religion. From the perspective of the majority group, communal autonomy supports political stability by providing nondominant (and unassimilable) groups

---

they were not perceived as religious, but as historical national symbols; their religious salience was low not only in the perception of the Jewish but also of the non-Jewish citizens." Ibid., 70. There are several reasons for the more violent history of the Thai government's relations with its Malay Muslim minority, but the one that is most relevant in this context is that Buddhism as a political presence has retained its religious significance, so that Muslims tend to perceive demands upon them as infringements upon their religion. "The Thai-Malay conflict, like that between Israel and the Arabs, is essentially a national and political one; but in Thailand it is expressed in a religious idiom, which in Israel, at least for the time being, it is not. It is this religious dimension of the conflict that endows it with its violent character." Ibid., 87.

[80] Ian Lustick has argued that a key to understanding the striking political quiescence of Israel's Arab minority (at least up to 1980) are the measures taken by the government to achieve religious fragmentation in the Arab community. "[T]he particular programs implemented by the regime with respect to the religious segmentation of the Arab population were designed to preserve these identities and encourage their use as meaningful political categories. These efforts must be understood as part of a general desire to inhibit the emergence of 'Arab' as the most meaningful category of political identity and association for Israel's non-Jewish population." Lustick 1980, 133. In this sense, the laws of personal status, as well as their earlier incarnation in the millet system, can be understood as the logical extension of a system that in various ways commits itself to the special concerns of a dominant group.

with mechanisms that enable them to minimize the effects of their inferior position in the larger society. To this end, the secular constitution assigns a meaning to equal protection premised upon the equal right of officially sanctioned communities to govern themselves in select areas of social life. While the State retains the authority to impose uniformity upon these communities, it does not follow a guiding, or "directive," principle to eliminate disparate communal legal experience.[81]

Thus there is no reliance in Israel's leading polygamy case on a constitutionally approved exception to an equal protection requirement of uniformity.[82] Discrimination among communities with regard to the legal proscription of polygamy was, as we shall see, justified in India on the basis of pragmatic considerations having to do with the need to pursue social reform in incremental stages. As long as the distinctions or classifications in the law were reasonable (e.g., recognizing one community as ill prepared for social reform), discrimination would be upheld. In the decision of the Israeli Supreme Court, the antidiscrimination norm was found to be unaffected by the legislative determination to allow a community-based variable application of the criminal law. The difference in the Indian and Israeli approaches is a subtle one, but revealingly suggestive of a greater acceptance in the latter case of differential treatment as a constitutive part of the solution to the problem of intercommunal diversity.

Yosifof, an Israeli Jew, had been convicted of the felony of bigamy. The core of his complaint was that the section of the Criminal Code ordinance under which he was convicted discriminated improperly among the inhabitants of Palestine.[83] In brief, it permitted a Muslim to have more than one wife but effectively precluded Yosifof from the same indulgence. Marriage, he claimed, was an institution common to all communities, and the

---

[81] This might fruitfully be contrasted with the early policies of the State regarding ethnic communities within the larger Jewish community. As Cohen-Almagor has shown, Israeli nation-building ideology emphasized the need to undermine cultural and traditional particularities in the interest of creating a new kind of Jewish person, the Sabra. Cohen-Almagor 1995, 466. Thus the elimination (or at least major modification) of disparate communal experience *was* consistent with political aspirations—but characteristically only within the Jewish community.

[82] *Yosifof* at 481.

[83] The case involved a statute passed under the mandate, a fact that does not undermine its comparative value, since it presents an underlying theory for the law of personal status that also applies to laws enacted subsequent to 1948. The statute did not absolutely forbid polygamy for Jews, but required that "a final decree of a rabbinical court of the Jewish community ratified by the two Chief Rabbis for Palestine and giving permission for the subsequent marriage, had been obtained prior to the subsequent marriage." Thus the statute sought to bring the criminal law of the state into conformity with Jewish and Muslim law. Because of the different attitudes of the religions toward polygamy, the effect of the law was to make it much more difficult for Jews to engage in the practice.

State (or mandatory power in this instance) could not legislate different principles for different communities. In upholding Yosifof's conviction, Justice Landau pointedly distinguished between the American and Israeli concepts of equal protection, noting, for example, that discrimination in the United States (and, we might add, in India too) "is permitted subject to the condition that it expresses itself in the form of a classification on a reasonable basis, while in our case discrimination is forbidden in all circumstances and is not limited by considerations of public order, and other considerations of a like nature."[84] Yosifof, then, cannot claim to be a victim of discrimination, even if as a Muslim he would be able legally to do what he cannot do as a Jew. How can this be?

According to Justice Landau, "The distinguishing feature implicit in the expression 'discrimination' is an attitude which is unequal and un-fair—*for different classes of people.*"[85] Placing the issue of differential treatment within the context of "the social realities of the country," he analogized the marriage law to the rule requiring that official court documents be issued in the language of the person to whom they are addressed. There is no discrimination involved in such a policy, only "a desire to confer equal status upon all the official languages."[86] With the issue of equality defined in terms of the status accorded to separate communities (and with no effort to distinguish language and religion), the fact that *individuals* experience a varied legal reality across communities does not substantiate a claim of discrimination. "We must ask ourselves whether the men and women of the same community regarded as one unit are discriminated against. The answer to the question cannot be otherwise than in the negative."[87]

Justice Landau was careful to emphasize the continuity of the challenged law with earlier practice under Ottoman rule, but his opinion is at least as noteworthy for its consistency with the logic of visionary secularism. "Wherein lies the discrimination upon race or religion in handing the final decision in regard to permission to marry more than one wife . . . to the competent Rabbis of the Jewish community?"[88] The power of the religious communities to issue binding decisions itself derives from secular law that is premised upon an equal protection principle specifically adapted to the circumstances of a culturally divided, differentially privileged, society.[89] This calls attention to Will Kymlicka's influential lib-

---

[84] *Yosifof* 1962, 185.

[85] Ibid., 184 (emphasis added).

[86] Ibid., 185.

[87] Ibid., 187.

[88] Ibid., 186.

[89] It should be noted, however, that the system of personal law existing in Israel is quite different from what prevails in India. As Marc Galanter and Jayanth Krishnan have pointed

eral argument for cultural rights. "A government that gives special rights to members of a distinct cultural community may still be treating them *as individuals*; the provision of such rights just reflects a different view about how to treat them as individuals and equals."[90] Along these lines, Justice Silberg's concurrence asserts that one of the appropriate functions of the state is "the maintenance and regulation of particular forms of living and cultural values in which that particular section of the community is interested, and which it holds dear."[91] Consistent with Kymlicka's liberal emphasis, the State's encouragement of cultural autonomy enhances and reinforces a sense of personal identity and capacity. Freedom of choice, the argument goes, is meaningful only within a secure cultural context. But for Justices Landau and Silberg, the identification of individual rights with the rights of groups also helps to legitimate the more particularistic aspects of Israeli nationhood. Because, as Landau said in *Rufeisen* of the Jewish people, "[N]ationalism and religion are inseparably interwoven," acknowledging the equal status of religions in matters of personal status advances the national aspirations of the religious community for whom the State was conceived as a homeland. Tolerance of alternative ways of life may render less objectionable the privileges associated with preferred status.[92] Or as a New Hampshire Anglican explained in 1790: "The pres-

---

out, in Israel the personal law is adjudicated and administered in religious courts that are an extension of religious institutions. In contrast, in India it is the responsibility of common-law judges functioning in regular State courts to rule on matters of personal law. Galanter and Krishnan 2000.

[90] Kymlicka 1989, 211. It is an argument that is developed further in a subsequent work. Kymlicka 1995a. See also Chandhoke 1999. For a nonliberal critique of the comprehensive liberal justification of cultural rights, see Deveaux 2000. For Deveaux, "[T]he value of cultural membership . . . does not reduce [as in Kymlicka] to the ways in which groups foster their members' personal independence." Ibid., 254.

[91] *Yosifof* 1962, 195.

[92] Consider in this regard the following comment by a Druze Arab member of the Knesset: "Of all the Arabs in the Knesset today, I'm the one who noticed something in the abortion law. This law was passed by the Knesset and therefore must apply to all citizens of Israel, including the Arabs. But the law is drawn from the Halakha. I rose and said: Fellow members, I don't want this to become a precedent in Israeli legislation, that a law drawn from the Halakha is applied to Moslems and Druze. . . . There was once a law prohibiting polygamy, but that law was not drawn from the Halakha." Quoted in Hareven 1983, 64. It is not surprising that an abortion statute passed by a predominantly Jewish legislature might have been inspired by Jewish law. It is also not surprising that this would be noticed by a member of a religious minority. The law's effect, however, is to cause this member to identify with an aggrieved national minority, the Arabs, thus displacing religion onto nationality in a manner that may call into question the legitimacy of the regime's fundamental distinction between rights and privileges. Maintaining abortion as an issue to be addressed within the separate religious domains of personal law might be morally problematic, but it can also be seen as serving the political purposes of the Jewish majority by minimizing the impact of religious nationalism. Thus it is significant that this Druze member of the

ervation of a religious, pure heart, is not less important; but becomes more so in a country where all religions are most justly tolerated, and ought and are promised to be protected."[93]

The British Mandate Ordinance has been superseded by a penal law that makes polygamy universally illegal in Israel. But policy concerning marriage and divorce remains essentially under the jurisdictional control of religious authorities. Unlike in India, where the Special Marriage Act provides an escape from the legal monopoly of the various personal law regimes, Israelis are much more constrained in their choices within these domains of intimate association. The proscription against civil marriages in particular is a major source of irritation and complaint within the non-Orthodox segment of the Jewish population.[94] As Smooha points out, the structural separation of religious communities in exercising authority over personal status "gave the religious sector a staggering lead in the struggle against the disestablishment of religion."[95] As suggested earlier, this lead has been maintained only in part through strategic electoral politics; its favored position is also an extension of the same logic that renders structural separation a fixture in the workings of the secular constitution. The difficulty reform-minded Jews have had in achieving intrareligious pluralism is to some extent the flip side of the constitutional commitment to group-oriented interreligious pluralism.[96]

Knesset specifically mentions the legal treatment of polygamy as less objectionable, because it was not derived from the Jewish law.

[93] Quoted in Hamburger 1993, 366.

[94] For some observers too they call into question the commitment of the polity to a secular constitution. For example, the Israeli constitutional scholar Amnon Rubinstein has written, "If religious freedom means not only the freedom to follow and observe one's religion, but also to be free from religion and religious rites, it exists in Israel only to a limited degree." Rubinstein 1967, 414. (As a Knesset member and government minister, Rubinstein has worked steadily to introduce constitutional protections for religious freedom.) Even more opposed is Gershon Weiler, whose objection extends to the whole concept of the personal laws. "The very idea of a personal status, something that attached to the individual citizen in addition to his status *qua* citizen, is in clear conflict with the idea of equality of citizens." Weiler 1988, 235. To see how these arguments connect to broader debates currently raging among political philosophers, see the collection of essays on multiculturalism and minority cultures in Kymlicka 1995b.

[95] Smooha 1978, 63.

[96] It also bears at least a faint resemblance to the early American experience, in which establishmentarians and dissenters debated over the best way to deal with the issue of diversity. Establishment writers argued with vigor and persistence that religious divisions were a threat to social and political unity. Hamburger 1993, 357. There is evidence, however, that constraints on religious pluralism are loosening somewhat. Thus, for example, it has been decided that secular organizations specializing in pluralist education will receive State funds for the first time. Also, the Supreme Court has ruled that the State must allocate funds to the Reform and Conservative Movements from the Religious Ministry's budgets for Torah culture and education. And in an eagerly awaited ruling in March 2002, the Court declared

In the words of a former chief rabbi: "Freedom of religion is intended for members of all religions, including the minorities, to enable them to pursue their own faith; this freedom of religion . . . is not intended to achieve an opposite objective, with the result that the dominant religion in the state, i.e., the Jewish religion, be jeopardized and torn asunder."[97] Such words from an orthodox rabbi are not surprising, although the allusion to domination is striking. But consider as well the words of a secular Jew, Israel Yeshayahu of the Mapai Party, who in support of the 1953 Rabbinical Courts Jurisdiction Law said: "If Israeli marriages and divorces are not in accordance with the traditional laws, . . . the *national identity* will be obliterated."[98] However exaggerated the concern voiced in this remark, it expresses a worry that seems inevitable in a situation where nationalism and faith converge to provide content to a critical dimension in the regime's political culture. Thus the prospect of fragmentation in the Jewish religious community casts a more ominous shadow in Israel than in the United States, where nationalistic forces do not exert a similar pressure on American Jewry to accept a monolithic religious front. As the journalist Yossi Melman has shrewdly observed, "Zionism was meant to offer a solution to the problems of the Jewish people as a whole and, ironically, not to those of the individual Jew."[99]

An important case in 1972 focused the Supreme Court's attention on the 1953 law. The Rogozinskys, claiming to be without religious belief, had been married in a nonreligious ceremony. As offspring of Jewish mothers, they conceded that they were Jews according to halakhic interpretation, but in accordance with their subjective view that they were *not* Jews, they insisted that their marriage fell outside the jurisdiction of the Rabbinical Court's statute. In essence their claim was that the State had no authority to force them to be Jews, and in the process deny them their "freedom of religion and conscience," as promised in the Declaration of Independence. The Court rejected their arguments, deferring to the 1953 law's adoption of Jewish religious law as the arbiter for determining who is a Jew. Thus their marital status could only be resolved by the Rabbinical Court.

Justice Berinson's opinion for the Court was an exercise in judicial self-restraint. "[I]t is clear that the Law of the State which turned over the matter of marriage and divorce of Jews in Israel . . . to the jurisdiction of the Rabbinical Courts, and directed that such marriages and divorces be

---

that the Interior Ministry was obligated to register Reform and Conservative converts to Judaism, converted by rabbis abroad or in Israel.

[97] Chief Rabbi Isaac Nissim, as quoted in Abramov 1976, 360.

[98] Quoted in Ibid., 194 (emphasis added).

[99] Melman 1992, 7.

conducted according to the law of the Torah, has preference over the principle of freedom of conscience, in the same way as every provision of a law interpreted differently prevails over everything else stated in the Declaration of Independence."[100] Berinson's understandable reluctance to challenge the principle of legislative supremacy cannot conceal the fact that the question at the heart of this case—who is a Jew?—is answerable only within a complex matrix of theological and political considerations. Ultimate reliance on religious law to provide an answer has a largely functional significance, as it establishes objective criteria for the concept of nationality that defines Jewish political identity. In this context the meaning of who is a Jew in the Jewish State is supplied by theological reasoning, but elsewhere, for example in the case of Brother Daniel, a distinctly secular meaning—the common understanding of the "ordinary simple Jew"— had greater instrumental value than a halakhic test for determining Jewishness under the Law of Return. Brother Daniel, after all, was the son of a Jewish mother; his assertion that, despite his conversion to Christianity, he still identified as a Jew was theologically correct but, because in this instance it unnecessarily complicated the test for establishing the nationality of a Jew, politically incorrect. For the Rogozinskys, on the other hand, personal subjectivity did not coincide with the objectivity of Jewish law, which to their misfortune permitted the law to deny them the right to act in accordance with a conscientiously held belief.[101]

Judicial outcomes such as this may cause one to reflect that "[T]he willingness of the Israeli public to tolerate the intolerance of the ultra-Orthodox calls into question its characterization as a liberal democracy."[102] But there are other cases that clearly establish that the scope and reach of religious law is ultimately a matter for secular determination, and that in this regard the liberal democratic aspirations of the Declaration of Independence often function as a set of "directive principles."[103] More-

---

[100] *Rogozinsky* at 135.

[101] Another way to approach this case would be to see its resolution as consistent with the more particularistic strand in the Declaration of Independence. Justice Berinson refers to the universalistic sentiments of the document and then indicates that they have no constitutional weight in negating the choices made by the legislative branch. But the choice made by the Knesset (to the extent that it reflected a principled determination) can itself be seen as drawing an inference from a particular reading of the Declaration's affirmation of the Jewishness of the State, and then applying it to the institution of marriage.

[102] Arzt 1991, 61.

[103] In this regard, Martin Edelman has usefully distinguished between cases where existing arrangements are not explicitly legislatively mandated and those where they are statutorily specified. Edelman 1996, 21. In the first category, the Court has generally supported outcomes favorable to religious freedom interests. Thus, for example, in cases involving the Ministry of Religious Affairs' supervision of kashrut, the Court has intervened on several occasions to limit its discretionary authority. In the second category, where the Knesset has

over, in a regime where there is no formal written constitution, they tend quite naturally to pull judges in the direction of judicial activism; whereas, as we will see in India, when directive principles are relegated to an unenforceable section of an otherwise reform-oriented document, they are just as likely to serve as a force for self-restraint.[104] Thus could an orthodox Supreme Court justice conclude that the exclusion on sexual grounds of a female candidate from a Jewish religious council "conflicts with the fundamental principle of the Israeli legal system, according to which gender discrimination is forbidden." "This fundamental principle," Justice Elon went on, "is stated in the Declaration of Independence, and is among the fundamental ideals that have been expressed in legislation [the 1951 Equal Rights for Women law], and is not merely an 'unwritten right' whose origin is in the judicial legislation of this court."[105] While there are "circumstances . . . in which the principle of gender equality is inapplicable," the administrative nature of the council's functions ensured that this was not one of them.

In his concurring opinion, Justice Barak went further, pointing out that in addition to being an administrative body, the religious council was also "concerned with religious services for all Jews—religious and secular."[106] Moreover, even if in accordance with halakhic interpretation a woman's membership on a religious council were forbidden (an interpretation that Justice Elon, to the consternation of his observant peers, disputed), the Declaration's principle of equality demanded deference. "It must not be forgotten that the chief rabbis also function in the context of the law and the principle of equality, which applies to everyone, applies to them as

---

laid down specific policies favoring Orthodox Jews, the Court has been reluctant to challenge the sovereign legislative will. Particularly with regard to many matters involving marriage and divorce, this restraint has been a source of great and festering frustration to many non-Orthodox Jews. Whether the newly claimed authority to exercise judicial review over laws passed by the Knesset (see chapter 8) will lead to significant changes in this area remains to be seen.

[104] The Israeli Supreme Court's use of the Declaration of Independence as a source for resolving constitutional questions has evolved over the years. The first Court, for example, said that the Declaration "contains no element of constitutional law which determines the validity of various ordinances and laws, or their repeal." *Zeev* at 89. However, it became a major source for judicial policy-making and judicial instruction in the principles of the polity. Indeed, judicial activism in Israel has meant pursuing the rights-oriented implications of the Declaration of Independence. In recent years, this activism has been reinforced by the 1992 adoption of a Basic Law on Human Dignity and Freedom, which, as interpreted by the Supreme Court (especially the chief justice), has inaugurated a "constitutional revolution" featuring judicial review over the actions of the legislature. Some implications of this revolution are explored in chapter 8.

[105] *Shakdiel* at 240.

[106] Ibid. at 272.

well."[107] For Justice Barak, the ambiguous language from the Knesset denying women the right to serve on religious councils meant that the secular law's antidiscrimination principle must take precedence over contrary religious law. Where the legislative will is not explicitly stated, the Court has an obligation to defend egalitarian principles of general applicability. Nothing, of course, prevents the Knesset from privileging a rival principle by committing additional sectors of Israeli life to the jurisdictional control of religious law. Thus unlike the United States, where "a state may not delegate its civic authority to a group chosen according to a religious criterion,"[108] this action always remains an option in Israel. While it is an option that, for a variety of reasons, will not often be exercised, the very existence of a discretionary authority of this kind is an expression of the complex, and occasionally conflicted, character of nationhood in Israel.

Conclusion

Tocqueville's famous insight that Americans possessed the distinct advantage of having "arrived at a state of democracy without having to endure a democratic revolution," no longer as uncontroversial as it once was, still clarifies comparative perspective on such matters as secular constitutional design and development. If he and his latter-day intellectual disciples, most notably Louis Hartz, exaggerated the differences between the United States and Europe, their emphasis on the absence of a feudal tradition in the former (the South excepted) was not misplaced. The Americans' fortunate circumstance of having been "born equal, instead of becoming so" meant that their social and political development could proceed largely in the absence of the bitterly divisive ideological battles that prevailed in most other places. As for their secular constitutional development, what is interesting is not simply the founding commitment to a secular polity, but that in order to achieve that goal, they did not have to break the chains (again with some local exceptions) of a dominant religion. By contrast, in having to overcome a feudal religious order, Indian constitutionalists understandably moved in the direction of a more transformative constitution, in which the commitment to secularism was directly related to the goal of social reconstruction. As for the third of our comparisons, the Israeli sociologist S. N. Eisenstadt's Tocquevillian contrast between his own country and the United States is very suggestive. "[T]he United States in many ways constitutes the most purely ideological society in the world. . . . Here . . . lies the greatest difference between the American revolution and the Zionist movement. The Zionist movement

---

[107] Ibid. at 277.
[108] *Kiryas Joel* at 2488.

was also highly ideological and highly revolutionary, but it combined these elements with the strong primordial and historical components of Jewish identity, with which its political aspirations were connected."[109] What Eisenstadt describes as "the almost total denial of the symbolic validity of hierarchy" in the American case is precisely what is present in the Israeli case, serving to set the parameters of its daunting project in visionary secularism.[110]

As we move on in the next chapter to consider the secular context of India's constitutional approach to religion and politics, another of Tocqueville's insights—this one explicitly focused on religion—invites consideration. Reflecting on the indirect influence that religious beliefs exert on political society in the United States, Tocqueville wrote: "Religion in America takes no direct part in the government of society, but it must be regarded as the first of their political institutions; for if it does not impart a taste for freedom, it facilitates the use of it."[111] The first part of that observation applies, at least in a formal sense, to all countries where religious authority is not expressly represented in the structure of governance. So it would not apply to Israel, but in India it would seem to hold, since the framers of the Constitution concurred in the sentiment behind Tocqueville's further claim that "The church cannot share the temporal power of the state without being the object of a portion of that animosity which the latter excites."[112]

But as to the second part, India presents an interesting contrast with the United States, and to a certain extent Israel. On the one hand, the argument is often made that Hinduism is a tolerant religion that "facilitates" freedom, an argument that demands to be taken seriously in addressing the world's largest democracy and its main religion. As exemplified by the teachings in the Gandhian tradition, Hindu religious ideas and practices need not contradict the fundamentals of secular democracy. Yet against this is the quite obvious way—one need look no further than the theologically sanctioned social stratification that has endured in India for centuries—in which religion on the subcontinent stands intransigently in defiance of a democratic way of life. A book entitled *Democracy in India* would be hard put to assert, as Tocqueville did about the United States, that "[N]o religious doctrine displays the slightest hostility to democratic and republican institutions."[113] Even discounting the extravagance of the claim as applied to the United States, one cannot help but be struck by a

---

[109] Eisenstadt 1992, 151.
[110] Ibid., 123.
[111] Tocqueville 1945, vol. 1, 316.
[112] Ibid., 321.
[113] Ibid., 312.

fundamental incongruity in the very notion of an easy compatibility between religion and politics in the Indian setting. That is not to say that the basic condition of Church/State relations has been one of unremitting hostility; indeed, State-sanctioned accommodation of religious needs will find a much more hospitable constitutional environment in India than in the United States. But that same environment will countenance, even encourage, the State's restriction of religious freedom in the interest of democratic freedom.

Tocqueville actually did write about India. While his commentary never matched his American opus in mass or style, it is clear in its depiction of a radically different political predicament, one that emphasizes circumstances much less fortunate for democracy than what he encountered in America. One might speculate that had he gone on to write a companion volume to his study of democracy in America, the substitution of India in the title would have been followed by a question mark. The Frenchman never visited India, but he understood very well the religious challenge to democratic institutions in that distant place. "India cannot be civilized as long as she conserves her religion and her religion is so intermingled with the structure of its social state, of its customs and of its laws, that one does not know how to destroy it. Religions of this sort survive long after people stop believing in them. It is a vicious circle."[114] The predictive value of this sentiment would depend to a large extent on the accuracy of another of Tocqueville's musings about India. "I am convinced that Hindus have never adopted anything from another nation. Everything in this culture is imprinted with the cachet of independence and originality."[115] As we shall see, the success of India's ameliorative project of constitutional secularism is at least partly contingent on proving Tocqueville wrong.

---

[114] Tocqueville 1962, vol. 3, 480. Tocqueville went on to describe Hinduism as *abominable*, although his complete appraisal of the religion is more restrained and mixed than that might suggest. However, he was more pessimistic than the founders of independent India regarding the prospects for significant government-sponsored social amelioration. "The immense majority of Hindus belong to the lower castes. No matter what happens, their birth has placed them poor and always on the lowest rungs of the social ladder where one has little to hope from the government and little to fear from it. They emerged from the foot of Brahma and not from his head; this misfortune is without remedy. What difference does it make to them who is their master! Revolutions are really only interesting to the upper castes, which are composed of a very small number of men. Thus is the power which rules millions of subjects definitely supported only by the interests or the efforts of a few individuals." Ibid., 448.

[115] Ibid., 544.

Chapter Four

INDIA: THE AMELIORATIVE ASPIRATION

"THIS COURT cannot be too cautious in upsetting practices embedded in our society by many years of experience."[1] The specific practice referred to by Justice Stanley Reed in this 1948 American case was a released time program enabling students to receive religious instruction without leaving their public school. Among the majority who voted to invalidate the program over Justice Reed's objections were several justices whose caution in exercising their judicial power had been well established over many years on the Court. They perhaps did not concur in their colleague's assessment of embeddedness, or if they did, believed their uprooting of the practice on First Amendment grounds would not entail significant societal disruption.

In India at about this time, a constitution was being framed that would present judges with a different perspective on this problem. Of the document that emerged from the Constituent Assembly, it would be fair to say that its framers were committed to "upsetting practices embedded in . . . society by many years of experience." So while cautionary admonitions could also appropriately be directed at Indian judges, the urgency of the advice might lack some of the accompanying jurisprudential logic present in the American context, where the Constitution is not devoted to social reconstruction.[2] The efforts of Indian judges to participate actively in the implementation of a transformational agenda was justifiable in a way that

---

[1] *McCollum* at 101.

[2] One qualification to this is perhaps in order. Cass Sunstein has forcefully argued that constitutional democracies are strongly committed to "the anticaste principle," which "forbids social and legal practices from translating highly visible and morally irrelevant differences into a systematic source of social disadvantage, unless there is a very good reason for society to do so." Sunstein 2001, 155. Obviously the principle has application to the United States, so in this sense there is a constitutional commitment to social reconstruction. But it is still worth distinguishing between polities where this commitment is part of the fundamental nature of constitutional democracies and those where it is more explicitly a part of the specific essence of a given regime.

would ring hollow for their American counterparts. Thus they could claim that their activism was true to the spirit of the charter that they had the responsibility to interpret.

On the other hand, the very explicitness of the constitutional recognition (especially in Article 25) that meaningful social reform required attention to the critical role of religion in Indian life might suggest the futility of judicial intervention. Problems of such complicated scope and intricacy would very likely defy Court-mandated solution. Moreover, the Constitution's recognition extended to other facets of Indian social reality, the most important being the entrenched character of communal affiliation, and with that, the consequent need to provide space for cultural and religious diversity.[3] Taken as a whole, the document evinces a complex awareness of the sometimes contradictory impulses that have figured so prominently in the Indian national experience. The common source of these impulses—to uproot and to preserve—is religion's thickness as a social phenomenon, the depth of its penetration into the fabric of Indian life. As Tocqueville observed, "[R]eligion is mixed up in everything and . . . everything is a religious act for Hindus."[4] Tempting, therefore, as it might be for judges to want to eradicate what they perceive to be the socially debilitating vestiges of ancient (and not so ancient) tradition, they would have to proceed cautiously, or risk underestimating the pervasiveness of primal group experience, and hence inadvertently inflame the ever-burning embers of communal antagonisms. In short, the founding commitment to the secular constitution could too easily be subverted if it became an invitation for judges to casually indulge their passion for individual rights and abstract equality.[5]

There is persuasive evidence that this indulgence has occurred. According to Rajeev Dhavan, "The nub of the issues in the freedom of reli-

---

[3] The Constitution makes a distinction between individual and collective freedom of religion. Under the latter heading all religious denominations have the right to manage their own affairs in matters of religion (Article 26). In addition, all minorities, religious and linguistic, have the right to establish and administer educational institutions of their choice (Article 30). Elsewhere, too, special provisions are included to address the particular needs of scheduled castes and scheduled tribes. And in Article 48, as one of the Directive Principles of State Policy, the State is urged to take steps to prohibit the slaughter of cows—a clear singling out of the Hindu population for special consideration.

[4] Tocqueville 1962, vol. 3, 537.

[5] A helpful contrast might be made here with the approach taken by Justice Robert Jackson in his famous opinion in the compulsory flag salute case. Jackson reminded his readers that the applicable principles "grew in soil which also produced a philosophy that the individual was the center of society." *Barnett* at 640. He then reflected on the need to protect individual rights in a different soil, in which the principle of noninterference no longer held sway. For the Indian judge, functioning within a legal culture where individualism was not rooted in the native soil, much greater sensitivity to group-related pressures was required.

gion cases has devolved away from religious freedom to a disorganized discussion of the legitimate areas of operation of a modern State. And the courts' answer to the question, 'How modern is the modern State?' appears to be, 'As modern as it wants to be!' "[6] If this is indeed the Courts' answer, it certainly resonates with a dominant strand in the Indian Constitution, exemplified by Article 25's limitation on religious freedom to accommodate the State's provision for "social welfare and reform." Highlighting this constitutional strand underscores the transformative dimension of Indian nationalism and the commitment to Nehruvian scientific rationalism with which it is frequently associated. Often drawing upon Western philosophical and jurisprudential sources, this vision of national unity relied primarily on social reconstruction to create one nation out of a multiplicity of peoples. For this experiment to succeed, popular religion had to be downplayed, constituting as it did the principal impediment in the path of integrating different classes and peoples into a modern nation-state.[7] As in the United States, subordination of religion was implicit in the dynamic of nation-building, but unlike the American example, it was to be a subordination that emphasized social transformation. Consistent with this emphasis, the secular constitution represented a commitment to fundamental social change, with an important presumption of constitutional legitimacy attaching to State intervention directed toward that end.[8] "India," Subrata Mitra has pointed out, "is virtually alone among post-colonial states in Asia to have adopted secularism as a key feature of her constitution and the cornerstone of her strategy of nation-building."[9]

But this is obviously not the whole story. Commentators on Indian politics and society, and not just critics of Western-style secularism like Nandy and Madan, present a much more complex, nuanced account of Indian nationhood, in which religion is not just an obstacle to be overcome but

[6] Dhavan 1987, 230.

[7] On this point see Ravinder Kumar 1987, 34.

[8] The significance of this presumption becomes clearer if considered in light of this observation by Harvey Mansfield Jr. about modern constitutionalism. "The subordination of state to society . . . is the main truth of constitutional government, which is shared by liberals, conservatives, and even radicals, despite the various pet projects of intervention in others' liberties cherished by all three parties. That these projects are known as 'intervention' indicates the general expectation that government be limited." Mansfield 1987, 3. Mansfield's point is that there is a general presumption in constitutional polities *against* the legitimacy of state intervention. A criticism that could be made of the prominent restrictive clauses in the Indian Constitution is that they reverse this presumption and thus threaten the viability of constitutional government. For some, no doubt, the plausibility of the criticism is rendered more obvious if Indian national identity is too closely associated with an ambiguous agenda of social reconstruction.

[9] Mitra 1989, 107.

a presence to be accommodated. "Except for those of the Marxist left, Indian dreams of the nation always take religion as one of the main aspects of national identity."[10] Indeed, while it is customary to contrast Nehru's national vision with that of Gandhi's, emphasizing in the process the latter's more spiritual and communitarian commitment, Nehru was hardly oblivious to the centrality of religion in comprehending the Indian nation. The sometimes harsh reality of extraordinary diversity probably guarantees that Indian national identity will always be tinged by artificiality; but to the extent that there is such a thing as the authentic voice of the Indian nation, incorporated in it will be a religious message(s) demanding to be heard.[11] What one hears will span the spectrum of substantive possibilities; in the end, acceptance of a specific definition of the secular constitution will be contingent upon who presides as arbiter of these contested meanings.[12]

I use the term *ameliorative secularism* to describe a model of the secular constitution as a conceptual projection of the multifaceted character of Indian nationhood. It is a term broad enough to encompass the layered meanings of Indian nationalism, including both its commitment to social reform and its mooring in rival and contentious religious/cultural traditions. Thus the Constitution seeks an amelioration of the social conditions of people long burdened by the inequities of religiously based hierarchies, but also embodies a vision of intergroup comity whose fulfillment necessitates cautious deliberation in the pursuit of abstract justice.[13] For example, the constitutional provision for a uniform civil code appears in the

[10] Van DerVeer 1994, 23.

[11] See Ninian Smart 1989, 28; and Anthony D. Smith 1991, 114.

[12] On the "contested meanings" of Indian national identity, see Varshney 1993, 227. Of course, not all of these meanings can plausibly apply to a constitution designated as secular. A major point of Varshney's essay is that "[S]ecularism, the ideological mainstay of a multireligious India, looks pale and exhausted." Ibid., 227. Thus should Hindu nationalism ultimately prevail, an outcome that can no longer be casually and confidently dismissed, the secular constitution would quickly turn into a phenomenon of largely antiquarian interest. The real choice, then, as far as secularism in India is concerned, is encapsulated in T. N. Madan's alternative vision: "[I]t should be realized that secularism may not be restricted to rationalism, that it is compatible with faith, and that rationalism (as understood in the West) is not the sole motive force of a modern state." Madan 1987, 754.

[13] For some this ameliorative solution entails an inherent contradiction in India's concept of secularism, a contradiction embodied in its "simultaneous commitment to communities and equal citizenship." Rudolph and Rudolph 1987, 38. Marc Galanter describes the constitutional commitment as including three principles: "1) a commitment to the replacement of ascribed status by voluntary affiliation; 2) an emphasis on the integrity and autonomy of groups within society; 3) a withdrawal of governmental recognition of rank ordering among groups." Galanter 1966, 289. Unlike the Rudolphs' view, Galanter sees these commitments less as a contradiction and more as a legal balance between the commitment to a substantial transformation of the social order and respect for the integrity of groups. Ibid., 310.

form of a hortatory appeal in a nonjusticiable section of the document, expressing by implication an awareness of at least one other important social condition requiring amelioration, namely the conflict and confrontation on multiple fronts among thickly constituted majority and minority communities. Ashis Nandy's charge, that "[s]ecularism has little to say about cultures," that "it is definitionally ethnophobic," makes sense as applied to the Indian Constitution only if there is a categorical exclusion of the regime of personal laws from the scope of secular calculation.[14] But while limited deference to the moral visions across religious communities seems to bespeak a nonsecular sensibility, in the context of the constitutional aspiration for national unity it reflects a prudent and quite secular regard for historic social realities.

"THE GOOD OF THE PEOPLE"

To move from the general to the particular, and to examine certain jurisprudential aspects of the ameliorative model, let us revisit the issue of polygamy, transposed now to the Indian environment. The struggle for the emancipation of women occupies a central chapter in the history of Indian nationalism and Hindu social reform.[15] The issue's constitutional significance is suggested in this excerpt from Raj Kumari Amrit Kaur's letter to B. N. Rau, included in the documentary history of the drafting of the Constitution: "As we are all aware there are several customs practiced in the name of religion e.g. *pardah*, child marriage, polygamy, unequal laws of inheritance, prevention of inter-caste marriages, dedication of girls to temples. We are naturally anxious that no clause in any fundamental right shall make impossible future legislation for the purpose of wiping out these evils."[16] And as it transpired, not *only* future legislation, for in 1952 the Supreme Court of Bombay, applying the provisions of the new Constitution, upheld the validity of the Bombay Prevention of Hindu Bigamous Marriages Act of 1946. Later, as part of the project of codifying Hindu law, the practice of plural marriages for Hindus was outlawed in the Hindu Marriage Act of 1955, the validity of which was also affirmed by the courts.[17]

[14] Nandy 1988, 179.

[15] See Heimsath 1964, 14.

[16] Government of India Press 1967, vol. 2, 146.

[17] However, as many commentators have pointed out, the statutory outlawing of plural marriages provided easily exploitable loopholes that have rendered the ban less effective than the text of the law might suggest. Thus as interpreted by the courts, proof that a second marriage was bigamous is a very difficult matter to establish under the law. It requires the testimony of witnesses who will certify that all rituals of the Brahminic religious ceremony were performed and scrupulously adhered to, which, given the elaborate details of tradi-

The ruling in the Bombay case[18] was handed down two years before Chief Justice Mukherjea's landmark opinion in *Ratilal*, where, recall, the distinction drawn in the American polygamy cases between religious beliefs and practices had been emphatically rejected. That distinction, complete with favorable citation of *Davis v Beason*, was relied upon in *Appa* to reach the conclusion that "religious practices must give way before the good of the people of the State as a whole."[19] If the state of Bombay chooses to compel monogamy, that choice must be respected as "a measure of social reform," and under Article 25(2)(b) of the Constitution, it must be upheld notwithstanding its infringement of religious liberty. However, Justice Chagla's opinion left unclear the rationale for distinguishing between belief and practice, particularly since the constitutional justification for intervention by the State does not in any way turn on that distinction. By contrast, in a polygamy case decided five years later (and three years after *Ratilal*),[20] the opinion for the Court appears to retreat from the dictum in *Appa*, conceding that religious practices are entitled to the same level of protection as religious beliefs. But the conclusion in the two cases is the same; in other words, the restricted reach of the social welfare rationale extends to all facets of religious engagement.

In another respect the two opinions display greater doctrinal consistency. In *Appa*, Justice Chagla observed that "[I]t is rather difficult to accept the proposition that polygamy is an integral part of Hindu religion."[21] In *Ram Prasad*, the Court similarly concluded that polygamy is not "an essential part of the Hindu religion."[22] Both Courts were responding to the claim that because the presence of a son is held to be essential to achieve religious salvation, Hindu tradition sanctions plural marriages as a sort of hedge against reproductive failure. But, the justices pointed out, the adoption of a male child would adequately satisfy the religious requirement, thus obviating the need to practice polygamy. It follows, then, that even if the motivation to engage in the legally proscribed practice is said to be religious, the erroneous assumptions underlying the behavior will suffice to deny it constitutional protection.[23] Not

---

tional practice, often proves impossible to demonstrate. As a result, what appears initially to be a case of bigamy turns out to be, at best, an instance of adultery.

[18] *Appa* 1952.

[19] Ibid. at 86.

[20] *Ram Prasad* 1957.

[21] *Appa* at 86.

[22] *Ram Prasad* at 413.

[23] The last thing I would seek to do is offer an opinion on this question. That it is, however, a complicated question is suggested by the fact that polygamy in India has persisted from Vedic times down through modern independence. Kapadia 1966, 7. It is pointed out that while the Vedic ideal of marriage favored monogamy, polygamy was socially approved. A. K. Sur mentions in his study of Indian marriage that there have been periods in Indian

that such a finding would be necessary, for "[e]ven if bigamy be regarded as an integral part of Hindu religion the impugned rule is protected under Art. 25(b) of the Constitution."[24]

These two jurisprudential tracks—determining the social welfare content of State action, and distinguishing essential from nonessential religious activity—enable the judiciary to encroach deeply into the domain of religious freedom. With regard to polygamy, the latter approach seems almost gratuitous, since the social welfare implications of the legislation require very little elaboration. Also, the judicial certification of reformist intent arguably raises fewer concerns in relation to the role of the courts than does establishing the presence of religious essences.[25] The validation of an Article 25 limitation on religious liberty entails little more than deference to the will of the legislative branch, precisely the sort of action that fits most comfortably within a framework of democratic expectations for the judiciary. On the other hand, as Derrett argues in reference to the alternative approach, "[T]he courts can discard as non-essentials anything which is not proved to *their* satisfaction—and they are not religious leaders or in any relevant fashion qualified in such matters—to be essential, with the result that it would have no constitutional protection. The Constitution does not say 'freely to profess, practise and propagate *the essentials* of religion', but this is how it is construed."[26]

---

history where polygamy was widely practiced. He calls attention to the *Mahabharata*, where Krishna is said to have had 1,016 wives and, in another place, 16,000. Sur 1973, 49–50. Hindu scriptures do indeed indicate that the need for progeny is the only reason for the institution of marriage. That any of this supports the view that plural marriage is integral to Hinduism is by no means obvious. But that it would be easy to generate a passionate argument over the matter *is* pretty obvious.

[24] *Ram Prasad* at 414.

[25] The question of the role of the courts in India will receive much more attention in part 2. With regard to the formal constitutional status of the Indian Supreme Court, the following details are worth keeping in mind: (1) The Court consists of a chief justice and a maximum of twenty-five additional judges. (2) The president of India appoints all judges, but is obligated to consult the chief justice and is encouraged to consult with others on the Supreme Court and the High Courts in the states. (3) There is a mandatory retirement requirement for judges reaching sixty-five years of age. (4) The Supreme Court has considerable original jurisdiction, including over disputes between the government of India and any state, and with regard to the issuance of writs for the enforcement of Fundamental Rights. (5) The Supreme Court has advisory jurisdiction, upon request of the president, to issue opinions on questions of law or fact on questions of "public importance."

[26] Derrett 1968, 447. Derrett is not alone in raising such concerns. See also, Galanter 1989, 249; and Dhavan 1987, 223–4. There is also this comparative assessment: "Although the Indian Court has adopted the American and Australian concept of free exercise of religion, it has considerably curtailed the freedom to profess, practice, and propagate religion. The freedom has been further curtailed by the Indian courts by propounding the view that the Constitution protects only such religious practices as are an essential and integral part of a religion." Srivastava 1992, 313. While the adoption of the American approach is more

Indeed it does not, and yet there is, intended or not, a revealing logic in the courts' embrace of an "essentials of religion" test. Their logic is consistent with the factors that make it difficult to sustain a belief/practice distinction when applying the Constitution's religion clauses. With a religious presence that is pervasive and deep, religiosity resists bifurcation into separate paths for action and opinion. Precisely for that reason, Indian legal circles may benefit from a further distinction that addresses more directly the ameliorative mission of the secular constitution. As a former Indian chief justice explained, "Because of the personal laws and the fact that religion plays such a profound role in people's lives, inquiring into the essentials of religion cannot be avoided."[27] Thus attempting to isolate what is integral to religion from what is not, however tricky and even dubious, proves necessary; otherwise, social reform efforts face overcoming religious-based practices not only considered a way of life, but also poised to claim undifferentiated theological significance.[28] To be sure, even essential religious practices are not guaranteed constitutional immunity if they obstruct social reform; nevertheless, limiting their impact to nonessential matters might enhance the legitimacy of judicially sanctioned social transformations.[29] As Dr. Ambedkar said at the Constituent Assembly:

> There is nothing extraordinary in saying that we ought to strive hereafter to limit the definition of religion in such a manner that we shall not extend it beyond beliefs and such rituals as may be connected with ceremonials which

---

complicated than Srivastava suggests, his reference is helpful in reminding us of the American reluctance to intrude into theological disputes.

[27] Interview with the author, March 10, 1999, New Delhi.

[28] An Israeli political philosopher has argued that "[I]t is not inconsistent to grant immunity to practices when they are conducted as part of religious life, while at the same time to prohibit those very same practices when they do not reflect components of such a way of life." Harel 1996, 118. As we have seen with the American case (and will revisit in the concluding chapter), much here depends on what one means by a "liberal perspective." Thus some who consider themselves liberals would not be comfortable making such theological distinctions and granting immunity accordingly.

[29] One must, however, give very serious consideration to the very reasonable concerns about the Court's involvement in the reform of Hinduism that have been raised by Marc Galanter. "Is the Supreme Court a forum for promulgating official interpretations of Hinduism? Is it a Supreme Court of Hinduism?" Galanter 1989, 252. Galanter points out the various reasons why judicial activism is appealing to the "educated reformist elite," chief among which is the goal of achieving national unity in the face of the diffuse and fragmented character of Hinduism. With unity may come modernity; hence the hope that judicial intervention, in which the Court serves as spokesperson for the religion as a whole, "will have a salutary unifying as well as reforming influence." Ibid., 252. His doubts center on the capacities of common-law judges to perform this role well, and on the nonself-evident assumption that the unification of Hinduism (even if attainable) would lead to national integration. "The successful breaking down of Hinduism's capacity to generate and tolerate internal differences may well lessen India's capacity to sustain pluralist democracy." Ibid., 255.

are essentially religious. . . . I do not see why religion should be given this vast, expansive jurisdiction as to cover the whole of life and to prevent the legislature from encroaching upon that field. After all what are we having this liberty for? We are having this liberty to reform our social system, which is so full of inequalities, discrimination and other things which conflict with our fundamental rights.[30]

In *Appa*, Justice Chagla pointed out that "The Hindu Bigamous Marriages Act is attempting to bring about social reform in a community which has looked upon polygamy as not an evil institution, but fully justified by its religion."[31] Demonstrating that polygamy is in fact *not* fully justified by the religion provides an alternative for judges reluctant to facilitate a secularly motivated legislature trumping a nonsecularly functioning society.[32] There are of course great risks in the strategy, vividly illustrated in the case of Justice Chagla, who, as a Muslim, was vulnerable to the charge that his authority in such matters was doubtful on two counts—as a judge and as a non-Hindu. But militating against these risks was the oft-noted absence among Hindus of a structured ecclesiastical authority, whose rulings on religious "essences" might command a respect within the secular community (including judges) that would tend to deflate the temptation to engage in theological second-guessing.[33] In contrast, the thought of even the most reform-minded of secularist judges in the United States questioning the religious significance of behavior that has been vouched for by ecclesiastical authority is scarcely imaginable. As a case in point, Justice William O. Douglas, in citing *Bombay v Appa* in some observations about Indian law, noted that "It comported with traditional concepts for the court to hold that bigamous marriages could not gain immunity from prosecution by being called a part of religion."[34]

[30] *Constituent Assembly Debates* 1989, 507–8.

[31] *Appa* at 88.

[32] Neera Chandhoke's distinction between "secular states" and "secularized societies" (1999, 81) bears upon this jurisprudential question. Judges who function in a context in which a secular state is in effect surrounded by a nonsecularized or deeply religious society may not feel as free to ignore theological questions as their counterparts who adjudicate in secularized societies.

[33] Donald Smith's work emphasizes the absence of coherent ecclesiastical structure in India. He develops a distinction between "organic" and "church" models of religiopolitical systems, with Hinduism falling within the first category. Smith 1970, 8. His argument is that Hinduism lacks effective organizational strength to reform itself, thus necessitating state intervention. See Smith 1963, 231; Caldorola 1982, 39; and Galanter 1998, 237. This is also the argument of N. J. Demarath and Phillip E. Hammond, who, following Weber, suggest that "Both Judaism and Catholicism (together with another Jewish offshoot, Islam) [and unlike Hinduism] have highly developed organizational forms as a way of fulfilling the mandate for aggressively ascetic action in the interests of large-scale social change." Demarath and Hammond 1969, 50.

[34] Douglas 1956, 316.

It was a case used appropriately by Justice Douglas to illustrate why "East and West often do not understand the other's actions."[35]

Here it is worth recalling the American Supreme Court's declaration that "The law knows no heresy, and is committed to the support of no dogma, the establishment of no sect." This observation marks the judiciary's acceptance of the binding nature of Church authority in all questions of faith and doctrine. But whereas in the United States the sentiment generally supports judicial passivity, in India a quite different interpretation pulls judges in an opposite direction. With specific application to Hinduism, an Indian version of the statement might read: "The law knows no heresy for the simple reason that the very concept of heresy has little practical import here; it is committed to the support of no dogma, because there is no official dogma to speak of; and it is committed to the establishment of no sect, because the dominant religion in India can only be described as a multiplicity of sects."[36] In this spirit, Justice Gajendragadkar suggested in his concurrence in *Appa* that the validity of the personal laws in India does not derive from their having been enacted by competent authority. "The foundational sources of both the Hindu and the Mohamedan laws are their respective scriptural texts."[37] What is implicit in his position is what Derrett has argued in another context, which is that "[I]t was never the case that the *sastra* insisted upon one way."[38] This flexibility, then, leaves the interpretation of these texts legitimately open to all, especially the judges.[39]

Gajendragadkar was one jurist who seized this opportunity. In a critique of his work, Dhavan found that for this reform-minded judge, the "essen-

[35] Ibid.

[36] George Bernard Shaw once commented that "Hinduism is so elastic and so subtle that the profoundest Methodist and the crudest idolators are equally at home in it." Quoted in Srivastava 1992, 22. That of course is a caricature, but its basic point about the heterodox character of Hinduism is a familiar one among students of India. For example, Max Weber noted that "the concept of 'dogma' is entirely lacking" in Hinduism. Weber 1958, 21. More authoritatively, particularly in relation to the law, is Derrett's observation that "Religious affiliation is not a question of an individual's belief, for on that footing he is free to believe or not believe in anything he likes, but of a social *belonging*." Derrett 1968, 58. More recently, Lloyd and Suzanne Rudolph point out that "The Hinduism of the 'Hindu majority' encompasses diversity of gods, texts, and social practices and a variety of ontologies and epistemologies. Without an organized church, it is innocent of orthodoxy, heterodoxy, and heresy." Rudolph and Rudolph 1987, 37.

[37] *Appa* at 90.

[38] Derrett 1968, 559.

[39] Not all Indian judges agree. As one current member of the Court pointed out in an interview with the author: "I'm with the American judges. We should not discuss essentials." Interview with Justice Sawant, March 3, 1999, New Delhi. His position makes sense in connection with another of his observations. "There cannot be a general reform movement as far as religion is concerned. . . . The reform movement has to come from the religions themselves."

tial practices" test had an *external* as well as *internal* requirement, meaning that in addition to being integral to a religion, a practice would have to be shown not to be the product of superstition.[40] This rationality requirement, which Dhavan fears now dominates the judiciary, is an important part of the direct effort to reform religion in the name of social progress. No doubt there have been jurisprudential excesses in the pursuit of progress (for some perhaps best exemplified by Gajendragadkar), but the Constitution itself, by abolishing untouchability and requiring that Hindu religious institutions of a public character be open to all Hindus, rather clearly establishes the importance of reformist intentions in the framing of the document.[41] In the important temple entry case, *Yagnapurushdasji v Muldas*, Gajendragadkar dismissed the claim of a religious sect that its members were not Hindus and were thus outside the mandate of access requirements. He provided a lengthy explanation for why it is "difficult, if not impossible, to define Hindu religion or even adequately describe it."[42] But, he went on to say, "[W]e must inevitably inquire what are the distinctive features of Hindu religion."[43] The result, which for Gajendragadkar was to link the religion's distinctiveness to the foundational commitment of the regime to social justice, produced misgivings for at least one authoritative observer as to whether it was appropriate for judges "to participate actively in the internal reinterpretation of Hinduism."[44]

These misgivings can profitably be considered in the context of some firmly and widely held American views on Church/State relations. Ac-

---

[40] Dhavan 1987, 224. Off the Court, Gajendragadkar wrote: "Whether or not polygamy should be allowed, what should be the line of succession, what should be the shares of different heirs, what should be the law of divorce, are matters which should be determined not by scriptural injunctions, but by rational considerations." Gajendragadkar, quoted in Baird 1981, 434.

[41] The question arises, however, as to what form these reformist intentions were expected to take. Vinit Haksar has called attention to the argument that a secular state should not be in the business of directly interfering with a religion in order to reform it. "However, it should be allowed to use principles of justice such as the principle concerning the amelioration of the lot of the worst off, even though a by-product of the implementation of such principles may be that certain religions will change in order to conform to the law. So it could permit temple entry of untouchables, in order to help the untouchables, without going into the question of whether untouchability is an essential part of Hinduism." Haksar 2001, 80. But more difficult would be instances where the Constitution is silent, leaving judges with the responsibility of assessing legislative encroachments on religion according to the social welfare provision of Article 25. Invoking Rawls's difference principle in such a context would not eliminate the jurisprudential advantage implicit in the application of an essential attributes of religion test. Thus ameliorating the lot of the worst off may be seen to have a clearer path if it does not cut through the heart of essential religious observance and practice.

[42] *Yagnapurushdasji* at 513.

[43] Ibid.

[44] Galanter 1989, 251.

cording to Laurence Tribe, for example, "[T]he most clearly forbidden church-state entanglement occurs when institutions of civil government use the legal process in order to discover religious error or to promulgate religious truth."[45] From the opposite end of the political spectrum, Richard Epstein seems to agree: "It is one thing . . . for a religious institution to yield its traditions through internal change in order to keep the consent and the loyalty of the governed. It is quite another for outsiders to impose their own external standards of right and wrong on these bodies."[46] Tribe and Epstein share more than a familiar liberal suspicion of collective impositions of the good life; their reluctance to intervene in the internal affairs of religious groups also reminds us that the relative thickness of religiosity has constitutional implications. Thus in the United States the cost of not extending the antidiscrimination principle governing public policy to the religious sector is minimal, and outweighed in any case by the benefits associated with free choice and association. If women cannot become priests, that denial will have very little far-reaching social significance, entitling one confidently to conclude that liberal principles are eminently affordable.[47] But indifference to the substance of religious belief is a much costlier indulgence when, as in India, it serves to legitimate an unjust status quo.

To be sure, Article 26 of the Indian Constitution protects religious denominations in their right "to manage [their] own affairs in matters of religion." In this connection, "it was not intended to enable the legislature to 'reform' a religion out of existence or identity."[48] As a result, in *Saifuddin* the Supreme Court upheld the authority of a religious sect to enforce its view of the essentials of religion through the mechanism of excommunication. In so ruling, the Supreme Court went out of its way to indicate that the State was not prevented from intervening in matters of religion to promote social welfare, although considering the details of the litigation (for example, those excommunicated lose their property rights),

---

[45] Tribe 1988, 1232.

[46] Epstein 1990, 402.

[47] Cass Sunstein might not think so. He has forcefully argued that religiously based sex discrimination does have far-reaching social significance in the sense that it inculcates values and norms that violate the anticaste principle essential to constitutional democracies. His conclusion: "If within-group deliberation promotes second-class citizenship for some, or contributes to the maintenance of a system with caste-like features, there should be no constitutional obstacle to reasonable efforts to supply correctives. Hence measures that attempt to promote sex equality by prohibiting discrimination within religious institutions should not be ruled entirely off limits." Sunstein 2001, 218. Without taking issue with his specific conclusion, a comparison with a place—India—where caste, rather than "caste-like features" is the historic reality, makes clear that among constitutional democracies there is a significant range in the extent of the costs involved in accommodating religious discrimination.

[48] Justice Ayyangar concurring in *Saifuddin* at 875.

one could easily imagine this to be just such a case.[49] However, the main lesson of this and related cases is that the Constitution is not a blanket endorsement of all reform efforts that may be politically contemplated, that even as it leans very heavily to accommodate such endeavors, the Constitution signals that competing interests may also have to be served. Inevitably, judges will disagree on how to weigh these interests; in the end, the balance struck will entail some revision of the American view that " 'religion' must be defined from the believer's perspective."[50]

Incrementalism is thus part of the spiritual core of *ameliorative* secularism, reflecting the cohabiting reformist and conservative components of Indian national identity. Even if it were so disposed, "[A] state," as Montesquieu points out, "cannot change its religion, manners, and customs in an instant."[51] The polygamy cases illustrate the dual character of this Indian incrementalism—its vertical as well as horizontal dimensions—by addressing the State's effort to ameliorate social conditions within the majority community while not exacerbating regime-threatening tensions between communities. In outlawing plural marriages (however difficult establishing that fact would turn out to be) as part of its codification of Hindu law, the State left Muslims free to continue practicing polygamy. In light of the equal protection guarantee of Article 14, this discrimination presented the Court with an obvious and very important constitutional question, which it answered in the following way: "The State may rightly decide to bring about social reform by stages and the stages may be territorial or they may be communitywise."[52] In this answer the Court felt it was honoring the intent of the framers of the Constitution, who had aspired to a regime with uniform laws, but who had not wished to accomplish this goal at any price.[53]

---

[49] An important constitutional issue in India involves the distinction between management of the property of a religious denomination and administration of religious matters. Dhavan's view is that there has been a "virtual takeover of the management of religious institutions." Dhavan 1987, 230. If there has, then Donald Smith, writing in 1963, will have been proven correct when he suggested that a "broad conception of corporate freedom is not recognized by the Constitution of India." Smith 1963, 247. Smith argues that this freedom presupposes the existence of well-organized churches, although Indian courts have tried to be protective of religious autonomy in connection with church endowments.

[50] Tribe 1988, 1181.

[51] Montesquieu 1966, vol. 2, 52.

[52] *Appa* at 87.

[53] Austin's analysis of the debates in the Constituent Assembly leads him to conclude that the placement of the provision for a uniform civil code in the nonjusticiable part of the Constitution was done largely to calm Muslim fears. Austin 1966, 80. By placing it among the Directive Principles, its realization was to be contingent upon legislative, that is, political discretion. This is not inconsistent with Srivastava's account of the Assembly debates in which, contrary to Muslim sentiment, the prevailing view was that the State should not be incapacitated in being able to legislate on any matter covered by the personal laws. Sriva-

"The State Shall Endeavor"

For someone like Justice Douglas, well steeped in the American tradition of equal protection, this resolution was deeply perplexing.[54] Indeed, Article 14 is phrased in the language of the Fourteenth Amendment of the American Constitution, an amendment that has never been permitted to tolerate such a blatantly discriminatory law. Some like-minded Indians entertain similar misgivings to those of Douglas, believing that "[P]ersonal law can have no place in a secular state."[55] They reject the Muslim-inspired position that was voiced at the Constituent Assembly, to the effect that "In a secular State, citizens belonging to different communities must have the freedom to practice their own religion, observe their own life and their personal laws should be applied to them."[56] If we reflect back on the American polygamy cases, the source of these reservations is clearly rooted in liberal constitutional principles requiring the subordination of religion to the civil law, albeit in the long-term interest of religion. The same constitutional logic that led to the Supreme Court's denial of the Mormons' right to an exemption from a law banning polygamy must raise doubts about the legitimacy of a system of personal law that treats groups of people differently. Soli J. Sorabjee has suggested that the main difference between India and the United States with regard to equal protection issues is that in India the source of discrimination has been religious personal law, whereas in the United States it has been the codification in state law of the prejudices of the powerful.[57] In effect, the Mormon challenge to State authority represented a campaign to introduce a regime of personal law into a politically and philosophically inhospitable constitutional environment. The legal response to that challenge reflected not

---

stava 1992, 242. Somewhat less convincing is his conclusion that "The recognition of heterogeneous personal laws, which tend to perpetuate social and religious division, is against the letter and spirit of the Constitution." Ibid., 263. Or at least this is a much more complex matter than is suggested by the comment. The dilemma confronting the framers was the same as that depicted by Varshney in his reflections on the contemporary scene. "Should the various religious groups in India be under a common civil code or under their distinctive religious laws? If secular nationalists claim that separate personal laws destroy national unity, they generate a reaction in the religious community whose personal laws are at issue. If, on the other hand, they promote personal laws on the argument that such concessions make minorities secure, they set off a reaction in the majority community that the state may have gone too far in minority appeasement, opening up fissiparous tendencies and undermining national unity." Varshney 1993, 238. Bhikhu Parekh has expressed similar concerns, worrying that the goal of uniformity "might become an unwitting instrument of avoidable disorder." Parekh 1992, 540.

[54] Douglas 1956, 316.
[55] Chatterji 1984, 223.
[56] Mahboob Ali Baig Bahadur, as quoted in Baird 1981, 404.
[57] Sorabjee 1990, 103.

so much concerns about social justice—the equal protection violations within the Mormon community—as concerns over political justice—the threat to the equal protection concept engrained in a liberally constituted government of law.[58]

Had the Mormons been a more formidable presence in American society, such that the community for which their regulative culture had been designed made up a substantial minority of the American people, and had this community, in addition, confronted a rival constitutive culture comprising the vast majority of the American people, the Court's response might very well have been different. Of course, under these conditions the American Constitution might also have been different. Perhaps, like the Indian Constitution, it would have included language of the following sort after its equal protection guarantee: "The State shall not discriminate against any citizen on grounds only of religion, race, caste, sex, place of birth or any of them." This language from Article 15, with special emphasis on the word *only*, was relied upon by the Court in *Appa* to uphold the community-based distinctions in the Bombay law. Thus by itself religion cannot be a basis for discrimination, but if other reasonable grounds are implicated, the Constitution does not necessarily preclude differential treatment according to group affiliation. As applied by the Court to the issue of polygamy, "One community might be prepared to accept and work social reform; another may not yet be prepared for it; and Art. 14 does not lay down that any legislation that the State may embark upon must necessarily be of an all-embracing character."[59] This incremental approach is present also in Justice Gajendragadkar's opinion: "So long as the State Legislature in taking gradual steps for social welfare and reform does not introduce distinctions or classifications which are unreasonable, irrational or oppressive, it cannot be said that the equality before law is offended."[60]

Somewhat obscured by the rhetoric concerning relative states of welfare preparedness are considerations of social comity. In today's highly

---

[58] It is rare that one encounters judicial sentiments in the American context that challenge this orthodox liberal constitutional view. One exception may be found in the dissenting opinion of Justice Frank Murphy in a case involving the application of the Mann Act to some Mormons who had transported their several wives across state lines. "We must recognize . . . that polygyny, like other forms of marriage, is basically a cultural institution rooted deeply in the religious beliefs and social mores of those societies in which it appears. It is equally true that the beliefs and mores of the dominant culture of the contemporary world condemn the practice as immoral and substitute monogamy in its place. To these beliefs and mores I subscribe, but that does not alter the fact that polygyny is a form of marriage built upon a set of social and moral principles. It must be recognized and treated as such." *Cleveland* at 26.

[59] *Appa* at 87.

[60] Ibid. at 95.

charged environment, in which the secular State is by many accounts under heavy assault from the forces of Hindu revivalism, deference to Muslim sensibilities over polygamy may engender passionate propaganda featuring India being overrun by the offspring of multiple Muslim wives.[61] The ease with which the fears of the majority can be aroused and manipulated is most vividly illustrated by the aftermath to the *Shah Bano* case, in which the government's efforts on behalf of Muslims upset by the Supreme Court's treatment of Islamic law provoked cries of appeasement and ultimately violent confrontation. In this famous and extremely controversial case, the Supreme Court decided in favor of a Muslim woman, granting her maintenance from her divorced husband. Muslim personal law had not required this support, and the reaction among many Muslims was to condemn the Court for endangering Islam in India with the imposition of a uniform civil code. Prime Minister Rajiv Gandhi then supported legislation that effectively reversed the Court's decision. While this gained him support within the traditional Muslim community, it enraged women, progressive Muslims, secularists, and Hindu nationalists. For the latter, the government's response to *Shah Bano* became a rallying cry that was part of the climate that led seven years later to the destruction of the Babri Masjid mosque by Hindu militants, who claimed that this temple in the city of Ayodhya rested on the birthplace of the Hindu god, Lord Ram. Indeed, the connection between *Shah Bano* and Ayodhya is frequently, if not always accurately, drawn.[62] Perhaps, then, it is easy to forget that the original vision (and accompanying understandings) of the secular constitution had emphasized the rights and sensibilities of religious minorities (especially Muslims), to the point that the *secular* ideal of religious freedom came to be inscribed, paradoxically, in both the aspiration for a uniform civil code and in the implicit invitation to frustrate its realization.

The *Shah Bano* ruling is in this regard revealing. According to Chief Justice Chandrachud, "We understand the difficulties involved in bringing

---

[61] See Thakur 1993, 649.

[62] Evidence for the connection continues to mount. Thus on June 13, 2001, the Union home minister, L. K. Advani, appeared before the Liberhan Commission, formed to inquire into the demolition of the Babri Masjid mosque in Ayodhya. Advani, of course, had been one of the principal organizers of the Ram temple agitation that had preceded the events on December 6, 1992. In his testimony before the Commission, Advani said that it was Prime Minister Rajiv Gandhi's vote bank politics that forced the BJP to join the temple movement. "The Supreme Court judgment in the Shah Bano case was reversed to appease the Muslim vote bank. And in order to appease the Hindu vote bank, the unlocking of the temple gates and shilanyas were allowed. We had no chance but to join the movement to fight the politics of the vote bank." Quoted in *Frontline* 2001. Advani's comment proves only that *Shah Bano* and its aftermath have come to serve as a rationale for the Ayodhya campaign, but that in itself is important in considering the constitutional politics surrounding these events.

persons of different faiths and persuasions on a common platform. But a beginning has to be made if the Constitution is to have any meaning."[63] This observation is accompanied by an exhortation to the State to exercise its "legislative competence" to enact a uniform civil code. Since, however, Chandrachud had already argued that the State's criminal statute (requiring financial provision for a wife who is indigent) takes precedence over any conflicting Muslim personal law, and that, moreover, a correct interpretation of the Koran makes clear that the secular law of maintenance is consistent with the rules of the *Shariat*, this exhortation was somewhat gratuitous. The latter interpretation, another example of judicial theological exegesis, obviated the need to enforce the Court's dictum that "morality cannot be clubbed with religion."[64] In the process, the Court illustrated how the exploitative conditions of women could be ameliorated without secularizing the personal law of the minority community.[65] Chandrachud's actions undermined the persuasiveness of his rhetoric: for "the Constitution . . . to have any meaning" does *not* require that the civil law apply in the same manner to all communities. The delicate balance of the secular constitution's dual commitment to social reform and the integrity of group religious life was achievable in the absence of legislation that, in the language of Article 44, "secure[s] for the citizens a uniform civil code throughout the territory of India."[66]

[63] *Shah Bano* at 954.

[64] Ibid. at 948.

[65] Chandrachud's opinion recognizes this but concludes that it is not a sufficient response to the injustice in the system. "Inevitably, the role of the reformer has to be assumed by the courts because, it is beyond the endurance of sensitive minds to allow injustice to be suffered when it is so palpable. But piecemeal attempts of courts to bridge the gap between personal laws cannot take the place of a common Civil Code. Justice to all is a far more satisfactory way of dispensing justice than justice from case to case." Ibid. at 954. While the argument here may be taken as a plea to the legislature to relieve the courts of the burden of judicial activism, it is more likely that it was intended as an expression of frustration at the incremental pace of social reform.

[66] This does not mean that, at least theoretically, there could come a time when this dual commitment could be better realized with the uniform codification of all law. But the constitution-makers seemed aware of the fact that this was, at best, a very long-term project. Krishna Prasad De cites the example of Turkey to illustrate by comparison how inadequate is an Indian commitment to secularism that maintains a system of personal laws. De, 1976, 131. The contrast is useful in distinguishing what I would call *reformist* secularism from the ameliorative secularism that best captures the Indian situation. But it also seems to pass too quickly over critical differences between the two countries. Marcie J. Patton, for example, points out that the Kemalist reforms embraced by the Turkish Constitution denied recognition to those groups that were threatened by the secular national project in nation-building. Patton 1995, 140. Perhaps this was possible in Turkey, but it is unimaginable as a solution for independent India. See also Nur Yalman's consideration of "[t]he cultural revolution in Turkey . . . as an early example of radical social and political reform in this hectic century."

The stakes in this balance are clearer if set against the backdrop of the American counterexample. In the United States, encroachment of religious identity upon the constitutive domain of political identity is, as has been argued, difficult to reconcile with the underlying premises of the secular constitution. In India, the constitutive domain of religion is, by the terms of the Constitution, open to encroachment by forces of political and social transformation; but the legitimacy of this undertaking is at least partially dependent on preserving political space for religious identity. Consistent with this solution, Kymlicka has urged the custodians of liberal regimes to acknowledge collective rights of minority cultural communities. His goal is to find room for the idea of group entitlements within the moral ontology of liberalism.[67] "Cultural membership affects our very sense of personal identity and capacity."[68] What he presents as an option for liberal regimes as a way of enriching the freedom of choice possibilities for their minority citizens is embraced as a necessity in India's secular constitution. To be sure, it is a cold embrace for advocates of major social reform, as historically it has meant legitimating much of the regressive and unattractive behavior that has inspired their outrage and sense of urgency.[69]

The alternative—accelerated implementation of the constitutionally stipulated goal of uniformity—runs the risk of undermining the frail consensus upon which even moderate reform is possible. The question confronting the Indian polity comes down, then, to one of determining how much of a risk to assume, of how strongly and how far to pursue the end of legal uniformity. But the question is not quite so straightforward, because those espousing the ameliorative aspiration are divided and un-

---

Yalman 1991, 241. Prasad's point about personal laws also fails to mention an important factual difference mentioned by Yalman. Turkey is a country that is 99 percent Muslim.

[67] Kymlicka 1989, 140.

[68] Ibid., 175.

[69] Tolerating intolerance would seem to be inevitable in any system that provides real autonomy for groups in the governance of their adherents. We have already seen with regard to governance in matters relating to religion that the secular constitution in the United States tolerates all sorts of departures from the norms associated with public law-making. However, with the partial exception of Native Americans, there is no autonomous rule-making authority conferred upon groups in matters of civil and criminal law. Formal equality takes precedence over a commitment to diversity that must entail some measure of infringement of individual rights. Kymlicka's argument is weakest in this regard. His advocacy of collective rights assumes that the groups exercising these rights will abjure intolerance. "[S]upporting the intolerant character of a cultural community undermines the very reason we had to support cultural membership—that it allows for meaningful individual choice." Ibid., 197. But if that is a reason for calling off the experiment in collective rights, it is hard to see where it would take hold. Surely Kymlicka's principle would deny a regime of personal laws in India, but even in the United States, where religious cultures are much "thinner," the prospects for tolerance would doubtless be disqualifying.

certain about the significance of adopting a uniform civil code for the achievement of social progress. To further complicate matters, some of the social activists supporting Article 44's directive have found themselves in the awkward position of agreeing with others' proclamations on behalf of the downtrodden they believe to be at best insincere, and at worst a cynical ploy to advance the cause to which these "allies" are genuinely attached—the inauguration of a Hindu Rashtra. The ensuing confusion reflects the fact that, as Susanne Rudolph has observed, "The idea of a uniform civil code carries no single meaning," that it "is what cultural critics would call a multi-valent signifier."[70] Thus Nehruvian nationalists see the code as critical to the project of modernist national integration, and advocates of civil rights see it (with some dissent in the ranks, especially among champions of women's equality) as vital to the expansion of opportunities for groups of people who have suffered under the regime of personal laws. At the same time, members of religious minorities—notably dominant members—perceive the code more ominously, viewing it as a threat to their cultural identity, while Hindu nationalists are suspected of welcoming it for that very reason, with the constitutionally defensible prospect of ending "special privileges" to minorities providing their leaders with potentially valuable political ammunition.[71]

The political ascendance of this latter group of course elevates the stakes surrounding the controversy over Article 44. While the fragility of the BJP's governing coalition demands policy moderation, those suspicious of the intentions of the reigning agenda setters are likely to find only limited comfort in this political reality. Indeed, the requirements of coalition building could sensibly be viewed by such skeptics as contributing to their adversaries' incentives for concealment. Thus they might anticipate hearing arguments for legal uniformity couched in a discourse that appeals to the natural inclinations of potential supporters of a code, namely broader national unity and enhanced civil rights. Absent would be the inflammatory rhetoric that often accompanies the Hindu right's initiatives in political mobilization.[72]

[70] Rudolph 1998, 20.

[71] A comparable American example may be found in the constitutional debate over sexual orientation. In *Romer v Evans* a state constitutional amendment nullifying local protective ordinances for homosexuals was successfully challenged in the Supreme Court. Justice Antonin Scalia argued in dissent that "The amendment prohibits *special treatment* of homosexuals and nothing more." *Romer* at 638. His position was that rights were already protected under general civil rights law (in effect a uniform civil rights code). Moreover, he saw nothing wrong with an amendment that expressed "animus" toward morally questionable conduct, a position that could be seen as connecting the constitutionally based argument over equality with political developments outside the courtroom.

[72] Tahir Mahmood expresses very well the sentiments of the skeptical partisans of minority rights. "When politicians and political parties search for 'election issues' in the ideals of

Within a political context characterized by bad faith and mutual distrust, little of importance can form a basis for common agreement. A Hindu politician soothingly declares that "When the BJP talks of a uniform civil code it does not contemplate imposing the Hindu law on the country."[73] In response, a Muslim civil rights advocate challenges the speaker's credibility, insisting that the "uniform civil code has been and remains a euphemism for Hindu law and a license for denigrating non-Hindu religions and personal laws, especially Islam and Islamic law."[74] A prominent spokesperson for the cause of Hindu nationalism invokes "the noble ideals which inspired our national struggle for freedom" as a rallying cry for replacing a system of personal laws that stands in the way of "the emancipation of and equality for women . . . that are clearly violated by these laws."[75] But this call for replacement, critics say, is a transparent ruse, one in which "[s]aving Muslim women from their oppression becomes the justification for not respecting the practices and beliefs of the Muslim community, and indeed, the basis for subordinating this community to Hindu rule."[76]

Ideally the decisions made about a uniform civil code should not be predicated on the promises and suspicions of political adversaries. Instead they should be made only after attempting calculations of how fulfillment of the Constitution's directive principle might affect progress in the achievement of ameliorative secular aspirations. To be sure, such calculations cannot ignore the stratagems and fears of the various contending interests, but neither can they rely too heavily upon them. For example, it may very well be that malevolent, or at least unfriendly, religiously based designs lie behind the BJP's and their allies' support for legal uniformity. Still, that would not ensure that any subsequent enactment of a uniform civil code would achieve the ends thought desirable by these proponents, or that a later assessment of the costs and benefits of codification would not yield acceptable results—and this despite the best intentions of some of its most ardent supporters. Thus reflection and debate over adoption of a uniform civil code, an arrangement that would supersede the existing personal laws of minority religious communities in India, should focus on a famous political question: Who gets what, when, and how?

---

the Constitution, the communal overtones of their selectivity in the matter are bound to prejudice those ideals and create insurmountable hurdles in the way of achieving those ideals by appropriate means." Mahmood 1995, 136.

[73] Lal Krishna Advani, as quoted in Ibid., 135.

[74] Ibid., 137.

[75] Shourie 1997a, 136.

[76] Kapur and Kossman 1995, 106.

A Conversion of Convenience

The third prong of the question—the *how* part—is perhaps the most intriguing, for it highlights Article 44's directing the State (which under the Indian Constitution refers specifically to the government and parliament) to endeavor to secure for its citizens a uniform civil code, while being silent with regard to the process through which to achieve it. What role should other non-State public institutions play—most prominently the judiciary—in securing the objective of the directive principle? The question of the Court's involvement is clouded by uncertainty over its institutional role in connection with a constitutional provision that is unenforceable and basically hortatory in nature. In the United States, for example, the norm against giving advisory opinions was established as early as the administration of George Washington, and while it has not prevented justices over the years from occasionally tendering their unsolicited advice to other public officials, the rule has essentially weathered the test of time. It is premised on the requirements of Article III, which limit the federal courts to actual cases that are subject to the granting of meaningful relief through judicial intervention.[77] That means enforcing constitutional limits where appropriate, as opposed to advancing constitutional goals to accompany advice on policies that may commend themselves to the judges, a practice that in the United States is nearly always inappropriate. But then there is no section in the American Constitution that is comparable to India's in enumerating principles according to which "it shall be the duty of the State to apply . . . in making laws."

That section's nonenforceability could be seen as committing the Court to a totally passive interpretive role. But it seems odd to remove an entire part of a nation's highest law from the purview of that nation's highest court. Could it not instead be taken as an invitation to the Court to function as an official constitutional gadfly? After all, the constitutional assertion of nonenforceability in Article 37 is immediately followed by the declaration that "[T]he principles laid down are nevertheless fundamental in the governance of the country and it shall be the duty of the State to apply these principles in making laws." Should the Court ignore this assignment of constitutional duty and in effect adopt a vow of silence on issues over which it has no power to enforce its judgments? With respect to Article 44, there is an indeterminate quality to the language of the provision—thus the State is not directed to secure a uniform civil code;

---

[77] Article 143 of the Indian Constitution provides explicitly for an advisory role for the Supreme Court. At any time that the president wishes advice with regard to a question of law or fact on a matter of public importance, he or she may refer the question to the Court for its consideration.

rather it is enjoined to *endeavor* to do so. It must, in other words, make a serious and determined effort to unify the laws of the polity, which presumably could be done without ultimately producing any actual codification. It seems, then, entirely reasonable for the Court to opine on the question of the seriousness with which the State is pursuing the effort to unify the civil laws of India. While the explicitly nonjusticiable nature of the substantive issue relieves the State of any concern that it will be ordered to proceed with codification against its better judgment, the moral authority that the Supreme Court brings to its normal adjudicatory obligations arguably should weigh heavily in the process through which implementation of the directive principle is achieved. But there are substantial risks in doing so.

Consider the case of *Sarla Mudgal v Union of India*, a 1995 Supreme Court decision that concerns one of the ingenious ways in which Hindu men have endeavored to circumvent the ban on polygamous marriages. Under Section 494 of the Indian Penal Code, a Hindu who marries while still married to someone else is acting illegally, an act that could result in the voiding of the second marriage and the imprisonment of the guilty party. By contrast, the same restriction does not apply to Muslims, who are free, as we have seen, to have multiple spouses. This disparity in legal treatment since the Hindu Marriage Act of 1955 had led to a rise in the number of apostates in India, with many polygamy-minded Hindus having concluded that conversion to Islam had at least one substantial virtue—the possibility of enjoying marital bliss with more partners than one. Among the resulting difficulties with this arrangement is that many loyal first spouses—loyal, that is, to Hinduism—understandably felt diminished by the more widely distributed bliss.

Their plight was given sympathetic consideration by the Court, which ruled decisively in favor of the non-Muslim spouse. Accordingly, the second marriage of a Hindu husband converted to Islam was held to be invalid.[78] The Court's emphatic rejection of the apostate's legal position was grounded in a ringing affirmation of the institution of marriage. "Marriage is the very foundation of the civilised society. . . . [It] is an institution in the maintenance of which the public at large is deeply interested. It is the foundation of the family and in turn of the society without which no civilisation can exist."[79] Using an abundance of precedents and a close analysis of the relevant statutory law, Justice Kuldip Singh's opinion for the Court proceeded quickly to the conclusion that a Hindu mar-

---

[78] The Court could rule on this question because a matrimonial dispute between a convert to Islam and his or her non-Muslim spouse was not subject to the jurisdiction of the Muslim Personal Law.

[79] *Sarla Mudgal* at 1533.

riage solemnized under the Hindu Marriage Act could not be dissolved on the basis of a conversion-facilitated second marriage, and that the logical result of taking seriously the Act's support for monogamy was invalidation of the Muslim marriage.[80] If a Hindu husband wishes to embrace Islam and then marry again, he must first dissolve the earlier marriage in accordance with legal requirements (cumbersome though they are) provided for Hindus seeking a divorce. The importance attached to this finding was underscored by Justice Singh's assertion that the Court's conclusion was dictated by "the rules of natural justice." So while it was clear that both positive law and *stare decisis* were sufficient to support the Court's decision, it was possible also to void the bigamous marriage as a violation of "justice, equity, and good conscience."[81]

Sarla Mudgal quickly became very controversial in India, but not because of the Court's ruling on the substantive merits of the case. Unlike *Shah Bano*, the decision was not burdened by judicial excesses of theological exegesis, and the loophole-closing outcome was widely seen as reasonable.[82] But as in the earlier case, the facts and issues in *Sarla Mudgal* presented the judges with an opportunity to advise the State on the urgency of adopting a uniform civil code. Justice Singh did not let the opportunity pass; indeed his opinion makes the dictum in the 1985 case look timid by comparison. Thus it commences not with a reference to the facts of the case at hand, but with a straightforward assertion of constitutional responsibility. "'The State shall endeavour to secure for the citizens a uniform civil code throughout the territory of India' is an unequivocal man-

---

[80] The actual commitment of the Act to monogamy (and to women's rights) is a matter of intense debate. For example, according to Flavia Agnes, "[T]he progressive sounding provision of monogamy not only turned out to be a mockery but in fact even more detrimental to women than the uncodified Hindu law which recognized rights of wives in polygamous marriages." Agnes 1999, 88. Like many feminists writing about India, Agnes emphasizes the loopholes available to bigamous husbands under the Hindu Marriage Act, which leads her to minimize the achievement of the Court in *Sarla Mudgal* for having closed only one of them. This critical view of the Hindu Marriage Act (and the Hindu Code in general) should be contrasted with Derrett's understanding that "[I]t was characteristically with the intention of equalizing [the sexes] that Parliament departed most radically from the ancient law." Derrett 1968, 333. More to the point, "[B]y far the most dramatic step towards equalizing the status of men and women was the abolition of plural marriages." Ibid., 337. A complete account of the Hindu Code's departure from ancient law would need to address the changes enacted with regard to religiously based caste privileges. As pointed out by Galanter, the Code "largely abandoned the shastric basis of Hindu law and established a more or less uniform law for Hindus of all regions and castes." Galanter 1966, 290.

[81] *Sarla Mudgal* at 1537.

[82] The Muslim civil rights activist Tahir Mahmood expressed the sentiments of many by saying: "What married Hindu men do and are helped with is a fraud on Hinduism, a disgrace to Islam, a cruel joke on the freedom-of-conscience clause in the Constitution of the country and a criminal scheming against the law of the land." Mahmood 1995, 60.

date under Article 44 of the Constitution of India which seeks to introduce a uniform personal law—a decisive step towards national consolidation."[83] A mention of the Hindu Code statutes of the 1950s follows, and next a sweeping declaration brings the opening paragraph to a close. "When more than 80% of the citizens have already been brought under the codified personal law there is no justification whatsoever to keep in abeyance, any more, the introduction of 'uniform civil code' for all citizens in the territory of India."[84]

However, as had surely been clear for some time, it was not only Indians from among the 20 percent of the citizens beyond the reach of the majority's codified personal law who would demur from the certainty of categorical pronouncements of this sort. For example, the eminent jurist (later attorney general of India) and scholar Soli J. Sorabjee wrote in response to the Court's decision: "It is unfortunate that the Supreme Court made these needless observations in the first place. It is more unfortunate that thereby an avoidable controversy was generated and political parties, especially the BJP, jumped into the fray to secure political mileage. . . . The moral of the episode is: where sensitive constitutional questions do not arise for determination, judicial silence is not an option but a constitutional compulsion."[85] Sorabjee's mention of "needless observations" referred to the feature of the Court's opinion that attracted the most criticism—the obiter dicta status of its importuning on the subject of a uniform civil code. His allusion to the BJP referred to that party's publicly expressed satisfaction in what its spokespeople portrayed as the Supreme Court's "directive" to the government to enact such a code, and their determination to feature it in the party's electoral campaigns. Finally, his articulation of the correct moral embedded in the story—the requirement of judicial silence—engages a familiar theme in contemporary constitutional theory, the possible damage to democratic institutions caused by an overextended and obtrusive judiciary.[86]

---

[83] *Sarla Mudgal* at 1532.

[84] Ibid. at 1532. The 80 percent figure can be questioned. Mahmood maintains, for example, that uniformity is more limited than Justice Singh suggested, with certain regions still experiencing conflicting traditional rules and certain subjects still uncodified. Mahmood 1995, 49. This is part of a broader critique that argues that enactment of the laws had very little to do with national unity or secularism. This should be contrasted with Derrett's view that the Hindu Code was "a half-way house to [the] end [of a single civil code]." Derrett 1968, 321. Derrett, however, also saw the motivations behind the laws to be complicated, involving class considerations more than religious ones.

[85] From an article in *Indian Express*, August 14, 1995, as excerpted in Mahmood 1995, 193.

[86] For anyone concerned about judicial activism, especially in the United States, a line quoted approvingly from *Shah Bano* by Justice Singh would provoke considerable anxiety. "Inevitably, the role of the reformer has to be assumed by the Courts because, it is beyond

The insistence on silence in the face of constitutionally inscribed direction is unconvincing. Consistent with the moral of Sorabjee's story, Tahir Mahmood has contended that the "[s]lightest chance of intended *obiter* being misunderstood or abused is a reason mighty enough to avoid it altogether." The concern behind this sentiment is clear. "Any idea or expression that can be pounced upon for its political overtone or cashed in by the communalists must never find a place in a court judgment."[87] In effect, then, the possibility of subsequent political mischief constitutes an argument for judicial muteness. Not reticence, or prudence, or caution, but absolute quiet. Yet embracing that argument would establish an unfortunate precedent, basically holding the Court hostage to the designs of others and potentially legitimizing a formula for judicial paralysis. To be sure, it is regrettable that the BJP portrayed the decision in *Sarla Mudgal* as *directing* the government to enact a uniform civil code when in fact what the Court said was quite different, specifically: "We . . . *request* the Government of India through the Prime Minister of the country to have a fresh look at Article 44 of the Constitution and 'endeavour to secure for the citizens a uniform civil code throughout the territory of India.'"[88] Must the Court censor itself in order to avoid its words being distorted in such blatant a fashion?

In a concurring opinion, Justice R. M. Sahai presented his own obiter dicta in the form of a response to Justice Singh's advice to the government. His argument included the familiar alternative in the Article 44 debate, namely that the achievement of a single code should not be attempted in the absence of the appropriate social and political climate. "[T]he first step should be to rationalise the personal law of the minorities to develop religious and cultural amity. The Government would be well advised to entrust the responsibility to the Law Commission which may in consultation with the Minorities Commission examine the matter."[89] This is an entirely reasonable point of view, but it can also be seen as playing into the hands of those within the Muslim community (and perhaps others as well) who wish to preserve the status quo, especially with regard to gender relations. Confident that they will be able to prevail over reformers within

---

the endurance of sensitive minds to allow injustice to be suffered when it is so palpable." *Sarla Mudgal* at 1538. An Indian response would have to factor in the knowledge of the Constitution as an explicitly social document. In this respect it is importantly distinguishable from its American counterpart.

[87] Mahmood 1995, 164. The sentiment is present in Madhu Kishwar's analysis. "[*Sarla Mudgal*] is not exactly a legal judgment but more of a political sermon on how the Muslim community should learn to behave and what ought to be its relationship to the Indian State." Kishwar 1998, 235.

[88] *Sarla Mudgal* at 1539 (emphasis added).

[89] Ibid. at 1540.

their religious group, they can be expected to find encouragement in a formulation of the problem that enables them to maintain indefinitely (for that is how a counsel of delay is likely to be read) the autonomy of their extensively accumulated corpus of personal law. Thus this part of the concurrence is equally susceptible to tendentious misreading and distortion, which under the logic of the Sorabjee teaching reduces it to a judicial intervention that would have been better left unsaid.

More productive than focusing on the appropriateness of pronouncements by judges on matters not directly before them would be to address the question of *how* the uniform civil code promises to advance the secular constitutional agenda of social amelioration. In this connection both of the opinions in *Sarla Mudgal* are disappointing. Repeating an argument from *Shah Bano*, the main opinion asserts the truism that a common civil code will help the cause of national integration. But the opinion fails to explain why a nation that achieves greater unification under a common set of laws is better off than one that does not. Is there a connection between uniformity and social justice? The concurrence answers affirmatively, insisting that "[A] unified code is imperative both for protection of the oppressed and promotion of national unity and solidarity."[90] But other than emphasizing that this relationship holds only if a process of rationalization within the minority communities precedes it, scarce light is cast on the question. Indeed, its point of emphasis could cause one to question whether the aggregate of progressive reform within the various religious communities would not be preferable to a single progressive system of civil law that treats all individuals uniformly. In other words, why not prefer a solution that satisfies cultural pluralists at the same time that it promises fulfillment to proponents of social justice? As Susanne Rudolph has noted, "India is heir to dual legal and political traditions, one making individuals the basic unit of society and polity and envisioning a universal and equal citizenship, another positing groups as the building blocks of society and polity with particular rights attaching to collective entities."[91]

Oddly, the significance of this duality appears to have eluded the reasoning of Justice Singh. The problem resides not in his strong recommendation for adoption of a uniform civil code, but in a serious misconstruction of Article 44 that bespeaks a broader failure of imagination regarding how one might conceptualize legal uniformity in the Indian context. Consider the following passage from his opinion.

[90] Ibid.

[91] Rudolph 1998, 1. This observation is the opening line in her essay. Her closing line is also worth quoting. "In an India whose constant political challenge is to reconcile diversity with integration, legal pluralism and legal uniformity are likely to continue as parties in a process of negotiation, to stand in dynamic tension rather than engage in a zero sum game." Ibid., 23.

Article 44 is based on the concept that there is no necessary connection between religion and personal law in a civilised society. Article 25 guarantees
religious freedom whereas Article 44 seeks to divest religion from social relations and personal law. Marriage, succession and like matters of a secular
character cannot be brought within the guarantee enshrined under articles
25, 26 and 27. The personal law of the Hindus, such as relating to marriage,
succession and the like, have all a sacramental origin, in the same manner as
is the case of the Muslims or the Christians. The Hindus along with Sikhs,
Buddhists and Jains have forsaken their sentiments in the cause of the national unity and integration; some other communities would not, though the
Constitution enjoins the establishment of a "common civil Code" for the
whole of India.[92]

Justice Singh was of course correct that a necessary connection between
religion and personal law is not a defining attribute of civilized society.
While the first sentence implies that there could be such a connection
(even if it is not necessary), the second puts forward the notion that, as
far as India is concerned, a radical separation of religion and law was
critical to the idea of civilized society. In the Court's view, the secular ideal
embedded in Article 44 sunders religion and social relations. Moreover,
much of this ideal has been realized in the codification of Hindu (and
Sikh, Buddhist, and Jain) law, in which the religious origins of personal
law were apparently transformed into a subject of chiefly antiquarian interest.[93]

But this conceptualization of the secular ideal in India is, as we have
seen, grossly misplaced. "[T]he concept of 'secular' versus 'religious' may
be valid in the West, but comes up against unexpected difficulties in India,
where the two main religious communities profess . . . a religion which
does not consider worldly or practical questions to be distinct from religion. No definition of Islam or Hinduism . . . could proceed on the assumption that the family regime was not ultimately a religious question."[94] When Radhakrishnan declared, "I want to state authoritatively
that secularism does not mean irreligion," he spoke for the vast majority
of his fellow constitution-makers. Understanding how deeply embedded

---

[92] *Sarla Mudgal* at 1538.

[93] This is couched in a patronizing way that clarifies the basis of some of the concern
provoked in the Muslim community over the opinion in this case. The reference to "some
other communities" displays an attitude of reproach toward minorities that have, in effect,
failed to move in the civilized direction of the majority, that is, Hindu, community. It should
also be noted that the secularization of marriage law is already manifest in the existence of
the Special Marriage Act, which offers an option for those wishing to avoid religious-based
marriage law. In terms of how most Indians lead their lives, however, it is an option not
realistically available to many citizens.

[94] Derrett 1968, 534.

the religious experience was in the lives of most of their compatriots, they sought to address the tensions between the temporal and the spiritual with a mix of solutions that implicitly or explicitly presumed the inextricability of the two spheres.

Justice Singh could presumably respond to such observations by pointing out that the Constitution's reference to a uniform civil code appears in the section of the document strictly devoted to goals and aspirations, which is to say, to the future. Thus when thinking about either the past or the present, a divesting of religion from social relations might very well indicate a worrisome detachment from reality, but given the futuristic orientation of the Directive Principles, imagining the eventual secularization of Indian society is at least plausible.[95] But Justice Singh contends that the adoption of a uniform civil code is long overdue, therefore implying that divestiture is a possibility today. If so, what is the evidence? Have important sectors of society been removed from the domination of religious institutions and symbols? In his opinion he writes of "[m]arriage, succession and like matters of a secular character." Does he mean this in a normative or empirical sense? If the former, then the act of codification will help transform these areas of family life into appropriately secularized activities; if the latter, then compliance with Article 44's directive will only confirm, clarify, and help to organize an existing reality.

In either case, Justice Singh may be faulted for not providing more argument and evidence for his less than obvious conclusions. This is particularly regrettable, since the logic of his reasoning affects the enjoyment of rights under the enforceable provisions of the Constitution's Fundamental Rights section. It is significant, for example, that these "matters of a secular character cannot be brought within the guarantee enshrined under articles 25, 26, and 27." In his determination to maneuver religion to the margins and interstices of the social order, Justice Singh has withdrawn matters that have (at minimum) a sacramental origin from the protective ambit of constitutionally guaranteed religious freedoms. But there is more. Because under the Constitution freedom of religion is always subject to State regulation on grounds of social welfare considerations, the effect of such a withdrawal is ironically to constrain the ameliorative authority of the government in the more targeted efforts it might undertake in pursuing social equity.[96]

---

[95] Which, as Neera Chandhoke reminds us, may or may not be a good thing, since "[i]t must be emphasized that there is a distinction between *secular states* and *secularized societies*." Chandhoke 1999, 81. Achieving the second may not guarantee the first.

[96] In this regard, consider these remarks of a Muslim scholar and editor: "It is just as well that it [India] is not secular in the western sense of complete separation between Church and State, for it reserves to itself the right to intervene in the interest of necessary social

Does this mean that Article 44 is unrealizable as well as unenforceable? Are the only viable alternatives either the passage of a uniform civil code on the basis of empirical assumptions that are unproven and seemingly at odds with a booming politics of cultural and religious assertiveness or the acceptance of the regime of communally based personal law that in time might reform itself through an internally generated dynamic of moral criticism? The Court's opinion does indeed present us with this option for social advancement, a choice subsumed within competing remote possibilities—Western separationism and indigenous communalism.[97] In so doing it perhaps obscures a third possibility: enactment of a uniform civil code that does not expend political capital in seeking to divest religion from social relations, but rather deploys it to mandate uniform standards without requiring uniform behavior. Such a possibility is consistent with the underlying premises of ameliorative secularism, both its commitment to social transformation and its accommodation to the demands of a thickly constituted religious presence. This is what is so attractive about S. P. Sathe's contention that a uniform civil code "does not necessarily mean a common law but different personal laws based on uniform principles of equality of sexes and liberty for the individual."[98] By shifting the focus from the goal of formal legal equality to that of substantive rights, Article 44's mandate assumes a meaning much more congruent with the fundamental suppositions of Indian constitutionalism. It also enriches the meaning of national integration, which should look much more attractive when it comes to be associated with the acceptance and enforcement of shared principles of social and political justice rather than the blanket imposition of a set of common rules.

CONCLUSION

"None of this had to be spelled out, no explicit orders given; people simply seemed to adjust naturally to an immutable pattern of expectations, where everyone knew his place and understood what he had to do."[99] This was the reaction of the Indian novelist and diplomat Shashi Tharoor upon returning to his grandmother's house in rural Kerala after spending most of his childhood years growing up in relatively cosmopolitan Bombay. Tharoor was reflecting on the "complicated hierarchies" of age, gender, and caste that seemed to be taken for granted by everyone. The first

---

reforms in matters which customarily come under the purview of religion." Quoted in Derrett 1968, 516.

[97] By *indigenous* I do not mean to ignore the role of the West in the development of Indian communalism and especially its system of personal laws.

[98] S. P. Sathe, quoted in Rudolph 1995.

[99] Tharoor 1997, 81.

two were easy to comprehend, even if life in the big city, where his mother "could hold her own at a Bombay party with a cocktail in her hand," had made the second seem to him less natural. But the entrenched discrimination of caste still pervaded the progressive state of Kerala, leaving Tharoor, who had not witnessed and experienced its "enshrined bigotry" in such a powerful way in the urban India with which he was most familiar, profoundly disturbed. Much as he wished he could deny it, the persistence of caste-related inequality was an unsettling reality fifty years after the inception of constitutional democracy.[100]

Inherent in the strand of ameliorative secularism that is prominent in Indian public law is a challenge to this threat to constitutional democracy. For democratic politics to work, the baneful effects of rigidly deterministic social hierarchy would have to be addressed. The constitutional solution was multipronged, reflecting the reality of caste as a phenomenon much broader than what might be subsumed under the specific concerns of secularism. For example, the Constitution's explicit commitment to caste-driven affirmative action accepts the existential fact of entrenched social segmentation without regard to its religious or secular character and origin. On the other hand, the broadest application of the term *caste*, in which, as Cass Sunstein has argued, any systematic social disadvantage attributable to morally irrelevant and highly visible differences would qualify, has a very obvious connection to a religious presence in India that is pervasive and deep. Tharoor's depiction of an "immutable pattern of expectations," particularly as this speaks to the question of gender relations, could very easily have led him to an extended rumination on the subject of religion and society.

The ameliorative aspiration is a constitutional commitment to diminish the social significance of caste in both its narrow and broad incarnations. The latter is in certain respects a much more difficult problem. The Constitution is explicit in its opposition to the vertical, hierarchical distinctions of caste, what Marc Galanter calls the "sacral view of caste" (i.e., Hinduism's *varna*-based gradations).[101] While this view has been "disestablished," the document's tolerance of "horizontal distinctions," in other words, its recognition of the claims of religious denominations that are not related to sacral ordering, makes for a much more complicated picture with regard to the broader conceptualization of caste. Within the protected spheres of

---

[100] Tharoor does not ignore the progress that has been made, pointing out, as many have done, that much of it is attributable to the constitutional irony of having caste officially recognized by the document for purposes of remedial action. Thus caste consciousness has remained high even while its objective burdens have been lessened to a limited extent. Some of this progress is of course also connected to the increasing importance of caste as a mobilizing factor in electoral politics.

[101] Galanter 1966, 309.

group denominations are laws and norms supporting patterns of expectation that over time have acquired the attribute of immutability. What we have seen in this chapter are some of the vexed constitutional questions surrounding the efforts of Indians to transform this seemingly natural attribute into an artificially constructed phenomenon that can more easily accommodate the demands of democratic social reform.

These efforts continue in the midst of political changes that present additional challenges to the project of constitutional secularism. The ascendance of the Hindu nationalist movement to the point where it occupies a predominant position in the coalition that governs the nation requires that we focus on some of the questions that this development has stimulated in connection with the essential commitments of Indian secularism. In part 2 I try to demonstrate that this challenge also offers an opportunity to sharpen and clarify our understanding of these essentials.

PART TWO

Constitutional Perspectives on the Challenge to Secularism in India

Chapter Five

RELIGION, POLITICS, AND THE FAILURE
OF CONSTITUTIONAL MACHINERY

THE YEAR IS 1825. United States President John Quincy Adams aggressively pursues the battle against slavery, exploiting the full range of his presidential authority. That includes removing the governments and dissolving the legislative assemblies in three states, Virginia, Mississippi, and South Carolina. A proclamation detailing the ways in which the elected officials of these states have forfeited their right to remain in office triggers the machinery of removal. The extreme measures are a response to the advancement of policies by the state governments in direct violation of the provisions of the Constitution as interpreted by authorities in Washington. Through their active support of slavery, the political leaders in the three states have subverted the basic structure of the Constitution; hence their power must be relinquished. Installed in their place will be regimes of President's Rule committed to the constitutional principle of human equality.

Of course this never happened. John Quincy Adams was, to be sure, a passionate foe of slavery, but he is celebrated only for his postpresidential efforts to do something about it. As president he did very little to rid the nation of the scourge of human bondage. In this respect his meager accomplishments mirror the record of the pre-Lincoln presidents, who, even if they had all been so inclined, possessed minimal political resources to dismantle the peculiar institution.

Were this story fact not fantasy, the evaluation of Adams's presidency no doubt would rest primarily on the success of his leadership in prosecuting the ensuing Civil War. His actions would have presumably precipitated such a war, for apart from the immediate threat to an entrenched way of life implicit in the political removals, the intrusions of the federal government into the domain of the states would surely have been viewed as an intolerable exercise of dictatorial power. The legal rationale for intervention—for example, the argument that under Article IV of the Constitution the administration in Washington had the responsibility to guarantee republican government in the states—would doubtless have been widely perceived as insubstantial and unpersuasive. While one could imagine a Supreme Court reluctant to intervene in matters deemed political, to the aggrieved parties the insufficient constitutional justification for such a massive encroachment upon local self-government would have created a need to respond appropriately, which is to say fervently and probably with violence.

Indeed, had such actions occurred, even those sympathetic to the motivations behind the removals might have questioned the legitimacy of what was done. The structure of federalism ensures that wherever it exists, local autonomy will be passionately defended against the expansionist proclivities (real or imagined) of central authority. This has certainly been the case in the United States. It is also true for India. But in India the scenario depicted above actually occurred, and not as the figment of anyone's overheated imagination. It culminated in a landmark Supreme Court decision upholding the dismissal of three state governments by the national administration in New Delhi; although at least as important was the Court's affirmation of the principle that extreme politics of this sort may be reviewed by the judiciary.

Considerably more was at stake in this case than the latitude available to the Central Government in the invocation of its emergency powers. Similar to the constitutional debate in nineteenth-century America, which was often argued in the abstract language of jurisdictional niceties, but which really had to do with the most fundamental questions of regime commitment, the contestants in the Indian dispute over the scope of state autonomy were confronting the critical and historically vexed issue of Indian national identity. Thus the dismissals of the governments in the states of Madhya Pradesh, Himachal Pradesh, and Rajasthan were predicated on the alleged failures of their administrations in implementing and respecting the constitutional commitment to secularism. Said the Court: "Secularism is a part of the basic structure of the Constitution. The acts of a State Government which are calculated to subvert or sabotage secularism as enshrined in our Constitution, can lawfully be deemed to give rise to a situation in which the Government of the State cannot be carried on in accordance with the provisions of the Constitution."[1]

But what is secularism? Counsel for one of the affected states pointed out, much as his nineteenth-century American counterpart might have done in speaking of the idea of human equality, that secularism is a vague, constitutionally ill-defined concept that would not bear the weight of the actions undertaken in its name. In particular, it could not furnish a basis

---

[1] *Bommai* at 149.

for taking action under Article 356, the provision of the Constitution that offers textual justification for the Central Government's deployment of emergency powers.[2] The conceptual ambiguity of the ostensible rationale for intervention reinforced the argument that it was politics and not emergency that had triggered President's Rule. If true, it would not have constituted an unprecedented abuse of the emergency power, as many of the one hundred or so previous occasions when it had been exercised had been accompanied by well-founded allegations of political manipulation and opportunism. As one careful observer has written, the "main consideration" in cases of President's Rule "has been the interest of the Congress Party at the Centre."[3] This instance was distinctive because the invocation of the power responded to a perceived threat to the underlying *principles* of the Constitution, rather than, as had been the pattern in the past, to a physical threat to the very existence of constitutional government. If something similar to this had occurred in the United States, if Abraham Lincoln, for example, had declared martial law in response to slavery's challenge to constitutional essentials and not only, as was done during a critical phase of the Civil War, in order to protect the physical integrity of constituted authority, we would have had an American version of *S. R. Bommai v Union of India.*[4]

That hypothetical Supreme Court case might very well have produced the definitive judicial commentary on the substance of American regime principles. Indeed, nothing short of a jurisprudential tour de force would have satisfied the judgment of history that due consideration had been given to the merits of such a unique and profoundly antidemocratic

---

[2] The key part of Article 356 reads as follows: "(1) If the President, on receipt of a report from the Governor of a State or otherwise, is satisfied that a situation has arisen in which the government of the State cannot be carried on in accordance with the provisions of this Constitution, the President may by Proclamation—(a) assume to himself all or any of the functions of the Government of the State and all or any of the powers vested in or exercisable by the Governor or any body or authority in the State other than the Legislature of the State; (b) declare that the powers of the Legislature of the State shall be exercisable by or under the authority of Parliament; (c) make such incidental and consequential provisions as appear to the President to be necessary or desirable for giving effect to the objects of the Proclamation, including provisions for suspending in whole or in part the operation of any provisions of this Constitution relating to any body or authority in the State."

[3] Quoted in Austin 1999, 607. A very important official analysis of President's Rule, known as the *Sarkaria Report*, recommended that Article 356 should be used only in extreme cases. Its findings reflected sympathy with the many submissions regarding the misuse of the provision to promote partisan political interests.

[4] (1994) 3 SC 1. The *Bommai* judgment consisted of a package of six cases involving the implementation of President's Rule, only three of which concerned dismissals of state governments for undermining the secular foundations of the Constitution. In the three other cases, one of which was Bommai's challenge, the Court found insufficient justification for the Central Government's resorting to Article 356.

course of action. How the judges would have responded to their special opportunity to clarify the meaning of American constitutional democracy can only be a matter of conjecture. In *Bommai*, on the other hand, we can consult actual adjudication. The Indian Supreme Court's review of the national administration's actions in dismantling three elected state governments ended in a compendium of opinions that included lengthy disquisitions on a range of topics, including federalism, judicial power, and most important, the nature of secularism in a plural democracy.

These opinions constitute, as one commentator has pointed out, "by far the most significant interpretation of the secular character of the Indian Constitution to date."[5] Their significance lies not only in the elaboration of these characteristics but also in the political circumstances that led to their articulation. Controversial issues of federalism and democratic legitimacy found themselves embedded in the debate over secular principles in ways that spoke to the uniqueness of the Indian predicament as well as to discussions about constitutional change that are of broader theoretical interest. Thus the inquiry by the Court into the meaning of the constitutional commitment to secularism in India also highlights a feature of that nation's jurisprudence that is, if no longer exceptional, still in many ways distinctive: the authority of the Supreme Court to assert the power of judicial review over amendments to the Constitution.[6] In *Bommai*, the dismissal of the state governments by the Center was upheld on the ground that officials of these governments had violated the Constitution's requirement of secular governance, a requirement substantial enough to be included by the Court among the unamendable "basic features" of the Constitution. The validity of this most intrusive kind of federal intervention ultimately rested on a judgment that the underlying promise of the constitutional project could be fatally compromised by the failure to act aggressively in the face of extreme provocation.

In the discussion that follows, I argue that the obligation of the Union Government to "ensure that the government of every State is carried on in accordance with the provisions of [the] Constitution" is, among other things, a directive to fulfill the ameliorative aspirations of Indian constitutionalism. It is a directive that, like the broader set of related Directive Principles, possesses a hortatory quality that, standing alone, cannot legitimate a result as extraordinary as the dismissal of a duly elected government. In concert, however, with a more legally enforceable legal principle,

---

[5] Panikkar 1997, 49.

[6] The Indian constitutional scholar Upendra Baxi suggested in 1985 that "The Indian Supreme Court is probably the only court in the history of humankind" to have asserted that power. Baxi 1985, 64. Developments in Germany and elsewhere have superseded this observation, but the Indian Court can still be said to have led the way.

such as the obligation of the State to treat all religions equally, it provides a theoretically compelling enticement for the invocation of President's Rule. In pursuing this argument I consider the Guaranty Clause of the American Constitution as the constitutional model for Articles 355 and 356. That Clause, which is as notable in the American context for its underuse as the analogous Indian provision is for its overuse, establishes the United States government as the guarantor of the republican form of government within the individual states. The very different histories of these clauses has much to do with the presence within their respective polities of alternative theories of Center-State relations; but the contrasting experience also mirrors critical conceptual differences in the role of a constitution in establishing political and social priorities within the larger society. With the cataclysmic events of late 1992, these priorities fell under a scrutiny unprecedented in postindependence India.

DEMOLITION, DISMISSAL, AND DEMOCRACY

In December of 1992, a wave of violence engulfed much of India, precipitated by a Hindu mob's destruction of the Babri Masjid mosque in Ayodhya, "the site of the most piercing assault ever faced by the Indian state, one that shook its basic political identity."[7] Not since Partition had so much blood flowed through the streets of Indian cities and towns. The orgy of Hindu-Muslim rioting and tumult was a chilling reminder of the awful circumstances that accompanied the birth of independent India. Communal carnage in Bombay attracted the attention of the world, but similar atrocities were being enacted throughout India, albeit on a smaller scale than in that unfortunate city.[8] One place lucky enough to have escaped the bloodletting was the small, mountainous, northern state of Himachal Pradesh. However, the absence of violence there did not prevent the government of that state, along with the governments of Rajasthan and Madhya Pradesh (where in both cases violence and killing had occurred), from being supplanted by President's Rule.[9]

---

[7] Khilnani 1997, 151. "No other event, barring Partition, in the history of twentieth century India has been as cataclysmic to the nation as the 'religious' rape at Ayodhya on 6 December 1992, by a mob of *kar sevaks* got together by the BJP, the VHP, the RSS and the bajrang Dal." Panikkar 1997, 171.

[8] Approximately twelve hundred lives were lost from December 6 through December 13. Maharashtra (including Bombay) had 259 deaths. There were 246 in Gujarat, 201 in Uttar Pradesh, 161 in Madhya Pradesh, 48 in Rajasthan, 15 in Delhi, and 24 in Bihar.

[9] The attack on the mosque occurred on December 6, leading on the same day to the dismissal of the BJP government of Uttar Pradesh (where Ayodhya is located) by the Central Government. That government had been heavily implicated in the events leading up to the demolition. The dismissal of the other three state governments took place on December 15

Himachal Pradesh, Rajasthan, and Madhya Pradesh had all formed BJP governments based on legislative majorities obtained in the elections of February 1990. The failure to dismiss governments in states in which similar incidents of violence had occurred, but where, unlike in these three places, there existed a correspondence between the ruling parties at the state and federal level, naturally led to the charge that the December 15 imposition of President's Rule had been a blatantly political act. Why do nothing about the Congress-ruled administration in Maharashtra (home of Bombay) while deposing the government in peaceful Himachal Pradesh? Could there be any doubt that emergency provisions were being selectively administered to gain political advantage?

The lawyers for the three states of course alleged that no alternative explanation was possible. In the end, the Supreme Court concluded otherwise, although the natural inclination of the judiciary to avoid the thicket of "political questions" argues for caution in reading their judgment as an outright rejection of the substance of the political allegations. The anomaly of Himachal Pradesh turned out, in effect, to highlight the main concern of the Court, which had less to do with governmental failure to keep the peace than it did with governmental malfeasance in undermining the secular precepts of the polity. Thus all three governments had made it unambiguously clear that their sympathies lay with those who had perpetrated the violence at Ayodhya; also that their active support for those actions and the ideas upon which they rested cast serious doubt on their willingness to conduct the business of government in accordance with the principles of the Constitution.[10]

To be sure, the Governors' Reports (sent by the state governors to the president of India requesting the invocation of President's Rule) emphasized in the cases of the two violence-plagued states the connection between official behavior and the limited possibilities for stemming the tide of disorder. In Himachal Pradesh the same sort of evidence was adduced— support by the state government (including the chief minister and his cabinet) for the *kar sevaks* who destroyed the mosque, membership in radical Hindu organizations such as the Rashtriya Swayamsevak Sangh (RSS) by the leaders of the government—without tying it to any demonstrable inability to preserve public order. These unique circumstances clarified

---

in response to reports from the three governors that the affairs of State could not be carried on in accordance with the provisions of the Constitution.

[10] In an interview with the author, Justice A. N. Ahmadi, author of one of the more thoughtful opinions in *Bommai*, cited these sympathies and this support as clearly establishing a constitutional rationale for distinguishing the situation of the three affected states from those others where violence had occurred, but where public officials had not been implicated in the actions culminating in the destruction of the mosque. Interview with the author, April 1, 2000, Toronto, Canada.

the essential meaning of the Court's decision as one pertaining as much to issues of constitutional principle as to matters of public emergency and crisis.[11] For those supporting the Court, the judgment was a great victory for secularism; for the Court's detractors, it represented the triumph of leftist ideology and rank hypocrisy. As a constitutional scholar with close ties to the BJP wrote: "[T]hey [the Left] had been in the forefront of demands for greater State autonomy and curtailing the powers of the Union Government. In a surprising somersault, their hatred and fear of a particular party made them forget their great concern for federalism and demand and justify the dismissal of three State governments in one go by an arbitrary order of the Union Government."[12]

The core of this argument is very much in line with what we have seen in the previous chapter: the appropriation by Hindu nationalist theoreticians of the discourse of liberal politics. Thus the State (in the case of Article 356, the Central Government) is obligated, in this account, to remain officially indifferent to the substance of ideology, an obligation that renders totally inappropriate the dismissal of any freely elected government on the basis of its political orientation. Accordingly, the only legitimate justification for invoking Article 356 powers is in the circumstance of a serious interruption in the workings of the democratic *process*. Therefore, a breakdown in the machinery of constitutional government, or the failure to act in accordance with the provisions of the Constitution, means only one thing: a duly elected government is, as a result of an arbitrary obstruction in the workings of the democratic process, manifestly unable to rule in fulfillment of its mandate.[13] "The basic issue is

[11] This distinction mirrors the language of Article IV, Section 4, of the American Constitution, which, as we shall see, bears directly on the Indian experience under Article 356. The Guaranty Clause reads: "The United States shall guarantee every State in this Union a Republican Form of Government, and shall protect each of them against Invasion, and on Application of the Legislature or of the Executive (when the Legislature cannot be convened) against domestic violence." The Domestic Violence Clause refers to federal action after the onset of hostile activities, whereas the guarantee of republican government can be read to envision preemptive action in advance of any overt and direct physical disruption. This of course raises the question as to whether there must even be a threat of violence to trigger federal intervention.

[12] Kashyap 1993. In an interview with the author, Kashyap made clear his belief that the politics of the Court had dictated the outcome in the case. Interview conducted in New Delhi on December 5, 1998. A principal advocate in the case for the States' position, Ram Jethmalani, was even more direct. "Most of the judges in the case were pro-Congress leftists." Interview with the author, New Delhi, February 26, 1999.

[13] Mark E. Brandon's typology of constitutional failure, developed in conjunction with his study of slavery and the American Constitution, is worth considering here. Brandon distinguishes between a failure of constitutional order, which is "unreflective and unselfconscious," and a failure of constitutionalism, which may involve "a failure to employ basic principles within a regime." Brandon 1998, 18, 20. As applied to a "failure of constitutional

whether the government has majority support."[14] That a government enjoying such support may have come to power promising to fulfill a party manifesto committed to the construction of a Ram temple at the very site where the Babri Masjid mosque stood is a constitutional irrelevancy insofar as the provisions of President's Rule are concerned. "It would be a clear fraud on the Constitution to use [Article 356] for dismissing stable governments with large popular mandates."[15]

The Court's rejection of this logic has ramifications that extend well beyond the particulars of the immediate case, suggesting at least that the official neutrality of the law on matters of great public import is not a constitutional obligation, perhaps even that elected officials *must* be correct about certain things. For example, the Indian government's white paper on Ayodhya had drawn attention to the role of campaign rhetoric in the destruction of the mosque. "The BJP in its [1991] campaign concentrated on the issue of construction of a Ram temple at Ayodhya at the disputed site."[16] Several justices emphasized this concentration in their opinions. Justice V. Ramaswamy wrote that "It is . . . a mandatory duty of every political party, body of individuals or association and its members to abide by the Constitution and the laws."[17] He and his brethren seemed to accept the government's claim that elected officials who had embraced manifestos that were antisecular could not be trusted to follow the secular commitment of the Constitution. Justice Sawant concluded that "Any profession and action that go counter to [secularism] are a *prima facie* proof of the conduct in defiance of the provisions of the Constitution."[18] Justice Reddy insisted, "[I]t is clear that if any party or organisation seeks to fight the elections on the basis of a plank which has the proximate effect of eroding the secular philosophy of the Constitution it would certainly be guilty of following an unconstitutional course of action."[19] In short, the Supreme Court's reaction to the Ayodhya debacle and the government dismissals that followed was framed within an explicitly articulated commitment to the protection of certain substantive principles against assaults—in speech as well as deed—that threatened to undermine their privileged status within the constitutional order. Apart from

---

machinery" in India, the distinction mirrors the dichotomy between those who would require a collapse of public order as a prerequisite for invoking Article 356 and those who would define failure more broadly so as to encompass a serious departure from the substantive principles that are constitutive of the regime.

[14] Interview with Subhash Kashyap, December 5, 1998.

[15] Kashyap 1993, 37.

[16] Government of India 1993, 16.

[17] *Bommai* at 172.

[18] Ibid. at 148.

[19] Ibid. at 821.

the Court's own powers of judicial review, the authority to enforce this commitment was grounded in Article 356, a provision with historic links to an unlikely source of inspiration—the American Constitution.

FEDERALISM AND REPUBLICANISM

For a whole host of reasons, the American Constitution has severe limitations as a resource for legitimating constitutional arguments in India, but in *Bommai* it came in handy. The widely renowned American solicitude for local authority was carefully noted as a predicate for observing that even the framers of the United States Constitution had provided for a safeguard against a "failure of constitutional machinery" in the states. Justice Sawant pointed out that Article 356 "was based on Article 4, Section 4 of the American document," and that "Article 356, like [the American clause], is not inconsistent with the Federal principle."[20] In the course of his argument, he also referenced Dr. Ambedkar, who, at a critical moment at the Constituent Assembly, had cited the American Guaranty Clause as a weighty precedent against opposition to the proposed provision for President's Rule as an indefensible infringement on the democratic authority of provincial electors.

In the debate over (what eventually became) Article 356, Ambedkar had first to respond to the charge that the dismissal authority projected for the Central Government was unprecedented in the power it envisioned, that it was some sort of novel and dangerous experiment in constitutionalism.

> [I] would like to draw . . . attention to the article contained in the American Constitution, where the duty of the United States is definitely expressed to be to maintain the republican form of the Constitution. When we say that the Constitution must be maintained in accordance with the provisions contained in the Constitution we practically mean what the American Constitution means, namely that the form of the constitution prescribed in this Constitution must be maintained. Therefore, so far as that point is concerned we do not think that the Drafting Committee has made any departure from an established principle.[21]

[20] Ibid. at 114.

[21] Constituent Assembly Debates 1949, 175. The point was echoed by another important delegate and future Supreme Court Justice, Alladi Krishnaswami Ayyar. "Such a provision is by no means a novel provision. Even in the typical federal constitution of the United States, where sovereignty is recognised more than in any other federation, you will find a provision therein to the effect that it is the duty of Union as the Central Government to see that the State is protected both as against domestic violence and external aggression. In putting in that Article, we are merely following the example of the classical or model federation of America." Ibid., 150.

Novelty aside, a more serious objection to the granting of a dismissal power to the Central Government was grounded in the fear that it would be implemented for inappropriate and insubstantial reasons. "I can understand," said one delegate, "drastic power being given when the existence of the State is threatened. But I do not like extraordinary power being given for a mere constitutional failure or a constitutional evil."[22] Another echoed these remarks by predicting that the legitimate interest of the Center in the maintenance of law and order in the states would be compromised by the temptation to interfere in the perceived maladministration of local affairs. "They will intervene not merely to protect provinces against external aggression and internal disturbances but also to ensure good Government within their limits. In other words, the Central Government will have the power to intervene to protect the electors against themselves."[23]

Phrased in this way, the objections to the language in the proposed article raise important philosophical concerns that transcend the more obvious, as well as historically understandable, sensitivity of Indians to the oppressive possibilities embedded in concentrated authority. They reveal that long before Ayodhya and the political ascendancy of the Hindu right, worries about the potential abuses of Article 356 powers were being expressed in the rhetoric of democratic aspirations. Thus the people, not distant elected officials, were to be the *guarantors* of good government, and it was for them to determine when and whether the conduct of public affairs by their chosen representatives required repudiation. Unless the "failure of constitutional machinery" possessed a purely procedural meaning, then, according to this view, a regime of President's Rule will by definition be an undemocratic regime. The worries voiced at the Constituent Assembly indicate that the delegates opposed to the language of Article 356 were fearful that "the provisions of the Constitution" would in fact be construed to have a more substantive meaning, thus possibly justifying Union of India intervention if a state were to be found in violation of the Center's broadly based understanding of constitutional obligation. And of course they were right.

Vindication of their position by the Supreme Court in *Bommai* was an occasion for little solace to those who had inherited these delegates' philosophical stance on the sanctity of majoritarian rule. "If democracy leads you in one direction and secularism in another, democracy should take precedence."[24] As we shall see, at least some of the *Bommai* justices were inclined to comprehend democracy and secularism as conceptually

[22] Statement by B. M. Gupte, ibid., 152.

[23] Statement by Pandit Hirday Nath Kunzru, ibid., 155.

[24] Subhash Kashyap, interview with the author, December 5, 1998.

intertwined, in effect rejecting a fundamentally process-based definition of "the provisions of this Constitution." Their critics, who thought it "a clear fraud on the Constitution to use this provision for dismissing stable governments with large popular mandates,"[25] bear an interesting resemblance to certain Americans in the nineteenth century who also cast their lot with the principle of democratic decision-making at the state level.

These Americans, like their Indian counterparts today, were engaged in a struggle over the meaning of membership in the civic community. In seeking to defend the states' exclusive control of slavery, they were determined to resist any move by the national government to undermine the authority of local officials. As William Wiecek has ably chronicled, one of the more absorbing issues of constitutional confrontation surrounding the slavery issue had to do with the meaning of the republican Guaranty Clause. On one side were the antislavery advocates, who saw in Article IV's promise of republicanism an opportunity to impose upon the slaveholding states the national government's understanding of political freedom and human dignity. Nothing was clearer to them than the incompatibility of slavery with the principles of the Declaration of Independence, principles that formed the core and essence of republican government. To the extent that the Constitution incorporated these principles (which all but the most radical abolitionists believed to be the case), then the duty of the federal government was clear—enforce the *guarantee* of republicanism on those states not acting (in the words of the Indian document) "in accordance with the provisions of the Constitution."

The other side insisted, much in the vein of the *Bommai* detractors, that the only provisions of the Constitution that were of any relevance to this issue were those that guaranteed self-government for the states free of federal interference. As Wiecek explains, the southern view was that "a republican form of government is one in which the people govern themselves, in the limited sense that some part of the State's residents exercise some choice in deciding who the elective officials of government shall be."[26] For John C. Calhoun this meant that "[T]he President would be obliged to support any extant legitimate regime."[27] There was, he wrote, no doubt that "the protection of the *Government* of the State is the object" of the constitutional provision.[28] "[T]hat the Federal Govern-

---

[25] Kashyap 1993, 37.

[26] Wiecek 1972, 149.

[27] Ibid., 135.

[28] Cralle 1855, vol. 6, 214. In recent years, protection of the states against interference by the federal government has moved to center stage in the agenda and priorities of the Supreme Court. Advocates of the states' rights position have pursued, with varying degrees of success, different constitutional strategies, with the Tenth and Eleventh Amendments providing them the most traction. But the Guaranty Clause has been given new life as well.

ment, in determining whether the Government of a State be, or be not republican, within the meaning of the Constitution, has no right whatsoever, in any case, to look beyond its admission into the Union."[29] Thus, in similar fashion to the Indian claims made a century and a half later, guarantees of republicanism that were contingent upon the enforcement of norms of right conduct from the political center were in essence a contradiction in terms. In Calhoun's words, "Give to the Federal Government the right to establish its own abstract standard of what constitutes a republican form of government, and to bring the Governments of the States, without restrictions on its discretion, to the test of this standard, in order to determine whether they be of a republican form or not, and it would be made the absolute master of the States. A standard more uncertain, or a greater or more dangerous power, could not be conceived."[30]

One scholar, for example, echoes Calhoun in affirming that "[T]he states cannot enjoy republican governments unless they retain sufficient autonomy to establish and maintain their own forms of government. The guarantee clause, therefore, implies a modest restraint on federal power to interfere with state autonomy." Merritt 1988, 2. For Merritt, the Clause "provides a more definite limit on national power than the ambiguous language of the tenth amendment." Ibid., 36. Those considering this effort to revive the Guaranty Clause might wish to ponder Wiecek's cautionary remarks: "If the clause is revived, it could possibly develop in a reactionary way, as a means of repressing any challenge to the *status quo* of state authority, no matter how outrageously anti-republican that *status quo* might be." Wiecek 1972, 293.

[29] Ibid., 219. Calhoun also responded to the problem of what should happen if the people themselves, acting according to constitutional and legal forms, subverted the republican form of government. "Against this danger, there is, and can be no guarantee. The reason requires but little explanation. The States themselves are parties to the guarantee; and it would be absurd to suppose that they undertook to enter into a guarantee against themselves." Ibid., 216. Ironically, this argument, which is premised on the political representation of the States in the national legislature, figured prominently (although without mention of Calhoun) in the Supreme Court's consideration of the powers of the federal government under the Commerce Clause. In *Garcia v San Antonio Metropolitan Transit Authority,* Justice Harry Blackmun defended an interventionist role for the Central Government with a similar argument to the one made by Calhoun in defense of the states. "[T]he Framers chose to rely on a federal system in which special restraints on federal power over the States inhered principally in the workings of the National Government itself, rather than in discrete limitations on the objects of federal authority. State sovereign interests, then, are more properly protected by procedural safeguards inherent in the structure of the federal system than by judicially created limitations on federal power." *Garcia* at 552. An argument like this was also voiced in the Constituent Assembly of India in the debate over Article 356 powers. K. Santhaman, a delegate supportive of granting dismissal power to the Center, said, "It must not be forgotten that in the Central Parliament the representatives of the State whose Government is to be superseded, will be here. . . . Therefore, it is not an infringement of the principles of democracy that these articles can be objected to." Constituent Assembly Debates, 153.

[30] Cralle 1855, vol. 6, 221.

On this assessment, at least, there was agreement on the other side, as was made clear by Charles Sumner, the leader for many years in Congress of its radical abolitionist faction. "There is no clause which gives to Congress such supreme power as [the republican guarantee] clause."[31] Thus while southern interests both before and after the Civil War wished to constrain interpretation of the Clause to meanings of self-government connected to explicit and specific constitutional language, antislavery forces were determined to pursue a more expansive and less textually confined goal of republicanism. It had been generally agreed in 1787 that the term *republicanism* possessed negative connotations, as in *nonmonarchical* and *nonaristocratic*; but the ambiguity of the word, as well as uncertainty over what it would take to guarantee it, ensured, as John Adams correctly predicted, "that successive predominant factions will put glosses and constructions upon it as different as light and darkness."[32] Slavery may have enjoyed a measure of constitutional protection by the original terms of the document, but it was inevitable that a "slave aristocracy" would eventually be held to be in violation of the original meaning of Article IV, Section 4. And if self-government—the antithesis of monarchy—was indeed the standard implicit in that Clause's constitutional requirements, then it is hardly surprising that very little time would elapse before the trafficking in and holding of human property—in other words the denial of *self*-government—would be seen as a massive repudiation of the spirit of the fundamental law.

Sumner repeatedly invoked this spirit to press for unlimited federal control over the defeated states of the Confederacy—in effect for a regime of President's Rule. Indeed Lincoln, much more moderate than the senator from Massachusetts, also cited the Guaranty Clause to justify the substitution of Union rule in the South. To Governor Andrew Johnson he wrote: "[Y]ou are hereby authorized to exercise such powers as may be necessary and proper to enable the loyal people of Tennessee to present a republican form of State government as will entitle the State to the guaranty of the United States therefor, and to be protected under such State government by the United States against invasion and violence, all according to the fourth section of the fourth article of the Constitution of the United States."[33] As it turned out, precisely because they were *defeated* states,

---

[31] Quoted in Wiecek 1972, 214.

[32] Quoted in Ibid., 72.

[33] Quoted in Randall 1963, 235. In India, Article 356 can only be invoked after the president receives a report from the governor of the state in question. Lincoln's statement was issued along the same lines, as it was sent in response to Governor Johnson's telegram to the president reminding him of the constitutional obligation of the United States to guarantee the states a republican form of government.

the Guaranty Clause was held not to apply, the Supreme Court ruling in *Coleman v Tennessee*[34] that the theory of conquest under international law, rather than Article IV, was the appropriate legal foundation for the exercise of federal power in occupied territory. So while the Guaranty Clause was one of the more intensely debated issues in the politics of Reconstruction, we do not have any instance, as an Indian scholar of President's Rule has noted, where "the American Government has suspended or interfered in a State Government on the ground that the latter had failed to perform its constitutional obligation."[35]

That we now have such a precedent in Indian law is attributable to several factors that distinguish the two constitutional systems, not the least of which is, as several justices pointed out in *Bommai,* that federalism in India was deliberately constructed to privilege the Center to a significantly greater degree than in the United States. Among those privileged prerogatives of the Center is what Calhoun so feared in the United States, but which has never been realized through the Guaranty Clause—"the right to establish its own abstract standard of what constitutes a republican form of government," or as the Indian Preamble puts it, "a sovereign democratic republic." Thus the government of a state that enjoys majority support in the assembly and "act[s] within the constitutional forms," but "flouts . . . constitutional principles [such as secularism]," may nevertheless be dismissed by the Union Government in order to remedy "a case of failure of the constitutional machinery."[36] What explains the triumph of Sumner over Calhoun in India? And what significance might this interpretive choice have for the constitutional status of secularism in India?

THE BROODING OMNIPRESENCE OF BASIC STRUCTURE

Article 139 of the Italian Constitution mandates that "The republican form of the State cannot be the subject of constitutional amendment." Article 112 of the Norwegian Constitution proscribes amendments that "contradict the principles embodied in this Constitution." They are among a minority of constitutions that provide explicit answers to the theoretically vexing conundrum of whether there can be such a thing as an unconstitutional constitutional amendment. Where such textual provision is absent (for example, in the United States and India), constitutional theorists spend time debating whether there are (and must be) implicit limits on the amending process.[37] In an interesting role reversal, American

---

[34] 97 U.S. 509 (1863).

[35] Harbir Singh Kathuria 1990, 6.

[36] *Bommai* at 189.

[37] See, for example, the collection of essays in Levinson 1995.

advocates of such limits enjoy the same rhetorical advantage as the Indian delegates at the Constituent Assembly who supported Article 356 powers: They can deflect the charge of novelty by pointing to foreign experience—of Indian constitutional development.

The Supreme Court's decision in *Bommai* should be viewed in the context of this development. Thus the Court's controversial affirmation of principle-based state dismissals is directly related to the politics of constitutional entrenchment. "There are certain *basic features* of the Constitution of India, which cannot be altered in exercise of the power to amend it, under Article 368 [India's version of Article V of the American Constitution]. If, therefore, a Constitution Amendment Act seeks to alter the basic structure or framework of the Constitution, the Court would be entitled to annul it on the ground of *ultra vires*, because the word 'amend', in Article 368, means only changes other than altering the very structure of the Constitution, which would be tantamount to making a new Constitution."[38] This summary encapsulates the essence of the Indian Supreme Court's ruling in the landmark case of *Kesavananda v State of Kerala*.[39] That decision modified an earlier ruling, *Golak Nath v State of Punjab*,[40] in which the Court had ruled that fundamental rights cannot be amended under Article 368. It chose in *Kesavananda* to affirm the existence of implicit limits on the power of amendment while providing a less textually based list of things that were protected from the amendment process.[41] Subsequent cases have added to the list of "basic features" that may not be amended out of existence. They now include such general features as the supremacy of the Constitution, the rule of law, the principle of separation of powers, judicial review, freedom and dignity of the individual, unity and integrity of the nation, the principle of free and fair elections, federalism, and secularism.

[38] Basu 1998, 153.

[39] A 1973 SC 1461 (F,B).

[40] A 1967 SC 1643. The Court's holding in *Golak Nath* that the fundamental rights provided for in Part 3 of the Constitution could not be amended by Parliament provoked that body to pass the Twenty-Fourth Amendment, which overrode the Court's decision by allowing for the parliamentary amendment of fundamental rights. *Kesavananda* upheld that amendment.

[41] The Indian constitutional scholar Upendra Baxi has written that "[T]he assertion of judicial review over the amendatory power is a remarkable feat of judicial activism, unparalleled in the history of world constitutional adjudication." Baxi 1985, 65. This assessment stems from his observation that "The Indian Supreme Court is probably the only court in the history of humankind to have asserted the power of judicial review over amendments to the constitution." Ibid., 64. That sounds like an exaggeration; for example, the German Court has asserted the same power. But given the length of the inferential leap necessary to establish the power as emanating from the text of the Constitution, Baxi's claim makes considerable sense.

Needless to say, a list of this sort lacks precision, which means that the Supreme Court has in effect deployed itself as official arbiter of what is textually changeable in matters constitutional. However tempting the role, the burden this places on the justices of the Court has not passed their notice; indeed temptation and doubt coexist for them in jurisprudential tension. For example, in the politically charged case of *Indira Gandhi v Raj Narain*, a justice who had voted against the "basic structure" doctrine joined a Court majority in striking down a constitutional amendment while declaring in the process: "The concept of a basic structure as brooding omnipresence in the sky apart from the specific provisions of the Constitution constituting it is too vague and indefinite to provide a yardstick to determine the validity of an ordinary law."[42] A colleague of his, who had also voted against the doctrine, aligned himself with both this sentiment and the accompanying disposition, opining that "The theory of basic structures is an exercise in imponderables. Basic structures or basic features are indefinable."[43] Nevertheless, the willingness of these justices to enforce the basic structure doctrine reminds one of what Justice Potter Stewart, with a mixture of frustration and resignation, famously said in connection with the American Supreme Court's belabored efforts to define obscenity: "I shall not . . . attempt . . . to define [it]. . . . But I know it when I see it."[44]

Arguably this type of enforcement is not strictly speaking a limit on the Parliament's power to amend the Constitution. "[T]he power thus conceded [to Parliament] is the power to make changes *in*, and not *of*, the Constitution of India."[45] As Walter Murphy has contended, an amendment, rightly construed (that is, following the Latin *emendere*), leads to correction or improvement, not reconstitution. "Thus changes that would make a polity into another kind of political system would not be amendments at all, but revisions or transformations."[46] These changes would

---

[42] Justice Mathew in *Indira Gandhi v Raj Narain*. Justice Mathew's thoughts about invoking the "spirit" of the Constitution are worth pondering in light of the interpretive stance taken by Sumner and others in the application of the Guaranty Clause to the issue of slavery. "The doctrine of the 'spirit' of the Constitution is a slippery slope. The courts are not at liberty to declare an act void, because, in their opinion, it is opposed to the spirit of democracy or republicanism supposed to pervade the Constitution but not expressed in words." Ibid., 2387. In his argument to the Court in *Bommai*, Ram Jethmalani, underscoring his claim that secularism was too vague a concept to trigger the invocation of President's Rule, "pointed out that the machinery of the Constitution does not refer to some spirit underlying the Constitution." Interview with the author, New Delhi, February 26, 1999.

[43] Justice Ray in *Indira Gandhi* at 2332.

[44] *Jacobellis* 1964.

[45] Baxi 1985, 65.

[46] Murphy 1995, 177. Murphy's argument follows the reasoning of earlier thinkers, most notably the nineteenth-century constitutional commentator Thomas M. Cooley. See his

entail the rejection and abandonment of regime-defining principles; therefore, when appropriately exercised, a court's decision to invalidate a legislature's actions under its vested authority to amend the document, in this understanding, nullifies a fraudulent effort to reconstitute the political order. Thus, for example, in *Bommai*: "The fact that a party may be entitled to go to people seeking a mandate for a drastic amendment of the Constitution or its replacement by another Constitution is wholly irrelevant. . . . We do not know how the Constitution can be amended so as to remove secularism from the basic structure of the Constitution. Nor do we know how the present Constitution can be replaced by another; it is enough for us to know that the Constitution does not provide for such a course—that it does not provide for its own demise."[47]

Murphy's claim with respect to implicit limits on the amending power is comparable to Sumner's position on the Guaranty Clause. "One might logically infer that, insofar as American tradition implants the nation's founding document, the Declaration of Independence, into the larger Constitution, natural rights impose binding standards on public officials."[48] Much as the natural rights principles of the Declaration provide the judiciary guidelines for limiting the amending process, so too do they establish for the elected branches of the national government republican standards by which to enforce Article IV, Section 4. "[O]fficials who take seriously their oath to support [the Constitution] are bound to try to give those norms practical effect."[49] Indeed, to the degree that such norms are recognized as legitimate for judging the validity of formal constitutional changes, their invocation by electorally accountable public servants in the execution of their assigned constitutional responsibilities logically follows. Thus officers of the United States are the agents of Article IV's guarantee, and to comply with their oath to uphold the Constitution, they must work toward the establishment in practice of, as Lincoln put it, that "standard maxim for a free society" enunciated in the Declaration of Independence.

For Lincoln, as for Murphy and some other contemporary constitutional theorists, this notion, that in the Constitution's hierarchy of values "substantive goals take precedence over process,"[50] negates the conven-

---

"The Power to Amend the Federal Constitution" 1893. Opposition to these views has been forcefully presented by John R. Vile, who argues that "To empower the courts not simply to review the procedures whereby amendments were adopted but also to void amendments on the basis of their substantive content would surely threaten the notion of a government founded on the consent of the governed." Vile 1995, 198.

[47] *Bommai* at 237.

[48] Murphy 1995, 180.

[49] Ibid., 181.

[50] Murphy 1978, 155. In Lincoln's case, the ordering of substance over process is best revealed in his opposition to the Kansas-Nebraska Act, which had achieved what the *Dred*

tional wisdom that the Supreme Court exercises a monopoly over constitutional interpretation. Lincoln, citing (with only partial accuracy) the examples of Presidents Jefferson and Jackson, had made it clear that "If I were in Congress, and a vote should come up on a question of whether slavery should be prohibited in a new territory, in spite of the *Dred Scott* decision, I would vote that it should."[51] His denial to the Court of an unqualified finality on constitutional questions was strenuously attacked in the debates with Stephen Douglas, but for the same reason that Sumner (and later Lincoln himself) used to invoke the Guaranty Clause in the struggle over the fundamental meaning of the Constitution, Lincoln continued to insist that legal interpretations must always remain open to political challenge. In both instances, the provisions of the Constitution incorporated an aspirational content that was accessible not only to judges but to other public officials whose first obligation was to advance the cause of the principles that defined this content.

Lincoln's views on interpretive finality were given new life with the adoption of the Civil War amendments and the enforcement provisions included therein. But as recently as 1997, the Supreme Court, in ruling on Congress's power under these provisions, voiced a deeply rooted skepticism over sharing its interpretive responsibility in constitutional matters.[52] However unpopular the particular decision (nullifying Congress's overturning of a free exercise of religion decision), the Court could doubtless perceive its judgment on institutional prerogative as fundamentally consistent with a longstanding legal and popular sensibility that had never been comfortably reconciled to the Lincolnian position. That sensibility, which is less sure than Murphy about the substance/process ordering in his constitutional hierarchy of values, nourishes a tendency to equate judicial review with judicial finality, and a proclivity for discouraging the invalidation of an elected government for noncompliance with substantive principles of republicanism. And it is likely to lead a Court to look with disfavor upon the concept of an unconstitutional amendment.

Scott decision later gratuitously accomplished—the repeal of the Missouri Compromise prohibiting slavery in the territories. The Act's theoretical rationale—the people should decide important questions directly through the political process—was condemned by Lincoln, whose opposition to the measure was grounded in purely substantive considerations, namely that slavery was irreconcilable with the liberty that the Constitution, following the Declaration, was bound to protect. As Harry V. Jaffa has observed, "Free government, according to Lincoln, was not the mere *process* of arriving at decisions without coercion by any formula embodying the principle of majority rule. . . . It was government of, by, and for a people dedicated to a certain proposition." Jaffa 1959, 348.

[51] Lincoln 1953, vol. 2, 495.

[52] *Boerne* 1997.

Of course, sensibility is all a matter of degree, not bright lines, as illustrated, for example, by the doctrine of nonjusticiability. Indeed, the "political question" doctrine has a historic association with the Guaranty Clause,[53] and one can readily imagine a Court sidestepping an effort by the national government to guarantee republicanism in a state by removing its elected government. More difficult to imagine, and ultimately more revealing in comparative terms, is the initiation of such an effort by the political branches, although Article IV, Section 4's, role as "a sleeping giant" in the constitutional scheme cautions against entirely foreclosing such a possibility.[54] Similarly, while the Court has never intimated that it possesses either the will or the power to declare a procedurally correct constitutional amendment invalid on substantive grounds, one could imagine a change emerging from the machinery of Article V so monstrous that a majority would feel that it had no choice but to strike it down. As for the maintenance by the Court of its exclusive authority to interpret the Constitution, there have already been instances where that exclusivity has been breached in practice even as the Court has insisted that its special prerogative remained unqualified.

So while the contrast between the American and Indian approaches in these matters should not be too sharply drawn, we should also recognize the alternative set of presumptions that operate within the two systems. The Indian Supreme Court has not abandoned its right to review implementations of President's Rule,[55] but in linking "basic structure" limitations on the amending process with Article 356 responses to failures of constitutional machinery in the states, it has cast the Central Government as a proactive player in the explication and enforcement of the constitutional essentials of the Indian republic.[56] Hence the insistence from the Court that "the manifesto of a political party should be consistent with

[53] *Luther v Borden*, 48 U.S. 1 (1849).

[54] "Sleeping giant" is what Charles Sumner called the Guaranty Clause in 1867. Wiecek 1972, 2.

[55] The judges in *Bommai* were in broad agreement that the President's Proclamation was justiciable; however, they reached varying conclusions on the extent of the justiciability. The key precedent on the question of justiciability and the exercise of power under Article 356 is *State of Rajasthan v Union of India*. That case, involving the dissolution of the state government in Rajasthan after national elections had returned members politically different from those in the state, is notable for its sweeping assertion of nonjusticiability in regard to declarations of President's Rule. However, the Court was careful to distinguish its assertion from other possible "basic structure" situations that might require judicial oversight.

[56] The matter of *essential* is important. As pointed out by Justice Reddy in *Bommai*, "[E]ach and every breach and infraction of [a] constitutional provision, irrespective of its significance, extent, and effect, cannot be treated as constituting failure of constitutional machinery." *Bommai* at 228.

... fundamental and basic features of the Constitution—secularism, socio-economic and political justice, fraternity, unity and national integrity."[57] The underlying sentiment here differs from that which led Justice Oliver Wendell Holmes Jr. to write of the Manifesto of the American Socialist Party: "It is said that this manifesto was more than a theory, that it was an incitement. Every idea is an incitement. . . . If in the long run the beliefs expressed in proletarian dictatorship are destined to be accepted by the dominant forces of the community, the only meaning of free speech is that they should be given their chance and have their way."[58]

Though Holmes's view was written in dissent, his philosophical commitments have largely prevailed in American jurisprudence, embedded today, for example, in the Supreme Court's requirement of "content neutrality" in First Amendment cases. The same animating assumption incorporated in this doctrinal orthodoxy—that a liberal society cannot tolerate the endorsement of an official or public philosophy—is to be found in conventional wisdom about entrenchment, the Guaranty Clause, and judicial finality.[59] Thus the person who believes that an unconstitutional

---

[57] Ibid. at 172.

[58] *Gitlow* 1925. In Israel, party manifestos are subject to substantial scrutiny. The Central Elections Committee has the authority, affirmed on several occasions by the Supreme Court, to exclude from the electoral process parties that deny the "existence of the State of Israel as the State of the Jewish people" or that deny the "basic foundations of the democratic regime in Israel." The legal situation in Israel pertaining to these matters reflects the *visionary* model sketched in chapters 2 and 3. In the early landmark free speech case, *Kol ha'am Co. Ltd. v Minister of Interior*, Justice Shimon Agranat wrote that "[I]nsofar as it [the Declaration of Independence] 'expresses the vision of the people and its faith,' we are bound to pay attention to the matters set forth in it when we come to interpret and give meaning to the laws of the State." *Kol ha'am* at 884. Agranat was a liberal jurist born and educated in the United States, and an admirer of Holmes. But unlike Holmes, his deference to the "dominant forces of the community" was in principle limited by the founding commitment to the vision of the polity as Jewish and democratic. As we shall see, reconciling this dual vision has been, to say the least, a formidable task.

[59] A contrast between Holmes and Lincoln is worth pondering. Holmes wrote in his famous *Abrams* dissent that "the best test of truth is the power of the thought to get itself accepted in the competition of the market." *Abrams* at 630. Inasmuch as the Constitution is not concerned with substantive goals, and judges are not to seek enforcement of fundamental values, this marketplace approach is the only reasonable one consistent with these assumptions. Said Lincoln in response to the charge that the Republican Party was a sectional party: "[I]t may be true that in some places we may not be able to proclaim a doctrine as clearly true as the truth of democracy, because there is a section so directly opposed to it that they will not tolerate us in doing so. Is it the true test of the soundness of a doctrine, that in some places people won't let you proclaim it? . . . Is that the way to test the truth of any doctrine?" Lincoln 1953, vol. 3, 222–3. Unlike Holmes, Lincoln's commitment to principles of natural right meant that he could be both liberal and intolerant, defining as subversive those ideas that are repugnant to the moral consensus necessary to support a liberal polity.

constitutional amendment is a contradiction in terms, that republicanism is too indefinite a concept to enforce via Article IV, and that the Constitution is what the Supreme Court says it is, is likely today to adhere to a set of jurisprudential precepts fundamentally opposed to the idea of a State-supported public philosophy. What Holmes had to say about the common law—that it is not "a brooding omnipresence in the sky but the articulate voice of some sovereign or quasi-sovereign that can be identified"[60]—applies with equal force to constitutional theorizing. The liberal constitutionalism that is presupposed by this positivist emphasis is much more congenial to process than to substance; accordingly, deference must be extended to the amendments that emerge from the procedures of Article V, the governments that are elected by popular voting in the states, and the decisions that are produced by majorities on the Supreme Court. That such outcomes would be deemed illegitimate on the basis of principles not explicitly specified by the text of the Constitution exemplifies a perspective incompatible with the requirements of neutrality associated with the liberal State.

This is the perspective that was vigorously argued in *Bommai* by counsel for the three dismissed governments. The Union Government could not take action under Article 356 on the basis of a vague concept such as secularism without rendering the Constitution a tool of nakedly partisan interests. Given the highly charged political climate in which the case was decided, there was little chance that the Supreme Court's rejection of this argument would not be seen as a blatantly partisan act. But it could also be seen as a recognition by the Court of the *omnipresence* of religion—not as a brooding presence in the sky, but as a constitutive reality that determines the shape and meaning of secularism as a basic feature of the Indian Constitution.

A SECULAR STATE: THE BASICS

After a detailed account of the sequence of events that culminated in the dismantling of the Babri Masjid mosque in Ayodhya, Justice Sawant concluded: "The destruction of [the] mosque was a concrete proof of the creed which the party in question [the BJP] wanted to pursue. In such circumstances, the Ministries formed by the said party could not be trusted to follow the objective of secularism which was part of the basic structure of the Constitution and also the soul of the Constitution."[61] By placing secularism under the rubric of *basic structure*, the Court established, following *Kesavananda*, a constitutional rationale for the govern-

---

[60] *Southern Pacific Co.* at 222.
[61] *Bommai* at 143.

ment's invocation of Article 356, and by suggesting that more than structural considerations were involved, the justices indicated that their task in *Bommai* was to define, or at least illuminate, the core of Indian constitutionalism. Thus there were features of the Constitution, such as federalism and judicial review, that were held to be so critical to *how* the system conducted its business that they required immunity against any effort to amend them out of existence. In the case of secularism, this immunity extended to constitutional commitments concerning *what* the system was all about. But precisely because this inquiry—how to understand the very soul of the polity—implicated issues falling along the deepest fault line in contemporary Indian politics, the Court's repudiation of the program of a major political party inevitably cast the judiciary as a partisan in a fiery and often ugly political debate.

However fair or unfair the casting, it raises an interesting question: How much of what the Court actually *said* in *Bommai* (as distinct from what it *did*) was contrary to the views on secularism espoused by the BJP and its allies in the *Sangh Parivar* (the coalition of Hindu nationalist groups)? As we have seen, leading theorists and proponents of the Hindu right, such as Arun Shourie, have repeatedly articulated positions on religion and politics that are often surprisingly consistent with liberal expectations regarding the appropriate configuration of Church/State relations in a constitutional democracy. It would be ironic if in the considerable space devoted in *Bommai* to the explication and elaboration of the Indian concept of secularism, the Court were to have said little that challenged the basic ideological assumptions of the perpetrators of the acts central to the case at hand. On the other hand, it would be quite helpful in advancing an understanding of the special character of Indian constitutional secularism to see if any of the Court's arguments highlighted relevant particularities. After all, to the extent that "Ayodhya was supposed to serve as a focus for a campaign to transform the very character of the Indian State,"[62] the dismissal of governments supportive of such a campaign might lead one to expect that a Court upholding these dismissals would undertake to defend the core principles of the beleaguered State.

In examining the arguments about secularism in the various *Bommai* opinions, common themes appear.[63] The dominant one is equal treatment

[62] Muralidharan 2000. In the same issue devoted to the Vishwa Hindu Parishad's (VHP) newly aggressive mobilization on the temple issue, Neera Chandhoke points out that "The 'liberation' of Ayodhya formed the dominant metaphor in a cluster of ideological formulations that challenged practically each one of the accepted themes that went under the heading of secularism—minority rights, freedom of religion, and equal citizenship." Chandhoke 2000.

[63] Justice Verma was the only justice who did not address the issue of secularism per se, a silence that will be taken up in chapter 7. His views, however, on the centrality of equal

of religions, often referred to in Indian tradition as *sarva dharma sambhava*. The justices cite eminent authorities to legitimate this principle, as, for example, in Justice A. M. Ahmadi's invocation of Nehru and Radhakrishnan, who are quoted respectively as saying: "I am convinced that the future government of free India must be secular in the sense that government will not associate itself directly with any religious faith but will give freedom to all religious functions."[64] And: "We hold that no one religion should be given preferential status, or unique distinction, that no one religion should be accorded special privileges . . . for that would be a violation of the basic principles of democracy."[65] In the same vein Justice Sawant emphasizes that "The State is enjoined to accord equal treatment to all religions and religious sects and denominations."[66] It is a theme echoed by Justice Reddy, who literally underlines the point by declaring that "*Secularism is . . . more than a passive attitude of religious tolerance. It is a positive concept of equal treatment of all religions.*"[67]

To the justices, the destruction of a Muslim mosque by a Hindu mob, which had been encouraged in the performance of its perfidy by the words (including the party manifesto) and deeds of government and party officials, was a clear violation of the equal treatment principle. However, apologists for Ayodhya were no less supportive of the principle, having either justified or rationalized the violence by the *kar sevaks* as the culmination of a long train of abuses (e.g., the capitulation on *Shah Bano* and the decision by the Central Government to implement the Mandal Report on reservations), that, through repeated acts of favoritism toward minorities, had compromised the aspiration for equality. As we have seen, the insistent refrain of Hindu nationalists (at least those in the BJP) was that they were the only authentic voice of secularism in India, that they were determined to expose as "pseudo-secularist" frauds those hypocritical opportunists who shamelessly practiced the politics of special or differential treatment. They believed the Supreme Court was tragically mistaken in its validation of President's Rule, but from their unique perspective little fault could be found in the guiding principles (as distinct from their application) that seemed to have driven the justices to their conclusion. Indeed,

---

treatment were made clear in the *Ayodhya Reference Case*, where he quoted extensively from several *Bommai* opinions, specifically the passages embracing the principle of equal treatment. In an interview with the author, Justice Verma made four related points: "(1) Our creed is *sarva dharma sambhava*; (2) the core value is that all religions are equal; (3) the State has no religion; (4) religion is a personal matter." Interview with Justice J. S. Verma, Ghaziabad, India, February 28, 1999.

[64] *Bommai* at 76.
[65] Ibid.
[66] Ibid. at 144.
[67] Ibid. at 233.

the Court's explicit rejection of counsel Jethmalani's strategic assertion of vagueness with reference to the concept of secularism was powerfully reinforced by the clarity with which the term had been repeatedly rendered in the past by Jethmalani's clients. And of course the irony was that this rendering bore a striking resemblance to the Court's consensus position on the meaning of secularism.[68]

But presented in this rather formal way, the equal treatment principle provides only limited insight into the underlying commitments of those who espoused it. One could, for example, imagine two judges voicing similar sentiments in the spirit of *sarva dharma sambhava* whose political and constitutional attachments were nevertheless quite divergent. The first might value the individualist ethos behind the guarantee of equality for its relationship to the formation of democratic majorities. That judge might adhere to this view out of a principled commitment to procedural liberalism or might recognize the utility of this position because it facilitates a desirable political objective, namely the subordination of minorities to majoritarian Hindu norms. The latter possibility does not match the anticommunal rhetoric of the several *Bommai* judges who discussed the concept of secularism in the context of the notorious party manifesto. That includes all the judges except Justice J. S. Verma, a subscriber to the precepts of *sarva dharma sambhava*, who nevertheless deemed the nonjusticiability of the Article 356 invocations such as to obviate any need to discuss either the merits of the case or the meaning of secularism.[69]

The second judge might apprehend the significance of the equal treatment principle differently. For this judge the essence of the Indian polity's commitment to secularism is, to be sure, embedded in the concept of

---

[68] Consider, for example, Arun Shourie's prescription for secularism: (1) The individual should be the unit for policies and laws of the State, and not the religion or caste to which he or she belongs or the region in which he or she lives; (2) nothing should be conceded to a religious-based group or organization that is denied or not available to a secular group or organization; (3) nothing should be conceded to a group or organization of one religion that is denied or not made available to groups or organizations of other religions. Shourie 1997a, ix. It is difficult to see how the judges in *Bommai* could find much, if anything, to disagree with in this list. Or, as Shourie writes in concluding several of his chapters: "What is the secular argument against these secular proposals?"

[69] Justice Verma's brief opinion is written for the purpose of drawing a line between himself and his brethren on the question of justiciability. Thus he argues for the narrowest understanding of justiciability in regard to the legal issues raised by the actions of the Central Government. "[O]nly cases which permit application of totally objective standards for deciding whether the constitutional machinery has failed, are amenable to judicial review and the remaining cases wherein there is any subjective satisfaction dependent on some imponderables or inferences are not justiciable because there are no judicially manageable standards for resolving that controversy; and those cases are subject only to political scrutiny and correction for whatever its value in the existing political scenario. This appears to be the constitutional scheme." *Bommai* at 85.

equality, but that commitment is meaningful only if equality is in turn situated within the context of the Constitution's broader objectives. In *Bommai*, Justice Reddy was one of the judges (along with Justice Rama-swamy) who endeavored to articulate this alternative understanding, try-ing in effect to loosen the principle of equal treatment from its comfort-able moorings in procedural justice. In this effort he found the views of Justice Gajendragadkar especially helpful.

> It is true that the Indian Constitution does not use the word *secularism* in any of its provisions, but its material provisions are inspired by the concept of secularism. When it promised all the citizens of India that the aim of the Constitution is to establish socio-economic justice, it placed before the coun-try as a whole, the ideal of a welfare State. And the concept of welfare is purely secular and not based on any consideration of religion. The essential basis of the Indian Constitution is that all citizens are equal, and this basic equality obviously proclaims that the religion of a citizen is entirely irrelevant in the matter of his fundamental rights. The State does not owe loyalty to any particular religion as such; it is not religious or anti-religious; it gives equal freedom for all religions and holds that the religion of the citizen has nothing to do in the matter of socio-economic problems. That is the essential characteristic of secularism which is writ large in all the provisions of the Indian Constitution.[70]

Specifically in response to Jethmalani's insistence in his argument be-fore the Court that secularism is a "vacuous word" and a "phantom con-cept," Reddy responds that it was "imperative in the Indian context" to "create a State secular in its outlook and egalitarian in its action."[71] To be sure, it is quite easy to conceptualize secularism and egalitarianism as distinct priorities (as some of the justices did),[72] but Reddy and Gajendra-gadkar emphasize the connection between the two. For them the "ideal of a welfare state" is not, in the narrow sense, a political choice; rather it is a constitutional obligation that has important interpretive conse-quences.[73] The promise of socioeconomic justice is explicitly laid out in Part IV of the Constitution—the Directive Principles of State Policy. These

---

[70] Ibid. at 234.

[71] Ibid. at 235.

[72] For example, in interviews with the author, Justices Sawant and Verma confirmed that their understanding of secularism stands separate from the egalitarian political aspiration.

[73] As Upendra Baxi has argued: "There is substantial difference between ideologies writ-ten into constitutions and ideologies proclaimed outside the constitutions. . . . The ideology written into the Constitution of India through the Directive Principles are a part of the Constitution. . . . The Directives furnish a technology of construction of statutes and consti-tution. . . . And any change or repeal of directive principles will invite invalidation on the test of essential features of the basic structure." Baxi 1985, 92.

principles, essentially an outline of moral precepts for the achievement of a welfare state, are not judicially enforceable, but, as Article 37 in this Part reads, "[T]he principles therein laid down are nevertheless fundamental in the governance of the country and it shall be the duty of the State to apply these principles in making laws." The sanction behind them is political; thus, as Dr. Ambedkar said at the Constituent Assembly, "[I]f any Government ignores them, they will certainly have to answer for them before the *electorate* at the election time."[74]

In retrospect Ambedkar's certainty may not have been justified, but in the context of the post-Ayodhya government dismissals, the political significance of Part IV's constitutional commitment deserves particular attention. By outlining a principled basis for constitutional interpretation, it provides the political branches additional support for using their Article 356 mandate to "ensure that the government of every State is carried on in accordance with the provisions of this Constitution." This is implicit in Justice Ramaswamy's observation that "Secularism . . . is part of the fundamental law and basic structure of the Indian political system to secure to all its people socio-economic needs essential for man's excellence with material and moral prosperity and political justice."[75] From this it would appear that the government is being invited to *act* in furtherance of the basic features of the Constitution, not simply to refrain from acting in situations where fundamental rights have been threatened or violated. When one reflects on the different experiences that Indians and Americans have had under their respective guarantee provisions, this invitation is illuminating. Perhaps the spare history of Article IV, Section 4, usage is a reflection, in part, of the fact that the political branches of the national government are not, as they are in India, constitutionally *directed* to pursue particular social and political ends. Consequently, in the United States any move to enforce the mandate of republicanism would very likely encounter a resistance born of specific expectations about the role of these institutions as passive, not proactive, implementers of constitutional policy goals.[76]

[74] Basu 1998, 142.

[75] *Bommai* at 170.

[76] Consider here the comments of an analyst of Indian and American federalism. "Unlike the classical federations of America and Switzerland, federalism in India has taken shape in the era of the positive state in which the financial and administrative resources of the entire nation have to be harnessed to the task of relieving economic development for general welfare. This is particularly true in India which must take great strides in order to leave behind the colonial legacy of poverty and backwardness." Kathuria 1990, 14. What needs to be added is that this unfortunate legacy has been intimately connected to religious practices, such that the purview of the positive State must encompass these practices as the govern-

It also clarifies a term that is favored by Justice Ramaswamy but which does not appear in the constitutional discourse on religion and politics in the American context: "positive secularism." As used by judges like Gajendragadkar, Reddy, and Ramaswamy, the term is intended to convey a sense of the constitutional role of the State in confronting religious impediments to social reform.[77] In his discussion of secularism, Justice Ramaswamy indicates that "The State . . . has a missionary role to reform the Hindu society . . . and dilute the beliefs of caste hierarchy."[78] Despite the emphasis in his opinion on the equal treatment principle, performance of this missionary role, with its singling out of the Hindu religion, does not apparently present a constitutional contradiction. Thus under the rubric of "positive secularism," *sarva dharma sambhava* is interpreted less formalistically than it is by both liberals, for whom sameness in the State's interactions with different religious communities is in itself a virtue, and Hindu nationalists, for whom any deviation from formal equality is viewed as a threat to the securing of majoritarian political results.

In these judges' account, the constitutional commitment to social reform means that governmental policies may be acceptable if their purpose is to eradicate social inequities traceable to religious practices, even if these policies are targeted at specific communities. The targeting does not violate the relevant legal requirement, because whatever group differentiation results, occurs within a context in which constitutionally sanctioned

---

ment embarks on the ameliorative course of action mandated by the Constitution. In an interview with the author, Justice M. N. Venkatachaliah, a retired chief justice of the Supreme Court, agreed with Justice Ramaswamy's view that socioeconomic egalitarianism is critical to secularism in India, and added: "There is a constitutional concept of equality that is the essence of secularism. It may vary depending on the stage of societal development." Interview with the author, New Delhi, March 10, 1999. This suggests that equal treatment as a constitutionally required component of secularism is a variable concept that can mean different things as society progresses. In other words, It may over time acquire a more procedurally oriented significance.

[77] On this point, see Verma 1986. Verma is more blunt than the justices. Thus he writes: "[T]he popular version of Indian secularism as 'sarva dharma sambhava' . . . simply leads to anti-secularism, as it goes, on the one hand, against modernisation and national integration, and, on the other, strengthens the existing socio-cultural structures." Ibid., 33. The sense intended by Verma and the justices is very different from the meaning assigned to the term by the BJP. Its 1998 election manifesto reads: "The BJP's concept of Positive Secularism is: Justice for All, Appeasement of None." The remainder of the paragraph is an attack on their "pseudo-secularist" opponents for their "shameless pandering" to minorities.

[78] *Bommai* at 169. This line may have been lifted without attribution from S. L. Verma's book on positive secularism, where the author writes: "The State under Indian secularism appears to have a missionary role to reform the Hindu society." Verma 1986, 10. Verma goes on to say that "It may have assumed this role due to lack of an organised church or unity among its various sects and denominations."

policy goals have been explicitly *posited* as the measure of equal treatment.[79] To see what is involved in this conceptualization, consider the opposite of "positive secularism," in other words, what prevails in the American setting. Here the actions of government are evaluated within constitutionally prescribed markers that define a playing field of *negative secularism*. Equal treatment under the Establishment Clause means either that government must take no cognizance of religion in framing its policies or, if it does, that it be scrupulously even-handed in its dealings with particular religions. Under the Free Exercise Clause, it means either that government must make no religiously based exceptions to compliance with laws of general applicability or, if it does, that as long as public order is not compromised, exemptions are to be granted to groups without any scrutiny of the merits of their conscientiously held religious beliefs. In the jurisprudence of both Clauses, Church/State issues are framed in such a way as to project a limited role for government: confining its business to the temporal world or, under the logic of the assimilative model, enabling it to secure (as in *make* secure) the favored status of certain constitutive secular political ideas.[80]

---

[79] There is a sense in which the issue in the government dismissals comes down to an assessment of how serious officials must be in pursuing these policy goals. According to Justice Reddy, "Any State government which pursues unsecular policies or an unsecular course of action acts contrary to the constitutional mandate and renders itself amenable to action under Article 356." Ibid., 897. According to this logic, could a state government be dismissed by the Central Government if it failed to follow the constitutional mandate of achieving an egalitarian society? It would be very hard imagining this happening, and if it did, expecting that the Court would be convinced by such a rationale for action. But what if it were shown that there was a direct connection between this failure and the support of actions undertaken in the interest of some religiously based cause?

[80] Consider in this context Jefferson's rough draft of the Declaration of Independence, which read: "That to secure these ends governments are instituted among men, deriving their just powers from the governed," whereas in the final version the word *ends* was replaced by *rights*. The change, as Morton White has demonstrated, is significant. In the first case the verb *secure* means "attain," whereas in the second case it must mean "make secure" or "guard," since, when speaking of rights, government need not "attain" what people already have. White 1978, 249. White's point is that the substitution represents a change in the intended purpose of government from that of abettor of people in the attainment of specific ends to protector of their unalienable rights. Ibid., 251. The distinction is analogous to the difference between positive and negative secularism. Thus in India the Constitution directs the State to secure certain ends—socioeconomic justice defined in egalitarian terms—that suggests an ameliorative role for government in its relations with religious groups. In the United States the Constitution embodies a set of constitutive political principles, the security of which is largely entrusted to the institutions of government, which are responsible for maintaining the proper balance between secular and religious life. Obviously there are some gray areas in making such a distinction, but the differences in fundamental orientation between the two polities can be usefully analyzed in this way.

"Our object," according to Justice Reddy, "is to ascertain the meaning of the expression 'secularism' in the context of our Constitution."[81] By itself, Reddy explains, secularism is "not capable of precise definition"; in effect Jethmalani was correct in his claim of terminological ambiguity, but only if one makes the mistake of extracting the concept from its constitutional surroundings. Reddy's method is to rely on what Charles L. Black Jr. once described as "structure and relationship in constitutional law." Black described Chief Justice John Marshall's approach in *McCulloch v Maryland* in much the same way as Reddy decides *Bommai*: "[J]udgment is reached not fundamentally on the basis of that kind of textual exegesis which we tend to regard as normal, but on the basis of reasoning from the total structure which the text has created."[82] Thus the Indian justice adverts to the 42nd Amendment to the Constitution, in which the words *Socialist Secular* were added to the Preamble and placed before the words *Democratic Republic*. This addition, he maintains, was to make explicit what had all along been implicit in the text as a whole, namely, that the constitutional commitment to secularism is to a great extent a commitment to the pursuit of "social justice" and "equality of status and opportunity."[83]

Seen in this light, the political support for the destructive campaign waged by Hindu activists in Ayodhya assumes a significance that extends beyond the immediate and obvious details associated with that event. What was most obvious, of course, was the unraveling of the nation's social fabric as a result of the communal violence perpetrated by members of the majority Hindu community against Indian Muslims. "When the ancient Babri Masjid was demolished, every Muslim of the country was shell-shocked and greatly pained, as . . . the decrepit mosque in the remote Ayodhya had emerged as a symbol of identity for the Indian Muslims."[84] Moreover, complicity in this ugly assault by public officials underscored the event's clear threat to secular values: How could religious freedom exist where one group was so evidently favored by those in power?[85] But

---

[81] *Bommai* at 232.

[82] Black 1969, 15.

[83] *Bommai* at 232. The interpretive significance of the Preamble is also present in Justice Ramaswamy's opinion. "Law should . . . provide a lead by holding forth the norms for continuity for its orderly march towards an egalitarian social order envisioned in the preamble of the Constitution." Ibid. at 162.

[84] Akhtar 1997, 234.

[85] Tahir Mahmood, Chairman of the National Minorities Commission, argues that President's Rule was justified by the attacks on members of a minority group. Such attacks constituted "a breakdown of constitutional machinery" on the theory that the failure of the governments involved to protect basic rights represented a compromise of Part III of the

in his *Bommai* opinion, Justice Ramaswamy suggests an additional threat: "The interaction of religion and secular factors . . . is to expose the abuses of religion and of belief in God by purely partisan, narrow or selfish purpose to serve the economic or political interest of a particular class or group or country. The progress of human history is replete with full misuse of religious notions in that behalf."[86] Applied to the Ayodhya debacle, Ramaswamy's observation is consistent with many subsequent analyses of the campaign to destroy the mosque, which have concluded that in its fundamentals it was a carefully planned effort at mass political mobilization, exploiting religious symbols to attain political power.

To what end? Certainly to extend and solidify the hegemony of Hindu cultural norms within the country. That in itself has alarming implications for secular institutions, although its proponents see it as fully aligned with the secular principle of majority rule. In addition, these proponents emphasize the Hindu tradition's well-known tolerance of other faiths to dispute any suggestion that a more pervasively Hindu society represents a threat to religious freedom. But even if true, "Hinduism . . . is quite different from other religions in one respect. No other religion is internally as intolerant and oppressive as Hinduism."[87] Many analysts to the right of the Marxist historian K. N. Panikkar would agree with his observation that "The emphasis on cultural nationalism, and the decision of the BJP to initiate a campaign for its dissemination, is an attempt to homogenize the Hindus by underplaying the fissures and contradictions within them."[88] A judge looking objectively at the political dynamic at work in the mobilization around Ayodhya could plausibly have concluded that the more profound threat to secularism resided not so much in the immediate damage to communal relations so vividly on display in the rubble that was Babri Masjid, but in the long-term consequences of unchallenged ethnoreligious nationalism on the prospects for social reform and reconstruction.

The infamous BJP manifesto does not forthrightly declare war on the constitutional commitment behind the Directive Principles. It does say: "BJP firmly believes that construction of Shri Ram Mandir at Janmasthan is a symbol of the vindication of our cultural heritage and national self-

---

Constitution, the section on Fundamental Rights. Interview with the author, New Delhi, February 8, 1999.

[86] *Bommai* at 164.

[87] Panikkar 1997, 49. However, this observation must be qualified by acknowledging the great diversity within Hinduism. Thus many who practice the religion would be appropriately upset by the suggestion that they are intolerant or oppressive in relation to other Hindus.

[88] Ibid., ix.

respect."[89] Against the backdrop of recent Indian history, a politically astute judge could very well have understood this affirmation as a classic example of the displacement of conflict phenomenon, where "[w]hat happens in politics *depends on the way in which people are divided* into factions, parties, groups, classes, etc."[90] As E. E. Schattschneider wrote in his classic text on American democracy, "The failure to understand that *unification and division are a part of the same process* has produced some illusions about politics."[91] Schattschneider reminded us that political outcomes depend on the achievement of a dominant position in the way in which societal conflict gets to be defined. As in other places, playing the communal card in India (as in the vindication of our cultural—that is, Hindu—heritage) can be a very effective means of maintaining the status quo in social and economic privilege.

Thus as Christophe Jaffrelot has well documented, the connection between Ayodhya and class and caste conflict, most notably with regard to the Central Government's decision to implement the recommendations of the Mandal Commission on reservations, is substantial and significant. The BJP's opposition to these recommendations (that 27 percent of positions in the central administration and public corporations be reserved for other backward classes [OBCs]) reflected its traditional base of support among the upper castes, but it also was a politically risky opposition given that 52 percent of Indians are comprised of OBCs. Consequently, support for the Ayodhya campaign presented an opportunity to obscure caste and class barriers under the banner of Hindu unity. "Hindu nationalist leaders and organs ... presented the Ayodhya movement as the means of uniting all Hindus in such a way as to defuse the OBCs' demands. By trying to make the OBCs regard themselves as Hindus first and foremost [the *Sangh Parivar*] could preserve the social *status quo*."[92] It would not, then, require an enormous interpretive leap to view the support of the Ayodhya campaign by officials in Rajasthan, Madhya Pradesh, and Himachal Pradesh as a tacit rejection of critical provisions of the Constitution, not simply because of the interreligious discord that it obviously represented, but because of the intrareligious social inequity that it was intended to reinforce.

But if such an interpretation had a major role in the judgment in *Bommai*, it was not readily apparent from the text of the various judicial opinions.

---

[89] Quoted in *Bommai* at 290.

[90] Schattschneider 1975, 60.

[91] Ibid., 62.

[92] Jaffrelot 1995, 431. See also Ashis Nandy et al 1997. Nandy et al write: "[A]bove all, the acceptance of the Mandal Commission recommendations threatened to split the political base of the BJP. The BJP had been working assiduously to expand its upper-caste support

The remarks of Justices Reddy and Ramaswamy reveal an appreciation for the ameliorative thrust of Indian constitutional secularism, but even their opinions do not seek justification for the invocation of Article 356 on the basis of a specific connection between the social agenda of Hindu nationalism and the alleged failure of constitutional machinery in the states. This, to be sure, is understandable in light of the potentially devastating impact such a justification would doubtless have on the scope and quality of debate on public issues. Moreover, the Hindu nationalists do not have a monopoly on the politics of conflict displacement; thus any move to hold them culpable for their blatant exercise of these tactics in connection with the Ayodhya debacle would present mind-boggling issues of judicial line-drawing when others resort, as they have in the past, to more subtle applications of the strategy.[93] After all, even an activist Court must confront the folly of judicial overreaching, particularly when there already exists a more readily comprehensible, manageable, and less politically divisive standard within the liberal constitutionalism of formal equality.

The reluctance to push the logic of the Reddy-Ramaswamy analysis of Indian secularism to its limits still leaves the substance of their argument essentially intact. Their discussion reminds us that Ashoka's Wheel consists of more than the spokes that symbolically represent the State's commitment to the legal equality of all religions. As a metaphor for secularism in India it invites us to consider the Wheel as an object constantly in motion, steadily proceeding along a course of progressive social reform.

---

by utilizing the ideology of Hindu nationalism. Its targets were primarily the numerically strong and politically mobilized backward classes." Ibid., 72.

[93] It is not only polemicists like Arun Shourie who accuse the so-called secular parties of participating in the same sort of communal politics as the BJP and its allies. See, for example, Bose 1997. Bose makes a convincing case that Congress, particularly under the leadership of Indira Gandhi and Rajiv Gandhi, has not been at all averse to playing the communal card for political gain. But he makes a deeper claim that points to an important irony in the Supreme Court's ruling in *Bommai*. He argues that Hindu nationalism *"is quite similar, in its basic emphasis and content, to the monolithic, unitary conception of Indian nationalism that has increasingly served as the official ideology of the post-colonial Indian state. . . . The 'secular' state and 'communal' politics, far from being binary opposites, have in reality been interwoven and implicated in one another: they are two sides of the coin of a monolithic and state-centralist conceptualization of Indian nationalism."* Ibid., 156–7. To the extent that this analysis is correct, it suggests that the outcome in *Bommai* will have an effect opposite from what was intended. By upholding President's Rule, and thus strengthening the authority of the Central Government, the Court's ruling, according to this analysis, will ultimately redound to the benefit of the Hindu nationalist cause. In this regard it is worth noting that in 1989 the BJP election manifesto asked for "a commission to examine the Constitution of India for making it an effective instrument for containing centrifugal tendencies." Quoted in Noorani 2000. Thus to complete the irony, the party whose repudiation by the Center was affirmed in *Bommai* had been calling in the period leading up to Ayodhya for constitutional revision in the interest of greater centralization.

But of course constitutional and political realities do not permit unobstructed access to the desired destination. While establishing that secularism is part of the basic structure of the Constitution, *Bommai* ultimately cannot stand for the proposition that any departure from the path of meaningful social reconstruction provides an adequate basis for dismissing governments whose stewardship has gone astray.

Nevertheless, the *Bommai* decision does mean that secularism is a feature of sufficient interpretive distinctiveness and precision that its exalted constitutional status can function as a predicate (or from the critics' perspective, a pretext) for undoing the results of the democratic decision-making process. The articulation of this predicate for action must, however, conform to a set of expectations deducible from the principle of *sarva dharma sambhava*. In the case of judges like Reddy and Ramaswamy, these deductions will include a substantive dimension reflecting an understanding of the ameliorative aspirations underlying constitutional arrangements for secularism. In some areas of constitutional contestation—for example, where social welfare considerations have dictated governmental action that restricts religious practices—this dimension will, in most instances, serve directly to justify the moves in question. However, in the case of an Article 356 invocation, which involves the most far-reaching example of counter-majoritarian political intervention permitted under the Constitution, the ameliorative aspiration as rationale for legitimating a dismissal will have to be collapsed and submerged under the broader and more politically acceptable criterion of equal treatment. Declaring "a failure of constitutional machinery" solely on the basis of projected political prospects for social reform would surely precipitate a crisis of constitutional legitimacy. And so prudent and clever judges intent upon using their judicial opinions to convey a clear sense of what is at stake in the pursuit of a secular polity in India will need to calibrate how far they can go in pushing the logic of positive secularism without jeopardizing the robust uninhibited debate and deliberation that is also essential to the basic structure of democratic institutions.

CONCLUSION

On February 1, 2000, the BJP-led Indian government announced the formation of a National Commission to review the working of the Constitution. The Commission's terms of reference were as follows: "To examine in the light of the experience of the past 50 years as to how best the Constitution can respond to the changing needs of an efficient, smooth and effective system of governance and socio-economic development of a modern India within the framework of the parliamentary democracy, and to recommend changes, if any, that are required, in the Constitution without interfering with its basic structure or features."[94] Concerns surfaced immediately that this commitment to noninterference would probably be honored in the breach.[95] Some of the negative reaction was predictably partisan, as reflected in a Congress leader's charge that "The BJP, in seeking to alter the basics of the beautiful document, wants to communalise and saffronise the country's polity."[96] There were multiple reasons for skepticism, not the least of which were the remarks made on January 28, 2000, by the Union law minister, in which the renowned lawyer suggested that the "misguided secularism" used by the Supreme Court as the basis for affirming the imposition of President's Rule needed to be "reviewed."[97] The minister, Ram Jethmalani, was of course very familiar with the case in which this imposition had been upheld.

How would it be possible to review the prevailing constitutional judgment on secularism and still respect the Commission's mandate to refrain from revising any of the document's basic features? One possibility would be to make a distinction between revision and clarification. If the Supreme Court had indeed been "misguided" in its understanding of secularism,

[94] Ministry of Law, Justice and Company Affairs (Department of Legal Affairs), Resolution No. A-45012(2)/98-Admn.-III(LA), February 22, 2000.

[95] For example, after reviewing a number of statements made over recent years by members of the government on the subject of the desirability of constitutional revision, A. J. Noorani concluded that "[T]he review commission is an instrument for implementing the BJP's hidden agenda." Noorani 2000. Similarly, the legal scholar and activist Rajeev Dhavan wrote: "The BJP's agendas are hidden and conspiratorial. . . . The tragedy is that this government has floated the idea of a review of the Constitution without so much as a policy statement or a white paper being issued on it. This is insidious and undemocratic. It surely gives rise to suspicions." Rajeev Dhavan, "Politician, Heal Thyself," *The Times of India*, February 29, 2000. Of course, those presently in the government were not anxious to arouse concerns about any hidden agenda. But statements such as the following by supporters outside the government were part of the background to the debate over establishing a commission on constitutional revision. "After securing freedom, we have to set up our own national state—A HINDU NATION-STATE. We have to discard the present Indian Constitution and give ourselves a new constitution of our own: then we can change almost all laws and policies and replace them by enacting new ones in keeping with our national ideals and interests." Chatterjee 1995, 6. During the last decade, the election manifestos of the BJP have called for a commission to examine the Indian Constitution, and these calls have been attached to demands for changes that clearly implicate features that have been placed under the rubric of basic structure. Noteworthy too was the posture of the president of India, who announced his opposition to the constitutional review on January 27, 2000, at the Parliamentary celebration of the fiftieth anniversary of the Indian Constitution. His point was that "[T]he Constitution of India has not failed us. We have failed the Constitution." President Narayan's distinction as the first Dalit president of India was probably not unrelated to his skepticism about the objectives of the reviewers.

[96] *Hindustan Times*, January 28, 2000.

[97] These remarks were reported on January 29, 2000, in several Indian newspapers, including *The Hindu*, *The Statesman*, and *The Telegraph*.

then as part of the project of revision, this basic feature of the Constitution should perhaps be clarified and given more precise definition. For Jethmalani and others in the government who had been disappointed by the outcome in *Bommai*, such an argument is not inconsistent with comments made in an interview by the chair of the new Commission, former Chief Justice M. N. Venkatachaliah: "So far as the basic features are concerned, the Supreme Court in the *Kesavananda* case, while dealing with what matters are amenable to the amending process under the Constitution, held certain constitutional fundamentals of the Indian Constitution as immutable in relation to the power of Parliament to change the Constitution."[98] Now, secularism may very well be an immutable principle, but what, as Counselor Jethmalani asked the Supreme Court in *Bommai*, *is* secularism? Would not Minister Jethmalani be in compliance with the Commission's terms of reference if he sought an amendation to the constitutional language that explained exactly what this unamendable feature actually meant? After all, since the judiciary is also constrained by the logic of *Kesavananda*, then Chief Justice Charles Evan Hughes's famous aphorism, that the Constitution, while supreme, is what the Supreme Court says it is, should not be used to preclude further clarification. Justices, after all, can get it wrong.

What, then, was "misguided" in the way secularism had been understood in *Bommai*? Surely it was not the Court's emphasis on *sarva dharma sambhava*, for, as we have seen, the losers in that case had been outspoken proponents of this very principle. Indeed, it had been at the core of their devotion to the cause of a uniform civil code and a featured component of their ideological arsenal in the struggle for political power. While they clearly believed that the Court had been "misguided" in the application of the principle to the case at hand, a failure in execution does not, in itself, justify a constitutional review—unless, of course, the failure is related to a fundamental misunderstanding of the meaning of the principle. Thus a more likely cause for their disillusionment was the additional emphasis in the extended opinions of Justices Reddy and Ramaswamy on the connection between secularism and the welfare-state aspirations of the Constitution.[99] This was the connection championed by Dr. Ambed-

[98] Venkatachaliah 2000.

[99] In an early call for a constitutional review, the author of a newspaper article wrote that "It should now be clear to everybody that the Constitution is not in tune with our national character." This provoked the following response a week later in the same publication. "Is it the Constitution which is not in tune with us or we who are not in tune with the Constitution?. . . . The Preamble of the Indian Constitution, pledging itself to the ideals of liberty, equality, fraternity, is 'foreign' to our socio-religious tradition." D. P. Das, 1998 "Change Leaders, Not Constitution," *The Pioneer*, August 14, 1998. The response reflects very well sentiments embodied in the ameliorative secular constitutional tradition.

kar, the principal architect behind the original document, whose legacy has long been aggressively challenged by polemicists on the Hindu right.[100] Constitutional revision that succeeded in severing this connection, that succeeded, in other words, in denuding secularism of its ameliorative aspirations, would be an achievement of historic significance.

---

[100] See especially Arun Shourie's book-length attack on Ambedkar, Shourie 1997b. It is perhaps worth noting in this regard that a number of the criticisms made against the National Commission focused on the overrepresentation of upper-caste Hindus in the appointed members.

Chapter Six

CORRUPT PRACTICES

Religious Speech and
Democratic Deliberation

SEVERAL YEARS AGO, the governor of Mississippi made what many people thought was an outrageous observation when he asserted that America was a "Christian nation." For the outraged, few statements could have matched the governor's in what it revealed about a political leader's fundamental disregard for the essentials of American democracy.[1] The governor, however, had no need to fear political retribution; after all, the intensity of the outrage precipitated by his statement correlated strongly with the distance one traveled from his state. Nor had he any need to fear any serious legal repercussions, it being quickly evident that a principled defense of his right to utter silly and offensive things was most likely to be found among those harboring the gravest misgivings about his questionable characterization. Moreover, he would no doubt have enjoyed the same immunity had he gone on to suggest that voters withhold their support from any candidate for public office whose faith was other than that of the favored Christian majority.

American social norms explain why the governor could feel politically secure in his job, just as American constitutional norms explain why there is no mystery in the governor's presumed confidence regarding possible legal liability. Thus we expect controversial speech to be sheltered by the speech clause of the First Amendment, and we assume further that the religious liberty guarantees of that Amendment would, in the case of the

---

[1] In a poll taken in 1996, 28 percent of the respondents supported the idea of a constitutional amendment to declare that "the United States is a Christian nation." Sixty-two percent were opposed. Just what to infer from this is unclear, since 60 percent agreed that "the United States [is] a Christian nation." Kohut et al 2000, 100. The most sensible interpretation is that a clear majority believes that empirically most Americans are indeed Christian, but that a minority believes in addition that this is the way it ought to be.

governor's remarks, augment this already considerable constitutional protection.[2] Justification for these expectations is well grounded in American constitutional jurisprudence. At the same time, skepticism about the normative standing of religiously inspired speech has become a subject of some controversy among contemporary theorists of liberal democracy.

In this chapter I remove this controversy from the realm of abstract theory and place it within a comparative constitutional framework. The comparative focus provides a richer context for a general understanding of the political interface of spiritual and temporal concerns, but also for its more particular manifestations, as in the vexing problem of religious speech in the public forum. Thus in India a politician who, while campaigning for office, voiced analogous sentiments to those expressed by the governor would be vulnerable to serious legal challenge. The possibility that such a challenge would be upheld by the courts provides an opportunity to further explore the constitutional implications of ameliorative secularism, and in the process to reconsider the argument for public reason, which, as it has been advanced by John Rawls and others, appeals to certain constitutional essentials of a liberal polity to derive guidelines for the appropriate discourse of democratic politics.

The Indian case suggests that the way in which we conceptualize the relationship between religious argumentation and democratic deliberation must take stock of the diversity of experience in constitutional arrangements for religion and politics. As we have seen, the commitment to secular democratic institutions may express itself in different ways, which means that the attempt to frame norms of public reason with reference to *the* constitutional essentials of a liberal polity will fail to explain why in some places these norms seem to require the sanction of law, while in others such sanctions would rightfully be judged illiberal and unconstitutional. In India, where certain kinds of religious rhetoric are proscribed as "corrupt practices," the justification for legally seeking to minimize the occasions in which elected officials exercise their powers on religious grounds needs to be premised on the particularities of the *Indian* experience in secular constitutionalism, rather than on general principles deducible from a liberal democratic polity. The corrupt practices approach of Indian law echoes a recurrent theme in political philosophy, in which the corruption of the State is linked to systemic structural inequalities, such that the civic virtue necessary to sustain a just and stable political order

---

[2] The key case is *Cantwell v Connecticut*. In reversing the conviction of someone who employed offensive and abusive speech in denouncing the Roman Catholic Church, the Court concluded that "[T]he people of this nation have ordained in the light of history, that, in spite of the probability of excesses and abuses, these [First Amendment] liberties are, in the long view, essential to enlightened opinion and right conduct on the part of the citizens of a democracy." Ibid. at 310.

is seriously and dangerously compromised.[3] As these structural inequalities are in India directly and profoundly implicated in religious belief and practice, they can only be addressed through policies that limit religious freedom—possibly including speech—in ways that would not pass constitutional scrutiny in a polity such as the United States, where religion is much less of a factor in configuring the shape of the temporal world.

This chapter and the next examine several companion cases decided by the Supreme Court of India, all of which involved appeals to religion to advance a candidate's electoral prospects. The office-seekers in these controversies had made little effort to conceal a principal objective of theirs, the dismantling of the dominant structure of state and national secular governance. The cases highlight a distinctive judicial approach to the challenge of religious advocacy in the public forum, one that in the end should arouse skepticism over the advisability of employing any univocal principle to govern the actual practices of liberal secular polities. The Court's invocation of Rawlsian reasoning to defend a law that in the United States would be found constitutionally infirm points to the limitations of abstract moralizing in addressing the problem of religious advocacy. To rectify this it is necessary to outline an alternative non-Rawlsian account for limiting "corrupt" speech in India that draws specifically upon the constitutional essentials peculiar to that polity. As we will see, the most convincing rationale for speech restrictions lies in the threat posed by religion to the achievement of substantive constitutional aspirations for equality, more so than in the political commitment to the *process* of democratic deliberation. To underscore this point I turn briefly to the "corrupt practice" of campaign financing in the United States, where the constitutional logic behind the Supreme Court's treatment of that issue reveals the alternative assumptions distinguishing Indian and American liberalism, and the implications that follow for religious speech in the public arena.

What Is Political Corruption?

On December 11, 1995, a three-judge panel of the Indian Supreme Court announced a set of related judgments that had potentially far-reaching implications for Indian politics. They all concerned the interpretation and application of a 1951 electoral law, the Representation of the People Act (RPA). Section 123 of the law detailed a number of activities that were designated as "corrupt practices," the commission of which subjected the

---

[3] On this point see J. Patrick Dobel 1978, 958. Dobel appeals to Plato, Aristotle, Machiavelli, and Rousseau for the view that "[T]he source of systematic corruption lies in certain patterns of inequality." Ibid., 961.

transgressor to serious legal consequence, including the reversal of an electoral victory. The Court found this section to be constitutional, interpreting and applying its two subsections in a way that produced mixed results in the specific cases under consideration.

To what activity did the language of corrupt practice apply? For Americans, whose recent elections have dramatically increased the level of public awareness of ethical abuses in politics, the statutory invocation of the term *corruption* in the regulatory context of campaign behavior has only one meaning: the improper use of money to secure electoral advantage.[4] In India the term has broader application; it includes not only money and politics irregularities but also covers the inappropriate use of speech to advance one's electoral prospects. Accordingly, in RPA a speech-related "corrupt practice" may be either of two things: (1) "The appeal by a candidate or his agent . . . to vote or refrain from voting for any person on the ground of his religion, race, caste, community or language or the use of, or appeal to, religious symbols . . . for the furtherance of the prospects of the election of that candidate or for prejudicially affecting the election of any candidate" or (2) "The promotion of, or attempt to promote, feelings of enmity or hatred between classes of citizens of India on grounds of religion, race, caste, community, or language, by a candidate or his agent . . . for the furtherance of the prospects of the election of that candidate or for prejudicially affecting the election of any candidate."

In its rulings, the Court held that Balasaheb K. Thackeray, the leader of an extreme Hindu nationalist party (Shiv Sena), could be barred from electoral competition on the basis of intemperate campaign rhetoric, including a reference to Muslims as "snakes." His remarks were found to be in clear violation of RPA's second corrupt practice category. But in companion cases the Court reversed findings against several other Hindu nationalist politicians, one involving a campaign pledge to turn Maharashtra (where Gandhi was from) into India's "first Hindu state," and another concerning appeals to voters on the basis of the candidate's support of "Hindutva," a term widely held to signify the religious faith of Hindus, but which the Court chose to interpret as referring to the culture and ethos of the people of India.[5] A rumination on the essence of Hinduism

---

[4] In the United States, religious organizations that participate in politics do run the risk of losing their tax exemption, but there is very little enforcement of this penalty. On those rare occasions when it is—as in the case of the Christian Coalition—the sanctions imposed have been more symbolic than real.

[5] As will be explored more fully in the next chapter, these decisions were extremely controversial. While they were applauded in Hindu nationalist circles, they were seen by others as a watering down of the provisions of the Representation of the People Act. For example, one commentator wrote: "Would the normal electorate in India understand that what is meant by Hindutva is the culture of all the people of India including those of non-Hindu

led the judges, ironically as we shall see, to conclude that "[N]o meaning in the abstract can confine it to the narrow limits of religion alone, excluding the content of Indian culture and heritage."[6] So "the term 'Hindutva' is related more to the way of life of the people in the subcontinent."[7] In short, by effectively blurring the distinction between religion and culture, the Court was left with insufficient evidence to substantiate the charge of corruption.

But why should the kind of speech detailed in RPA—especially that of the category 1 variety—be construed as a form of corruption? Until we have an answer to that question, the irony in the Court's reflections on Hinduism will go unappreciated, and the comparative and theoretical significance of the Indian approach to religious speech in the public arena (one upheld by the Court as both constitutional and wise) will not be apparent. In pursuing the question, however, we should not be constrained by the narrow understanding of corruption most evident in common usage (including the social science literature), namely the betrayal of the public trust for private (generally financial) benefit. Instead, it will be useful to embrace an older view, one with a respectable lineage in the tradition of political philosophy, and perhaps best expressed in Montesquieu's observation that "The corruption of every government generally begins with that of its principles."[8] Accordingly, a corrupt practice should be understood in the light of regime principles, those constitutive commitments that establish a polity's constitutional identity. Critical here is the concept of *integrity*, as applied both to our modern intuition about corruption as the abuse of a public trust and to its conceptualization here, where it speaks to a lack of fit between a given practice and the animating precepts of the surrounding constitutional order.[9] How helpful, then, is the Court's constitutional defense of the Representation of the People Act?

---

faiths? Obviously, by Hindutva most of the voters would understand the culture of Hindus including their religious faith, and not the faith and culture of non-Hindus." He concluded: "These decisions of the Supreme Court Bench are thus highly derogatory to the principle of secular democracy and the letter and spirit of Section 123(3) of the Representation of the People Act, 1951." V. M. Tarkunde, "Hindutva and the Supreme Court," *Hindustan Times*, January 10, 1996, 13. Said another scathing review: "The judgment is yet another instance of a widespread confusion in the discourse on secularism, pluralism, and humanism." Nauriya 1996. Criticism of the Court for its interpretations of RPA extended to judgments in earlier years as well. See, for example, V. S. Rekhi 1993.

[6] *Prabhoo* at 159.

[7] Ibid. at 159.

[8] Montesquieu 1966, 109. For an interesting discussion of corruption as it has been understood in political philosophy, see Dobel 1978; see also Euben 1989.

[9] Integrity as a virtue in liberal political theory has been most fully developed by Ronald Dworkin. "Integrity becomes a political ideal when we make the same demand of the state or community taken to be a moral agent, when we insist that the state act on a single,

The defense began reasonably enough with an approving account of statutory intent. "Obviously the purpose of enacting the provision [in RPA] is to ensure that no candidate at an election gets votes only because of his religion and no candidate is denied any votes on the ground of his religion. This is in keeping with the secular character of the Indian polity."[10] But the meaning of this legitimation, as clear as it may on first inspection seem, ultimately must rest upon a matter of inflection left unresolved by the Court's imprimatur. Is the law in keeping with the *secular* character of the Indian polity, or rather with the secular character of the *Indian* polity? We know of course that the secular character of other polities (including the American) has not led to the regulation of campaign rhetoric featuring sectarian religious appeals. So either these other polities have not done what they should in order to adequately support their commitments to secularism, or there is something special about the secular character of the Indian polity that in this case at least justifies restrictions on religious speech as an appropriate response to corrupt practices. As we see in the next section, the latter understanding best comports with what is distinctive about Indian constitutionalism. But we need first to see how the Court's discussion assumes an idealized model of liberal democratic politics more than it does the particularities of the Indian experience.

In emphasizing the sustaining features of a secular polity (i.e., where "the State has no religion and the State practices the policy of neutrality in the matter of religion"),[11] the Court appealed to language from an earlier decision. "No democratic political and social order, in which the conditions of freedom and their progressive expansion for all make some regulation of all activities imperative, could endure without an agreement on the basic essentials which could unite and hold citizens together despite all the differences of religion, race, caste, community, culture, creed, and language."[12] What these "essentials" are may be gathered from the fact

---

coherent set of principles even when its citizens are divided about what the right principles of justice and fairness really are." Dworkin 1986, 166. Corruption, in short, represents the loss of integrity. J. Peter Euben's discussion of corruption in Aristotle's thought also captures this sense of integrity. "When a constitution systematically falls short of the paradigms of action, character, and justice which give it unity and definition, it is corrupt." Euben 1989, 227.

[10] *Prabhoo* at 145. "Section 123(3) is a provision which is in consonance with the policy of the framers of the Constitution to make India a secular State, a State which has no religion of its own and which refrains from discrimination on grounds of religion." Tripathi 1974, 499. As in most discussions of the electoral law, only a superficial consideration of the Indian secular State is provided, leaving unresolved an explanation for the comparative uniqueness of the statute.

[11] Ibid., 147.

[12] Ibid., 149. The quote was taken from Justice Beg's opinion in *Ziyauddin Burkharrudin Bukhari v Brigmohan Ramdass Mehra and Others* at 24. Obviously the reference to caste speaks directly to the Indian experience, but for present purposes its connection to religion

that "In order that the democratic process should thrive and succeed, it is of utmost importance that our elections to Parliament and the different legislative bodies must be free from the unhealthy influence of appeals to religion, race, caste, community, or language."[13] Thus the success of the democratic project is predicated on the exclusion of certain forms of argumentation from the electoral arena, specifically those that appeal to voters on the basis of ascriptive affiliation. But what precisely is it that is "unhealthy" in such appeals? The Court said, "*[O]ur democracy can only survive if those who aspire to become people's representatives and leaders understand the spirit of secular democracy.* That spirit was characterized by Montesquieu long ago as one of 'virtue.' . . . *For such a spirit to prevail, candidates at elections have to try to persuade electors by showing them the light of reason and not by inflaming their blind and disruptive passions.*"[14]

The Court's understanding of a corrupt practice relies on a normative view of politics in which the presence of procedurally correct reasoned deliberation becomes the measure of viable secular democratic institutions. Those activities that depart from this defining norm are therefore corrupt in the sense adverted to earlier; that is, they tend to undermine the essential principles of secular democratic governance. In this regard, the specific invocation of Montesquieu reminds us that the "spirit of the laws" is not self-sustaining; rather it requires the support of law, in this case the statutory prohibition against certain kinds of campaign rhetoric. The intent behind the Section 123 prohibition may not have been to guarantee that elected officials would exercise their powers on a nonreligious basis, but, as one analysis of some early RPA decisions suggests, probably it was to minimize that possibility.[15] In clearly endorsing this interpretation, the Court's argument bears a striking resemblance to formulations advanced in contemporary liberal political theory which, as Ronald Thiemann aptly puts it, "grant[s] virtual axiomatic status to the belief that religious convictions must be limited solely to the realm of the private."[16] This segmentation is essential for a "liberalism of reasoned respect," the goal of which is a structured society that places a premium on the virtue of civility.[17]

---

is so intimate that the general argument in which it appears may still be viewed as derivative from the nature of a secular polity and not just the Indian case.

[13] Ibid. at 160.

[14] Ibid. at 150. This language was again borrowed from *Bukhari*. The italics that the Court used to emphasize its point in the later case do not appear in the original.

[15] Mansfield 1989, 223. Mansfield, however, does not investigate the reasons for this policy objective, something I take up in the next section.

[16] Thiemann 1996, 89.

[17] Weithman 1997, 4. Weithman argues that the liberalism of reasoned respect is addressed to advanced democracies, one manifestation of which is that reasoned discourse,

The derivation of these limitations in contemporary liberal theory mirrors the structure of the Court's arguments, in which democracy's survival is placed in jeopardy by the presence of irreconcilable group-based differences (or comprehensive views), only to be maintained and preserved by a shared commitment to basic essentials, including a process for reaching public decisions by the light of reason. For example, in *Political Liberalism*, Rawls tackles the pluralist conundrum of "[h]ow [it is] possible for there to exist over time a just and stable society of free and equal citizens, who remain profoundly divided by reasonable religious, philosophical, and moral doctrines[.]"[18] While Rawls rightly assumes that all societies with aspirations to political justice confront this vexing dilemma, it is of course a question with special significance for India, arguably the most diverse society in the world.[19] For this reason the Indian Court had a very easy time upholding the constitutionality of that section of the RPA under which the Shiv Sena leader, Mr. Thackeray, had been prosecuted. Thus political rhetoric that promotes enmity and hatred among different classes of citizens must be appraised in India against that country's sad history of religiously and ethnically inspired violence. Appropriately, the constitutional guarantee in Article 19 of freedom of speech and expression includes a public order exception, in accordance with which restrictions on group-directed assaultive speech, especially in the highly charged setting of an electoral contest, could be (and were) comfortably accommodated.[20]

The Constitution also includes a "decency and morality" exception, which is the provision the judges appealed to in order to uphold RPA's other prohibition on religiously inspired speech. This affirmance could

---

rather than the prevention of civil strife, is the animating concern driving its proponents. Ibid., 33. This of course raises the obvious question as to the appropriateness of the principled application of the scheme to a place such as India.

[18] Rawls 1993, 4.

[19] Rawls's philosophic method is occasionally insufficiently sensitive to questions of degree as they relate to societal division. He says, for example, that "Liberty of conscience and freedom of association, and the political rights of freedom of speech, voting, and running for office, are characterized in more or less the same manner in all free regimes." Ibid., 228. Much depends on the meaning of "more or less," but as the differences between India and the United States on the issue of religious expression illustrates, free regimes can differ rather significantly on constitutional essentials in light of their alternative pluralist experiences. I pursue these differences in detail in *Apple of Gold: Constitutionalism in Israel and the United States*, ch. 6.

[20] There are, in addition, many cases concerning provisions of the Penal Code in which restrictions on religious speech have been upheld under the Article 19 exception. However, as John Mansfield points out, "[T]he struggle between conflicting values——freedom of speech in matters of religion on the one hand and the protection of public order, religious sensibilities and religious identities on the other—has continued at the level of statutory interpretation." Mansfield 1989, 211.

not be obtained as straightforwardly as was the hate speech proscription, and so it became necessary for the Court to rely on interpretive ingenuity, which in this instance meant abjuring the narrow, if more obvious, sexually oriented intention behind the exception, in favor of a meaning more consonant with liberal norms of political propriety. "Thus, seeking votes at an election on the ground of the candidate's religion in a secular State, is against the norms of decency and propriety of the society."[21] What is here given constitutional mooring is presented in Rawls as a morally desirable, but not legally enforceable, standard for liberal polities as they confront the critical pluralist challenge. "[I]t is normally desirable that the comprehensive philosophic and moral views we are wont to use in debating fundamental political issues should give way in public life."[22] The Indian Court's "norm of decency and propriety" is in essence a corollary of Rawls's ideal of public reason, a norm deducible from the fundamentals of the liberal democratic polity. While the norm, as incorporated in RPA, is intended to cover only the specific kind of political appeal delineated in the statute (and thus not to cover religiously articulated perspectives on public issues in general), its basic logic is fundamentally consonant with the Rawlsian aspiration.[23] "[T]he ideal of public reason . . . hold[s] for citizens when they engage in political advocacy in the public forum, and thus for . . . candidates in their campaigns and for other groups who support them. It holds equally for how citizens are to vote in elections when constitutional essentials and matters of basic justice are at stake."[24] Although there is no citation of Rawls in the Court's judgment, the author of the opinion, Justice J. S. Verma, was familiar with the argument of *Political Liberalism*, having cited it two years earlier in his majority opinion in the *Ayodhya Reference Case*. His opinion there quotes a speech of a judicial colleague, in which the latter said: "In a pluralist, secular polity law is perhaps the greatest integrating force. A cultivated respect for law and its institutions and symbols; a pride in the country's heritage and achievements; faith that people live under the protection of an adequate legal system are indispensable for sustaining unity in pluralist diversity. Rawlsian pragmatism of 'justice as fairness' to serve as an 'overlapping consensus' and deep seated agreements on fundamental questions

---

[21] *Prabhoo* at 153.

[22] Rawls 1993, 10. "[T]he ideal of citizenship imposes a moral, not a legal, duty—the duty of civility—to be able to explain to one another on those fundamental questions how the principles and policies they advocate and vote for can be supported by the political values of public reason." Ibid., 217.

[23] "[A] democratic constitution," Rawls writes, "is a principled expression in higher law of the political ideal of a people to govern itself in a certain way. The aim of public reason is to articulate this ideal." Ibid., 232.

[24] Ibid., 215.

of basic structure of society for deeper social unity is a political conception of justice rather than a comprehensive moral conception."[25]

Rawls's ideal has been the subject of withering critique and flattering emulation. Its detractors have found it intolerant of illiberal views whose very divisiveness should be present in public debate;[26] mistaken in its assumption that shared premises are the prerequisite for public deliberation among contestants holding widely disparate views;[27] illusory in its presumption of having transcended religious-like dogma;[28] impractical in its rendering of liberalism inaccessible to those most in need of its principles;[29] and opposed to a life of integrity in its insistence on refashioning arguments to make them conform to the dictates of reason.[30] On the other hand, theorists of note have borrowed from and refined the Rawlsian ideal, as they have developed reciprocity-based exclusions of religion from the jurisdiction of political action;[31] formulated a "principle of secular rationale" to govern advocacy in the public forum;[32] and established limiting principles for the intervention of religious convictions in the making of political choices.[33]

In reflecting on the Indian Court's consideration of political corruption, these perspectives can be deployed in supportive or critical ways. One need not take a position here on the merits of these claims, except to observe in regard to both sides of the debate that their focus, like that of Rawls's, is on the criteria appropriate for secular democracies in general. The Court's constitutional evaluation of RPA proceeds in similar fashion, as it develops an understanding of corrupt practices on the basis of theoretically driven liberal aspirations to a just political order. In so doing, however, it fails to provide an adequately textured account of political corruption, one that conveys a fuller sense of why it is that an appeal to voters to exercise their democratic freedom on the basis of religious considerations threatens the core principles of *this* secular regime; and how the *legal* proscription of such appeals may possess a logic consistent with secular democratic expectations. In the next section I suggest what such an account might look like.

[25] *The Ayodhya Reference* 1995, 36. When asked about his use of Rawls, the colleague, Chief Justice Venkatachaliah, explained that it is entirely appropriate to use concepts from Western philosophical liberalism in Indian constitutional cases, because there are universals that apply to all societies. Interview with the author, New Delhi, March 10, 1999.

[26] Perry 1997.

[27] Waldron 1993.

[28] Galston 1994.

[29] Hurd 1995.

[30] Wolgast 1994.

[31] Gutmann and Thompson 1996.

[32] Audi 1989.

[33] Greenawalt 1988.

RELIGION, EQUALITY, AND CONSTITUTIONAL ESSENTIALS

The ideal of public reason in Rawls is meant to apply to the discussion of constitutional essentials and matters of basic justice. Constitutional essentials are of two kinds: (1) fundamental principles specifying the general structure of government and the political process and (2) equal basic rights of citizenship, including rights connected to voting and political participation, conscience, thought and association, and the rule of law.[34] Specifically excluded by Rawls from this enumeration are principles regulating basic matters of fair opportunity and social and economic inequalities.[35] Though important, these latter are questioned more often, and answered less urgently, than the essentials dealing with basic freedoms.

Upon first glance, the Indian Constitution addresses Rawls's constitutional essentials. As we saw in chapter 2, Part III of the document contains a detailed enumeration of the sort of fundamental rights mentioned by Rawls in (2), followed in Part IV with a listing of the Directive Principles of State Policy. Included in this latter section are the directives to the State concerning the achievement of social justice. "The State shall strive to promote the welfare of the people by securing and protecting as effectively as it may a social order in which justice, social, economic and political, shall inform all the institutions of the national life." (Article 38) But as the preceding Article states, this section, unlike Part III, is not enforceable by any court; while important, it is essentially hortatory in nature. Thus one might suppose that the principles contained therein are both more contestable and less urgent than those specified in Part III.

Such a supposition, however, is unwarranted. If under the rubric of constitutional essentials in India are not to be found principles regulating basic matters of social and economic inequality, then much of the history of the Indian Constitution will need to be rewritten. And more directly to the point of this chapter, the regulation of these matters is deeply enmeshed in constitutional policy concerning religious freedom, so much so that to imagine one without the other is radically to misconstrue the essence of Indian constitutionalism.[36] Thus, as noted earlier, the nonjusticia-

---

[34] Rawls 1993, 227.

[35] Ibid., 228. The relevance of Rawlsian philosophy to the Indian setting is considered in Rajan 1998. Rajan does not consider the question of religious speech in relation to the argument for public reason, but does use Rawls to urge a more principled separation of Church and State in India. For example, Rajan argues that the adoption of a uniform civil code is required by Rawlsian philosophy, and that "[A] logically coherent application of Rawlsian theory . . . would require radical changes in existing power structures." Ibid., 207.

[36] In this holistic conception, the distinction between the secular and the religious largely disappears. It is a disappearance that, in the case of India, renders problematic (as we shall see) the application of Rawlsian public reasoning, which, predicated on the existence of a

ble aspirations of the directive principles are in fact manifest in the explicit limitations attached to constitutionally guaranteed rights, such as are to be found in Article 25's protection of religious freedom.

The application of the term *corrupt practice* to religiously framed campaign rhetoric is therefore consistent with the underlying logic of these limitations. The constitutional essentials of the Indian polity were forged out of the tension between religion and equality. To the extent that political corruption represents an erosion of the core commitments of a given polity, then the most compelling interpretation of RPA is that it seeks to reinforce the special character of *Indian* secular constitutionalism. Officials responsible for the enforcement and interpretation of the law need to reflect on the contemporary challenge to these constitutional essentials in light of the fundamental purposes of the election law.

Corruption's Conceptual Expansion

Not surprisingly the historical antecedent for the Indian election law is to be found in England. The corrupt practices provisions of the Representation of the People Act are traceable to an 1883 British statute, which became the model for the Government of India Act of 1919. There, for the first time in Indian law, sanctions were detailed for the violation of provisions regulating corrupt election practices. Postindependence legislation was also modeled after the British example, as Section 123 of the Representation of the People Act of 1951 was "basically a by-product of the English law on corrupt practices."[37] With only minor changes, the Indian approach incorporated the substance of British law as promulgated as late as 1949 in the British Representation of the People Act. But there was one significant departure from the list of corrupt practices borrowed from the British experience: Unlike in England, electoral corruption in India may involve abuses associated with religious speech.

The departure is no mystery. As the Court said in *Bukhari*, "[T]he provisions [of Section 123] . . . seem wider in scope [than English law] and also contain specific mention of what may be construed as 'undue influence' viewed in the background of our political history and the special conditions which have prevailed in this country."[38] Justice Beg clearly had in mind the terrible violence generated over many years by the ethnic and

---

distinct secular realm, insists on separating what may be indivisible. For an insightful analysis of Rawlsian theory and the anthropological view, see Stolzenberg 1997. Stolzenberg focuses on the Satmar Hasidim of Kiryas Joel, where, she argues, "The conventional distinction between the religious and the secular realms is not a part of the Hasidic vocabulary." Ibid., 309.

[37] Jhingta 1996, xiii.

[38] *Bukhari* at 25.

religious divisions in the country. The attachment of significant costs to the use of rhetoric that increases the likelihood of such occurrences is a legal and political response to this historically based Indian social reality. Surely in 1951, with the horrific images of Partition and its aftermath still vivid in people's minds, the dampening of the violent impulses that were known to cause incalculable destruction and harm would understandably be a high priority on the legislative agenda. But along with these concerns were others relating to "special conditions," specifically that religion in India had been a massive impediment to the achievement of social reform.

The appeal in *Bukhari* to "the spirit of secular democracy" clearly resonates with the ameliorative aspirations of the document, providing guidance for the work of constitutional interpretation.[39] One interpretive opportunity presents itself in the linkage of those aspirations and RPA's corrupt practices provision. Thus to "persuade electors by showing them the light of reason" has both substantive as well as procedural possibilities. One way in which the State can take the initiative to pursue its reconstructive ambitions is to minimize religiously based electoral interference with that pursuit. The connection between constitutional aspiration and regulatory purpose is personified by Dr. Ambedkar, the prime mover behind both the adoption of the Constitution and the passage of the Representation of the People Act. As minister of law he navigated the complex elections law through Parliament, although very little of the debate occurring during the seven months between introduction and signing pertained to the speech-limiting provisions of Section 123, and of that much less actually illuminates the question of legislative intent.

Indeed, Ambedkar's own interventions raise as many questions as they answer. For example, on May 9, 1951, during a critical phase of the debate, he said: "I think that elections ought to be conducted on issues which have nothing to do with . . . religion or culture. A political party should not be permitted to appeal to any emotion which is aroused by reason of something which has nothing to do with the daily affairs of the people."[40] The apparent clarity of this remark cannot prevent one from asking: What

---

[39] As we have seen, the *ameliorative* model embraces the social reform impulse of Indian nationalism without ignoring countervailing impulses within the entrenched religious diversity of Indian society. Some accounts attach much greater emphasis to these countervailing impulses, seeing the commitment to group autonomy as more prominent than egalitarian justice. See, for example, Mahajan 1998. Consistent with this view, Mahajan's interpretation of the *Hindutva Cases* differs from mine. She understands the rulings to be an affirmation of the constitutional value of group autonomy. "The interpretation of the Supreme Court has . . . affirmed the autonomy of the religious domain, including its right to participate in the political domain. . . . By refusing to restrict the use of religion in politics, the Supreme Court has ensured that religious denominations and institutions are not excluded from or disadvantaged in the public realm." Ibid., 67–8.

[40] *Parliamentary Debates—Parliament of India* 1985, 8365.

could this possibly mean? After all, Ambedkar's role in Indian history and politics, including his work at the Constituent Assembly, is in essence a reflection of his profound awareness of the constitutive place of religion in the "daily affairs of the people." The idea that religion should be excluded from the rhetoric of campaigns on the basis of its remoteness from the concerns of the temporal world makes no sense at all, unless, that is, it was intended to express a normative rather than an empirical point. Suppose, in other words, Ambedkar had said: "A political party should not be permitted to appeal to any emotion which is aroused by reason of something which *should have* nothing to do with the daily affairs of the people." Such a sentiment would at least display a discernible consistency with the radical impulses that had impelled Ambedkar to confront the injustice of a society in which gross inequities were predominantly an expression of historically evolved religious experience.

This normative gloss allows the logic of Indian constitutional secularism (which Ambedkar had been instrumental in configuring) to manifest itself in legislation that, for all practical purposes, is an extension of the Constitution. Article 327 provides for the power of Parliament to make provision with respect to elections. RPA flows from this delegated authority. Its superintendence is, according to Article 324, placed under the aegis of an Election Commission headed by a chair and however many (currently two) additional commissioners Parliament may choose to appoint. While the actions of the Commission are not entirely unreviewable, its powers are very substantial, and widely recognized as such within the Indian political system. The Commission's considerable authority stems in large measure from its justly perceived independence; its incorruptibility and impartiality are of inestimable value to the political system. With respect to its role in enforcing the corrupt practices provisions of RPA, in particular the sections relating to improper religious appeals, it can easily jeopardize its reputation for objectivity by getting sucked into a vortex of controversy in this inherently polarized political arena.[41] This possibility, however, has not prevented the current chair, Dr. M. S. Gill, from emphati-

---

[41] Thus A. G. Noorani asks, "What business is it of the Election Commission or for that matter of any external authority but the party members and electorate at large to sit in judgment on changes in a party's 'policies'? Or its 'principles' or 'aims and objects'?" Noorani 1996, 235. It should be noted here that the jurisdiction of the Commission has been broadened since 1951. This has been done by amending the law to strengthen the exclusion of religion from political life. For example, in 1961 the scope of the provision on religious appeals was enlarged by deleting the word *systematic* from Section 123(3), thereby making even a single such appeal a corrupt practice. In 1989 Section 29A was added to RPA, requiring registration of all political parties, accompanied by a commitment "to the principles of socialism, secularism and democracy." In 1993 a proposal to strengthen 29A was extensively debated but never enacted into law. It would have banned associations bearing religious names from electoral competition. The proposal flowed from the widely perceived

cally endorsing the ameliorative understanding of corrupt practices. "Religion is a conservative force in society. Religion, all religions, cover injustice. Ambedkar was right to think in those terms [as a social reformer] and to frame the law [RPA] accordingly."[42]

The *Bukhari* case illustrates Gill's point. It concerned an election in Bombay between two Muslim candidates, one supported by the Muslim League and the other by Congress. Bukhari, the Muslim League candidate, stridently attacked his opponent, declaring in his campaign oratory that voters would become objects of divine displeasure if they supported Chagla, the candidate of Congress. The latter was an advocate of Muslim personal law reform, which, according to Bukhari, rendered him unfit to get the support of "any Muslim."[43] The Court found his diatribes to be in violation of RPA. "The whole outlook revealed by the speeches of Bukhari is that of a medieval crusader who had embarked on a Jehad for the extirpation of . . . heresy . . . which, in Bukhari's imagination, was represented by Chagla and his party. We do not consider such speeches to have any place in a democratic set-up under our Constitution. Indeed, they have none in the world of modern science which has compelled every type of religion, for its own survival, to seek securer foundations than child-like faith in and unquestioning conformity or obedience to an invariable set of religious beliefs and practices."[44]

Justice Beg went out of his way to make clear that the Court's objection to the speeches was not content specific. "We are not concerned so much with the real nature of what is opposed or supported as with the grounds on which a candidate claims support over a rival. We have to primarily examine the cloak which the appeal wears to parade in and not only what lies beneath it."[45] What lie beneath it of course are issues of social justice that in India extend well beyond the concerns and confines of the Muslim community. Emphasizing the packaging of the message rather than its substance is consistent with the public reason motif of the opinion as a

---

paradox that while RPA prohibited religious appeals, it permitted the formation and activities of parties (such as the Sikh Akali Dal) that had a religious or communal basis.

[42] Interview with the author, New Delhi, December 16, 1998. This is a point made also by some Indian scholars. For example, S. L. Verma writes: "In practice, religions are a conservative force. As such, they hamper economic growth, neglect material aspects of life, and obstruct growth of nationalism as a vehicle of modernization and development." Verma 1986, 33. It is important to point out here that much of the debate in 1951 relating to passage of the Representation of the People Act was directly concerned with the general issue of equality in Indian political life. Thus many of the provisions were argued in the context of the generally accepted commitment to limiting the influence of the wealthy in elections.

[43] *Bukhari* at 28.

[44] Ibid. at 31.

[45] Ibid.

whole and its understandable anxiety over the divisive potential of rhetoric that "whip[s] up low herd instincts and animosities."[46] However, this
process-oriented gesture did little to conceal the Court's evident concern
with substantive issues. The "medieval crusader" has no "place in a democratic set-up under [the Indian] Constitution," for his intolerant ways
are clearly offensive to the norms by which such a polity is expected to
conduct its business. But he is also out of place in a modern democracy
in which the spirit of science has seeped into the fabric of political life.[47]
His "unquestioning conformity or obedience to an invariable set of religious beliefs and practices" puts him in a confrontational position vis-à-
vis the democratic commitments of the Constitution. This "child-like
faith" in traditional religious beliefs and practices expresses itself not simply in Bukhari's condemnation of one who advocated reform of the Muslim personal law, but in his consignment of all those who support such
advocacy to the sorry predicament of divinely sanctioned subordination.
Beg suggests that modern science is the key to the survival of religion.
What seems more likely, however, is that absent a scientifically assisted
reform of society, the survival of Indian democracy will be at risk. And
given the centrality of religion to any reasonable assessment of the societal
status quo, RPA's corrupt practice provisions become useful tools in the
service of a legitimate, as well as worthy, constitutional cause.

The Contemporary Challenge

This brings us back to the irony of the Court's rumination on the dominant religion of India. Correctly construing Hinduism as much more than
theology, as a social and cultural presence that requires treatment as "a
way of life," it then went on to reverse holdings against politicians who
had promised to establish a Hindu State and commit it to the essentials
of Hindutva. But it is precisely the fact that religion in India *is* so pervasive
and all-encompassing, with consequences deeply problematic for the egalitarian objectives of the Constitution, that provides RPA's campaign restrictions with a measure of coherence and principled consistency.[48] Thus,

[46] Ibid. at 24.

[47] "[Modern scientific man] does not permit his religion, which should be essentially his
individual affair, to invade what are properly the spheres of law, politics, ethics, aesthetics,
economics, and technology, even when its administration is institutionalised and it operates
as a social force." Ibid. at 32.

[48] V. S. Rekhi's criticism of earlier rulings on RPA is predicated on the recognition of this
all-encompassing religious presence. "No opinion of the Court shows an awareness of the
relation of religion to social structure either in general or in particular relation to elections."
Rekhi 1993, 200. In particular, Rekhi is dismayed by the Court's failure to appreciate that
religion may be the only way for the have-nots in India to organize politically in pursuit of

the very conflation of religion and culture that the Court then proceeded to find exculpatory as applied to the charge of political corruption is what provides a compelling policy rationale for RPA. Moreover, it is a rationale that fits comfortably within the secular logic and commitments of the Constitution, the latter aptly characterized by an observation from an earlier opinion cited by the Court, but not fully appreciated by the judges for the implications it contains. "The concept of secularism is one facet of the right to equality woven as the central golden thread in the fabric depicting the pattern of the scheme in our Constitution."[49] One does not have to embrace wholeheartedly the late nineteenth-century Indian social reformer K. T. Telang's indictment of Hinduism for "preach[ing] not the equality of men but their inequality," and for being in a state of "war against the principles of democracy," to grasp the significance in India of religion's challenge to the secular State and its reconstructive aspirations.

That challenge, of course, is most evident in the resurgence of Hindu nationalism, a movement that should never be viewed as representing Hindus generally (an impossibility, given the radically heterodox nature of the religion), but one that voices a sociocultural agenda that historically qualifies as the foil of Indian nationalism. The democratization of a rigidly hierarchical social order that is correlated strongly with a thickly constituted religious presence had always been an animating principle of the Indian independence movement, one that continued to give meaning to postcolonial constitutional politics. Hence it must be observed with more than just passing interest that historically the spirit of Hindu nationalism has been nurtured by high-caste Hindus who have been notable in their insensitivity to India's downtrodden. "Hindutva is a political movement for upper caste hegemony, based on Hinduism."[50] As Christophe Jaffrelot has pointed out, "Hindu nationalism . . . largely reflects the Brahminical view of the high caste reformers who shaped its ideology."[51] Indeed it has been the pervasiveness of this ethic in both ideology and practice that explains why it has had only minimal success in attracting support from

---

their interests. While perceptive in its critique of the Court's failures, his analysis is insufficiently attentive to the ways in which religious practices and discourse serve to limit the socioeconomic progress of the disadvantaged, and thus the reasons why a consistent application of RPA may reasonably be seen as serving these people's long-term interests.

[49] *Prabhoo* at 148.

[50] Ram 1996, 519.

[51] Jaffrelot 1996, 13. See also Sarkar 1996, 277. "The votaries of Hindutva have tended to come in the main from high castes quite self-conscious about their status privileges." And Arun Patnaik and K.S.R.V.S. Chalam point out that the discourse of Hindutva "aims at a reaffirmation of the Hindu caste order." To the extent that "[I]ndian history is a history of unfinished tasks set by the critics of Brahminism," the Hindu nationalists can rightly be viewed as historically retrograde. Patnaik and Chalam 1966, 268, 263.

low-caste Hindus.[52] Even the efforts to reshape the movement's appeal to disadvantaged Hindus by capitalizing on resentments against Muslims have been notably unproductive as exercises in mass mobilization. In this respect Hindu nationalism, if not unique, is distinguishable from most contemporary religious nationalist movements in not being a populist-based movement directed against the entrenched economic power of established interests. The threat in all of this to the ameliorative constitution, which is to say secular constitutionalism in India, is clear.[53]

What, then, is wrong with this bit of nasty campaign rhetoric from Mr. Thackeray? "We are fighting this election for the protection of Hinduism. Therefore, we do not care for the votes of the Muslims. This country belongs to Hindus and will remain so."[54] The Court found this sentiment in violation of RPA's proscription against speech that promotes enmity and hatred against classes of citizens, which it most assuredly does. But it might also be seen as a verbal assault on secular democracy in India, because indirectly it serves to perpetuate an unjust status quo structured around a radically skewed distribution of wealth, status, and influence. Votes gained as a result of an attack on the Muslim minority are votes that surely will, if sufficient in number, translate into policies adverse to the interests of lower-class Hindus (as well as Muslims and others), and so may be seen as violating the spirit of secular democracy as outlined in the Constitution. What qualifies this speech as a "corrupt practice" is only partially revealed by its explicit attack on Indian national unity; a complete account must also clarify the meaning of its implicit attack on ameliorative secularism.

Indeed, this attack is evident in some of the journalistic reactions to the Supreme Court decisions by Hindu nationalist writers. "It is unfortunate," said one, "that fault is being found with a clear, rational, fair, incisive and sound enunciation of law, constitution and culture of India by the apex court."[55] This approval provided an opportunity to claim vindication for longstanding political positions. Thus Arun Shourie pointed out, "A major sin of the judgment for the secularists arose from the fact the Court accepted, indeed adopted in toto the definition of Hindu, of Hindutva which the RSS and the BJP have been maintaining is what they

[52] Jaffrelot 1995, 47.

[53] As Sumit Sarkar points out, "A construction of Hindu unity that evaded rather than sought to reform or even significantly ameliorate hierarchy needs for its sustenance the notion of the Muslim as an ever-present, existential threat, actualized and renewed, furthermore, in recurrent communal riots." Sarkar 1996, 289.

[54] Quoted in *Prabhoo* at 139.

[55] Jagmohan, "Hinduism and Hindutva: What the Supreme Court Says," *Hindustan Times*, January 8, 1996.

have meant whenever they have used these expressions."[56] The author then revealingly moved from approval to advice, expressing the hope that one day the Court will examine, as part of its interpretive role in relation to the illegalities of corrupt practices, the solicitation of votes on the basis of class antagonism. "How come that, while it is an offense under our laws to spread hatred or solicit votes on the basis of religion, caste, etc., it is perfectly all right to spread hatred and enmity, and to solicit votes on the basis of class?"[57] To which the secularist disturbed by the Court's obliviousness to the ameliorative logic of RPA might respond with wry admiration—as well as contempt—for his opponent's clever effort to steer the Court toward the embrace of an opposing logic.

We now have a plausible non-Rawlsian answer to the question of why Section 123 seeks to minimize the occasions for elected officials to exercise their powers on religious grounds. Or at least it is an answer that illustrates that the norms of public reason must be framed in such a way that culturally specific iterations are given their due. Indian restrictions on religious speech can be justified according to content-neutral principles that conform to contemporary conceptualizations of the liberal State; but those principles do not readily conform to the nonneutrality of the Indian State as delineated in the nation's Constitution. It is only when political liberalism is identified with neutrality that the alternative rationale for these restrictions—one that finds in the substance of religious belief and practice a reason for action—will be deemed illiberal. And as taken up in the next section, notions of corrupt practices ingrained in legal precedent

---

[56] Shourie 1996. But this vindication provided only partial satisfaction. "The Court's formulation is also evidence of our state—namely that the only way in which references to Hinduism in election speeches can be defended is by defining Hinduism out of existence. . . . It can be small satisfaction that a formulation that came to be put out as a defensive reaction is now to be the official definition of the faith, that is, by which it is not a faith at all." The author then shrewdly employs the logic of the Court's obfuscation of the distinction between religion and culture to defend the nationalist position against the Court's criticism of its campaign rhetoric. "As the word Hindu is not to be understood in terms of narrow-minded religion, as Hindutva, . . . how come it became despicable to say that Maharashtra shall be the first Hindu state, by what reasoning did the expression merit the disdain of the Court?" In an interview with the author, Shourie explained that such a statement may well be grounds for an RPA violation, but only, he claimed, if the law is applied uniformly. But because, he maintained, Muslim politicians are permitted to say things that Hindus running for office are not, Shourie questioned the appropriateness of overturning the election result in this case. Indeed, the official Sangh Parivar line on RPA appears to be nominal support for the law as long as it is narrowly and uniformly applied. Thus in the Parliament debate in 1993 over the banning of religiously based parties, L. K. Advani said, "I would never object to [RPA]. I think this is a sound law." *Lok Sabha Debates* 1993, 518. He then went on to vigorously denounce the proposed addition to the law.

[57] Ibid.

reinforce the noninterventionist constitutional requirement of contemporary liberalism while providing a sympathetic, if ultimately unsuccessful, hearing for the Rawlsian case for public reason.

CORRUPTION: PROCESS AND SUBSTANCE

Section 298 of the Indian Penal Code makes punishable whoever "with the deliberate intention of wounding the religious feelings of any person, utters any word or makes any sound in the hearing of that person." It is the sort of regulation that may remind Americans of some campus speech codes, most of which are widely seen, since the Supreme Court's decision in *R.A.V. v St. Paul*, as unconstitutional viewpoint-based violations of the First Amendment. *R.A.V.* was the case cited by the Court in *Rosenberger v University of Virginia*, where it held that a public university could not withhold funding for a Christian publication while providing support to other student publications. In his majority opinion, Justice Anthony Kennedy wrote, "The government must abstain from regulating speech when the specific motivating ideology or the opinion or perspective of the speaker is the rationale for the restriction."[58] There was much in Justice Kennedy's opinion that the minority contested, including the application of this principle to the case at hand; with the doctrine, they generally agreed.

Viewpoint neutrality has become the axiomatic precept of First Amendment jurisprudence, as well as the *grundnorm* of the "procedural republic." It need not distinguish between religious speech and other types of expression, since in a liberal polity a religious point of view is in principle no different from any other perspective one chooses to embrace. This follows from what Michael Sandel refers to as "the voluntarist justification of neutrality," the requirement that "[G]overnment should be neutral toward religion in order to respect persons as free and independent selves, capable of choosing their religious convictions for themselves."[59] Sandel of course is critical of this ascendant view. "Protecting religion as a lifestyle, as one among the values that an independent self may have, may miss the role that religion plays in the lives of those for whom the observance of religious duties is a constitutive end, essential to their good and indispensable to their identity."[60] In the American context this argument leads to deference and accommodation in the face of religious obligations that compete with State policies. In India just the opposite is true; where

---

[58] *Rosenberger* at 829.
[59] Sandel 1996, 63.
[60] Ibid., 67.

it more readily may serve to legitimate an unjust status quo, such accommodation is a much costlier indulgence.

As we think about restrictions on religious speech in Indian penal and electoral law, the case for their reasonability turns on the sociopolitical implications of deeply encumbered selves. The Indian Constitution's various exceptions to "First Amendment" freedoms are an implicit rejection of the American neutrality axiom, since religion as a lived experience is, for most people in India, much more than a constellation of views and beliefs that one chooses to adopt. Hence State indifference to the substance of ideas cannot so easily be justified as it can in the United States. Interestingly, Justice Kennedy's opinion in *Rosenberger* acknowledges that the doctrine of viewpoint neutrality possesses a certain awkwardness when applied to religious speech. "It is, in a sense, something of an understatement to speak of religious thought and discussion as just a viewpoint, as distinct from a comprehensive body of thought. The nature of our origins and destiny and their dependence on the existence of a divine being have been subjects of philosophic inquiry throughout human history."[61] But there is nothing in this acknowledgment to the effect that religious expression, though comprehensive, is anything more than "a vast area of inquiry,"[62] that it might constitute, in Justice Gajendragadkar's phrase, "a way of life and nothing more."[63] It is this characteristically American separation between comprehensiveness and consequence that makes a principled commitment to judicial agnosticism relatively uncontroversial.

Viewpoint neutrality has a connection as well to political corruption. In the United States, the constitutional debate over corrupt practices centers on statutory restrictions on campaign financing. Nothing in this debate bears directly on questions of religion; nevertheless American judicial scrutiny of these restrictions shows why the notion of *corruption* is important to a comparative analysis of religious speech in the public arena. The same principle that protects candidates and politicians who publicly proclaim the Christian content of American identity also protects the unlimited expenditures of those who support their political ambitions.

Consider in this regard Justice Scalia's criticism of a majority opinion upholding a Michigan limitation on corporate campaign expenditures. "Under [the Court's] mode of analysis virtually anything the Court deems politically undesirable can be turned into political corruption—by simply describing its effects as politically 'corrosive,' which is close enough to

---

[61] *Rosenberger* at 831.

[62] Ibid.

[63] *Yagnapurushdasji* at 513. Or as another justice said while sitting as a delegate in the Constituent Assembly that framed the Constitution, "[Y]ou can never separate social life from religious life." Government of India Press 1967, vol. 2, 266.

'corruptive' to qualify."[64] Scalia was objecting to the Court's discovery of a "New Corruption," found to exist in the distortive effect of massive infusions of corporate wealth into the political process. According to the Court, there was no correlation between immense aggregations of corporate wealth and the public's support for the corporation's ideas, a lack of association that constitutionally justified the State's representation-reinforcing restriction. Scalia's critique parallels Martin Shapiro's argument that "By calling various inequalities corruption we can ignore the risks to freedom that are endemic in the pursuit of equality."[65] Underlying the criticisms of both Scalia and Shapiro is the latter's further observation: "Americans enjoy an ambivalent relationship with freedom of speech. They believe in it for the good guys but not the bad guys. There was a time when the bad guys were on the left and the hated danger was 'subversion.' Today the bad guys are on the right and the danger is 'corruption.'"[66]

From this perspective the judicial abuse of the term *corruption* represents a departure from the constitutional requirement of viewpoint neutrality. It is a perspective perhaps reflective of what has been called "the liberal transvaluation of corruption," a development traceable to Hobbes, in which "[t]o call a regime corrupt is to say something about the speaker's preferences, not about the regime itself."[67] Just as subversion was a term used in the past to delegitimate ideas on the left, the term *corruption* has assumed a similar role today in attacking the system opposed by the left. In both instances the terms should be applied narrowly by judges only to specific acts of malfeasance, for example, a conspiracy to overthrow the government or a bribe offered to a public official. Scalia's sharply worded dissent in *Austin* seeks to restore to the law of campaign finance restrictions the logic behind the Court's landmark decision in *Buckley v Valeo*, in which the meaning of corruption was to be limited to quid pro quo arrangements (or the appearance thereof) connected to large contributions. Or as Chief Justice William Rehnquist wrote in *Federal Election Commission v NCPAC*: "Corruption is a subversion of the political process. Elected officials are influenced to act contrary to their obligations of office by the prospect of financial gain to themselves or infusions of money into their campaigns. The hallmark of corruption is the financial *quid pro quo*: dollars for political favors."[68] This quid pro quo emphasis had led the Court in *Buckley* to strike down limitations on independent expendi-

---

[64] *Austin* at 684.
[65] Shapiro 1989, 393.
[66] Ibid.
[67] Euben 1989, 230.
[68] *Federal Election Commission* at 497.

tures, since the implicit meaning of corruption contained in such limitations was a broader political one having to do with the best way to organize a society. "[T]he concept that government may restrict the speech of some elements of our society in order to enhance the relative voice of others is wholly foreign to the First Amendment, which was designed . . . 'to assure unfettered exchange of ideas for the bringing about of political and social changes desired by the people.'"[69]

What, under this account, can we say of the Indian use of the term *corrupt practice* to refer to certain kinds of religiously inspired speech in electoral campaigns? Following the argument in the previous section, we might conclude that the validity of the usage hinges on the fact that the Constitution itself is a principal agent of social change, not just the people, as suggested in *Buckley* about the American scheme. Moreover, in the spirit of ameliorative secularism, it is a specific kind of social change that is constitutionally prescribed, so that corruption—the departure from the politics of first principles and collective self-understanding—need not be subject to the American-like limitations of viewpoint neutrality. Where, in the United States, "[p]olitical corruption violates and undermines the norms of the system of public order which is deemed indispensable for the maintenance of political democracy,"[70] in India a more ambitious democratic agenda serves to broaden the scope of corrupt practices to cover, as we have seen, campaign speech that advances the prospects that governmental policy will be based on religious considerations.[71]

To be sure, the Court in *Austin* ignored Justice Scalia's concerns about the New Corruption and extended the mantle of corrupt practices beyond the narrow quid pro quo focus of *Buckley*. But the Court's extension stays well within the procedural boundaries of representative government. The infirmity of massive corporate expenditures to advance particular policy objectives is found in the disjunction between political speech and the amount of public support for the funded positions. This introduces a distortion into the political process that may be legislatively corrected consistent with constitutionally mandated First Amendment requirements, including viewpoint neutrality. As Dennis Thompson notes, "The idea that corruption involves bypassing the democratic process is not partial to-

---

[69] *Buckley* at 48.

[70] Berg, Hahn, and Schmidhauser 1976, 3. This is fairly typical of the definitions found in the literature of political corruption in the United States.

[71] The one empirical study that examines opinion on the use of religious and caste appeals in elections shows a strong majority of respondents believing that such appeals interfere with the right to vote. Interestingly, this belief is correlated with caste affiliation, with scheduled caste respondents most opposed to the use of these appeals and Brahmin respondents least opposed. Jhingta 1996, 282.

ward any particular view about democracy."[72] Removing the distortion opens the way to a fuller realization of what Rawls refers to as "a political conception of justice for the main institutions of political and social life."[73] Indeed, as one commentator points out, "[W]e can best explain *Austin's* redefinition of political corruption by returning to some basic legal and political theory," namely Rawls's principle of an equal right to participation, a principle of course included among the constitutional essentials for a liberal and just polity.[74]

Another finds in *Austin* support for Thompson's deliberative theory of liberal democratic governance, in which Rawlsian public reason considerations are evident. "[I]f representation involves deliberation about the public good, then contributions that influence representatives are a corruption of the democratic process."[75] Genuine reflection will not occur if representatives are, by virtue of their obligations to contributors, essentially unreachable through reasoned argument. What Thompson refers to as "the improper use of public office" can mean both the pursuit of private gain through official misconduct, and the subversion of the democratic process with obstacles that preclude reasoned deliberation. It is this second invocation of the language of impropriety that links campaign financing and religious speech, since the excesses of both have in common the tendency to undercut the liberal polity's ideal of public reason. "A belief in the importance of public deliberation is essential for a reasonable constitutional regime, and specific institutions and arrangements need to be laid down to support and encourage it."[76] Acting on this belief might cause one to favor limitations on activities that lead to public decisions based on "nonpublic reasons"—as arguably would be the case for the legislative recipient of large amounts of money and for the exponent of a comprehensive religious doctrine.[77]

---

[72] Thompson 1995, 29. Thompson focuses on what he calls "the modern conception of corruption," which he suggests is more limited in scope than the traditional conception in its emphasis on the pursuit of private purposes rather than on broader social and economic forces. The distinction, however, could be misleading if it deflects attention from critical differences ingrained in the constitutive choices of different constitutional polities. As the Indian example suggests, the relevant distinction has less to do with contrasting *conceptions* of corruption than with the fact that alternative conceptions of *democracy* produce contrasting understandings of what constitutes a corrupt act. In both cases, though, corruption involves an attack on regime principles.

[73] Rawls 1993, 175.

[74] Edwards 1996, 20.

[75] Burke 1997, 148.

[76] Rawls 1993, lix.

[77] Or as Gutmann and Thompson write, "Deliberative democracy asks citizens and officials to justify public policy by giving reasons that can be accepted by those who are bound by it. This disposition to seek mutually justifiable reasons expresses the core of the process of deliberation." Gutmann and Thompson 1996, 52.

Of course, despite this connecting logic, it is extremely doubtful that an American court would ever use the "new corruption" as a constitutional impetus for upholding restrictions on religious speech in the public arena. Were the judges all political liberals in the Rawlsian sense, they very likely would still value untrammeled speech rights over public reason-inspired legal limits on expression; but they would undoubtedly see the restrictions as having some principled foundation. Yet if they were so inclined, they could view their efforts as responsive to corrupt practices, as a judicial defense of the constitutive commitments of a liberal polity. That indeed is what the Indian Court appears to have done in upholding the constitutionality of RPA's regulation of religious speech in campaigns. The fact that the Court then proceeded to overturn the convictions of Hindu nationalist politicians prosecuted under the statute suggests very strongly that the principled underpinnings of the constitutional ruling were more in line with Rawlsian assumptions about liberal constitutionalism than with the logic of ameliorative secularism. But the Court never made clear why the need to govern "by the light of reason" required legally enforceable sanctions, why unlike other secular democratic polities such as the United States, reliance on other mechanisms would not be sufficient. Indeed Rawls himself does not advocate the legal codification of his ideal of public reason. The most telling criticism of the Court's rulings—that together they constituted a "watering down" of the provisions of RPA and "a very severe blow to the principle of secular democracy"—derives whatever force it may have from the special needs of *this* secular democracy and not from the constitutional essentials of political liberalism.[78]

CONCLUSION

Suppose a familiarity with Indian law persuaded American lawmakers of the wisdom of enacting an RPA in the United States. Let us assume further that after its enactment into law, it is quickly applied to the governor of Mississippi, who has persisted in pushing his Christian nation claim. For example, in campaigning for one of his followers who is running for Con-

---

[78] The criticism is taken from V. M. Tarkunde, "Hindutva and the Supreme Court," *Hindustan Times*, January 10, 1996. The weakness of Tarkunde's argument is precisely that it does not explain *why* "an appeal for the creation of a Hindu State is obviously contrary to the principle of secular democracy and is a corrupt practice." Clearly the creation of such a State, just as the creation of a Christian State, would conflict with secular democracy; but why the speech itself is a corrupt practice requires an argument that connects the expression to the specific aims of secular democracy in India. One version of such an argument may be found in Martha Nussbaum 1997. Focusing on India, she argues that all religious discourse that encourages the denial of equality to women should be viewed as unacceptable within a constitutional democracy.

gress, he is quoted as saying: "Joe deserves your support because he understands the meaning of America, that it is and has always been in essence a Christian nation. I can promise you that in all that Joe will do as your representative, he will be guided by the precepts of his Christian identity." Joe then gets elected but is deprived of his victory for having permitted his campaign to run afoul of the new law.

How might the United States Supreme Court respond to this result? Consider three possibilities. (1) The finding against Joe is reversed, and the statute under which his election was denied to him is held unconstitutional. The law violates both the freedom of speech and free exercise clauses of the First Amendment. (2) The finding against Joe is reversed, but the statute under which the election was denied to him is held constitutional. Joe has done nothing wrong since his Christian identity is a cultural affiliation, not a religious calling. The law, however, is consistent with the spirit of the Constitution, specifically its secular commitment to reasoned deliberation in the public arena. (3) The finding against Joe is upheld, and the statute under which his election was denied to him is constitutional. The First Amendment is not an absolute, and the rights guaranteed under it are bounded by important public welfare considerations, among which is the discouragement of religious motivations in the making of public policy.

Option (1) is the obvious candidate for selection for reasons that should be quite evident. It fits all the expectations Americans bring to the case based on prevailing precedent and doctrine. But it is worth considering why (2) and (3) appear on their face to be implausible choices; doing so will highlight the major point of this chapter, that the effort to derive guidelines and principles for the regulation of religious discourse in the public sphere cannot proceed only from an exercise in abstract moral reasoning, but must confront as well the diversity of experience in secular constitutional arrangements.

Option (2) represents the approach taken by the Indian Supreme Court in the RPA cases. It involved a decision by the Court to understate the religious significance of Hinduism in favor of a cultural understanding, thereby freeing the defendant Hindu nationalists of legal liability in the face of a statute that legitimately seeks to structure campaign debate according to a constitutional norm of reasoned deliberation. In the American context this norm (deduced from the essentials of a liberal polity) must, unlike in India, confront the categorical language of the First Amendment without the support of any exception clauses that might be viewed textually as a convenient constitutional location for asserting the relevant ideal. An additional (and more interesting, if debatable) obstacle resides in the greater difficulty one would have in making a cultural claim on behalf of Christian identity, which much more so than its Hindu counterpart is something one experiences as a matter of faith rather than (at least in most instances) as a way of life. So an American court would have even less success than an Indian one in eliding the religious significance of a candidate's promise to pursue a sectarian agenda grounded in religious tradition.

Option (3) looks like a coherent and perhaps sensible solution for India, but makes very little sense for the United States. Not only is there much less warrant for perceiving the majority religion in the United States as a way of life, but to the limited extent that it can be so viewed, its role in structuring social institutions and relations hardly compares in magnitude with the role in that regard of the majority religion in India. Therefore, the legally sanctioned discouragement of religiously motivated public policy has minimal constitutional standing when, as in the United States, it is not necessary for the attainment of public welfare objectives that are at once urgent and constitutionally directed. To be sure, the secularization of political discourse can always be asserted to have policy consequences. And occasionally, as, say, in the case of legislation affecting people's sexual behavior, religious arguments may play a critical role in explaining, for better or worse, the evolution of policies. But to imagine something comparable to the Indian situation would require viewing the historic systematic subordination of a class of people in the United States as having been the result largely of religious beliefs and practices that are now illegal by dint of constitutional mandate.

It is quite revealing that when public welfare considerations *are* introduced in the United States as an occasion for limiting religious freedom, it occurs in response to someone's claim for an exemption on religious grounds from an otherwise unexceptionable law. Since the Supreme Court's controversial decision in *Employment Division v Smith* (and its subsequent invalidation of the Religious Freedom Restoration Act), upholding the public welfare, defined neutrally as the need to reinforce civil authority, does not require the demonstration of a compelling State interest. The Indian Constitution, on the other hand, defines with unmistakable certainty what *constitutes* a compelling State interest.[79] So clear is its incorporation of the egalitarian ideal into the text of the document that the meaning of corruption as having something to do with the direct (or as in the case of RPA, indirect) frustration of that aspiration is not a fanciful

---

[79] In chapter 9 I argue that *Smith* might have been better decided had the Court been more sensitive to egalitarian considerations that are more familiar within the Indian Church/State jurisprudential tradition. However, as we shall see, in the United States these considerations push in the direction of a more expansive interpretation of religious freedom in the face of State regulation.

notion. This suggests that the appeal of public reason as an ideal for liberal polities is more variable than any abstract account of its virtues might lead one to presume. Indeed it turns out that the case for limiting certain kinds of religious speech in democratic deliberation is strongest when it is identified with the defense of constitutional essentials that are not recognized as such in the articulated premises of political liberalism.

Chapter Seven

ADJUDICATING SECULARISM: POLITICAL LIBERALISM OR RELIGIOUS REVIVALISM?

THE PHILOSOPHICAL LIMITATIONS of political liberalism in providing a strong rationale for regulating religious rhetoric in the electoral arena is only one part of the story of judicial engagement in the *Hindutva Cases*. The remainder of the story is also concerned with liberalism's significance in the constitutional politics of Indian secularism. But in this installment—which could be titled *The Mystery of the Hindutva Cases*—our concern is less with the formal structure and internal coherence of the opinions and more with possible judicial uses of liberal argumentation in the ongoing power struggle over the meaning of Indian national identity.

Much of the mystery surrounding these cases concerns the behavior of Justice J. S. Verma, the author of all the Supreme Court's opinions in the election law cases. The opinions are subject to alternative interpretations, which in itself is neither mysterious nor enigmatic. What distinguish the puzzling aspects of these decisions from the interpretive uncertainties surrounding the results of routinely complex constitutional adjudication are the questions they raise about the role of the judiciary in the campaign to reconstruct the foundational blocks of Indian secularism. It is an effort, which as we have seen in chapter 3, involves the very clever appropriation of the discourse of constitutional liberalism to advance the agenda of Hindu nationalism. While the occasional need to mobilize the *Sangh Parivar's* political base ensures that the more extreme, visceral appeals to Hindu solidarity and privilege will not soon disappear from the rhetorical landscape of Indian politics, the basic arithmetic of electoral ascendance and governing continuity means that these appeals will be muted in favor of arguments more acceptable to moderate sensibilities within the broader Indian electorate. In this connection the courts are vitally important as a potential source for legitimating some of the more contested aspects of religious and cultural nationalism.

For this reason alone the reaction to the judgments in the *Hindutva Cases*—enthusiasm within saffron circles and disappointment among many secularists—commands our attention. The Court, of course, cannot be held responsible for the manner in which its judgments are received. Interests on both sides of an issue can usually be expected to offer tendentious readings of judicial decisions; moreover, unattractive results flowing from the deployment of entirely reasonable (and benignly chosen) interpretive principles of constitutional adjudication are quite common. Nevertheless, the possibility that the Indian Supreme Court has become, wittingly or unwittingly, a medium for the achievement of antisecular aspirations cannot be ignored.[1]

Hence our second look at the election law cases of 1995. The focus in the previous chapter was on the reasoning that led the Supreme Court to uphold the constitutionality of the Representation of the People Act's regulation of electoral appeals to religion. That outcome can be viewed straightforwardly as a victory for the opponents of Hindutva, who succeeded in protecting an important weapon in the arsenal of their legal defense of secular institutions. But as has already been suggested, there is a certain hollowness in that victory, one that stems from the absence in Justice Verma's opinion of an argument rooted in the ameliorative commitment of the Constitution's secular blueprint. Now it is necessary to refocus from the constitutionality of the law to its specific applications, largely to determine whether that absence has a significance beyond the purely heuristic value inhering in an inquiry into the scope and possibilities of philosophical liberalism. We need to move, in other words, from the domain of constitutional essentials to the domain of political essentials.

But the story line attached to this second domain requires a different narrative presentation. Indeed, it requires three separate, if interrelated, narrations, each displaying an alternative version of what the real story is about. Thus one possibility is that the ultimate outcomes in the *Hindutva Cases* represent a principled extension of the argumentation underlying the judgment on RPA's constitutionality, that in the end what emerges is a tale of liberalism ascendant. In a different telling, liberalism remains central to the plot, which, however, thickens in such a way as to lead to a confounding of expectations and a consequent reduction of that

---

[1] At the outset it is important to be clear about the meaning of antisecular aspirations. So-called communalists often argue that they are the only dedicated secularists in India. Their opponents, they say, are "pseudosecularists," political opportunists who reveal their hypocrisy in a variety of ways, most notably and egregiously in their incessant pandering to religious minorities. In the extreme cases, such as Rajiv Gandhi's capitulation in the aftermath of *Shah Bano*, the charge of pseudosecularism rings true, but the more general polemical critique within which such instances are enumerated fails to give sufficient attention to the special features of Indian, which is to say, *ameliorative* secularism.

political orientation to a distinctly subservient role in the advancement of Hindutva politics. And in yet a final version, the driving force behind the actions in the story is neither liberalism nor the politics of Hindutva, but a jurisprudential theory whose implementation can lead to results either liberal or illiberal, which is to say, compatible with the endings in both of the other stories.

Story I: Liberalism Ascendant

Not long after he delivered the judgments in the *Hindutva Cases*, Justice Verma received some unsolicited praise for his efforts from the legal philosopher Ronald Dworkin, who happened to be in India at the time of the decisions. Coming from such a pedigreed source, as well as someone unaffected by any interest in the outcome of the litigation, the evaluation was especially welcome as a confirmation of the justice's self-perception as a liberal jurist doing the necessary, if not always popular, work of providing justice within a politically charged environment.[2] Indeed, occurring near the conclusion of a lengthy judicial career, Verma's role in the *Hindutva Cases* may be viewed as the culmination of a distinguished tenure as a judicial voice of reason and liberal values.

A number of significant legal engagements provides support for such a characterization. Verma himself is most proud of what he accomplished as a member of the High Court in Madhya Pradesh during the dark days of Indira Gandhi's rule in the mid-1970s. "I think I was the first judge in the country to have rejected the Government's argument that the Emergency proclamation took precedence over the right to life and liberty. I was even short-listed to be transferred out of MP as a penalty for not falling in line."[3] This image of a resolute fighter for governmental accountability has been a recurrent one in the justice's subsequent history, most notably in his critical intervention in the exposure and investigation of the "Jain hawala" government corruption scandal in late 1994. Verma's tenacious and unprecedented pursuit of governmental malfeasance attracted enormous attention, accompanied by extraordinarily favorable assessments of his performance. "This was a case," according to the Su-

---

[2] Interview with the author, February 28, 1999, Ghaziabad, India. On another occasion, Justice Verma met with Justice Antonin Scalia of the American Supreme Court, who pointed out to the Indian judge that "You and I have a different approach." Inasmuch as Dworkin and Scalia have written extensively of the differences in their respective approaches to constitutional jurisprudence, the value attached by Verma to the approval of his work by Dworkin is quite understandable.

[3] *India Today*, March 15, 1996, 118. Said G. P. Singh, former chief justice of the Madhya Pradesh High Court, "The mettle of the judges was really tested during the Emergency. And Verma showed courage of conviction." Ibid., 117.

preme Court advocate and constitutional scholar Rajeev Dhavan, "where the rule of law seemed to have gone off the rails. Verma steered it back."[4]

There is a consistency between these high-profile instances and judgments rendered by Verma in less notorious cases. For example, in a 1991 challenge to a state government's dismissal of government employees without reason, the Supreme Court, in an opinion by Justice Verma, reinstated the workers amidst a ringing rebuke of the state for its indefensible actions. "We have no doubt that the Court does not envisage or permit unfairness or unreasonableness in State actions in any sphere of its activity contrary to the professed ideals in the Preamble."[5] In a sense the ruling anticipates the judgments of the *Hindutva Cases*, which also involved the dismissal of governmental employees, in this instance officials whose electoral victories had been overturned on the basis of alleged violations of the Representation of the People Act. One of the officials was the chief minister of the state of Maharashtra, whose "despicable" campaign rhetoric could not erase the fact that he had, after all, been selected for his job in accordance with the sovereign will of the people. "When you unseat . . . the Chief Minister of a State . . . the standard of proof required [must be very high]."[6]

In fact, the standard of proof appropriate for the review of an election petition should, according to Justice Verma, be the same as what is required in a criminal case.[7] It is easy to see why. While a violation of the election law does not subject the perpetrator to criminal liability, the penalty that may be invoked—denying the winner of an election the fruits of victory—has a punitive impact extending well beyond the hardship imposed on the successful candidate. It represents a short-circuiting of the democratic process at its most critical moment, depriving a majority of

---

[4] Ibid., 115. This comment appears in a cover story on Justice Verma published in India's leading English-language news weekly. As illustrated by the following sorts of comments, it is a story of sustained and unremitting adulation. "Verma has given a new and powerful dimension to activism, and, in the process, enhanced the prestige of the Supreme Court as well as that of the country." Ibid., 114. "Law is what the courts and public officials do with it. . . . If the Jain hawala case is one of breaking the law to run away with the silver, Verma has shown that even if public officials fail, the Court can ensure that the law won't." Ibid., 118. It should be noted here that Verma's actions in forcing the Central Bureau of Investigation (CBI) to investigate all the accusations against some of the highest political figures in India did attract some criticism, focusing on what was considered to be a rather heavy-handed and potentially dangerous use of judicial power.

[5] *Shrikekha Vidharthi* at 549.

[6] Interview with the author.

[7] Interview with the author. Respected authority supports this position. "It is settled law that the charge of corrupt practice is to be proved like a criminal charge and that the same standard of proof as is required in a criminal case is to be applied in the testing of the evidence of corrupt practice in an election petition." Jain and Jain 1998, 1.432.

voters the right to be governed in accordance with their freely expressed collective judgment. As John Hart Ely has argued, "[U]nblocking stoppages in the democratic process is what judicial review ought preeminently to be about."[8] What it decidedly should not be about is the exercise of "ultimate sovereignty over society's substantive value choices."[9]

Thus even though a particular electoral outcome may owe to a successful campaign propagating morally and politically questionable ideas, including ones connected to improper religious themes, this should not be reversed without incriminating evidence. It had been argued before the Court that the provocative and incendiary speeches delivered by a party leader made the candidate of that party legally liable, because the nature of the speaker-candidate relationship implied his or her consent. If the statute was intended to protect the electoral process from undue corruption, then, it was contended, permitting candidates to benefit from an improper appeal for votes simply because others spoke on their behalf would undercut this objective. Indeed, such a position had been accepted, and even given a distinctly robust formulation in the opinion of Justice Variava of the Bombay High Court: "[W]here the plank has been declared by the leader of the party, once it is proved and held that the plank declared by the leader amounts to a corrupt practice, every candidate of that party will be bound by that plank."[10] To which Justice Verma of the Supreme Court responded that the requirement of consent in the statute had to be strictly construed to mean that "it must be free consent given by the giver of consent, of his own volition."[11]

But if one of the constitutional essentials of a liberal democracy is that "candidates at elections have to try to persuade electors by showing them the light of reason and not by inflaming their blind and disruptive passions," should it then matter that the inflaming is done by one person while another, who happens to be the actual candidate, is off to the side nodding in approval? Does Verma's construction create a huge loophole through which the polluters of the electoral environment can easily violate the sanctity of the deliberative process? Despite the ease with which it is possible to answer the first question negatively and the second positively, a commitment to liberal political values, rather than a desire to alleviate the rhetorical burden of the Hindu right, lies behind the overturning of

---

[8] Ely 1980, 117.

[9] Ibid., vii.

[10] *Ramakant Mayekar v Celine D'Silva*, 17.

[11] *Manohar Joshi* at 677. As for the relevance of party planks, Verma writes: "The so-called plank of the political party may at best be relevant only for appreciation of the context in which a speech was made by a leader of the political party during the election campaign, but no more for the purpose of pleading corrupt practice in the election petition against a particular candidate." Ibid. at 678.

the lower court's interpretation. Having used public reason-based arguments to uphold the constitutionality of Section 123 of RPA, the Court may have understandably concluded that this speech-limiting provision be confined in its application to the most unambiguous examples of corrupt practices. As Ely has reasoned, "Where the evil the state is seeking to avert is one that is thought to arise from the particular dangers of the message being conveyed . . . the hazards of political distortion and judicial acquiescence are at their peak. . . . That means, where state officials seek to silence a message because they think it's dangerous, that we insist that the message fall within some clearly and narrowly bounded category of expression we have designated in advance as entitled to protection."[12] The goal, accordingly, is to achieve a healthy balance between the quality and quantity of political debate.

Such a balance arguably reflects an effort to bring together two liberal principles that are often in tension with one another. If Rawls's norms of public reason lead one to consider appropriate limits on speech to free public discourse from corrupting passions, then Ely's "representation-reinforcing" norms discourage even well-motivated efforts to limit speech for fear that they will improperly exclude unpopular voices from the political arena. But neither of these principles is presented as an absolute demanding doctrinaire constitutional implementation. Indeed, both are committed to the workings of the democratic process, emphasizing representational and participatory goals that are essential to liberal constitutional development.

In the most controversial of the *Hindutva Cases*, the Supreme Court reversed the voided election of Manohar Joshi, Bal Thackeray's handpicked choice for chief minister of Maharashtra. Joshi, a candidate of the BJP–Shiv Sena alliance, had been elected in a Legislative Assembly district of Greater Bombay by a vote of 47,737 to 24,354. With regard to the controversial speeches made on his behalf by Thackeray and other Shiv Sena leaders, the failure to produce evidence of formal consent placed their diatribes outside the reach of RPA's legal ambit. Joshi, however, had not been content simply to let others speak for him, and so at a February 2, 1990, meeting held in Bombay's Shivaji Park, he told his audience that "[T]he first Hindu State will be established in Maharashtra." While expressing "disdain at the entertaining of such a thought or such a stance in a political leader of any shade in the country," Justice Verma ruled that the sentiment did not warrant imposing the punitive sanctions of the election law. "In our opinion, a mere statement that the first Hindu State will be established in Maharashtra is by itself not an appeal for votes on

[12] Ely 1980, 112.

the ground of his religion but the expression, at best, of such a hope."[13] Others were less sure. "'Will be established,'" wrote the political commentator A. G. Noorani, "is not an expression of hope but a pledge by a Shiv Sena leader at a meeting in a predominantly Hindu locality. If this is not seeking votes 'on the ground of his religion,' what is?"[14] And from a senior Supreme Court advocate, P. Ram Reddy: "To say that Maharashtra will be the first Hindu State means that others will follow. If this is not a corrupt practice, nothing could prevent Muslims in Kashmir from declaring in an election campaign that it would be the first Muslim State or Islamic State, and Sikhs in Punjab could follow suit."[15]

As these critical comments suggest, it is difficult to argue that Joshi had not been engaged in a rather blatant effort of using ascriptively based assertions to procure votes from a particular religious constituency. To suggest otherwise, as Verma does, seems oddly out of touch with political reality. Even if Joshi's comment is relegated to wishful thinking, the particular object of his musing—the establishment of a state identified with the religion of a majority of Indians—should render the speaker liable to sanction under a fair construction of RPA. At a minimum, it expresses a "hope" which, if realized, would produce a state of affairs very much in conflict with certain "basic features" of the Constitution. And this leads to the anomalous conclusion that if *Chief Minister* Joshi, rather than Candidate Joshi, had publicly expressed the aspiration for a Hindu state of Maharashtra, a dismissal of his government under President's Rule could, following *Bommai*, plausibly be upheld by the Supreme Court.

Nevertheless, one can understand why Justice Verma would be reluctant to overturn a landslide election result on the basis of this comment. "Disdain," after all, is not *disgust*, which is how one should react in response to the things that Bal Thackeray had said about Hindus and Muslims, and for which his punishment was left undisturbed. In one speech, for example, Thackeray proclaimed: "We are fighting this election for the protection of Hinduism. Therefore, we do not care for the votes of the Muslims. This country belongs to Hindus and will remain so."[16] On one level the difference between the two quotes is negligible, as they both display, albeit with varied modulation, a problematically pro-Hindu bias. However, on a different level there is a principled distinction to be made between them, certainly one that a judge committed to liberal values might want to take very seriously. To hope for, even to promise, a Hindu *Rashtra* introduces a highly suspect, but at least debatable, subject for

[13] *Manohar Joshi* at 684.
[14] Noorani 1995, 170.
[15] Reddy 1996, 182.
[16] *Prabhoo* at 139.

public discussion. One can imagine ways of arguing for it, all invoking a controversial conflation of Hinduism and the way of life of the Indian people that avoid an unambiguously hostile agenda toward Muslims and other minorities. On the other hand, Thackeray's remark is not only overtly hostile toward a particular group of people, it is harshly antagonistic toward the very process of democratic deliberation. To debate the proposition advanced by Thackeray is implicitly to extend it a measure of legitimacy that is simply unwarranted. Its exclusionary presupposition violates the norms of public reason, which should be construed as an invitation to all rational actors to deliberate about the public good. Having employed these norms as a philosophical rationale to uphold the corrupt practices provision of RPA, Justice Verma is consistent in his deployment of the same logic to distinguish these two alleged violations of the statute.

Taken together, then, the *Joshi* and *Thackeray* decisions display an admirable sensitivity to an array of constitutional concerns that are often difficult to reconcile coherently. In reflecting upon these cases, Upendra Baxi, whose liberal and secular credentials have never been questioned, has noted, "The hard issue before the nation is: how to achieve a balance between the constitutionally evolved notions of secularism on one hand and respect for the precious, but precariously held, fundamental human rights to speech, conscience, religion, language and culture on the other."[17] Regarding the *Hindutva* litigation he asks: "Should the law disqualify and punish candidates because they express un-constitutional and anti-constitutional hopes? . . . Should Manohar Joshi have been disqualified because of his advocacy of a Hindu Rashtra? . . . Should the election law prohibit advocacy of political utopias?"[18] There are aspects of Verma's handling of these cases that trouble Baxi, but in stressing that a constitutional democracy must create sufficient political space for the airing of direct challenges to its own foundational suppositions, he finds considerable merit in the justice's choices. Baxi's emphasis on *advocacy* echoes a familiar doctrine in American free speech jurisprudence that is intended to preserve a critically important distinction between constitutionally protected speech and legitimately proscribable action. As applied to the Indian context, and in particular to the contested status of religion in social and political life, the speech/action distinction clarifies the several steps taken by the three-judge panel in its response to the Hindutva challenge. They can be summarized as follows: (1) Establish a constitutional basis for civility in political discourse. Here it is necessary to articulate reasons for limiting speech in the name of liberal virtues, specifically ratio-

---

[17] Baxi 1996, 213.
[18] Ibid., 211.

nality and personal autonomy. Verma accomplishes this, as we saw in the previous chapter, by employing Rawlsian arguments to uphold the statutory exclusion of dangerously divisive campaign rhetoric from the political arena. (2) Apply strict standards of statutory construction to the interpretation of the provisions of the law defining corrupt practices. This helps to ensure that in the enforcement of the law, the worthy goal of enhancing the quality of deliberative democracy is not perverted into an occasion for political manipulation and abuse. Verma pursues this avenue in his insistence on employing demanding evidentiary standards borrowed from the criminal law. (3) Extend an exculpatory benefit of doubt to any ambiguous set of facts involving an alleged violation of the corrupt practices provisions. The concern at this stage is to minimize the risk of either inadvertent or deliberate censorship of controversial ideas, or identically, to maximize the possibility that the public will have before it the full range of ideas concerning the optimal way to pursue the public good. Verma's strategy here is to offer a reading of the factual record that is most sympathetic to a secular version of the speech in question; in other words, a reading that provides ample latitude for people to respond to provocative ideas short of acting destructively in reaction to blatantly primordial electoral appeals.

In short, three steps to liberalism ascendant.

STORY II: LIBERALISM SUBSERVIENT

The importance of the issues raised in the *Hindutva Cases* is reflected in the prominence of the opposing lead counsel, Ashok Desai and Ram Jethmalani. They were familiar courtroom adversaries, having faced off against each other many times before in landmark cases. Each enjoyed the reputation of a gifted and influential senior advocate, whose elite status within the Indian legal community ensured a steady incoming flow of high-profile cases. Desai is a former attorney general of India, who argued, on behalf of the defeated candidates, that the decisions by the Bombay High Court to overturn the "corrupt" elections should be upheld. Jethmalani, who went on to become Minister for Urban Affairs and Employment in the BJP-led government, and later law minister, represented the BJP's aggrieved Shiv Sena political allies in Maharashtra.[19]

---

[19] Jethmalani's regal status among the Supreme Court bar can be gauged by the loftiness of the praise that is heaped upon him on those testimonial occasions that mark the achievement of personal milestones in a well-regarded individual's life. The most recent such occasion was a celebration of his seventy-fifth birthday that saw an array of legal and political luminaries offer their glowing assessments of Jethmalani's career. Included among them was ex-Chief Justice J. S. Verma, who praised his friend as "a crusader for freedom of speech and expression." Verma 1999, 3.

Jethmalani had also represented one of the dismissed state governments in *Bommai*. He of course lost that case, having failed to persuade the Court that what he considered to be the vague, constitutionally ill-defined concept of secularism could not be relied on to invoke President's Rule under Article 356. As stated in an interview, he believed that *Bommai* was a profoundly ill-conceived judgment. To those who suspect the judges in the *Hindutva Cases* of political bias, Jethmalani countered emphatically that "It was the *Bommai* judgment which was colored by political prejudice."[20] Indeed, he elaborated, "Most of the judges were leftist and pro-Congress."[21] Jethmalani was therefore pleased that the opinions in the decisions concerning Thackeray, Joshi, and their associates made no mention of *Bommai*.

Others, however, were less happy. A consistent line of criticism among Justice Verma's detractors targets his failure to cite this case, which is widely believed to contain the most thoughtful, and perhaps definitive, analysis of secularism in Indian constitutional history.[22] "[A] careful reading of the hindutva decision reveals many inconsistencies with the spirit of secularism affirmed by the Supreme Court [in *Bommai*]. The conclusion on the meaning of hindutva, and on the secular nature of the speeches of the Hindu right, are fundamentally at odds with the conclusions of the full constitutional bench of the Supreme Court on both the meaning and importance of secularism, and the unsecular nature of the strategies of the Hindu right."[23] This inconsistency was also noticed by a judicial colleague of Justice Verma, who sat for several years on the Court with him, and who was the author of one of the lengthy disquisitions on secularism in *Bommai*. "It made me wonder," said this justice, "why they did not refer to this case at all."[24] He was not alone in wondering, as is reflected in the comment of another prominent member of the bar: "It is unfortunate that [the] 1994 verdict was not brought to the notice of the court."[25]

But of course it *had*. Ashok Desai expressed "astonishment" that Justice Verma had made no mention of *Bommai*.[26] Like Jethmalani, Desai had argued *Bommai*, and he was determined to have the election reversals upheld on the basis of that precedent. In his brief to the Court, Desai

---

[20] Interview with the author, February 26, 1999, New Delhi.

[21] Interview with the author.

[22] Typical of this belief is the comment of Tahir Mahmood, the chairman of the National Minorities Commission: "The world has seen *Bommai* as the most articulate and trend-setting judgment of the Supreme Court of secular India on separation of religion and politics." Mahmood 1996, 312.

[23] Cossman and Kapur 1996, 2624.

[24] Author's interview with Justice P. B. Sawant, March 1, 1999, New Delhi.

[25] Reddy 1996, 182.

[26] Interview with the author, January 30, 1999, New Delhi.

contended that "A party which rides to power on such speeches [of the kind at issue before the Court] or manifestos will also act accordingly when in Government. This was the danger which was recognised in the decision of *S. R. Bommai.*"[27] He pointed out that "In [that case] Mr. Jethmalani . . . raised issues very similar to those argued in the present case on the nature of Section 123(3) and 123(3-A). The interpretation suggested by him, however, was not accepted."[28] He then quoted at length from several of the opinions in *Bommai*, including those passages that refer specifically to Sections 123(3) and 123(3A) to establish that "an appeal to the Electorate on the grounds of religion offends the scheme of democracy."[29]

In oral argument, Justice Verma specifically instructed the attorneys not to argue *Bommai*. Desai responded that he felt compelled to do so, whereupon to the justice's evident displeasure, the former attorney general read from the judgment—obviously to no avail, as "Verma refused to recognize that nine judges had said that an appeal on the basis of religion was contrary to the basic features of the Constitution."[30] Desai found this behavior "very peculiar," adding somewhat mysteriously that the "reason will not be found in the law reports."[31] What the law reports do present is Verma's official explanation for ignoring the 1994 decision, which may be found in a subsequent "clarifying judgment," decided in response to the controversy engendered by the *Hindutva* rulings. In the clarification, Verma brusquely asserted that *Bommai* was inapposite because nothing in that case "is of assistance for construing the meaning and scope of sub-sections (3) and (3A) of section 123 of the Representation of the People Act."[32] Verma of course knew that a great deal was said exactly to the meaning and intentions of those provisions; his branding this discussion irrelevant obiter dictum allowed him to evade the substantive objection that the earlier Court's consideration of RPA did indeed have profound implications for the appeals by the Hindu right politicians.[33]

Though part of a nine-member unanimous Court in *Bommai*, Justice Verma was one of only two justices who did not use the occasion to write

---

[27] *Submissions of Shri Ashok Desai, Senior Advocate on Behalf of the Respondent No. 1 on Constitutionality of Section 123(3) and Section 123(3A) of the Representation of the People Act, 1951,* 24.

[28] Ibid., 46.

[29] Ibid., 48.

[30] Interview with the author.

[31] Interview with the author.

[32] *Mohd. Aslam* at 239.

[33] Moreover, as Tahir Mahmood has pointed out, the rejection of *Bommai* as irrelevant did not prevent the Court from heavily relying, for its interpretation of the discourse on Hinduism/*Hindutva*, on two precedents that had absolutely nothing to do with the corrupt practices clauses of the election law. Mahmood 1996, 313.

about secularism and the Constitution. His decision to uphold the dismissals of the state governments on more narrow grounds does not in itself signify any disagreement with the sentiments expressed in his colleagues' opinions; it did, however, provide him greater leeway to affirm their irrelevance in the case at hand.[34] It also did not prevent him from reflecting on the nature of secularism; without referring to *Bommai*, he quoted from his own opinion in the *Ayodhya Reference Case*. "It is clear from the constitutional scheme that it guarantees equality in the matter of religion to all individuals and groups irrespective of their faith emphasising that there is no religion of the State itself. . . . The concept of secularism is one facet of the right to equality woven as the golden thread in the fabric depicting the pattern of the scheme in our Constitution."[35] As we have seen earlier, linking secularism and equality would not, as an abstract matter, find disfavor in the writings of speakers from the Hindutva camp, for example Arun Shourie. "The discursive strategies of the Hindu right have been based on bringing a very particular understanding of equality to the popular understanding of secularism, with powerful results."[36] But the very success of these politicians in using the equality theme to legitimate their agenda means that, lacking additional information, no inference of concurrence with that agenda ought to flow from any individual's similar use of the concept of equality. So the question is whether there is further evidence that might, in this instance at least, clarify the intentions and commitments underlying the Verma-led trio of judges.

The most accessible evidence is in the public record, in one of Justice Verma's opinions, ironically the case upholding the sanctions against Bal Thackeray. It is here that the justice addressed the vexing question of Indian national identity in a manner that courts often studiously avoid, namely by weighing in on one side of an argument that is the source of bitter conflict within the polity. Thus Verma wrote: "[N]o precise meaning can be ascribed to the terms 'Hindu', '*Hindutva*' and 'Hinduism'; and no meaning in the abstract can confine it to the narrow limits of religion alone, excluding the content of Indian culture and heritage. . . . [T]he

---

[34] In light of the following observation made by Justice Verma, it is difficult to understand exactly why *Bommai* is irrelevant to the specific issues raised in the *Hindutva Cases*. "The so-called plank of the political party may at best be relevant only for appreciation of the context in which a speech was made by a leader of the political party during the election campaign, but no more for the purpose of pleading corrupt practice in the election petition against a particular candidate." *Prabhoo* at 84. Perhaps what the Court in *Bommai* said about these matters was obiter dictum, but it seems to contradict Verma's assertion about what constitutes a corrupt practice under the law.

[35] *Dr. M. Ismail Faruqui*. The entire opinion is included in *The Ayodhya Reference* 1995, 36.

[36] Cossman and Kapur 1996, 2622.

term '*Hindutva*' is related more to the way of life of the people in the sub-continent. It is difficult to appreciate how in the face of [prior rulings] the term '*Hindutva*' or 'Hinduism' *per se*, in the abstract can be assumed to mean and be equated with narrow fundamentalist Hindu religious big-otry, or be construed to fall within the prohibition in sub-sections (3) and (3A) of Section 123 of the R. P. Act."[37]

How freighted this comment is with divisive potential is apparent in the political rhetoric of a BJP Manifesto of early 1999. The document stated that "Every effort to characterize Hindutva as a sectarian or exclu-sive idea has failed as the people of India have repeatedly rejected such a view and the Supreme Court, too, finally endorsed the true meaning and content of Hindutva as being consistent with the true meaning and defini-tion of secularism."[38] The manifesto then drew a connection between these "true meanings" and the event that has come to symbolize the deep-est fault line in contemporary India. "It is with such integrative ideas in mind, the BJP joined the Ram Janmabhoomi movement for the construc-tion of Shri Ram Mandir at Ayodhya. The greatest mass movement in post-Independence history reoriented the disoriented polity in India and strengthened the foundation of cultural nationalism."[39] It is a strengthen-ing noted as well on the other end of the political spectrum—though with considerable distress—when it was pointed out that a major "feature of Justice Verma's judgment is its gloss on *Hindutva* in order to purge it of its current and established meaning, give it a benign one, and put on it the imprimatur of the approval of the country's highest court."[40]

Justice Verma acknowledged in an interview that "I got a lot of flak when I said Hinduism is a way of life."[41] But, he maintained, "Understood in the abstract, philosophically, Hinduism is a way of life."[42] This observa-

---

[37] *Prabhoo* at 159.

[38] As promulgated on January 19, 1999.

[39] Ibid.

[40] Noorani 1995, 169.

[41] Interview with the author. He pointed out, however, that "Both sides misused the opinion."

[42] In this interview, Justice Verma went on to note with satisfaction that "A most interest-ing thing happened recently. Sonia Gandhi (widow of Rajiv Gandhi and leader of the Con-gress [I] Party) said that Hinduism is a way of life." The reference was to a resolution adopted on January 16, 1999, by the Congress Working Committee (CWC) and chaired by Mrs. Gandhi. The resolution states that "Hinduism is the most effective guarantor of secu-larism in India." It was preceded several weeks earlier by a speech in which Mrs. Gandhi observed that "India is secular primarily because Hinduism, both as a philosophy and as a way of life, has been based on what ancients said truth is one, the wise pursue it variously." The BJP immediately seized upon these sentiments by mischievously claiming that the Con-gress had come around finally to its point of view. J. P. Mathur, the BJP vice president, asserted that the Congress resolution echoed "the BJP's conviction that Hindutva is the bedrock of Indian nationalism and national identity." It was also construed as an affirma-

tion is consistent with the understanding of the constitutive significance of Hinduism in India explored in chapter 2. It is therefore reasonable to suggest that, while Hinduism *is* a religion, it is other things as well, so that it would be a misguided reflex to automatically apply the corrupt practices sanctions of RPA to any given campaign invocation of Hindu themes. But while the flak received by Justice Verma did indeed have a lot to do with his interpretive reliance on a particular *way of life* in India, it is the linking of this phenomenon with Hindutva, not Hinduism, that provoked the most strenuous objections. They are for the most part well taken, raising intriguing questions about the political sympathies of the ruling judges. But it is the seemingly more benign depiction of *Hinduism* as a way of life that has deeper implications for the issue of illegal corrupt practices, and for Indian secularism generally.

The Conflation of Hinduism and Hindutva

Justice Verma became a lightning rod for criticism (as well as commendation) by failing to distinguish between Hinduism and Hindutva. For example, in the Thackeray case he wrote: "Considering the term 'Hinduism' or '*Hindutva*' per se as depicting hostility, enmity or intolerance towards other religious faiths or professing communalism, proceeds from an improper appreciation and perception of the true meaning of these expressions."[43] And this: "Unless the context of a speech indicates a contrary meaning or use, in the abstract these terms are indicative more of a way of life of the Indian people and are not confined merely to describe persons practising the Hindu religion as a faith."[44] Verma conceded that these terms can be abused, specifically by rendering them synonymous with religious fundamentalism; and should that occur their debasers can "be curbed with a heavy hand to preserve and promote the secular creed of the nation."[45] This concession places a judicial imprimatur upon a politically useful fiction, that the interchangeability of Hinduism and Hindutva is justifiable in light of the absence in both of a necessary connection to

tion of the Supreme Court's view that Hindutva was a way of life. Two months later, at the national executive meeting of the RSS, Mrs. Gandhi was again praised for her recognition of the virtues of Hindutva. These tongue-in-cheek compliments for Sonia Gandhi cleverly elide the distinction between Hinduism and Hindutva, an elision that parallels what the Court did in the *Hindutva Cases*. And that the author of the opinions in those cases should see fit to echo the refrains of the BJP and RSS as a way of justifying his actions is at least worth pondering.

[43] *Prabhoo* at 161.
[44] Ibid.
[45] Ibid. at 162.

religious extremism. This in turn reinforces the larger fiction that liberalism is the animating force behind the Court's decision.

Preventing religious fundamentalism from intruding into the public arena was of course the rationale for upholding the constitutionality of the contested provisions of RPA. On this account "the secular creed of the nation" essentially means keeping religious faith at a safe distance from the governance of the nation. Justice Verma was correct to suggest that Hinduism and Hindutva are not naturally conjoined with religious fundamentalism. For him this was reassuring as far as safeguarding secularism—defined narrowly in his formulation—is concerned. What he did not note is that this nonreligious affiliation is the case for very different reasons—in the first instance because, as we have seen, the radically heterodox character of Hindu belief and practice diminish its propensity for doctrinaire pronouncement, and in the second because Hindutva is, in its essence, not a religion at all. As Sumantra Bose puts it, "[H]indutva politics is far more an *explicitly modern political interpretation of pan-Indian nationalism* than a manifestation of atavistic religious fundamentalism. . . . Hindutva ideology is above all an extreme form of state-led nationalism."[46]

Distinguishing between Hinduism and Hindutva is a relatively simple matter and is central to much of the critical commentary directed at the Court. V. D. Savarkar himself, as the originator of the term *Hindutva*, referred to the "unfortunate misunderstanding that owes its origin to the confusing similarity between the two terms."[47] It has become, however, a politically useful misunderstanding that the Court either wittingly or unwittingly embraced. Having done so, the judges found themselves exposed to a barrage of criticism of the following sort. "Hinduism is ancient. *Hindutva* is modern. The former is a matter of faith. *Hindutva* belongs to sordid expediency."[48] "Was it really necessary . . . to make all the general remarks about Hinduism and appear to give respectability to Hindutva by using it interchangeably with Hinduism?"[49] "Unlike Hinduism . . . Hindutva is not a religion. It is not concerned with the salvation of the soul but with the racial, national and cultural aspects of a state system, distinguishing individuals not on the basis of their moral stature but their

---

[46] Sumantra Bose 1998, 145, 157. Consider too the point made in the *Organiser*, the journal of the RSS: "The Supreme Court has put its seal of judicial imprimatur on the Sangh ideology of hindutva by stating that it is a way of life or state of mind and that it is not to be equated with religious fundamentalism." *Organiser*, December 24, 1995.

[47] Savarkar 1969, 4.

[48] Noorani 1995, 169.

[49] Nauriya 1996, 11.

roots and love for the fatherland."[50] Such criticisms are telling; certainly they diminish the possibility of Verma's opinion becoming an authoritative pronouncement on religion and politics in India. But as arguments for a more effective enforcement of the corrupt practices provision of the electoral law, they are at best incomplete.

Thus one of the more thoughtful critiques of the decisions concludes: "When used in the context of electoral politics, hindutva is an appeal to religion, and as such, ought to constitute a violation of sec. 123(3) of the RPA."[51] Perhaps. However, a plausible argument can be made that it ought *not* to constitute an illegal act, that those who campaign under the Hindutva banner are advocates of cultural, rather than religious, nationalism; moreover, their opponents may only help matters with their equally plausible insistence that this campaign is all about political power and the attempt to capture the Indian State for ends antithetical to both liberal democracy and Hinduism properly understood. Obviously if candidates were to say, "All Hindus should vote for me because I will bring us closer to the golden era of the Hindu Rashtra (i.e., the triumph of *Hindutva*)," then there is little doubt that those candidates are engaged in a blatantly illegal religious appeal. But if they say, "Vote for me, I'm the candidate who will give us what we need—*Hindutva*," then it is far less certain that they have run afoul of the law.[52] In this instance the appeal invites judges—those who are actively sympathetic to the Hindutva agenda as well as those whose main concern is the right of free speech—to minimize, in conformity with prevailing wisdom, a candidate's legal liability by relegating religion to the sidelines.

In the case of Justice Verma, when asked why his opinion conflated the distinction between Hinduism and Hindutva, he responded: "There may be an academic distinction between Hinduism and *Hindutva*. But how many people who hear the election speeches [make it]?"[53] In other words,

---

[50] Amulya Ganguli, "Hinduism and Hindutva," *The Hindustan Times*, February 8, 1999. "Hinduism is only a derivative, a fraction, a part of Hindutva. . . . Hindutva embraces all the departments of thought and activity of the whole being of our Hindu race."

[51] Cossman and Kapur 1996, 2619.

[52] A comparable result presents itself in the United States with regard to the issue of pornography and the First Amendment. Having had some success in persuading people that pornography is about politics and power relations rather than sex, feminists have had to confront the fact that the shift in categorization has lessened the chances that restrictions on such materials will be upheld. The reason: Political speech is entitled to the highest level of protection under prevailing First Amendment doctrine, whereas sexual expression gets much less.

[53] Interview with the author. Or as he puts it in his opinion: "Care must be taken to remember that the public speeches during election campaign ordinarily are addressed to an audience comprised of common men and, therefore, the manner in which it would be understood by such an audience has to be kept in view." *Prabhoo* at 145.

whether the speaker refers to Hinduism or Hindutva, the average listener at an election rally will hear the same thing, presumably a message about the way of life of the Indian people. If the context couching those words does not convey a more specific message that clarifies that the speaker is exploiting religion for electoral advantage, then to attach an improper and illegal construction to the remarks is unfair to the candidate.

To be sure, the average listener at an Indian political rally has a good idea of what the speaker has in mind when he or she uses the term *Hindutva*. In fact, Verma himself reflected this popular understanding when he said that "[T]he word '*Hindutva*' is used and understood as a synonym of 'Indianisation,' i.e., development of uniform culture by obliterating the difference between all the cultures co-existing in the country."[54] In short, most members of the audience will have little difficulty identifying the speaker with a set of political and social views, whose proponents have long been vying for political respect and acceptability in both preindependent and postindependent India. While the particulars of the agenda flowing from these views may vary within Hindu nationalist circles, the core ideology—that, as delineated by one of its advocates, "*Hindutva* and Indian nationhood are synonymous terms"[55]—is a familiar staple of Indian electoral politics.[56]

The problem with Justice Verma's description of the commonly held understanding of Hindutva lies not in the accuracy of the rendition but in its equation with Hinduism. Hinduism as a religious phenomenon is a part of Hindutva, but as both the founders of the concept as well as its current practitioners and critics have emphasized, it is *only* a part. And since its content defies singular interpretation, its rhetorical invocation would doubtless leave most members of even a nonacademic audience able to

---

[54] Ibid. at 159. Justice Verma relies heavily on a Muslim writer, Maulana Wahiduddin Khan, to support his equation of *Hindutva* with the Indian way of life. However, A. G. Noorani has shown that Verma presented a misleading account of Khan, portraying him as a supporter of what he was describing, whereas in fact he had clearly indicated his disapproval of the concept of *Hindutva* as Indianization. Noorani 1995, 172–3. In another critical review of Justice Verma's opinion, Soli J. Sorabjee wrote: "It would be utterly unrealistic to believe that the persons who heard speeches extolling *Hindutva* from candidates of Shiv Sena–BJP alliance would regard them as an exposition of the way of life of the Indian people and the Indian culture or ethos." Sorabjee 1995, 157. But it surely would *not* be unrealistic for them to regard such speeches as expressing the aspiration that Hindu culture become the way of life of the Indian people. Indeed, that is the essence of *Hindutva*.

[55] V. K. Malhotra, "Religion and Politics," *The Hindustan Times*, February 2, 1996, reprinted in Tahir Mahmood, ed., *Religion and Law Review*, 209.

[56] How radical the inevitable assimilationist assault on minorities that is implicit in the basic ideology should be depends on the extent of cultural uniformity thought to be necessary. Here speaker and audience can easily disagree, perhaps with consequences affecting the results of any given election.

appreciate that it need not be, and probably is not, synonymous with Hindutva. Hinduism, like Hindutva, can be considered a way of life, but not, as the advocates of the latter contend (or perhaps desire), for all the people of the subcontinent. For example, implicit in the fact that Hindus who convert to other religions often do so because they feel the way of life embodied in much of Hindu practice is socially regressive is the expectation that their new way of life will differ significantly from the experience of their previous socioeconomic incarnation, which is to say that Hinduism must not be the way of life of the Indian people. That this group includes among its number Dr. Ambedkar, who, with many of his followers, converted to Buddhism to escape the social constraints of the religion of the majority, is symbolic testimony to a constitutionally salient point, namely that secularism in India (as several provisions of the Constitution indicate) assumes the existence of a composite rather than uniform culture. In other words, the distinction between the two terms may be derived from the Constitution of which Ambedkar was the principal author.

But should that mean that any appeal to Hindutva constitutes grounds for reversing the results of an election? The answer lies at least as much in the realm of prudence as it does in the dictates of clear statutory intent. Justice Verma's decision that it should not is defensible in light of the prominent political and cultural features embedded in the Hindutva electoral option and the consequent reluctance to remove such a broadly programmatic choice from the public's democratic right to choose a "way of life." On the other hand, it is less defensible if it reflects a disregard for secular considerations vital to constitutional aspiration and design. For that we turn to Verma's discussion of Hinduism as a way of life.

Hinduism as a Way of Life

This discussion was introduced by Justice Verma in order to address the alternative interpretations of Hindutva submitted to the Court in the briefs of Ashok Desai and Ram Jethmalani. Desai had emphasized the religious underpinnings of Hindutva, whereas Jethmalani had stressed culture. In supporting Jethmalani's version, Verma offered an extended analysis of Hinduism, omitting any explanation of the pertinence of that inquiry for the controversy surrounding RPA's application to Hindutva. His analysis relied heavily upon Justice Gajendragadkar's opinion in *Yagnapurushdasji v Muldas*, which was, as we saw in chapter 3, an elaborate effort to interpret Hinduism in a useful way, namely to facilitate the realization of some of the ameliorative aspirations of the constitutional commitment to secularism.

The key passage quoted by Justice Verma reads as follows: "When we think of the Hindu religion, we find it difficult if not impossible, to define

Hindu religion or even adequately describe it. Unlike other religions in the world, the Hindu religion does not claim any one prophet; it does not worship any one God; it does not subscribe to any one dogma; it does not believe in any one philosophic concept; it does not follow any one set of religious rites or performances; in fact, it does not appear to satisfy the narrow traditional features of any religion or creed. It may broadly be described as a way of life and nothing more."[57] This emphasis on the uniqueness of Hinduism was helpful to Verma in two ways: First, it minimized the risks to secularism associated with an appeal to Hinduism; and second, it supported the claim that because there is much more to the "religion" than religion, caution must be exercised in how one defines a corrupt practice violation of the law.

These two arguments are interrelated, connecting secularism with the way of life of the Indian people. Thus the strength of Hinduism resides in its tolerant ways, in the secularist orientation that is intrinsic to its very ethos. "Secularism in the Constitution," Verma explained in an interview, "is merely a reaffirmation and continuance of this aspect of the Indian way of life."[58] In effect, then, the constitutional commitment to a secular society is a codification of a spirit of tolerance that is engrained in the Hindu way of life. "The aim of the Constitution is the same as the aim of the Indian society [from] time immemorial."[59] The implication is that the constitutional way of life—as it relates to the goal of a secular society— is consistent with the way of life embodied in India's dominant religion. It is, however, essentially at odds with a premise that had been fundamental to the reasoning of Gajendragadkar in *Yagnapurushdasji*. His contention in the temple entry case that "[T]he democratic way of life [had been] enshrined in the provisions of the Indian Constitution" and that "[S]ocial justice is [its] main foundation" pointed to a tension with his characterization of Hinduism as a way of life. For Gajendragadkar and the judiciary, the reconciliation of these two ways of life was a task of great importance, one requiring creative jurisprudence, including potentially controversial efforts to define the "essentials of religion."

Justice Verma's foray into religious essentialism served a very different agenda. Two judicial observations appearing in the *Bommai* case reveal how different. In the first, Justice Reddy quotes from a speech given by Justice Gajendragadkar: "[The Constitution's provisions] are inspired by the concept of secularism. When it promised all the citizens of India that the aim of the Constitution is to establish socio-economic justice, it placed before the country as a whole, the ideal of a welfare state. And the concept

---

[57] Quoted in *Prabhoo* at 155.
[58] Interview with the author.
[59] Interview with the author.

of welfare is purely secular and not based on any consideration of religion."[60] The second comes from the opinion of Justice Ramaswamy: "The Constitution has chosen secularism as its vehicle to establish an egalitarian social order. . . . Secularism, therefore, is part of the fundamental law and basic structure of the Indian political system to secure to all its people socio-economic needs essential for man's excellence."[61] Verma was straightforward in his rejection of this understanding of secularism in the Constitution. "Ramaswamy's [mistaken] view would indicate that there was a constitutional innovation [in the understanding of secularism]."[62] But since, according to Verma, the document only codifies what is, and always has been, immanent in the way of life of the nation's majority—a commitment to secular ideals—it is erroneous to suggest that the framers of the document intended to introduce something new to the established understanding of secularism. "Secularism has been a key value in India much before the adoption of the Constitution."[63] While acknowledging that the Constitution held out the promise of an egalitarian society, "[T]hat has nothing to do with secularism. . . . Social justice is something one must talk about in a context different from secularism."[64]

This too is creative jurisprudence. Gajendragadkar's discussion of Hinduism was appropriated by Verma in order to advance an understanding of religion and politics that is sharply divergent from the intentions of the earlier jurist. Both understandings employ the concept of equality to provide structure and meaning to the constitutional definition of secularism. For Justice Verma, secularism means equal treatment under law, whereas for Justice Gajendragadkar, the constitutional aspiration of equality may justify the active intervention by the State into the spiritual domain (in violation, perhaps, of formal equality) in order to achieve an objectively more egalitarian society. Verma's model is consistent with familiar Western norms of liberal democracy, most notably because it encourages a much cleaner separation of Church and State than does the alternative model. As Cossman and Kapur suggest, the conceptual relationship between secularism and equality is not a trivial matter. "There

---

[60] *Bommai* at 234.

[61] Ibid. at 170.

[62] Interview with the author.

[63] Interview with the author.

[64] Interview with the author. This separation between social equality and secularism is a matter of contention even between like-minded jurists. For example, the chief justice at the time of the *Hindutva Cases*, M. N. Venkatachalia, indicated in an interview with the author that Ramaswamy was correct in making the connection between egalitarian aspirations and the constitutional guarantees relating to secularism. Chief Justice Venkatachalia is a close friend and associate of Justice Verma, who is generally supportive of the outcome in these cases. He did, however, mention that perhaps the Court could have been a bit more restrained in its controversial discussion of religious essentials.

has been surprisingly little attention to [the] meaning of equality within the dominant vision of secularism. The continuing silence on the underlying conception of equality is no longer a harmless oversight. . . . It has become a dangerous silence that the Hindu right has been only too willing to exploit in its quest to claim the terrain of secularism as its own. The discursive strategies of the Hindu right have been based on bringing a very particular understanding of equality to the popular understanding of secularism, with powerful results."[65] Why did the proponents of Hindutva find so much to celebrate in the reasoning of Justice Verma? Because it legitimated two key parts of their political message: First, that they are the authentic voice of secularism in India, relying as they do on the inherent tolerance of the Hindu religion; and second, that they are also the only genuine practitioners of liberal democracy, committed as they are to a version of equal justice that condemns any special treatment for either majority or minority groups.

But there is more. Though the blurring of the distinction between religion and culture may have potentially exculpatory implications for the enforcement of RPA, as I argued in the previous chapter, the most compelling and coherent policy rationale for the Act's corrupt practices provision is that it reinforces the ameliorative aspirations of the secular constitution. Had Verma been more faithful to the concerns animating Gajendragadkar's investigation of Hinduism, he might have proceeded to evaluate the various campaign appeals to Hinduism and Hindutva in light of the specific substantive issues that lie at the core of the Indian model of secular constitutional development. The Hindutva campaign is, as Thomas Blom Hansen has argued, at its core a "conservative revolution," a reaction against social democratic transformation that threatens the status entitlements of those who have benefited from class and caste inequities.[66] Thus Verma might have raised some questions about the substantive implications of establishing the first Hindu State in Maharashtra. (He never, for example, explained *why* it would be a "despicable" thing.) But had he done so, he would doubtless have disappointed the Hindu right, whose caste and class loyalties do not coexist comfortably with the reconstructive ambitions of the Gajendragadkar model of secularism.

POSTSCRIPT FOR STORY II

We have already seen that the *Sangh Parivar* was not disappointed by the outcome in the *Hindutva Cases*. (*India Today* observed that "This is the most direct compliment the Sangh Brotherhood has got from the judiciary

[65] Cossman and Kapur 1996, 2622.
[66] Hansen 1999, 4.

since the Bahri tribunal lifted the ban on the RSS in '93 saying it was a 'nationalist' organisation."[67]) But the political opportunities it found in Justice Verma's opinions extended well beyond the electoral arena. For example, after the BJP came to national power in 1998, supporters of a Hindu Rashtra decided to apply their energies to the task of character development for the body politic of the future. *Sangh* affiliates submitted unsolicited school curriculum suggestions to the Human Resource Development Ministry (HRD), strongly advocating that education from the primary to the highest levels be "Indianized, nationalized, and spiritualized."[68] Among their specific recommendations: making Sanskrit compulsory from Class III to Class X, emphasizing the Vedas and Upanishads at all curricular levels in the school hierarchy, and amending Articles 29 and 30 of the Constitution, which grant autonomy to minorities in the running of their educational institutions. These proposals had a logical connection to the salutary result in the *Hindutva Cases*. According to one account of the educational enhancement effort, "[T]he Parivar also felt that they could stretch the Supreme Court ruling of three years prior that defined Hindutva as a way of life and not a religion."[69]

These recommendations were quite radical, so it is not surprising that given the political realities of fragile coalition governance, they were not, despite their obvious appeal to those running the Ministry, adopted. But shortly thereafter, HRD did formally constitute a committee to submit to the government of India "suggestions to teach fundamental duties to the citizens of the country." The committee was set up in response to concerns that there had been an ominous deterioration in public morality, including a specific worry emanating from the judiciary that the "Fundamental Duties" enumerated in Article 51A of the Constitution had not been given the attention they deserved. The individual chosen as chair of the committee was the author of the ruling of three years prior, the now retired ex-chief justice of India, J. S. Verma.[70] The appointment was made by the minister of HRD, the Honorable Murli Manohar Joshi, a prominent Hindu nationalist political figure best known for his outspoken views on the virtues of Hindutva and for having been, along with the now minister

---

[67] *India Today*, 15 January 1996, 51.

[68] *Secularism Alert* 1998, 50.

[69] Ibid., 51.

[70] The Committee consisted of Verma and five distinguished public servants, one of whom, Subhash C. Kashyap, a former secretary-general of the Lok Sabha, was "co-opted" by the Committee in order "to avail the benefit of the contribution he had already made in the field." No mention was made of what that contribution was, but Kashyap had been a member of the earlier group that had urged adoption of the controversial curricular proposals. January 30, 1999 letter from J. S. Verma to Murli Manohar Joshi, included as part of the Committee's Interim Report.

of Home Affairs, L. K. Advani, the leader of the massive populist agitation against the Babri Masjid mosque in Ayodhya.[71] The perverse symmetry in all of this is hard to miss: Justice Verma, the author of the *Ayodhya Reference Case* judgment, which, according to the justice's personal assessment, "saved the nation,"[72] is asked by the government of India to submit a report on good citizenship to Minister Joshi, the man whose rabble-rousing efforts precipitated the catastrophic events of December 1992.[73]

STORY III: JURISPRUDENCE

"[E]veryone will agree that a judge is likely to share the notions of right and wrong prevalent in the community in which he lives; but suppose in a case where there is nothing to guide him but notions of right and wrong, that his notions of right and wrong differ from those of the community—which ought he to follow—his own notions, or the notions of the community?"[74] The American legal philosopher John Chipman Gray gave a categorical answer to his own question. "I believe," he wrote, "that he should follow his own notions."[75] To which Benjamin Cardozo responded in his

---

[71] Joshi was a leader of the hardline faction in Hindu nationalist circles and was identified with upper-caste politicians who opposed inclusion of lower-caste individuals into the apparatus of party governance. See Hansen 1999, 182.

[72] Interview with the author. It should be noted here that the Verma opinion in the *Ayodhya Reference Case* was, for reasons considered in chapter 4, widely viewed at the time as a pro-Hindu ruling. His argument that the right to pray at a mosque was not a constitutionally protected right, because it was an unessential practice of the Islamic religion, struck many as both gratuitous and insulting. For example, Rajeev Dhavan, who argued the case before the Court, commented that "[W]hen all is said and done, the majority judgment is not a juristic victory for secularism; and may trouble the secular cause for years to come." Dhavan 1994, 3038. On the other hand, Arun Shourie was encouraged by Verma's effort. "[N]ot just on the specific question of mosques but on the general question of what Islamic law in India is to be, the new judgment opens up many opportunities for creative jurisprudence." Shourie 1995, 161.

[73] Joshi received an Interim Report from the Committee on January 31, 1999, and he used the occasion to suggest the establishment of sensitization programs, seminars, orientation programs, and fairs to deal with issues concerning fundamental duties. Verma marked the occasion by sending a letter to the state chief ministers pointing out that "[A]t this juncture of history, the nation needs to reemphasize [basic human values necessary for the upliftment of Indian society] in a pragmatic manner for inculcation by all generations to ensure a better future for the nation." The letter was sent on December 28, 1998, and was included as an appendix to the Interim Report. The report itself was notably vague on specifics. For example, in connection with the fundamental duty "to cherish and follow the noble ideals which inspired our national struggle for freedom," its discussion of secularism simply endorsed the concept of *sarva dharma sambhava*, that is, tolerance and the equality of all religions.

[74] John Chipman Gray, as quoted in Cardozo 1969, 107.

[75] Ibid., 108.

classic book on the judicial process: "My own notion is that he would be under a duty to conform to the accepted standards of the community, the *mores* of the times."[76]

To a great extent, this question and the two replies it elicited frame the debate within which the discourse of twentieth-century jurisprudence has proceeded. The common premise of both answers is that something other than transcendent principles of justice ought to guide the actions of the judge, be it a personal code of ethics or the judgment embodied in the moral sense of the community. Moreover, as Cardozo, perhaps the key figure in the development of the school of legal realism, pointed out, the dichotomy between personal predilection and the dictates of the community is usually overdrawn. "The spirit of the age, as it is revealed to each of us, is too often only the spirit of the group in which the accidents of birth or education or occupation or fellowship have given us a place."[77] Most judges, he maintained, were themselves unaware of "the subconscious element in the judicial process." In focusing attention on this neglected factor in judicial decision-making, Cardozo wanted to make judging a more reflective enterprise, with the expectation that heightened awareness of the craft would enhance judicial performance.

In the person of Justice Verma, we have a case study in the subtle workings of the judicial process, allowing one to see his performance in the *Hindutva Cases* as understandable in jurisprudential terms. To be sure, the role of jurisprudence in directing the adjudication of courts is, to say the least, a historically vexed topic. Whether legal philosophy is a convenient device to rationalize a private agenda or a genuine principled commitment that propels a judge to this or that outcome will be debated as long as there are courts deciding cases that matter. What we have observed thus far in Stories I and II provides ample material for speculation about such possibilities. Is Justice Verma a principled liberal pursuing justice without regard for the specific consequences flowing from that commitment, or is his embrace of principle designed both to conceal and facilitate a controversial political agenda? Whatever one's answer to that question, one may interpret the judgments in the *Hindutva Cases* as an exercise in legal theory, specifically Cardozo's sociological jurisprudence. Indeed, the judicial methodology in these cases, viewed against the backdrop of Verma's normative and personal reflections on the role of the judge in a democratic polity, provides an important additional perspective for understanding the involvement of the courts in delineating the essentials of Indian secularism.

[76] Ibid.
[77] Ibid., 175.

Problem-Solving

Some judges are eager to use their authority to tackle the problems of society, whereas others seek to avoid this role in the belief that courts lack the practical and moral resources to justify the intervention. Justice Verma readily aligns himself with the judicial problem-solvers. "[P]articularly in the field of human rights, the Court in a democracy governed by the Rule of Law has been required to find solutions to human problems within the legal framework. This exercise has given rise to the need for judicial creativity to find suitable remedies for myriad problems in the society."[78] Indeed, the creativity of the Indian Supreme Court in the postemergency period is an oft-observed phenomenon.[79] The Court's activism has steadily increased with the rise of public interest litigation, the relaxation of rules limiting access to the judiciary, and the manifest failures of the other branches of government in addressing pressing societal needs. "Acceptance of the role of the judges as 'law makers' is occasioned . . . by the change in the concept of the role of the courts from a mere instrument of governance to an instrument of society."[80] Verma's acceptance of the role was unabashed and unapologetic. "I'm identified with judicial activism in the 1990's more than anyone else."[81]

Two of the most difficult challenges confronting the Indian polity are corruption and communal discord. The accuracy of Verma's claim is evinced by the closeness of his connection to both of these subjects. As noted earlier, Justice Verma was instrumental in exposing the "Jain hawala" corruption scandal, the biggest such political scandal in the nation's history. When asked how it felt "to have shaken the entire polity," he responded with a striking mixture of humility and immodesty: "Well, it proves that even an average man like me can achieve extraordinary results by making extraordinary efforts."[82]

Should additional evidence in support of Verma's observation of what an average man can accomplish be required, one need look no further than the *Ayodhya Reference Case*. There "the sensitivity of the issue in a pluralistic society was evident from the fact that the dispute had generated

---

[78] Verma 1997, 1–2.

[79] See, for example: Baar 1992; Cassels 1989; Madon 1984; Baxi 1985; Bhagwati 1985; and Epp 1998.

[80] Verma 1997, 1.

[81] Interview with the author. Justice Verma was appointed a judge of the Supreme Court in 1989. He became chief justice of India in 1997 and retired from the Court one year later.

[82] *India Today*, March 15, 1996, 122. Ultimately immodesty won out over humility. "Whenever there has been a crisis in the form of a failure of some agency, the people of this country have raised the issue in such a manner that somebody with the capacity and the will to find a solution has been available." Ibid., 120.

communal disharmony between two sections of the society. The decision required judicial statesmanship to preserve communal harmony."[83] Specifically it meant that in his opinion for the Court, Verma would have to perform "a lot of gymnastics to save the law." Why? "Because I knew that if I struck down the law, the central government would have lost its authority." That, according to the justice, would have precipitated a "bloodbath" and "free-for-all." Indeed, had the Court minority prevailed, "there would have been a holocaust." So even while some commentators criticized what they considered the pro-Hindu bias of the opinion (thus concurring with the dissenters), Verma knew at the time exactly what had to be done, even if it meant exposing himself to scathing attack from the sidelines. In the end, however, he could take pride in the fact that "Many Muslim leaders [told him], "Sir, you have saved the nation."[84]

These experiences may help to explain why in the *Hindutva Cases* Justice Verma allowed himself to be drawn into the judicial quagmire of theological disputation. The criticism that the cases could have been decided without the extended inquiry into the nature and essence of Hinduism, that this exercise was entirely gratuitous and ultimately harmful, is more likely to impact those less confident in their remedial authority than Justice Verma. In the *Ayodhya Reference Case*, the solicitor general had urged the Court to use its decision to solve the communal crisis confronting the nation. He could not have chosen a better audience for such an appeal, for in Justice Verma he faced a judge with very few doubts about the capacity of the courts to respond to even the most intractable of problems. Given what Verma believed was his exemplary record in the creative use of judicial power, he could easily have seen the Hindutva challenge as an occasion for problem-solving at the highest level of urgency. In contem-

---

[83] Verma 1997, 13.

[84] All quotes are from an interview with the author. A subsequent chapter in the tragic saga of Ayodhya would provide Justice Verma an opportunity to reinforce his portrayal of himself in this heroic guise. In February 2002, communal violence in Gujarat claimed over seven hundred lives. The bloodshed was precipitated by a Muslim assault on a train filled with Hindu activists returning from a pilgrimage to Ayodhya, where they had threatened to revive the struggle over the disputed temple. The extensive killing that followed is now part of the sequence of communal rioting flowing from the original Ayodhya-related violence of December 1992. This new carnage was followed by a Supreme Court ruling, in which Justice Verma's 1994 opinion was interpreted by the justices to disallow the latter-day Hindus the right to participate in a symbolic *puja* on the site of the proposed temple. It also led to an investigation of the rioting (and the alleged complicity of the BJP government in Gujarat) by the National Human Rights Commission (NHRC), whose chairperson was none other than ex-Chief Justice J. S. Verma. The fact that the *Sangh Parivar* filed a petition in the Gujarat High Court questioning the jurisdiction of the Commission could only enhance the justice's reputation as a defender of human rights against the threat represented by the forces of communalism.

porary India, the problem of defining the national identity despite a glob-ally unrivalled diversity arguably tempts those in positions of authority to do something that would significantly change the life of the polity. Moreover, in light of the repeated ineptitude of elected officials in taking advantage of such an opportunity, confident judicial activists might well have imagined that they could fill the political vacuum left by others.[85]

Verma's confidence lay in an optimistic assessment of the institutional capabilities of the judicial branch of government, but also in the states-manlike attributes he felt he brought to the issues requiring attention from the Court. "[The judicial power] is like a sharp-edged tool which has to be used as a scalpel in the hands of a skilled surgeon to cure the malady. Not as a Rampuri knife which can kill."[86] One of the talents of a skilled surgeon (as well as an effective judge) is knowing when a procedure should best be left to someone else, so Verma cautioned against acting "as a knight in shining armour waving his sword all around."[87] Another is abjuring ad hoc judicial interventions. "I dare say I have never made any innovation in an ad hoc manner. Every order of mine is based on some legal principle."[88] These remarks would surely have delighted Car-dozo, who in an oft-quoted observation wrote: "The judge, even when he is free, is still not wholly free. He is not to innovate at pleasure. He is not a knight-errant roaming at will in pursuit of his own ideal of beauty and goodness. He is to draw his inspiration from consecrated princi-ples."[89]

Thus the judicial profile of Justice Verma that emerges is of someone whose experience has provided positive reinforcement for pursuing an active role where, as he has stated, the "public interest is involved";[90] and whose sense of his own abilities encourages him to proceed with alacrity. But an eagerness to solve problems in the public interest is one thing, defining its content and then adopting a judicial methodology for securing

---

[85] The situation that the judges found themselves in may remind one of the American Supreme Court at the time of the *Dred Scott* decision. The Court in 1857 really believed that its opinion would go a long way toward solving the crisis over slavery. Chief Justice Taney's opinion was sharply attacked for its gratuitous commentary on the moral and politi-cal status of people of African descent, but the Court was looking beyond the specific facts of the case, which meant that what many viewed as inappropriate *obiter dictum* was seen by the Court majority as necessary if the larger problem was to be successfully addressed. One is not required to make an equivalence between the American and Indian cases to recognize a similar judicial mind-set at work in both instances. On the *Dred Scott* case see Fehrenbacher 1978.

[86] *India Today*, March 15, 1996, 121.

[87] Ibid.

[88] Ibid.

[89] Cardozo 1969, 141.

[90] Interview with the author.

it is quite another. Both the Indian judge and his American counterpart embraced what the latter called a "teleological conception of his function." For Verma, "[T]he aim of law primarily is the public good."[91] For Cardozo, "The final cause of law is the welfare of society."[92] But what is the public good? What is the welfare of society? Where does a judge go for answers?

The Method of Sociology

To fulfill this teleological function, Cardozo offered the "method of sociology," which was an attempt to steer a middle course between the two dominant schools of jurisprudence of his time, analytical positivism and natural law. He found in the application of ethical considerations by the natural rights theorists, and in the abandonment of such considerations by the analytical positivists, a similar detachment from the realities of the social situation. In the first case, ethics was not grounded in experience, and in the second, reality was distorted by the failure to understand the ethical imperatives implied in experience. Cardozo's objective was to establish an empirical jurisprudence that included a consciousness of the moral basis of law.[93] In developing his preferred solution—the sociological approach to legal interpretation—Cardozo likened the role of the judge to that of the legislator, but he was careful to confine the application of the analogy to the interstices of the law. "[The judge] legislates only between gaps. He fills the open spaces in the law."[94] In the domain of "creative" jurisprudence, the choices made determine the quality of judicial craftmanship. Cardozo's most important teaching considered what ought to govern these choices. "[W]hen the question is one of supplying the gaps in the law, it is not of logical deductions, it is rather of social needs, that we are to ask the solution."[95]

　　Justice Verma too has given thought to what constitutes creative jurisprudence, and, like Cardozo, he focused on "gaps in the existing enacted law."[96] "Existing law will always be behind the needs of society." The judge's job is "to equate law with justice by filling the gaps in the existing law."[97] The equation "Law plus X = Justice" sets the terms of judicial creativity; the judge's task is to "reduce X as much as possible," thereby

[91] Verma 1997, 2.

[92] Cardozo 1969, 66.

[93] I have discussed this point at length in Jacobsohn 1977, chapter 4.

[94] Cardozo 1969, 113.

[95] Ibid., 123.

[96] Interview with the author.

[97] Verma 1997, 2.

achieving an equivalence that will best serve the needs of society.[98] Unlike Cardozo the legal philosopher, Verma has not articulated a systematic account of the methodology by which one achieves the desired correspondence of law and justice. However, his actions in the *Hindutva Cases* are strikingly consistent with the jurisprudential norms prescribed by Cardozo.

How, then, does one identify the welfare of society? The sociologically oriented judge relies on what Cardozo called the "mores of society," a term that is integral to his definition of the public good: "[T]he social gain that is wrought by adherence to the standards of right conduct, which find expression in the *mores* of the community. In such cases, its demands are those of religion or ethics or of the social sense of justice, whether formulated in creed or system, or immanent in the common mind."[99] The "social sense of justice" is of course quite different from how justice had been conceptualized in the dominant tradition of Western political philosophy and jurisprudence, the goal there having been to systematize ideas of right and wrong according to some absolute, universal doctrine. Cardozo's pragmatic understanding redirects the search for the source of justice to "the prevailing standard of right conduct," which in this account is derived directly from the mores of the community. It is a shift in focus consistent with the meaning given to this source by the renowned American sociologist William Graham Sumner, whose writings were familiar to all serious scholars of society in the early part of the twentieth century. In his most important work, *Folkways*, Sumner explained that "It is important to notice that, for a people of a time and place, their own mores are always good, or rather that for them there can be no question of the goodness or badness of their mores. The reason is because the standards of good and right are in the mores."[100] For Cardozo's ideal judge, the identification of justice with the social mores carried with it an obligation to translate the prevailing standards of right conduct into law, irrespective of their agreement or disagreement with an absolute ethical standard.

Sumner, a conservative thinker, adhered to a social philosophy antithetical to Cardozo, who, like most subsequent judicial practitioners of the "method of sociology," anticipated progressive results flowing from their

---

[98] Interview with the author.

[99] Cardozo 1969, 72. Elsewhere he says, "Law accepts as the pattern of its justice the morality of the community whose conduct it assumes to regulate." Cardozo 1928, 37.

[100] Sumner 1907, 58. Consider in this context this observation by Nirad C. Chaudhuri: "A Hindu's exclusiveness is social: it is created, in the first instance, by his birth which makes him an individual among a chosen people by divine right, and after that by his *mores*, which he regards as superior to everybody else's." Chaudhuri 1979, 148. If correct, then an appeal to the mores by a Hindu judge may be attributable to both jurisprudential as well as religious or cultural considerations.

efforts. But the philosophical neutrality of the method could not guarantee one result over another; for example, the judgment in the landmark segregation case of *Plessy v Ferguson* was obtained by reasoning consonant with what Cardozo was later to recommend. Indeed it is a textbook illustration of the application of sociological jurisprudence in constitutional adjudication. In upholding racial segregation, the Supreme Court appealed to "the established usages, customs, and traditions of the people" in order to determine the reasonability of a statutory separation of the races.[101] Justice John Marshall Harlan's famous dissenting opinion applied a more traditional understanding of reasonability, according to which segregation was unconstitutional because it offended principles of justice that were not dependent for their meaning on the mores of the community. "[I]n view of the Constitution, in the eye of the law, there is in this country no superior, dominant, ruling class of citizens. There is no caste here."[102] Segregation, he contended, was "inconsistent with the guarantee given by the Constitution to each State of a republican form of government,"[103] which meant that, like the assault on secularism in India, it violated a "basic feature" of the Constitution and thus could not stand. Much as the Indian Court in *Bommai* eschewed any reliance on established usages to issue its mandate on secular obligations, Harlan understood that a dependency on the mores of the community would essentially validate the views of the "superior, dominant, ruling class of citizens."[104]

This jurisprudential context helps to clarify Justice Verma's actions in the *Hindutva Cases*. In essence his conclusions in these cases concerning the meanings of both secularism and Hindutva are deducible from the societal mores, which makes the established usages and traditions of the community (the superior, dominant ruling class of citizens?) the critical factor in identifying the public welfare and hence the path of legal growth. Much like what occurred in *Plessy*, reliance on the mores of the community in effect worked to the advantage of "a kind of 'conservative populism' that mainly attracted more privileged groups who feared encroachment on their dominant positions, but also 'plebeian' and impoverished groups seeking recognition around a majoritarian rhetoric of cultural pride, order, and national strength."[105] For filling the gaps in the law Verma appealed to "the audience comprised of common men," not the discussants in an academic debate who prefer abstractions to ordinary meanings. Labeling himself an "average man" is less significant as a pro-

---

[101] *Plessy* at 550.
[102] Ibid. at 559.
[103] Ibid. at 564.
[104] Ibid. at 559.
[105] Hansen 1999, 8.

fession of humility than it is as a reassuring signal that he, a member of the judicial elite, is nevertheless qualified to divine the thinking and sensibilities of the average member of the community.

But what are the mores of the community? Moreover, what is the community? Cardozo was rather vague about these matters, and it is perhaps the greatest deficiency of his theory that such little attention was devoted to them. Especially in India, these questions defy simple answers. The "Hindu community" itself incorporates a kaleidoscope of lesser communities, such that most efforts to generalize on that basis will entail so many qualifications and exceptions as to prove counterproductive. The cultural and religious diversity within the Hindu segment of the population also includes an economic dimension, as is readily apparent from the burgeoning literature relating to the behavior and attitudes of the Indian middle class. So when Verma suggested that the average person listening to a speech about Hindutva does not distinguish between the use of that term and a reference to Hinduism, which person belonging to which specific community was he talking about? Clearly the unemployed Hindu from Bombay is more likely to respond favorably to the anti-Muslim and Christian messages suggested by the invocation of Hindutva themes than is the successful Hindu entrepreneur from Delhi. Verma, one suspects, was quite aware of these class-based variations, but did not fear they would negate his essential point, that both individuals, despite their very different circumstances, will understand the two words to refer to a distinct culture and ethos, in short, the Indian way of life.

Verma's unwillingness to delegitimate all Hindutva campaign advocacy is accordingly a reflection of his intention to reinforce what he saw as the legitimate sociopolitical aspirations that many people associate with the use of the term. The "way of life" to which he repeatedly referred was in his view deeply engrained in the mores of the majority, expressing itself as a yearning for a common collective identity. The content of this identity will vary widely; for some it manifests itself in hostility to minorities, while for others it more positively embraces matters of national pride, rather than overtly subordinating non-Hindus. In looking to the mores of the majority, Verma appealed to a rather vague and undifferentiated set of norms and assumptions that reflect the aspirations for a uniform culture held by many, perhaps most Hindus in India.[106] For some these aspirations fall benignly under the rubric of Hindutva, and as long as they do not get expressed in explicitly antiminority terms—as in the case of Bal Thackeray—there is no violation of the election law. Recognizing the

---

[106] See in this regard Madhu Kishwar 1998. Kishwar points out that the *Hindutva* agenda has become increasingly important as a political force because it is part of a worldwide wave of nationalism. "Its agenda is an internationally respected agenda." Ibid., 254.

spectrum of possible meanings obviates the need to be more specific about community differentiation within the larger Hindu fold. Thus middle-class Hindus, as Pavan Varma has argued, have their own reasons for seeking the "certitudes and simplicities of an idealized past," if only to provide an "accessible crutch to stand up to the unpredictability of . . . rapid and demanding [societal] transformation."[107] These reasons are distinguishable from the motivations of other groupings of Hindus to favor similar general yearnings. For Verma, such distinctions should be the preoccupation of academics and should not deflect judges from concentrating on the more generally applicable aspects of the mores of the majority. To the extent that the mores of this dominant sector of Indian society are broadly consonant with the positive-*sounding* features of the Hindutva agenda, a judge's provision of legal sanctuary for outspoken advocates of the Hindu nationalist cause constitutes a commendable advancement of the welfare of society.

To be sure, in all of this there is a somewhat selective reliance on the social mores. Madhu Kishwar has observed that the *Sangh Parivar's* "various grouses against the Muslims are unfortunately shared by most people in India today."[108] This assessment appears to contradict Justice Verma, who maintained in an interview that "Most of the people practicing Indian religions are basically secularist."[109] But it is possible that both views are correct, and that most of the Hindus who bear some resentment toward Muslims (and may be consciously unaware that they do) do not favor antisecularist policies.[110] It is possible, in other words, that the social mores of the majority community are a complex amalgam of sentiments, ideas, and emotions that are in tension with each other, but which do not pose a direct threat to the secular foundations of the polity. Verma clearly chose to mute the socially discordant notes of the Hindutva appeal and, in the process, remove the sanction of criminal liability from rhetoric that explicitly avoids its more problematic evocations.

---

[107] Varma 1999, 138. This argument is also spelled out by Hansen, who suggests that social transformation "challenged the sense of security, status, and competence in the middle classes, already shattered by the gradual retreat of the Indian state from the economic and regulative model of which it had been the main beneficiary." Hansen 1999, 145.

[108] Ibid., 255.

[109] Interview with the author.

[110] A number of commentators have noted that the main difference between the BJP and Congress is that the latter's communal appeals are more subtle, indicating a desire to capitalize politically on the prejudices of the majority without necessarily wanting to do anything about it. Sumantra Bose, for example, has observed that "[T]he Hindutva brand of state-led nationalism is simply a more explicit and extreme version (and in some cases a logical culmination) of the officially-sanctioned, 'secular' Congress ideology and practice." Bose 1998, 147. Secularism, then, may coexist, much as we may wish to deny it, with a range of deep-seated prejudices that are latent in the population that supports it.

So doing, his approach is consistent with Cardozo's sociological method. Thus Cardozo wrote that "[T]he judge in shaping the rules of law must heed the *mores* of the day."[111] But he added, "It is the customary morality of right-minded men and women which he is to enforce by his decree."[112] The implication is that judging is more than being a slavish follower of the mores of the community; instead it entails exercising interpretive freedom to present those mores in their best light. "The law will not hold the crowd to the morality of saints and seers. It will follow, or strive to follow, the principle and practice of the men and women of the community whom the social mind would rank as intelligent and virtuous."[113] That is in essence what Justice Verma did in the *Hindutva Cases*. The audience for Bal Thackeray's diatribes may have responded enthusiastically to his nastiness and vitriol, and they may have understood his verbal assault on Muslims as defining the essence of Hindutva. But Verma was under no obligation to accept their specific understanding, even if it flowed from a source prevalent in most members of the majority community, namely the aspiration for a common identity that marked as unique the way of life of the Hindu people. After all, the "intelligent and virtuous" members of the Hindu community could never accept this understanding, if for no other reason than that they define Hindutva as the way of life of "the people of the sub-continent." Since those physical boundaries include Muslims and other minorities, the essence of Hindutva cannot logically be associated with any meaning that featured targeted vilification of ascriptively defined groups residing therein. Rather, for someone of intelligence it would have to be associated with a more elevated and edifying message, highlighting aspirations for cultural unity that emphasized positive aspects of the Hindu tradition. That there are those who believe this emphasis could lead to cultural imposition by the majority on the minorities, and that such a development would be a bad thing, is not a matter that should concern the Court. Its assignment is to interpret the law, filling in its gaps, as circumstances require. If the results of its work are found wanting, the solution is to make new law.

CONCLUSION: LIBERALISM, COMMUNALISM, AND JURISPRUDENCE

Not long ago the *Hindustan Times* conducted an interview with a well-known Indian musician and entertainer, Pandit Jasraj, a brief segment of which reads as follows: "Q: Are you for a culture the Sangh Parivar wants or are you a liberal? A: I am a liberal but in favor of Indian culture.

---

[111] Cardozo 1969, 104.
[112] Ibid., 106.
[113] Cardozo 1928, 37.

Q: What is Indian culture for you? A: That which is in our Vedas and Upanishads. Our moral strength should come from these texts."[114] There is no reason to think that the newspaper interviewer was trying to trap Mr. Jasraj into exposing himself as a sloppy thinker or a hypocrite. Nevertheless he managed to elicit from the musician a set of responses that display strikingly antithetical sentiments, while also revealing Mr. Jasraj to be quite unaware that he was possibly contradicting himself. Of course there is no conflict in supporting both liberalism and Indian culture, nor would there necessarily be a problem in favoring liberalism and Hindu culture. But to identify the sacred texts of the dominant religion in India with the culture of a nation that includes innumerable other religious groups is an unambiguously illiberal move.[115]

One would not be surprised to learn that the contradictory commitments held by this person of culture and refinement are common to many members of the Indian intelligentsia, including judges. The pervasion of Hindu culture into the fabric of Indian society invites identification of one with the other with or without consciously illiberal intentions, even if this conflation is something that liberally inclined individuals should try to counteract. As the chief justice who appointed the panel in the *Hindutva Cases* suggested with pointed reference to Cardozo, "Statesmanship is the art of resisting one's subconscious loyalties."[116] He was agreeing with the American's observation that "The training of the judge, if coupled with what is styled the judicial temperament . . . will help to broaden the group to which his subconscious loyalties are due." However, Cardozo continued, "Never will these loyalties be utterly extinguished while human nature is what it is."[117] Thus even the greatest of American judicial statesmen, John Marshall, was exaggerating when he declared, "Judicial power is never exercised for the purpose of giving effect to the will of the judge; always for the purpose of giving effect to the will of the legislator; or in other words, the will of the law." "It has a lofty sound," noted a skeptical Cardozo, "it is well and finely said; but it can never be more than partly true."[118]

---

[114] *Hindustan Times*, March 21, 1999.

[115] In response it might be said that Jasraj was simply trying to make the point that the moral strength of the Indian people ought to come from the universally applicable teachings found in those sacred texts. But even if that had been his intent, it would not have negated the fact that such general teachings are to be found as well in the scriptures of the other great religions of India. Not all of which is in the Vedas and Upanishads is common to all religions, so it is reasonable to interpret the observation as implying that Indian and Hindu cultures are one.

[116] Interview with the author.

[117] Cardozo 1969, 176.

[118] Ibid., 169.

Cardozo's skepticism is itself susceptible to gross exaggeration; indeed the excesses of the school of judicial realism have been well documented. But his insights into the psychological dynamics of the judicial process can be helpful in making sense of certain perplexities, including apparent contradictions in the three stories we have just told about the *Hindutva Cases*. The final story drew our attention to similarities between Cardozo and Verma, and explained the outcome in these cases as having been dictated by broader jurisprudential considerations. The difference—an important one—is that unlike Cardozo, Verma's application of the sociological method lacks an introspective dimension, so that his judicial pursuit of the public welfare proceeds without much attention to the personal factors that accompany the work of adjudication. When asked whether he saw himself as a crusader for justice, Verma responded, "I can't sit in the court in the morning and lead a *dharna* in the evening. I can't use the trappings of my office to carry out my private agenda." How, he was asked, could he be so confident that extraneous considerations would not guide this pursuit? "All the precautions I take, all the questions I put, are meant to obviate such a danger. I leave no scope for that."[119]

But to whom are these questions put? Cardozo understood that "The great tides and currents which engulf the rest of men do not turn aside in their course and pass the judges by."[120] In effect he counseled judges to ask themselves how much of what they do is accidental, the product of associations, experiences, and sympathies that shape the mind-set of even the most self-reflective jurist. Verma may well have taken precautions that limited the likelihood of his private agenda coming to dominate his official duties. But his categorical assertion of judicial rectitude betrays an unawareness of "the forces so far beneath the surface that they cannot reasonably be classified as other than subconscious."[121] Defining the social mores critical in evolving the law may depend as much on the subtle ways in which a judge's own situational embrace of those mores has unknowingly configured his perceptual screen as it does on the ostensibly objective judicial inquiry that he undertakes to find out what they are.

Indeed, "It is often through these subconscious forces that judges are kept consistent with themselves, and inconsistent with one another."[122] If, then, we were to imagine a fourth story, in which the salient components of the previous three renditions were to be brought together to form a coherent narrative, it would emphasize the importance of the forces to which Cardozo called our attention and to which Justice Verma gave

---

[119] *India Today*, March 15, 1996, 121.
[120] Cardozo 1969, 168.
[121] Ibid., 12.
[122] Ibid.

short shrift. It would feature a judge whose self-image as a liberal and a problem-solver had been reinforced and validated at numerous points in a long career that culminated at the pinnacle of the Indian judicial hierarchy. As a member in good standing of the judicial elite, this judge had the good fortune of enjoying the professional esteem of colleagues who valued the institutional benefits flowing from the legal consequences of his twin commitments. But one of those commitments—the jurisprudential one—provided space for the entrance of influences that were in tension with liberal justice; and the other—the commitment to liberalism itself—may inadvertently have advanced the cause of its opposite.

This fourth story is necessarily more complicated than the preceding three. Rather than offering a univocal interpretation of events, it presents the facts surrounding the *Hindutva Cases* in a way that suggests a different reality, one that posits the coexistence of seemingly incompatible explanatory themes. The broader context for this less straightforward account is a political system, including all major political parties, that has failed to provide effective leadership in resolving (or even seriously addressing) the question of Indian national identity. That failure has created a political vacuum that an increasingly powerful judiciary, which, through the agency of strong-willed activist judges, has been only too willing to fill. In entering the thicket of disputation over religious and political identity, the Supreme Court has, however, often further clouded the waters; in part through the attempt to satisfy the expectations of dual constituencies—the legal elite, whose fealty to the rule of law requires deference to traditional norms of philosophical liberalism—and the Hindu majority—whose confusion over the role of religious identity in constituting the Indian polity inevitably distorts the clarity with which liberal ideals are articulated. This in turn works to the benefit of yet another constituency, the Hindu minority of aggressively ascriptive nationalists, whose illiberal agenda is at this moment best achieved through the propagation of formulaic liberalism.

Justice J. S. Verma is again of course the main character. The driving force behind his actions in the *Hindutva Cases* are not known for sure, but they have clearly become an occasion for him to honor both his jurisprudential and his philosophical commitments. In the process, however, he honored a third commitment, the one that is bound up in his membership in the majority culture. He perhaps would agree that "[A] judge is likely to share the notions of right and wrong prevalent in the community in which he lives," yet believe that his training and experience have enabled him to distance himself from those notions when acting in his judicial capacity. But that his commitment to "the group to which his subconscious loyalties are due" can ever be "utterly extinguished" is doubtful, especially, as we have seen, when the judicial methodology employed in the cases in question encourages its recognition.

That methodology anoints the judge as conduit for the transmission of community mores to the legal arena, specifically directing them to the gaps within the law. The "predilections and the prejudices" of one realm make their way into the other by way of judicial interpretation; how much the transmission link will filter problematic excesses varies from individual to individual. In Justice Verma we have someone whose performance of this role is facilitated by the fact that his own sensibilities are harmonious with the mores of the community of which he is a part. Like Pandit Jasrit, he can be both a liberal and a believer in the Indian way of life, which, as it happens, is also the Hindu way of life. It is a way of life that, according to the prevailing majority view shared by Verma, is not only consistent with secularism but is the basis for its success in India.

That also alleviates the burdens of coexistence with liberalism, which, as understood by Verma (as well as many contemporary philosophers), is distinguished by its process-oriented conception of justice. Upholding the norms of public reason and the guarantees of free speech need not threaten the cultural aspirations of Hindutva, provided that those aspirations are given an affirmative articulation that avoids overtly divisive appeals to primordial loyalties. Justice Verma *can* sit in the court in the morning and lead a *dharna* in the evening. He can be a conscious and conscientious liberal in his public role while fully committed to a Hindu way of life in his private capacity.[123] In fact, such is the situation today of millions of Indians who comfortably wear the trappings of upwardly mobile contemporary lifestyles while retaining very traditional roles and beliefs within the sanctity of their personal space.[124] "It is important to go backstage . . . because it is there, hidden from public view, that we are likely to find, beyond the 'tidiness' of the middle class' own image of itself as a modern and rational entity, the scattered but powerful inheritances of the past, and the evidence of their patchy interface with the present."[125] Seen in this light, Verma's judicial resolution of the challenge posed by Hindutva to the sanctity of the democratic electoral process is

---

[123] To say that he *can* be is not to say that he necessarily *is* truly committed to the advancement of liberal ideals. Story II suggests that, despite his denial, his office is being used to carry out his private agenda, that, in other words, liberalism is essentially a front for the pursuit of illiberal ends favored by the Hindu right. But the actual evidence available does not at this point justify reaching such a conclusion.

[124] "[T]here can be no real assessment of some of the identifiable traits of the Indian middle class without taking into account the legacy that Hinduism—the religion of the overwhelming majority of the middle class—has bequeathed and the influence it continues to have." Varma 1999, 123.

[125] Ibid.

one that reflects the prevailing position of the "enlightened" segment of the Hindu middle class in India, which is a complex admixture of cosmopolitan and communal ideas whose equilibrium has survived the countervailing pulls of alternative visions. More important, it is a reflection of the very particular condition of Indian secularism—an institution that, for better or worse, is destined to remain tethered to the way of life that it seeks to regulate.

Chapter Eight

SO YOU WANT A (CONSTITUTIONAL) REVOLUTION? LESSONS FROM ABROAD

INDIA AND ISRAEL have recently marked a half-century of national independence, and the United States joined both countries in celebrating the democratic successes of these experiments in statecraft. Often the tributes became effusive when noting the extraordinary obstacles surmounted in order to achieve this success. But precisely these obstacles will cause many to temper their enthusiasm for fear that, even after fifty years, the validation of democratic accomplishment may yet come to be seen as premature. While each obstacle alone—for example, living in a hostile neighborhood—threatens to disturb the equilibrium of democratic practice, the specter of religious and ethnic nationalism casts the most ominous shadow over the future of constitutional democracy in these two countries.

In India the establishment of the State of Israel was celebrated only among those outside the mainstream of the Indian independence movement. In pointed disagreement with the official position of Nehru's Congress Party, Veer Savarkar, on behalf of the Hindu Sanghatanists, extended to the new State in the Middle East "their moral support to the establishment of the independent Jewish State in Palestine on moral as well as political grounds."[1] Without concealing his contempt for the very different political arrangements adopted in his own country, Savarkar

[1] Savarkar 1967, 221. These attitudes toward the State of Israel continue to this day. For example, Mani Shankar Aiyar, a prominent Congress official and writer, speaks disparagingly of Israel as a way of castigating followers of the BJP. "There is the Zionist State of Israel where Judaism is the official religion—and the majority Muslim Palestinian population has been driven out of the country or deliberately reduced to second-class status." Aiyar 1995, 32. On the other hand, the BJP politician and writer Arun Shourie points out that when he tells Indian audiences that India should develop closer ties with Israel, he always gets enthusiastic applause. Interview with the author, New Delhi, November 19, 1998. And Ram Jethmalani, law minister in the BJP-run government and defender of the Hindutva legal cause, takes pride in his reputation as Israel's best friend in India. Interview with the author, New Delhi, February 26, 1999.

wrote: "After centuries of sufferings, sacrifices and struggle the Jews will soon recover their national Home in Palestine which has undoubtedly been their Fatherland and Holyland. Well may they compare this event to that glorious day in their history when Moses led them out of the Egyptian bondage and wilderness and the promised land flowing with milk and honey came well within sight."[2]

For Savarkar the occasion of the establishment of the Jewish State was as much an opportunity to irritate Muslims as it was to identify with the plight of the Jews. As the key figure in the development of Hindu nationalist ideology, much of his work as a theoretician and political leader (he headed the Hindu Mahasabha from 1937 to 1942) was formulated as a response to the purported vulnerability of the Hindu majority in India in the face of Muslim assertiveness. Moreover, as an admirer of Hitler's occupation of the Sudetenland because its inhabitants shared "common blood and common language with the Germans," Savarkar will never be mistaken as a friend of the Jews.[3] But this only underscores the obvious, that the attractiveness of the Israeli venture for Hindu nationalists lay in the example it set for the establishment of the Hindu *Rashtra*, rather than in any sentimental attachment to the Zionist cause.[4] And doubtless the added attraction of tweaking the Muslim minority was a factor of no small significance.

The Israeli model—a State that serves as official homeland for a particular religious group—has understandable appeal for many in India who espouse the cause of Hindu nationalism. They would rejoice if the constitutional reality in India were such as to enable a mainstream Supreme Court justice to declare that "There is no Indian nation separate from the Hindu people." Indeed, were such a moment to come to pass, commenta-

---

[2] Savarkar 1967, 219. He went on to say: "In justice . . . the whole of Palestine ought to have been restored to the Jews." Ibid., 220.

[3] Jaffrelot 1995, 53. As Jaffrelot makes very clear in his discussion of the RSS, a good bit of the ideological inspiration behind Hindu nationalism in the 1930s and 1940s had its origins in Nazi Germany. Ibid., 50–58.

[4] Admiration for the Israeli model is frequently evident in the writings of Hindu nationalists. For example: "As for the Jewish nation, they had in fact completely lost hold of their motherland. For nearly 2000 years, they remained separated from their traditional homeland. But even that did not cause extinction of the nationhood of the Jews. The Jews remained a nation and despite so much of persecution and tyranny, they reestablished their own state in their traditional homeland after 2000 years. Hindus too have remained a nation." Chatterjee 1995, 6. This stands in marked contrast with views expressed in a journal known for its intense disagreement with the Hindu nationalist position. "[A] state based on a religious identity and which effectively stands for a two-nation theory within Palestine is not and cannot be your ally . . . for assertion of a modern, secular basis of nationalism. . . . Israel is not only not a secular state but, what is worse, it is no less fundamentalist in its approach to matters of religion and politics." *Economic and Political Weekly*, January 19, 2002, http://web@epw.org.in.

tors would surely be justified in portraying the development as marking the occasion of a constitutional revolution. It was M. K. Gandhi, after all, who said, "In no part of the world are one nationality and one religion synonymous terms; nor has it ever been so in India."[5] In the terminology of our study, this departure would represent a radical transformation in the foundations of constitutional secularism: visionary precepts replacing ameliorative ones.

But should it? What would be the probability of it culminating in secular constitutionalism, in a political reality that provided genuine religious freedom for those unaffiliated with the favored religion of the State? The above formulation is patterned after Justice Shimon Agranat's observation that "There is no Israeli nation separate from the Jewish people."[6] As pointed out in chapter 2, the author of the remark was no wild-eyed religious nationalist harboring dangerous extremist ambitions, but a secular Jew identified with the cause of civil liberties. If not a universally shared sentiment among Israeli Jews, Agranat's assertion is well within the mainstream of Zionist (if not post-Zionist) thought, expressive of the broader commitments animating the founders of the State.

In Israel, the ethnoreligious nationalism that has dominated the politics of the State since its inception has been relatively benign as far as religious tolerance and freedom are concerned, largely because the social demands it makes of religion are basically peripheral to its political objectives. To be sure, Orthodox Judaism is unambiguously thick in the sense that it effectively governs all aspects of its adherents' lives. But because the number of its adherents in Israel is relatively small, with many of these people having dissociated themselves from the business of the State, the prevailing pattern of religiosity is one in which a theocratic threat to personal liberties is quite remote. While the secular majority in Israel is not, as we have seen, unencumbered by halakhic regulation, ultimately it retains control over the reach and extent of religious imposition. Moreover, the extent of secular complicity in the intrusion of religion into public and private domains renders the issue of coercion a very complicated matter, certainly defying any casual attribution of theocratic motivation.

The threat posed by religious nationalism to principles of secular constitutionalism may take several forms, varying in their magnitude according to the theological precepts of particular religions. If all we know are general assumptions about the convergence of spiritual and temporal power, the identification of the State with a specific religious group tells us—and more important, other religious groups—very little about the impact of that identification upon the prospects for religious liberty. Thus the an-

---

[5] Quoted in Justice A. M. Ahmadi's opinion in *Bommai* at 76.
[6] *Tamarin* at 201.

swer to the question of whether a Hindu State would bear a close resemblance to a Jewish State hinges on the nature of the similarities and differences of the two religions (at least with respect to how they would be interpreted by those wielding political power) in matters marginal to affairs of state. For example: Are they proselytizing religions? Are their proclivities assimilative or detached on questions of coexistence with nonmembers?

Because of the radically heterodox character of Hinduism, answers to such questions defy singular responses. Gandhi, for example, was murdered for his policies of tolerance and peaceful coexistence toward fellow Indians of Muslim descent. But to the non-Gandhian Hindu nationalists who are so prominent and vocal in the contemporary discourse of Indian politics, that is to say, to the descendants of Savarkar who see in the Jewish State an intriguing model for emulation, the reconstituting of India into a Hindu State would introduce a type of assimilation quite different from the political assimilation that characterizes, say, American secular constitutionalism. Thus as Ashutosh Varshney points out, the generic Hindu nationalist argument is that to become a part of the Indian nation, Muslims would have to agree to a number of things, including an acceptance of the centrality of Hinduism to Indian civilization and a relinquishment of all claims to the maintenance of religious personal laws.[7] In the words of Madhav Sadashiv Golwalkar, who along with Savarkar developed the ideology of Hindutva, "Non-Hindus must be assimilated to the Hindu way of life."[8]

In contrast, the nonassimilative character of Judaism in Israel arguably enhances the prospects for religious freedom among non-Jews, introducing a political climate in which benign neglect sets the terms for religious minority relations with the state. Such terms represent an imperfect realization of liberal ideals, but they do afford significant safeguards for religious beliefs and practices. In this regard, Gershon Weiler is correct to see the very idea of personal status in Israel in conflict with the idea of equal citizenship.[9] But opposition to personal status need not connote a principled commitment to equal citizenship; indeed it may, as I have argued earlier, be part of an agenda of religious and political subordination. Thus the insistence by the BJP and its allies on a uniform civil code is more a reflection of their determination to require Muslim acceptance of Hindu tradition than it is an affirmation of the principles of liberal constitutionalism. Much as constitutionalism is a category broad enough to include nonliberal variants, ethnorepublicanism may incorporate

---

[7] Varshney 1993, 231. "They must assimilate, not maintain their distinctiveness."
[8] Quoted in Sarkar 1996, 289.
[9] Weiler 1998, 235.

under its rubric both secular and nonsecular possibilities. There are powerful normative arguments why we should not lightly countenance constitutional experiments that embrace ethnoreligious distinctions in national self-understanding; while not categorically precluding such arrangements, a proper regard for the conditions that nurture and sustain a commitment to secularism should suggest appropriate limits on our tolerance for experimentation.

But sustaining a commitment to *Indian* secularism, that is, to the ameliorative goals that inspired the original work of constitution-making, would likely be lost in the pursuit of the ascriptively driven nationalist dream. Democratizing a rigidly hierarchical social order had always figured centrally in the constitutional aspirations of the Indian independence movement, and this imperative continued to give meaning (not always through its realization) to postcolonial constitutional development. This stands in marked contrast to the experience of modern Israel's founding fathers, who, like their Indian counterparts, were for the most part committed to broadly egalitarian socioeconomic objectives; but in the Israeli case these goals could be pursued in tandem with the construction of a Jewish State. More to the point, in Israel, unlike in India, the dominant cohort in the nationalist movement that won the struggle for independence had not been charged with the additional responsibility of reforming a social structure that bore the imprint of the newly emergent nation's dominant religion.[10]

They *had been* charged of course with establishing a homeland for the religion of the majority, but their visionary Zionist aspirations were circumscribed by a countervailing commitment to universalistic norms of liberal justice. A regime in which visionary *secularism* prevails must by necessity be moderate in the pursuit of its religiously constituted vision. Unlike, for example, the Islamic revolution in Iran, which Mark Juergensmeyer rightly depicts as having set "the standard for religious revolution throughout the Muslim world," the Israeli homeland for the Jewish people can at best be described "as the expression of an incomplete form

---

[10] By this I do not mean to suggest that there was *no* ameliorative dimension involved in the realization of Zionist aspirations. Indeed, to the extent that the Jewish national movement's historic roots can be traced to rebellion against traditional Judaism, its hopes for a Jewish State in Israel were implicated in a project in social reconstruction. See in this regard Cohen-Almagor 1995, 465. But the contrast with India in this regard represents a difference in kind and not merely magnitude. For example, David Ben-Gurion often spoke of Jewish revivalism in cultural terms, but this cultural agenda did not preclude a large presence for the State in social and economic policy. In India, "None of the [Hindu revivalists] would ever suggest a radical change in the Hindu social structure. . . . The economic implication of this revivalistic nationalism is the assertion of non-interventionism. . . . It does not sponsor the concept of State interference in economic life." Varma 1964, 358–9.

of religious nationalism."[11] But for similar reasons, the other side of the political equation—Israel's democratic institutions—must also be depicted as incompletely realized, leaving partisans of each commitment unfulfilled with regard to their respective revolutionary ambitions.

This lack of fulfillment expresses itself in various forms, including the constitutional jurisprudence of the Supreme Court. In this chapter I examine the role of the Israeli Court in connection with the judicial campaign to achieve a kind of revolutionary fulfillment through the legitimation and institutionalization of constitutional review. The term *constitutional revolution*, as it has been used in Israel, signifies, among other things, the resolution of contradictions in the nation's founding legacy that are directly related to the absence in that polity of a comprehensive written constitution. In contrast with India, where "[t]here was no religious lobby to stand in the way of constitutional formulation of secular state sovereignty,"[12] the feasibility of constitution-making in the Jewish State has always been constrained by the political imperatives of religious identity.

So too has the role of the Court within the framework of Israeli governance. What has been said of India—that "judicial activism is . . . in a very real sense a constitutional imperative"[13]—can be said of Israel only by appending so many qualifications as to vitiate the conclusion. To the extent, therefore, that the visionary model is viewed by some in India as a plausible, and even enticing, candidate for emulation, it commands our scrutiny, not the least because of the possible implications that might follow for the functioning of the judiciary. Bearing in mind Upendra Baxi's sober reminder that "[T]here can be only theories about judicial roles, never a single cross-cultural theory about the judicial role,"[14] what lessons can be gleaned from the Israeli experience?

REVOLUTIONS AND THEIR CONSTITUTIONS

In an address commemorating the fiftieth anniversary of the adoption of the Indian Constitution, a former chief justice (and author of one of the *Bommai* opinions) observed: "The multi-dimensional jurisprudence woven around the Preamble has a revolutionary thrust as it seeks to transform the socio-economic structure of our society."[15] A leading student of Indian constitutional origins has suggested that from the earliest days of independence, the Indian judiciary had been considered "an arm of the

[11] Juergensmeyer 1993, 50, 63.
[12] Chatterjee 1997, 149.
[13] Baar 1990, 85.
[14] Baxi 1985, 4.
[15] Ahmadi 2000.

social revolution."[16] And an analyst of the "rights revolution" in comparative perspective has concluded that since 1978, "[T]he extent of change in constitutional interpretation wrought by the [Indian] Supreme Court is difficult to overstate. Commentators typically describe it in revolutionary terms."[17] The common emphasis in these accounts is something most students of the judicial process consider rather counter-intuitive: a high Court's exercise of judicial review to advance a broadly encompassing societal transformation.

Indeed, the conventional wisdom has not been exactly undermined by the Indian experience. Thus the former chief justice completed his observation by pointing out that "[E]ven though more than a half a century has elapsed since independence we have yet to see it [the revolutionary thrust] bloom in the direction of providing the promised social order envisioned by our constitution makers."[18] The comparative analyst adds that "In spite of all the sound and fury after 1977 regarding the Supreme Court's egalitarian judicial activism, the Court has not developed sustained attention to individual rights."[19] And however much the Court might have been regarded in the projection of its framers as an "arm of the social revolution," the fact is that it failed for nearly thirty years to live up to such expectations, and when it finally began cautiously to align itself with revolutionary aspirations, it encountered a political reality that made it exceedingly difficult to capitalize on its newfound judicial role. In short, if judicial activism in the service of revolutionary goals is a constitutional imperative, there is scant evidence to suggest that this mandate has had much to show for the effort.

Unsurprisingly, the gap between aspirations and achievement should concern those committed to the elimination of social inequities; but there is at least one reason to view it positively. Thus a Court that functioned as the arm of a totally successful social revolution might very well cause one to wonder if the law had not become a mere extension of the authoritarian will of the State. Upendra Baxi has distinguished between the "*written* Constitution of India" and the "*unwritten* constitution," the first referring to the social justice ideology that animates and informs the document, the second to the antireform ideology of the privileged classes

---

[16] Austin 1966, 164.

[17] Epp 1998, 89. Epp shows that the Court was very much in the forefront of these changes. "[W]ithin the sphere of activity staked out for social action litigation, the justices did all they could to develop an egalitarian, due process revolution. And there is little doubt that judges rather than public interest activists originated the development." Ibid., 88. Jamie Cassels reaches the same conclusion with respect to the Court's leadership role in the legal aid/public interest movement in India. Cassels 1989, 495.

[18] Ahmadi 2000.

[19] Epp 1998, 90.

and castes, who, he argues, have been quite successful in entrenching their version as constitutional orthodoxy.[20] He interprets the judicial activism of recent decades as an effort by some influential judges to reestablish the ascendancy of the first over the second. However, says Baxi, "The ascendancy will not be total; in the very nature of things a *total* ascendancy of the written over the unwritten Constitution will itself constitute a revolution in Indian state and politics."[21] Stated differently, the revolution that would follow a total ascendancy of the written constitution (including the Directive Principles) would itself consist of a societal transformation so extensive as to entail a total restructuring of existing relations in civil society.

But "total revolution" is a concept hard to reconcile with Indian secularism, which, as we have seen, incorporates the view widely held at the Constituent Assembly that "[W]e cannot dissociate our social life from our religious environments." "Total revolutions, such as the one in France that began in 1789 or in China throughout much of this century, aim at supplanting the entire structure of values and at recasting the entire division of labor."[22] When successful, they "alter the social system from one major archetype to another."[23] As part of this process, there is a change in basic political consciousness that may involve people ceasing to regard themselves as members of religious communities and instead embracing membership in the national community.[24] The Indian Constitution clearly envisions these transformations, but only in attenuated forms, as both its commitment to democratic values and its sensitivity to religiously based affiliations preclude their total revolutionary embrace. So the existence of at least a small gap between aspiration and achievement is in this respect a good thing, bespeaking the presence of a moderate political sensibility that is a necessary, if not sufficient, condition of constitutional secularism.

Nearly forty years ago Chalmers Johnson distinguished "simple revolutions" from "total revolutions." Simple revolutions are usually aimed at "the normative codes governing political and economic behavior, which are thought to be in need of change."[25] They are "restricted to fundamental changes in only a few values—for example, values governing access to the statuses of authority."[26] Johnson pointed out that "In some cases, the goals of simple revolutions can be achieved through promulgating or rewriting a political constitution for the system, as in the case of General

---

[20] Baxi 1985, 18.
[21] Ibid., 20.
[22] Johnson 1966, 139.
[23] Ibid.
[24] Ibid., 141.
[25] Ibid., 140.
[26] Ibid., 139.

de Gaulle's seizure of power in 1958 or, to a large extent, in the American Revolution."[27] Like total revolutions, they include a "conscious espousal of a new social order," but their limited reach leaves alternative values in the system intact, even if at some point "deliberate reinterpretations of [these] values" become necessary "in order to maintain a coherent and integrated social structure."[28] "On the other hand, a simple revolution intended to resolve certain dissynchronized conditions may produce new conditions which the elite is unable or unwilling to relieve through policies of change, thereby setting the stage for a later total revolution." One way to understand the revivalist resurgence of Hindu nationalism in recent years is to see it as a reaction by segments of the elites to pressures from below, with the long-term objective of moving India from simple to total revolution. "[N]o one among the exponents of Hindu revivalism would plead for a radically equalitarian casteless society. They would plead for the restoration of the Vedic principles of the functional organization of society."[29]

Political realities obstruct the way of such a restoration; for example, the Commission on Constitutional Review was constrained in its capacity to produce a constitutional revolution. But the probability of the ameliorative secularist commitment of India's simple revolution, as presently codified within the pages of its lengthy Constitution, being increasingly challenged and modified by countervailing commitments, is also quite real. To the extent that this process continues, with the original constitutional aspirations encountering contradictory pressures that tend to obscure the underlying purposes of the document, neither *simple* nor *total* are categories that seem appropriate for the emerging political reality. Therefore I suggest that we consider a third type—*complex revolution*, in which strands of both simple and total revolutions coexist in uncertain constitutional equilibrium. These strands need not (and probably will not) be equally represented, but their presence must be such that they are more

---

[27] Ibid.

[28] Ibid., 138–9.

[29] Varma 1964, 360; see also Aloysius 1994. Aloysius sees the extraordinary efforts by the Hindu right at political mobilization as a response to "the threat . . . to the upper caste vested interests, mostly from the egalitarian and pluralistic aspirations of the masses within formal democracy." Ibid., 1452. "Hindutva," he claims, "has no place for the numerous lower caste Hindu traditions, cults and sects that represent ways of life at variance with the upper caste orthodoxy." Ibid., 1451. Even the efforts to reshape the movement's appeal to disadvantaged Hindus by capitalizing on resentments against Muslims (for example, following the *Shah Bano* controversy) have been notably unproductive as exercises in mass mobilization. In this respect Hindu nationalism, if not unique, is distinguishable from most contemporary religious nationalist movements in not being a populist-based movement directed against the entrenched economic power of established interests. The threat to the ameliorative constitution, which is to say secular constitutionalism in India, is clear.

than token factors in the mix of goals comprising the regime's aspirational agenda. This ensures that a competition between factions identified with each of the strands will persist, at least until revolutionary clarity is reached through the unambiguous emergence of one dominant orientation. Perhaps the best example of the phenomenon of complex revolution is Israel, distinguished as it is by the ongoing competition between the particularistic and universalistic filaments in its constitutional constellation.

This complexity is evident in the disjunct between Israel's historical situation—resulting in its incomplete realization of the liberal constitutionalist ideal—and the dichotomy of simple and total revolution. Standing in the way of its completion is the Jewish identity of the State, which has prevented, or at least postponed, the promulgation of a constitution. Thus the typical path to securing the goals of a simple revolution has been absent in Israel. On the other hand, only the most hostile critics of the Zionist State would find in the label "total revolution" an apt characterization of Israel's modern origins. That a visionary, ascriptive element was present at the founding of the polity does not justify any equation, in revolutionary typology, between Israel and, say, Iran, where in 1979, "supplanting the entire structure of values" had indeed been the centerpiece of revolutionary upheaval. To be sure, all revolutions are complicated affairs in which labels such as "simple" and "total" do not do justice to conceptual understanding. But the Israeli case shows that they can be useful starting points, as their lack of fit in this instance is so obvious that no mere qualification of one or the other category will effectively serve an analytical purpose. And so we turn to the recent efforts in Israel to resolve the contradictions in the constitutionalism of that polity through the institution of judicial review. That will enable us to speculate about the possible consequences of greater complexity in Indian constitutional secularism.

Judicial Revolutionaries

Only a brief interval separated the signing into law of the two Basic Laws of 1992 and the rhetorical elevation of that moment to revolutionary significance. However, the use in Israel of the term *constitutional revolution* to describe the addition of the Basic Laws on Freedom of Occupation and Human Dignity and Freedom to the corpus of Israeli fundamental law was destined to have more than rhetorical significance. Had the characterization been made by someone other than the next president of the Supreme Court, it might have attracted a modicum of public attention before fading from view, perhaps to be remembered only as a felicitous example of wishful thinking. But Justice Aharon Barak's effusive reaction to the Knesset's higher law-making merited careful scrutiny if only because his leadership of the Court—intellectual and administrative—provided opportunity for transforming wishful thinking into self-fulfilling prophecy. The necessity for scrutiny acquired greater urgency after Barak's repeated invocation of the phrase became the rhetorical centerpiece of the justice's opinion in the landmark *Gal* decision of 1995.[30]

The decision is considered a "turning point in Israeli constitutional law" because it provided unambiguous affirmation for the existence of substantive judicial review of legislation.[31] Although the Supreme Court reversed a lower court's invalidation of a law passed by the Knesset, it did so while accepting the authority of Israeli courts to perform such acts. Despite the differences among the justices regarding the status of the Basic Laws in relation to the still controversial constitution-making powers of the Knesset, the practice of judicial review is now a political reality.[32] Also a reality is the constitutional standing of certain fundamental rights, which, according to Justice Barak, means that they now "enjoy normative superiority."[33] This reconceptualization of the status of rights—and all that it entails—has provided Israel with its "constitutional revolution."

The attribution of revolutionary significance to the Knesset's adoption in 1992 of the two Basic Laws is best understood as a clarion call for the commencement of a postrevolutionary constitutional jurisprudence. "The revolutionary ingredient, immanent in the Zionist project," Shlomo Avineri has observed, "is a redefinition of Jewish identity in a post-Enlightenment world. Nurtured by the ideas of the Enlightenment, Zionism inherited also the burden of its dialectics: Having both liberalism and nationalism as its pillars, Zionism and Israel embody all the contradictions of the modern nation-state—how to achieve self-determination as well as how to transcend nationalistic particularism within a universalistic framework."[34] The revolutionary content of the 1992 acts inheres less in the actual substantive changes introduced by the enactments than in the latent possibilities for creative judicial intervention in the unresolved dilemma of regime definition. Its meaning is ultimately traceable to the first great act of constitutional inaction in Israel: the decision to delay adoption of a formal written constitution. As was argued in the First Israeli Knesset by a member of the governing Mapai party: "One does not create a consti-

---

[30] *United Mizrachi Bank plc* at D. 221.

[31] Editorial Commentary 1997, 765.

[32] Some would say that judicial review had been established in 1969, in the famous case of *Bergman v Minister of Finance* 1969. For example, Chief Justice Shamgar wrote in his *Gal* opinion that "[I]t has been recognized, at least since the *Bergman* case, that the Court is competent to decide on the invalidation of legislation that contradicts or violates a provision of a Basic Law." *United Mizrachi Bank plc* at 288. For a variety of reasons, however, including the fact that the author of the *Bergman* opinion, Justice Moshe Landau, repeatedly denied that his narrow ruling in this case legitimized any major expansion of judicial authority in constitutional matters, the political reality of judicial review had not been established in that case.

[33] Ibid. at 353.

[34] Avineri 2000, 82.

tution at the beginning of a revolution, but when it is completed. All constitutions are an attempt to 'freeze' certain principles, to preserve them, inasmuch as it is possible to preserve any particular thing in the life of a nation."[35] The actions of the Knesset in 1992 led Justice Barak to attempt to close the door on the Israeli Revolution.

There were of course other well-documented reasons for the failure of the Constituent Assembly to produce a constitution for the new State in fulfillment of the promise of the Declaration of Independence. But one did not have to look very far beyond the Declaration's conflicting visions of national development to appreciate the logic of constitutional postponement. Thus if the basic nature of the regime was in doubt (a Western state? a state of the Jewish people? a Jewish State? all of the above?), it was reasonable to postpone constitutionalizing, which is to say "freezing," a set of principles around which no consensus had yet congealed.[36] To be sure, a vigorous case was made at the time for moving forward by doing what most successful revolutionaries have done, namely seizing the opportunity to codify the fruits of victory. But most revolutionary victories have produced coherent agendas that are codifiable with only minimal effort. In this, of course, timing is everything, and in Israel framing a judicially enforceable constitution would require patience. "We are not at the end of a revolutionary process but at its beginning."[37]

Unlike the American experience, in which a written constitution represented the final legitimation of a Revolution that had effectively given birth to a new people, the wisdom of entrenching a body of principles that would, through constitutional mandate, rigidly constrain the course of future political development was less compelling in a setting in which independence had left the core issues of political identity unresolved.[38]

---

[35] Rabinovich and Reinharz 1984, 45.

[36] This postponement can also be understood as a manifestation of the consociational basis of Israeli democratic institutions. For example, Asher Cohen and Bernard Susser argue that refraining from clear decisions is necessary to achieve political legitimacy in a place like Israel, where deeply divisive issues threaten to destabilize the polity. "Irresolution, adopting elusive formulas (such as maintenance of the status quo), and allocating sufficient resources to all parties preserve the secular-religious divide in a state of negotiated balance that prevents a potentially ruinous Kulturkampf from erupting." Cohen and Susser 2000, 8.

[37] Ibid., 42.

[38] It has been pointed out that the American Constitution is a paradigmatic example of how constitutional arrangements tend to accompany transformative historic events. "[T]he prototypical constitutional revolution is an offspring of a historic revolution. It occurs at a 'historic moment.' " Barak-Erez 1995, 350. Barak-Erez relies on Bruce Ackerman's theory of constitutional moments to account for the revolutionary significance of the enactment of the 1992 Basic Laws. Thus these laws, she maintains, can be viewed as a response to the "unrestrained politics" of the time, in which a "constitutional moment" necessitated fundamental constitutional changes. Ibid., 351. A similar kind of argument is advanced by Robert A. Burt, who understands the emergence of judicial review in the United States and Israel

But leaving the future relatively unfettered by constitutionally designed principled constraints was not a condition comfortably to be endured, particularly by those professionally committed to the rule of law. Over the years Israeli justices have managed to maneuver quite effectively within the limitations of parliamentary supremacy, employing various interpretive strategies to enact and enforce a de facto judicial bill of rights. Always, however, the reach of their influence was measured by the sufferance of the legislature, a political reality that doubtless afforded them a unique perspective on the downside of unfinished revolution. Closure, then, might well have represented an enticing prospect.

Nearly forty years ago Hannah Arendt noted that "[R]evolutions are the only political events which confront us directly and inevitably with the problem of beginning."[39] But revolutions (real or imagined) are as much about endings as they are about beginnings. What happens after the revolution depends on the way things have been concluded, on the details of resolution. While a "constitutional revolution" is by some interpretations a classic oxymoron,[40] it is a term that draws our attention to these details; moreover, the very strategy of deploying it in a campaign to enhance the role of the courts as authoritative interpreters of the Basic Laws is in itself politically significant.

Revolutionary Possibilities

"Revolution is a game any number can play."[41] It is, as Bruce Ackerman has pointed out, "one of the slipperiest words in the modern political vocabulary."[42] Through its familiarity in contemporary usage, the word

---

as an institutional response to the presence of fundamental societal conflict. Burt 1989, 2013. For a critique of this argument see Jacobsohn 1993, 110–24.

[39] Arendt 1963, 13.

[40] For example, Paul Schreker stipulates that a condition of revolution is that it shall be illegal. "In the realm of politics we can . . . define revolution as an illegal change of the constitution." Schrecker 1966, 38. A *constitutional* revolution, therefore, is a contradiction in terms, although with a different inflection (a constitutional *revolution*), we can accommodate the use of the reference as it was introduced into the Israeli political debate by Justice Barak. For a theoretical consideration of the term see Lipkin 1989, 701. Lipkin's conceptualization is quite broad; thus "A constitutional revolution occurs when the Court pragmatically creates a formal or substantive principle of constitutional adjudication." Ibid., 718. This can occur, for example, "when the Court gives meaning to a vague or indeterminate constitutional provision such as due process or equal protection." Ibid., 748. While this formulation is, in my opinion, too broad to successfully support the language of revolutionary activity, Lipkin is more helpful when he points out that "Generally, a revolutionary constitutional decision is a response to a perceived constitutional or social crisis." Ibid., 745.

[41] Ackerman 1991, 170.

[42] Ibid., 201.

has acquired, he suggests, a banality that diminishes its analytical power. It is a point echoed by Jacques Barzun, who writes that "We have got into the habit of calling too many things revolutions."[43] The term may, however, be useful in other ways. According to Robert Dahl, "A large part of politics consists of purely expressive actions with little or no consequence for social, economic, or political change, and to roll the word revolution trippingly off the tongue appears to be particularly cathartic."[44] Thus the rhetoric of revolution may possess significance separate from the objective changes introduced by the phenomenon to which the word applies.[45]

In the case of the "constitutional revolution" in Israel, it is surely premature to render definitive judgment concerning the type or magnitude of the change associated with the 1992 additions to the Basic Laws. Moreover, it is probable that, like the "Warren Court Revolution" in the United States, the impact of the revolution will for a long time remain a subject of intense debate within the legal and scholarly communities.[46] Early assessments have emphasized a neoliberal economic orientation in the Israeli Supreme Court's postrevolutionary adjudication of the new Basic Laws,[47] but how enduring this development is, and how prominent among other as yet undeclared commitments it turns out to be, is anybody's guess. What Thomas Kuhn said about the scientific domain applies

[43] Barzun 2000, 3.

[44] Dahl 1970, 3.

[45] As Dahl reminds us, the prominence of revolution in the political vocabulary of a nation is a poor predictor of the degree of transformation one should expect to find. "Some of the most profound changes in the world take place in a quiet country like Denmark, where hardly anyone raises his voice and the rhetoric of revolution finds few admirers." Ibid., 4. In the United States the term *revolution* is often applied to critical junctures in electoral politics: After the 1980 election, many heralded the arrival of the "Reagan Revolution," just as earlier in the century the "New Deal Revolution" functioned in similar fashion as a rallying cry for social and political change. The fact that basic continuity rather than fundamental change could more accurately describe the achievements of both revolutions has not given rise to any serious efforts to revise the descriptive nomenclature.

[46] The controversy surrounding Gerald N. Rosenberg's book *The Hollow Hope: Can Courts Bring About Social Change?* (1991) is the best example of the nature of the debate that revolutions in constitutional law can engender over the question of impact. Impact aside, however, the role of the Court in political life is likely to be fundamentally transformed. As Robert G. McCloskey wrote of the "constitutional revolution of 1937": "The Court's relationship to the American polity had undergone a fundamental change. Quite probably the judges themselves did not understand how great a withdrawal was portended by their about-face in 1937. But within a few years it would be plain to all that another constitutional era had ended and a new one had begun." McCloskey 1994, 119. There is good reason to believe that in Israel too debates about impact will proceed into the foreseeable future at the same time that general agreement will coalesce over the changed relationship of the Court to the Israeli polity.

[47] See in this regard Hirschl 1998, 427; Gross 1998, 80; and Mandel 1999, 259.

equally well to the constitutional: "[I]f a new candidate for [revolutionary recognition] had to be judged from the start by hard-headed people who examined only relative problem-solving ability, the sciences would experience very few major revolutions."[48]

Not only is it premature to focus on objective changes, but it may be, in a certain sense, beside the point. Catharsis seems far from the purpose of Barak's frequent references to revolution, but these invocations do convey an essentially expressive intent: to affirm a particular political reality, the broad acceptance of which, it is believed, will lead to desirable consequences and, most important, the achievement of constitutional politics. Judicial review over actions of the legislature gives formal recognition to this achievement, but it is not secured without the commitment of "large numbers of people to invest their energies and identities in the collective process of political redefinition."[49] The existence of a constitution is one thing; its revolutionary significance in constituting a regime of democratic freedom is another. Or as Justice Barak has put it, "The existence of a constitution conferring rights on the individual has not yet been sufficiently clarified in Israeli society."[50]

In this regard, consider the American analogue to the *Gal* decision. Chief Justice Marshall's argument for judicial review in *Marbury v Madison* is premised on the logic of a written constitution. Although the Constitution is silent as to the existence in the courts of a substantive supervisory power, there is, as far as we can tell from Marshall's opinion, nothing revolutionary about the official recognition of judicial review. In Kuhnian terms, judicial enforcement of constitutional rights represented normal politics.[51] What *was* revolutionary (although Marshall does not refer to it in this way) is the following:

> That the people have an original right to establish, for their future government, such principles, as, in their opinion, shall most conduce to their own happiness is the basis on which the whole American fabric has been erected.

---

[48] Kuhn 1970, 157.

[49] Ackerman 1991, 204.

[50] Barak 1998, 10. For a thoughtful comparative study that questions a "constitution-centered" view emphasizing constitutional rights guarantees as the precondition for a rights revolution, see Epp 1998.

[51] A contrary view on the revolutionary significance of *Marbury* has been advanced by Robert Justin Lipkin, who declares it to be "a paradigmatic revolutionary decision." Lipkin, 1989, 756. Lipkin believes Marshall's opinion to be revolutionary "because it read into the Constitution a particular substantive political philosophy, not a neutral or objective principle of constitutional law." Ibid., 773. My view that the decision is better represented as entailing normal politics is premised on the understanding that it (the argument for judicial review) follows from the substantive political philosophy already present within the document.

The exercise of this original right is a very great exertion; nor can it, nor ought it, to be frequently repeated. The principles, therefore, so established, are deemed fundamental. And as the authority from which they proceed is supreme, and can seldom act, they are designed to be permanent.[52]

This is the sentiment that clarifies what Hannah Arendt had in mind when she referred to constitution-making as "the noblest of all revolutionary deeds."[53] Upon first glance, this may seem odd. After all, in the United States revolutionary deeds are more often associated with the likes of Thomas Paine than John Marshall. Nevertheless, although Paine and Marshall were men of different political persuasions, the chief justice's opinion makes clear that he embraced the former's claim that "A constitution is not the act of a government, but of a people constituting a government."[54] The power of the people to bind the future through the entrenchment of principles that *constituted* the people as the legitimate source of sovereign authority was the essence of the revolutionary achievement. In their concurrence on this point, the advocate of revolutionary action and the defender of constitutional government were thus brought together, Paine initiating a process that Marshall consolidates through an act of legal benediction.

It may be "difficult," as Arendt put it, "to recognize the truly revolutionary element in constitution-making."[55] It may be even more difficult to clearly articulate this element in the Israeli context, where constitution-making is a much vexed and uncertain subject. However, in his *Gal* opinion, Justice Barak does effect a close approximation of Paine's teaching. "[A] constitution is not an act of government which grants a constitution to the nation. A constitution is an act of the nation which creates the government."[56] In so declaring, Barak was drawing a distinction between himself and Chief Justice Meyer Shamgar, who, rather than join his colleagues in applying the doctrine of constituent authority, had based the constitution-making authority of the Knesset on the theory of legislative sovereignty. Thus for Shamgar, "The doctrine of unlimited sovereignty of the Knesset is based on the view that the Knesset is the supreme legislative authority and that its powers are unrestricted, barring those limitations which it establishes for itself."[57] Without delving into the question of

---

[52] *Marbury* at 175.

[53] Arendt 1963, 157.

[54] Paine 1985, 185.

[55] Arendt 1963, 142.

[56] *United Mizrachi Bank plc* at 390.

[57] Ibid. at 284. On the question of sovereignty, Justice Barak's position is that legislative supremacy has never prevailed in Israel. "The truth is that the Knesset was never sovereign. Sovereignty belongs to the people, not to their representatives. However, the Knesset was supreme in its legislative power. It has now been clarified that the supremacy is that of our

which of these interpretations best reflects the views of Israel's founders, it is clear that the Barak position is the more revolutionary of the two, at least in the Arendtian sense of the term.[58]

But Arendt's usage may not travel all that smoothly to Israel. She wrote of the American Constitution that it "finally consolidated the power of the Revolution, and since the aim of revolution was freedom, it indeed came to be what Bracton had called *Constitutio Libertatis*, the foundation of freedom."[59] This is what led her to appreciate Woodrow Wilson's description of the Supreme Court as "a kind of Constitutional Assembly in continuous session."[60] As the final authority on the meaning of the Constitution, the Court, in this rendering, was an embodiment of the original constitutive will of the people, which meant that it also represented the spirit of the Revolution and its commitment to freedom. For Arendt, everything depended on this commitment. Where it was not present (or at least dominated by other aspirations), as in the French Revolution and the great revolutions of the twentieth century, "disaster" and/or political disillusionment followed.[61]

In connection with Israel, I have already suggested that delay in constitution-making was partially a by-product of the difficulty Israelis encountered in consolidating the conflicted meanings of the Zionist ascendance to power. David Ben-Gurion, for example, distinguished between the revolutionary experiences of Israel and the United States by pointing out that "There the people rose against the government and a change in government signified attainment of the people's aim. But not we. We rose against a destiny of the years, against exile and dispersion, against deprivation of

---

new Constitution." Barak 1997, 4. This tends to weaken the revolutionary meaning of the acts of 1992, in that their effect is, at least in this regard, to clarify rather than to change.

[58] Arendt argued that the difference between constitutions that are acts of government and constitutions by which people constitute a government is critical. The issue is one of legitimacy. She looked at the experience of constitutional government in the twentieth century and found that there is "an enormous difference in power and authority" when constitutional limitations emerge through acts of popular sovereignty as opposed to governmental imposition. Arendt 1963, 144. As for the use of the term *constitutional revolution* by Justice Barak, it refers specifically to the elevation to constitutional status of human rights in Israel, an elevation which, even in Justice Shamgar's account, would make them, according to Barak, "constitutional supra-statutory rights." *United Mizrachi Bank plc* at 352. In other words, Barak deflects attention from the revolutionary significance of the derivation of the rights to the fact that they now exist as functioning parts of the Israeli constitution.

[59] Arendt 1963, 152.

[60] Ibid., 201.

[61] Arendt distinguished between the American and French Revolutions in a manner suggestive of Chalmers Johnson's distinction between simple and total revolutions. Johnson, however, was a critic of Arendt, having found her use of the ideal of freedom to define revolution to be imprecise and narrow. Johnson 1966, 118.

language and culture."[62] In other words, the revolutionary legacy bequeathed to future Israelis incorporated a strong revivalist component, which itself was understood in radically different ways by secular and observant Jews. Many (but certainly not all) of the former were committed to the other powerful strand in the legacy, democratic institutions; but only a minority of the latter subscribed to its principles.[63] As for the secular democrats, most were not beholden to the type of popular sovereignty approach spelled out in the *Gal* decision by Justice Barak. Rather, they would probably have found Chief Justice Shamgar's views on parliamentary sovereignty more compatible with their fundamentally State-centered political orientation. It is a measure of the ideological distance traveled over the years since independence by the political elite—especially the judiciary—that Shamgar's was the lone voice on the Court for the older perspective. How much of a distance yet remains between the judicial elite and the body politic is a matter of immense importance to the fate of the constitutional revolution.

In this respect Justice Barak's rhetorical skills will be sorely tested. His use of the term *constitutional revolution* can be understood as an effort to transform a complex revolution into a simple one by muting, if not eliminating, the discordant notes in the revolutionary legacy.[64] Justice

---

[62] Ben-Gurion 1954, 377. For Israel, then, the revolutionary experience was revivalist in nature, falling into a category of what Anthony Wallace referred to as a movement "profess[ing] to revive a traditional culture now fallen into desuetude." Wallace 1956, 275.

[63] The numerical and political dominance of those committed to liberal democracy, a fragile coalition comprising a majority of the secularists and a minority of the observant, dampened whatever theocratic impulse there may have been in the founding commitment to ascriptively driven nationalism. I discuss this in detail in Jacobsohn 1996, 1.

[64] The enactment of the two Basic Laws in 1992 was a galvanizing event that enabled those so committed to imagine how they might finish the project in constitutionalism begun decades ago. The question, however, is whether the effort to deploy the resources of judicial power to consummate the unfinished work of politicians will enhance the quality of the constitutional experience in Israel. In reflecting on this question, it is perhaps worth keeping in mind that unfinished work can be of exceptionally high quality. If this were not true, Schubert's *Eighth* (or *Unfinished*) *Symphony* would be a minor footnote in music history. Instead it "is rightly recognized as a pinnacle in the history of the symphony and in the history of music, a supreme poetic vision in sound." Newbould 1992, 207. No audience feels shortchanged by its incompleteness, despite "the absurdity of a Classical symphony . . . beginning in one key and ending in another." Ibid., 182. We may never know for sure why Schubert did not finish his masterpiece, but whatever dissatisfaction may attend that uncertainty is more than compensated for by the sublime pleasure of experiencing its mellifluous tonalities. If the logic behind Justice Barak's "intention of achieving unity and constitutional harmony" were not immediately evident, Schubert's achievement is surely instructive in clarifying the virtues of coherence and integrity. "[B]y now we have come to accept the two extant movements of the *Unfinished* as a complete and organic whole, and this because it is one of the few large-scale works of Schubert's where a central idea makes for compelling

Cheshin found his colleague's words to be "filled with exaltation and elation," but he worried that "labels—in themselves—may sometimes be blinding and invite wishes to be perceived as reality."[65] The "reality" here is revolutionary clarity, in which the inner tensions of Israel's dual constitutional aspirations are happily resolved, thereby enabling unity of purpose to be brought to bear on a constitutional future that resembles the progress of other liberal democracies. The conversion of a complex revolution into one of the other two possibilities reflects the inherently transitional character of this political type, although a stable equilibrium in the constitutive elements that comprise it can give it a finished or permanent appearance. A genuine constitutional revolution would mean that the equilibrium has broken down, effectively ending the period of complexity, and providing a solid foundation for constructing a constitutional edifice appropriate for the new political reality. On the other hand, a construction effort that was based on a constitutional revolution in name only (i.e., one that only imagined a new political reality) could pose a threat to valued institutional assets of the "transitional" polity.

---

unity. The moods of the two movements are so complementary, so much the outcome of one particular emotional experience, that we no longer have the feeling of incompleteness." Carner 1947, 64. In contrast, of course, the two "movements" in the constitutional legacy of Israeli independence coexist in competitive tension, and the disagreement over a central idea underscores for many the feeling of incompleteness. The internal contradictions of Israel's unfinished constitution mirror the historic divisions within the body politic, just as the seamlessness of the unfinished work of art reflects the unified genius of its creator. Aspirations for a compelling unity are what inspired the constitutional revolution and also the judges today who are motivated by the possibility of its culmination in a finished charter. Justice Barak, however, is not Franz Schubert. Nor for that matter is any other judge, even one who might perchance embody the "Herculean" virtues of Ronald Dworkin's ideal jurist. Dworkin 1977. Had Schubert completed his symphony, the effort might very well have produced a work superior to his unfinished gem, although one must reckon with the possibility that the factors that contributed to its interrupted completion would have somehow also diminished the quality of the final achievement. In the case of the Constitution, evaluation of the finished product requires looking beyond the enhanced coherence of the document and the decisions based upon it, and considering as well how the process by which consummation was achieved might affect the nation's democratic prospects and the legitimacy of its institutions. Completing a constitution is not like completing a symphony, in part because the results of the first activity, as Aristotle's famous distinction between ideal and attainable constitutions teaches, must be judged according to standards shaped by the demands of actual circumstances. Thus the good lawgiver and the genuine statesman must know what perfection is, but understand the necessary political constraints on seeking its achievement. For the judicial statesman in Israel it means participating in a political process directed toward shaping a public consensus supportive of genuine constitutional transformation. The discordant notes of complex and unfinished constitutionalism can be rearranged to achieve harmonious results, but not in the manner of a Schubert composition, where the only circumstance necessary to ensure success is the towering genius of the composer.

[65] *United Mizrachi Bank plc* at 567.

Constitutional Harmony

The Constitutional Revolution has led to a change in the judiciary's status. Great responsibilities have been imposed upon it. It must fill the mould created by the "majestic generalities" in the new Basic Laws. The judiciary must be aware of the fundamental values of the people. It must balance them in accordance with the values of the "enlightened general public" in Israel. It must reflect the general public's conscience, the social consensus, the legal ethics and the value judgments of society with regard to acceptable and unacceptable behaviour. Constitutional interpretation should not be formalistic or pedantic. It should be purposive. It should be done from a wide perspective and adopt a substantive approach. A constitution is a living organism, and its interpretation must express the deep "I believe" of the society. This interpretation must base itself on the historical continuance of the nation's creation, with the intention of achieving unity and constitutional harmony.[66]

Drawing a connection between the institution of judicial review and the spirit of revolution is not unprecedented. For example, in his famous argument in the *Writs of Assistance* case, James Otis defiantly argued, "As to Acts of Parliament, an Act against the Constitution is void: and if an Act of Parliament should be made, in the very words of the Petition, it would be void. The Executive Courts must pass such Acts into disuse."[67] Upon hearing these words in 1765, the young American revolutionary John Adams wrote: "Then and there the child Independence was born."[68] Associating an act of constitutional transgression with the birth of a new nation (dedicated, as Lincoln later said, to a certain proposition) has both symbolic and real significance where the institution of judicial review is concerned, namely that its legitimacy, in the end, inheres in advancing those ideas that nourish the American conception of nationhood. Twenty-two years later, in Philadelphia, the child observed by Adams came to maturity, but the occasion—the constitutional revolution of 1787—curiously did not make explicit provision for judicial review. Much like in Israel, that revolutionary innovation emerged from the handiwork of judges.

In the United States, judicial review was in a profound way tied to the presence of a pervasive and dominant political creed that was expressive of the philosophy of the American Revolution. As Louis Hartz put it, "Judicial review as it has worked in America would be inconceivable

---

[66] Barak 1997, 5.

[67] Quoted in Grey 1978, 843, 869.

[68] Ibid., 869. As Thomas C. Grey has noted, "John Adams' romanticized recollection has more than anecdotal significance; it shows that one of the central figures in the founding of the nation could look back and find in such an argument the first articulation of the essential spirit of the Revolution." Ibid.

without the acceptance of the Lockian creed, ultimately enshrined in the Constitution, since the removal of high policy to the realm of adjudication implies a prior recognition of the principles to be legally interpreted."[69] In effect judicial review functions as an instrument designed by the architects of American constitutionalism to validate and preserve the Revolutionary accomplishments of the first generation of Americans. Like the Basic Laws in Israel, the Constitution is filled with much contested "majestic generalities." However, the disagreements over such wordings as "due process" and "equal protection" have not expressed fundamental divisions over the constitutive principles of the regime, leaving the Supreme Court's interpretations and rulings vulnerable to critique but not to the more destructive attacks that call into question the Court's very legitimacy.[70]

In the case of Israel's *complex revolution*, "unity and constitutional harmony" are goals to be "achiev[ed]," not a foundation upon which to construct the institution of judicial review. Thus the Basic Law on Human Dignity requires upholding "the values of the State of Israel as a Jewish and democratic State." Critics of the legislation worry about the burden this places on the courts. "[I]t is a mistake," according to Dan Avnon, "to embrace a constitution that in one swift move burdens the judiciary with the enormous responsibility of formulating the resolution of a schism that is an immanent feature of Jewish social existence."[71] Ruth Gavison suggests that "[I]n rifted democracies courts should be reluctant to determine specific arrangements and priorities, especially in areas of social controversy, where the grounds of judicial action are not clear."[72] Such concerns are surely not alleviated by Justice Barak's interpretive commitment regarding the dual obligations of the Basic Law. In construing those pas-

---

[69] Hartz 1955, 16.

[70] The one great exception is of course the *Dred Scott* case.

[71] Avnon 1998, 543. Avnon also fears that unburdening representative institutions of responsibility for advancing the cause of principled reconciliation will weaken the deliberative capacity of popular governance.

[72] Gavison 1999, 218. "The deeper the rifts in society, the more cautious the courts should be, because there is greater danger of a serious break-down in the cohesion of society." Ibid., 253. As applied to Israel, Gavison makes a very interesting point about the use of judicial power that bears directly on the category of complex revolution. "The clearer it is that an arrangement is indeed the result of a complex compromise, the more reluctant the court should be to pronounce the compromise illegal." Ibid., 255. She then distinguishes between secular-religious divisions and Jewish-Arab divisions, only the first of which is a product of negotiation and compromise, and notes that contrary to the deference that the Court should display in cases of complexity, it has instead taken a problematically active stance. On the other hand, the Court, she argues, has been too passive in cases involving the second type of division, where arrangements are products of unilateral Jewish decisions.

sages, "The content of the phrase 'Jewish state' will be determined by the level of abstraction which shall be given it. In my opinion, one should give this phrase meaning on a high level of abstraction, which will unite all members of society and find the common ground among them. The level of abstraction should be so high, until it becomes identical to the democratic nature of the state."[73]

Reliance on a high level of abstraction to achieve a unified view may fuel the anxiety of some that the "enlightened general public" from which guidance in values is to be found is likely to be a liberal, generally secular intellectual elite, widely perceived as unrepresentative of Israeli public opinion. The term *majestic generalities* was first used in an American case, *Fay v New York*,[74] in an opinion by Justice Robert Jackson involving race, juries, and the Fourteenth Amendment. To "fill the mould" created by that Amendment's general language, scholars and judges have also reasoned on a high level of abstraction, often drawing connections between the meaning of its famous clauses and the universalistic principles of American founding documents, notably the Declaration of Independence. What distinguishes such reasoning from its Israeli counterpart is the extant constitutional harmony upon which it rests; thus, for example, the Warren Court's "judicial revolution" was innovative in the expansive meanings it assigned to consensual principles. Controversial as these innovations were, the fact that they rested *on* secure principles, and were not intended *to* secure principles, meant that the threat of counterrevolution was of less ominous potential consequence than if these innovations had implicated the very soul of the constitutional polity. Earl Warren was assaulted by billboards; Aharon Barak confronts assaults of a much more targeted variety.[75]

But the project of deploying the judiciary to achieve closure for a complex revolution should not be deterred by the threat of extremist overreac-

---

[73] Barak 1992–93, 30.

[74] *Faye.*

[75] One of Gerald Rosenberg's contributions in *The Hollow Hope* is his consideration of how Court decisions usually mobilize opponents much more than supporters, which in turn limits the societal impact that the decisions are likely to have. The mobilization of opposition takes on another order of magnitude when the output of the Court is viewed as a threat to what are perceived to be the underlying principles of the regime. The following remark is suggestive of what is at stake. "Aharon Barak is the driving force behind a sophisticated campaign against Jewish life in Israel. We must not waste our shells. We must take off the gloves and argue with him up front. To present him as he really is, as one who is creating a 'judicial revolution.' " Quoted in the *New York Times*, August 28, 1996. In their consociational interpretation of Israeli politics, Cohen and Susser argue that the courts are crucial to the stability of a divided society, but only if they continue to be perceived as a politically disinterested institution. "[C]onstitutional pitched battles are precisely what consociational politics seeks to avoid." Cohen and Susser 2000, 92. They worry that Barak's revolutionary

tion. On the other hand, legitimate concerns over the possible impact of the project for the long-term influence of the Court in Israeli political life does caution against proceeding full throttle. Shlomo Avineri has said that "It is impossible to ignore the fact that when the Supreme Court makes decisions in matters of values and morals over which there are legitimate political differences, it is hard to prevent a deterioration in its status."[76] In fact, however, it is not so hard to imagine a Court overcoming the immediate decline in its status occasioned by the loss of support from the losing side in a debate over morals and values. If it can weather the storm by first sharing the institutional burdens of decision-making, and then educating the public in the wisdom of its principled vision, then it may not only recover but also in the long run perhaps enjoy an enhanced level of status in the broader polity. How likely is it, then, that these conditions will be met in the aftermath of the constitutional revolution?

Judicial Finality

The existence of a moral consensus embodied in a written constitution may help to legitimate the exercise of judicial review, but the possibility of error or willful distortion also suggests why it is problematic to vest in the Supreme Court an unqualified finality in constitutional interpretation.[77] Thus even in the United States, where the view that the Constitution is what the judges of the Supreme Court say it is represents an aphoristic approximation of a serious and widely held jurisprudential position, sober voices (notably Lincoln's) have insisted on the necessity of constitutional interpretation as a collaborative enterprise. Such an insistence does not require relinquishment of primary institutional responsibility for clarifying and elaborating meanings that define the nation, but it does argue for humility and restraint.

---

effort, by altering the perception of the Court as nonideological, will undermine its ability to maintain control over politically charged conflicts concerning religion. Ibid., 75.

[76] *Jerusalem Post*, September 2, 1996.

[77] The question of judicial finality pushes one to consider the Canadian case and its much discussed legislative override provision. In a thoughtful article, Lorraine Eisenstat Weinrib analyzes Canada's constitutional revolution, occasionally comparing it to the Israeli revolutionary experience. "In points of convergence and divergence alike, Canada's Charter and Israel's new Basic Laws mark a parallel transition from the legislative state to the constitutional state." Weinrib 1999, 50. Weinrib does not view the construction of a constitutional culture as predicated on the existence of constitutional consensus. Ibid., 50. For this reason, perhaps, she does not pursue the comparative implications of her observation that "It will take time for Canadian judges to work out the Charter's full substantive and institutional coherence and to integrate its norms into the larger framework of Canada's constitutional order." Ibid., 37. It will take time, she says, because transitions of the magnitude of what has occurred in Canada and Israel are very difficult. Because of her devaluation of constitutional

The absence of a consensus in the constitutionalism of a complex revolution deepens the logic of restraint; in these circumstances judicial modesty means avoiding or deflecting judgments of finality in the absence of a final settlement of regime principles. But modesty is less of an imperative where the specific results of immodesty possess a politically tentative or intermediate status in the elaboration of regime principles. As Justice Sussman of the Israeli Supreme Court said a number of years ago, "[T]he judicial restraint in favor of which Justices of the United States Supreme Court preached, lest the national patterns be determined by people whom the public did not choose . . . this restraint is unnecessary in Israel, whose legislature is all-powerful."[78] Sussman's observation calls attention to a paradox in the politics of judicial review, which is that the constraints imposed on the courts by the presence of parliamentary supremacy may serve to legitimate a more active role for the Court in construing the law. Or as Menachem Hofnung has argued, "[T]he previous 'weakness' of not having formally defined review powers, made it possible for the Court to incrementally increase its influence without being perceived as threatening the other branches of government."[79] The development of a de facto bill of rights through statutory interpretation and administrative review had left the rights thus secured vulnerable to the vagaries of politics, but that vulnerability could also be a source of boldness, as it provided the judiciary a protective shield against assaults launched from the high ground of democratic accountability. Thus the Court could pursue with admirable determination the more libertarian aspirations of the nation's founding agenda, knowing in advance that the Knesset stood ready to parry what the legislators viewed as the excesses of liberal enthusiasm. If, however, constitutional revolution means that such perceived excesses will cement themselves in the rulings of an institution brandishing final interpretive authority, the prospects for constitutional accommodation between competing visions of national purpose are likely to diminish accordingly.[80]

---

consensus, she does not consider how much more difficult it is in Israel, where "substantive and institutional coherence" is much less a constitutional reality than it is in Canada.

[78] Quoted in Barak 1987, 194.

[79] Hofnung 1996, 604.

[80] In this regard, Alon Harel has pointed out that opposition to the constitutional revolution is not confined to those who might be expected to resist effort to extend the coverage of constitutional rights in Israeli society. "Liberal counter-revolutionaries are convinced that a judicial constitutional revolution exposes the courts to political pressures. Courts which have to defend their very constitutional powers to review statutes are less able vigorously to defend human rights. Ironically, under this view, the Court's declaration of dejure constitutional power weakens its de facto power and consequently undermines its ability and commitment to the protection of human rights." Harel 1999, 148. See also Barak-Erez

Teachers to the Citizenry

"The judge does not merely adjudicate. He also has an educational role."[81] Justice Barak has long been an advocate of a judicial role that to some extent parallels the figure of the spiritual leader in rabbinic tradition. In this account the courtroom functions simultaneously as a classroom. In his *Gal* opinion, he suggested that "It is possible that the constitutional transformation will be internalised; that human rights will become the 'daily bread' of every girl and boy, and that the awareness of rights . . . will prevail, and that we will be more sensitive to the rights of a human being as a human being."[82] Ultimately, then, the larger achievement of the constitutional revolution will be inscribed in the hearts and minds of people, in their embrace and understanding of the principles that are the substance of the new constitutional harmony.

The basic thought here is that "[A]djudication is not only declarative but also constitutive."[83] This constitutive act also serves the pedagogical purposes of the Court, so that adjudication is not only a declarative act but also an educative one. In the United States, opponents of constitutional ratification widely believed that omitting a bill of rights represented a lost opportunity for civic education. It was thought that a specific written enumeration of rights would facilitate the task of popular education in a new republic. "We do not by declarations change the nature of things, or create new truths, but we give existence, or at least establish in the minds of the people truths and principles which they might never otherwise have thought of, or soon forgot."[84] The supporters of the Constitution disagreed with this view of the instructional value of a specific enumeration of rights, indeed insisting that it would in fact misinstruct the American people about the Constitution and its purposes. They felt that reducing rights to a compressed inventory would encourage a shallow jurisprudence and thus an essentially unenlightened teaching. But that judges should be engaged in civic instruction, that they should play the role of "republican schoolmaster," was a point on which both opponents

---

1995, 353. "The value of invalidating a law will have to be weighed against the counter-majoritarian difficulty and against the problem of legitimacy. The additional power granted to the Court will have to be accompanied by an added sense of self-restraint. The Court will have to 'earn' its legitimacy."

[81] Barak 1987, 221. Or as Ralph Lerner pointed out in a well-known essay, "Whether the Justice should teach the public is not and cannot be in question since teaching is inseparable from judging in a democratic regime." Lerner 1968, 180.

[82] *United Mizrachi Bank plc* at 448.

[83] *Ressler* at 458.

[84] Federal Farmer 1987, 458.

and supporters of the Constitution could agree. While contesting the most effective vehicles for instruction, they believed the principles of the Revolution, as codified in the Constitution (whatever that might turn out to be), should be at the core of a citizen's education. But for a Court to conduct a national seminar that aimed to internalize the principles of the Revolution, those principles should be characterized by coherence and consistency; otherwise the effort is likely to founder under widespread suspicion of the motives and agenda of the presumed educator. To the extent that the moral authority of educators depends on a high level of trust in their nonpartisan ambition, then the identification of the Court with one side of the divided legacy of a complex revolution could prove fatal to the educational project.[85]

In his important study of the educative mission of the justices of the early American Supreme Court, Ralph Lerner quoted John Adams on the subject of the Constitution and its relation to public opinion. "[A]s its administration must necessarily be always pliable to the fluctuating varieties of public opinion, its stability and duration by a like overruling and irresistible necessity, was to depend upon the stability and duration in the hearts and minds of the people . . . of those principles proclaimed in the Declaration of Independence, and embodied in the Constitution of the United States."[86] This administration, we might add, faced a daunting task of extraordinary delicacy and deftness, as it involved balancing the vagaries of public opinion with enduring principles emerging from the Revolution. If, in addition to effecting such a balance, it had also been necessary to reconcile unresolved tensions within the legacy bequeathed by the Revolution, then we might wonder whether the endeavor would have collapsed under its own weight. This, in short, is the predicament confronting the Israeli Supreme Court in the wake of its constitutional revolution. If the Court is successful in realizing the "possib[ility] that the constitutional transformation will be internalised," then the magnitude of its achievement will have historic significance. But if it fails, then the ordeals of revolutionary complexity will continue, with prospects for their elimination perhaps put off even further into the distant future.

---

[85] Ruth Gavison writes that "[T]he courts should elaborate, articulate and implement the shared commitments of the society they serve—the values reflected in the laws of the society—as opposed to the values which judges personally or as members of distinct groups within society, uphold." Gavison 1999, 218. Alon Harel makes the same point with more specific reference to the Israeli situation. "[T]he Court in Israel is perceived by some as insufficiently representative of the complexity of views and ideologies and consequently granting the power of judicial review to the courts may be perceived as the political victory of a secular ideology over a religious or nationalist one." Harel 1999, 156.

[86] Lerner 1968, 178.

Reverse Images

David Ben-Gurion's revivalist characterization of the Israeli revolutionary experience as one in which a people rose up to reclaim their past presents an interesting contrast with India. There as well, severance of the ties of political subordination to the British empire meant that cultural roots of ancient lineage could once again flower unhindered by the intrusive grip of an alien presence. "One of the remarkable developments of the present age," wrote Nehru shortly before independence, "has been the rediscovery of the past and of the nation."[87] But as Nehru's invocation of Ashoka at the Constituent Assembly suggests, Indian nationhood was imagined by the principal leaders of the independence movement as a composite culture consisting of much more than the particular ethnoreligious affiliation of most Indians. This of course contrasted sharply with the Israeli experience.

The Hindu nationalist challenge to the idea of a composite culture is typically portrayed as nonthreatening because of what its votaries assert is an abiding spirit of tolerance lying at the core of the religion.[88] It is indeed nonthreatening, but in a very different sense, namely by not imperiling the dominant class and caste interests in Indian society.[89] In the context of the political drama unfolding in contemporary India, it displays the characteristics of a "religion of the status quo," the goal of which, according to Bruce Lincoln, is "ideological hegemony throughout the state . . . in which it is active. . . . [T]o this end it energetically proselytizes, attempting to disseminate its contents to all segments of society."[90] Its threat is to the "lower socioeconomic strata," those "whose sufferings are too great for the solace extended by the religion of the status quo."[91] So

---

[87] Nehru 1959, 515.

[88] For a sample of the Hindu right's critique of the idea of a composite culture, see Narain 1990. Says Narain: "In point of fact, Hindu culture alone deserves the credit of recognition as *the* national culture of this country, as the culture owning and possessing this great nation, along with other India-born cultures like Buddhist and Jain cultures as its subcultures, Muslim and Christian cultures being in the nature of tenant-cultures, parasitic cultures, or out-and-out counter-cultures." Ibid., 35.

[89] Empirical findings from a study in Uttar Pradesh speak directly to the issue of threat. "[A] general pattern: the higher the position in the socio-economic hierarchy, in terms of land-ownership, education and economic status, the more frequent the position that India belongs to the Hindu community, and that Muslims should be treated as second-class citizens. To be more precise: more than one-third of the rich Hindus rejected the idea of Hindu-Muslim equality in a secular Indian State. Among the poorest households, this idea was practically absent. These findings do suggest that the zeal for hindutva is likely to be informed by the class position." Lieten 1996, 1415.

[90] Lincoln 1985, 272.

[91] Ibid.

if there *is* a composite culture in India it is confined to this strata, which is to say that it need not be taken seriously. As a prolific exponent of Hindutva has written: "[C]ulture has two strata: culture of the aristos and culture of the demos. It is the former which represents and defines society, imparts its own identity to it, and determines the course of events in it. There is little notable difference among the different cultures of the demos. The culture of the demos has no appreciable form of its own, wherefore it is comparatively easy for it to intermingle with other cultures."[92]

We have seen in Justice Verma's equating of Hindutva with "Indianisation"—referring to a uniform national culture obtained through the assimilation of minority cultures into a Hindu way of life—that the challenge to the original secular ideal of a composite culture has found a sympathetic hearing on the Supreme Court. We have also seen how this represents a challenge to the ameliorative secular commitment of India's simple revolution. Juxtaposed against trends in the Israeli polity, we now see that whereas the constitutional revolution in the Jewish State is essentially about the effort to achieve greater clarity and coherence in the face of revolutionary complexity, the political and legal pressures in India to legitimate a primordial-based conception of nationhood would, if successful, have the opposite effect. In other words, Indian constitutional jurisprudence would confront the challenge of revolutionary complexity.

Mindful of the pitfalls in extrapolating from the Israeli experience, what can we learn that possibly illuminates the Indian situation? We might begin with Chief Justice Barak's statement that "[C]onstitutional interpretation must base itself on the historical continuance of the nation's creation, with the intention of achieving unity and constitutional harmony." In the Israeli case the uncertainty about the Supreme Court's revolutionary pronouncements reflected a concern that the achievement of unity and harmony would turn out to be more transparent than real, and that the divided legacy of that nation's creation was so enduring and deep that the Court's commitment to bridge (or obfuscate) it would end up undermining its own authority. Since the effectiveness of judicial review is strongly associated with the existence of a pervasive and dominant political creed, expanding the judiciary's formal powers in the absence of genuine constitutional consensus on basic issues of nationhood could jeopardize its real power within the political system. The danger lies in the potential for people to identify the Court with the agenda of one side

---

[92] Narain 1990, 3. In this regard, consider the question raised by G. Aloysius: "Why pick on a community that is hardly a threat to anybody, as the enemy of Hindutva? The explanation lies more in the socio-economic and political similarity of the Muslim to the lower-caste masses than in their exaggerated religio-cultural dissimilarity to the Hindus in general." Aloysius 1994, 1452.

of an unresolved debate over constitutional essentials, thus diminishing the requisite moral authority to perform some of its critical roles, not the least of which is the valued one of educator to the citizenry.

India too, of course, is a deeply rifted society, but the early rejection of the two-nation theory made it possible not only to codify constitutional arrangements, but also to formalize within them a commitment to secularism that was a corollary of the political imperative of social reform and communal harmony. To be sure, the Hindutva theme had always been a background presence in Indian constitutional politics, but the question is whether its emergence as a more competitive strand in the foreground of constitutional and political disputation will affect the functioning and legitimacy of the Indian judiciary. At this point we can only speculate as to the answer. However, the Israeli experience may cause us to wonder if in India any substantial move toward revolutionary complexity will subject the Court to the sort of political pressures that, as in Israel, will require it to navigate jurisprudential waters with a heightened level of risk and constraint.

To put these musings into a more concrete setting, consider again the Supreme Court's involvement in the Ayodhya story. We have looked closely at the landmark cases concerning applications of Article 356 and the Representation of the People Act. The first dealt directly with the tragic circumstances flowing from the destruction of the mosque in Ayodhya, and the second with the subsequent electoral participation of individuals who had been implicated—through direct acts and inflammatory rhetoric—in the violence associated with that event. In yet a third high-profile judgment, popularly known as the *Ayodhya Reference Case*, the Supreme Court focused directly on the very ground upon which the mosque had rested. It addressed two related questions: (1) the constitutional validity of the Acquisition of Certain Area at Ayodhya Act and (2) the Special Reference made by the president of India under Article 143(1) of the Constitution seeking an opinion of the Supreme Court on the question of whether there had been a Hindu temple existing on the site where the disputed structure stood.[93] The Court's ruling, written by Justice J. S. Verma, was handed down on October 24, 1994, chronologically placing it between the *Bommai* and *Hindutva* decisions.

In brief, the government of India had acquired the controversial Ayodhya site and adjacent land in order to use it at some future date in an

---

[93] Article 143(1) reads: "If at any time it appears to the President that a question of law or fact has arisen or is likely to arise, which is of such a nature and of such public importance that it is expedient to obtain the opinion of the Supreme Court upon it, he may refer the question to that court for consideration and the court may, after such hearing as it thinks fit, report to the President its opinion thereon."

appropriate way given what had previously and tragically occurred on this location. The question submitted to the Court under the Special Reference was an attempt to determine what that would be. The reasons given by the Central Government for these actions emphasized the necessity of restoring communal harmony in the aftermath of the most devastating rupture of Indian society since the time of Partition. Such was the high prestige and widely perceived impartiality of the Supreme Court that its judgment in this matter was sought in order to begin the process of national healing and reconciliation. According to the solicitor general, the "[g]overnment will treat the finding of the Supreme Court on the question of fact referred under Article 143 of the Constitution as a verdict which is final and binding." He went on to say that the "[g]overnment is confident that the opinion of the Supreme Court will have a salutary effect on the attitudes of the communities and they will no longer take positions on the factual issue settled by the Supreme Court."[94]

However sincere the stated motivations of the Congress Government in acquiring the property may have been, many in the Muslim community were outraged and offended by the move. They saw the acquisition as part of an attempt to deprive Muslims of an important place of worship in order to deliver it into the hands of the majority Hindu community. As such, it was a clear violation of secularism, a basic feature of the Constitution. In Justice Verma's summary of the Muslim objection, "[T]he Act read as a whole is anti-secular being slanted in favour of the Hindu community and against the Muslim minority since it seeks to perpetuate demolition of the mosque which stood on the disputed site instead of providing for the logical just action of rebuilding it, appropriate in the circumstances."[95] Indeed, a statement by the Central Government announced shortly after the demolition, in which a pledge had been made to rebuild the mosque, was cited by counsel for the Muslim side in order to establish the impropriety of the subsequent acquisition and presidential reference.

It was therefore naive or disingenuous for the government to project a confident tone in predicting a positive public response to any decision by the Supreme Court. Perhaps sensing this, the Court declined to provide an answer to the question included in the reference, thus depriving both sides of an occasion to celebrate a decisive victory. But in the case of the Hindus (more specifically, the Hindu nationalists), a partial victory was proclaimed, whereas the Muslim community found very little solace in the Court's decision. The disparate reactions reflected the fact that a 3–

[94] *The Ayodhya Reference* 1995, 19.
[95] *Dr. M. Ismail Faruqui* at 29.

2 majority upheld the constitutionality of the Acquisition Act, thereby permitting Hindus to continue worshipping at the site of the demolition, where, the faithful believed, a new Ram temple would eventually be constructed. One commentator on the Hindu right referred to the judgment as a "judicial backlash" against the earlier verdict to uphold the government dismissals in *Bommai*.[96] He and other like-minded commentators applauded the Court's constitutional finding; they also found comfort in the very promising reasoning contained in the opinion of Justice Verma.

The justice sought to demonstrate why the government's acquisition was consistent with the constitutional guarantee of secularism. After copiously quoting from several of the opinions in *Bommai*, Verma, referring to the "communal holocaust" precipitated by the leveling of the mosque, said: "Any step taken to arrest escalation of communal tension and to achieve communal accord and harmony can, by no stretch of argumentation, be termed non-secular much less anti-secular or against the concept of secularism."[97] While the dissent challenged this reasoning on the ground that the preservation of public order was an insufficient justification for acquiring a place of worship (especially in light of the circumstances attendant here), the language of Article 25 of the Constitution gave Justice Verma a more than credible basis for his claim.[98] Thus its provision for religious freedom is preceded by a public order exception, sufficient, so it would seem, for the State to exercise its sovereign prerogative power to acquire property in pursuit of the public good.

Justice Verma went on, however, to make a further claim. "The protection under Articles 25 and 26 of the Constitution is to religious practice which forms an essential and integral part of the religion. A practice may be a religious practice but not an essential or integral part of practice of that religion."[99] There was no question, he asserted, that prayer or worship is a religious practice protected by the Constitution, but whether it is essential that this practice occur at a particular location was a matter for judicial determination. And as far as the Court was concerned: "A mosque is not an essential part of the practice of religion of Islam and Namaz (prayer) by Muslims can be offered anywhere, even in [the] open. Accordingly, its acquisition is not prohibited by the provisions in the

---

[96] Jaitley 1995, 107.

[97] *Dr. M. Ismail Faruqui* at 41. In addition, Justice Verma argued, it would unwittingly support the forces responsible for the events of December 6, 1992.

[98] In fairness, the dissent was very much concerned about public order, but that only meant that the State had the constitutional obligation to use whatever means necessary to prevent the disorder that had occurred at Ayodhya. To demonstrate its concern for public order after the fact would be, in effect, to reward the perpetrators of the dastardly acts of violence.

[99] *Dr. M. Ismail Faruqui* at 54.

Constitution of India."[100] Needless to say, the two dissenting judges, both of whom were Muslims, had an understanding of the obligations of Islamic practice that differed sharply from their three Hindu colleagues in the majority.

We have seen before the risks associated with judicial insinuation into the essentials of religion. Even when justified, these interventions invite criticism of the sort that is potentially most damaging to the Court, calling into question the legitimacy of its role as objective arbiter in matters central to people's most fervently held beliefs. Rajeev Dhavan, who represented the Muslim side in the litigation, wrote subsequently: "The Court's verdict that the right to pray at a mosque (as opposed to prayer in the open) was not to be regarded as a constitutionally protected practice of particular significance must gnaw at the roots of any version of plural secularism, surrendering the property and practice of a faith to extensive interference by the State and annihilating the diversity of local practices which make the Indian subcontinent what it is."[101] Inasmuch as this version of plural secularism has long been the target of the BJP and its allies, it is not surprising that their leading theoretician and polemicist, Arun Shourie, has noted that the *Ayodhya Reference Case* "judgement opens up many opportunities for creative jurisprudence. . . . For as it can now no longer be asserted that even praying in a particular mosque is a practice essential and integral to Islam, how can it be maintained that to have four wives and to have the power to throw them out, without any maintenance, by uttering just one word are practices essential and integral to the practice of Islam?"[102] Making the prospects for such creative jurisprudence more promising is the fact that the majority emphasized the supremacy of Indian courts, rather than Muslim law as interpreted by Muslim legal authorities, in determining the essentials of Islamic practice. "The touchstone is the extent to which the claim conforms to the principles enshrined in our Constitution, the extent to which it conforms to what has been approved by our courts."[103]

[100] Ibid. at 56.

[101] Dhavan 1994, 3038.

[102] Shourie 1995, 161, 164. As for jurisprudence, it is interesting in light of the discussion in the previous chapter that Justice Verma's opinion was applauded because, according to one commentator on the Hindu right, it tacitly endorsed Oliver Wendell Holmes's notion that the "first requirement of a sound body of law is that it should correspond with the actual feelings and demands of the community, whether right or wrong." Dasgupta 1995, 94.

[103] Shourie 1995, 160. Acknowledging the supremacy of the courts in resolving questions pertaining to the essentials of religious practice is more situational than Shourie's comment would suggest. For example, eight years after the Court's decision, the Ayodhya issue flared up again, this time involving the threat by the VHP to proceed with the construction of the Ram temple at the disputed site. The issue was quickly thrust into the hands of the courts, and when asked what the VHP would do if the verdict went against them, its working

Despite the possible insensitivity of one judge who perhaps went a bit too far in his efforts to restore communal harmony to a fractured nation, there was, one would think, very little reason for committed secularists to be frightened by the specter of judicial supremacy. After all, it was the Supreme Court which had, with eloquence and passion, recently articulated the precepts of secularism that define the essence of Indian constitutionalism. Even the dissenting justices indicated that "Ayodhya is a storm that will pass." "The dignity and honour of the Supreme Court," they pointed out, "cannot be compromised because of it."[104] So if Arun Shourie was comforted in the assertiveness of the Court (in spite of its refusal to answer the specific question submitted to it) with respect to its prerogatives concerning theological matters, why should anyone much care?

But imagine a slightly altered chronology. Suppose the *Hindutva Cases* had preceded the *Ayodhya Reference Case* rather than followed it. Suppose, in other words, that Justice Verma's opinion upholding the Central Government's acquisition of the disputed acreage had appeared after his controversial affirmation of core Hindu nationalist ideology? Under these circumstances, would we be as inclined to dismiss Shourie's ruminations about the future benefits of the Court's "creative jurisprudence" as mere wishful thinking? More important, would the dissenters in the *Ayodhya Reference Case* have been so confident that the honour and dignity of the Supreme Court would emerge unscathed from the brutal winds of Hurricane Ayodhya?

Chronological manipulation provides an opportunity to revisit the essentials of the religion question within the comparative jurisprudential context of constitutional revolutions. In chapter 4 we observed how the constitutional logic of ameliorative secularism demanded an approach by the Indian judiciary that often required it to intrude into the sensitive domain of theological belief and practice. There I pointed out that unless the attempt was made to isolate what is integral to religion from what is not, social reform efforts will be obliged to carry the extra burden of overcoming religiously grounded practices that not only enjoy the status of a way of life but also can lay claim to exalted theological importance. To the extent that judicially sanctioned social transformations were limited to nonessential matters, their legitimacy, as well as that of the Court itself, would arguably be enhanced by such classification. Thus as controversial as this judicial practice was, the fact that the constitutional commitment to ameliorate the regressive practices associated with some religious traditions was so clearly revealed in constitutional history and text

---

president, Ashok Singhal, replied: "Courts have no importance in this matter. It is a matter of faith. Matters of faith are not justiciable." *Deccan Herald*, February 1, 2002.

[104] *Dr. M. Ismail Faruqui* at 87.

allowed Indian judges to exercise significantly more latitude than would be the case in most other places.

In other words, this judicial practice is compatible with the political creed of India's simple revolution. Louis Hartz's observation regarding judicial review in America, that it would be inconceivable without the constitutional enshrinement of principles that enjoyed prior recognition, is also applicable to India. If we substitute the social reform ethos of Parts III and IV of the latter's Constitution for the Lockean creed of Hartz's famous account, then the acceptability of essentialist interventions in Indian Church/State jurisprudence is readily comprehensible. But if, as was done in the *Hindutva Cases*, this creed is called into question by, or at least placed into competition with, an alternative creed based upon ascriptive foundations, then this sort of judicial intervention is likely to be assessed quite differently, and in ways that could undermine the effectiveness of the courts. Justice Verma's excursion into Islamic theology in the *Ayodhya Reference Case* might, then, incur criticism from those questioning his knowledge, but the absence of a predicate for questioning his motives enables the Court's methodology to survive this problematic application. Altering the chronology, and thereby establishing a clear foundation for suspecting that the justice's motivations stem from an attraction to the precepts of the alternative creed, produces a situation of increased probability that the criticism generated will be more destructive and, in the end, debilitating. Under these conditions the Court's inquiry into what is integral to a religion and what is not appears, rightly or wrongly, as part of a judicial strategy to advance the agenda of the Hindu right. As far as traditional secularists are concerned, this transforms Arun Shourie's prognostications from a matter of indifference to one of substantial concern.

Applying the lessons from Israel, two issues stand out. The first concerns the role of the Supreme Court as an "arm of the social revolution." We have noted in regard to Israel that the lack of a consensus in the constitutionalism of a complex revolution may encourage tentativeness in the exercise of judicial authority, an inclination to avoid or deflect judgments of finality in the absence of an ultimate settlement of regime principles. In Israel the absence is symbolized by the failure to adopt a comprehensive constitutional document, whereas the lengthy Indian charter, including an ideologically coherent set of Directive Principles, suggests the presence of a largely settled commitment to regime-defining principles. But even without formal constitutional change, the document is supple enough to enable a determined judicial effort toward creative jurisprudence to engineer a constitutional revolution that could unsettle those very principles. If that were to happen, it might be seen—much as revolutionary "constitutional moments" in the United States have been seen—

as a reflection of broader trends and developments in the political evolution of the system, beginning, in India, with the ascendance of the BJP in national politics.

Should the traditional secular understanding of a composite culture come under sustained judicial assault, thereby suggesting that Justice Verma's views on "Indianization" had become entrenched in the orientation of a major faction on the Court, then, in order to avoid a corrosive politicization of that institution, its members would be pressured into adopting the more cautious judicial profile associated with a regime of revolutionary complexity. This could easily reflect itself in a greater hesitation to intrude into the combustible arena of theological disputation for fear that any ruling on religious essentials would be caught in the crossfire of disputed versions of political essentials, resulting in a dangerously wounded institution. In time, given the constitutionally legitimated role of judicial review in Indian politics, the generally activist orientation of the Supreme Court as an agent of social change would surely be modified in evolving recognition of the diminished capacities of an obviously politicized Court.[105]

Finally, the same newly aroused suspicions of the motives and agendas of justices who are widely identified with one or the other side of a bifurcated political blueprint would doubtless also impair these justices' ability to use their unique position to educate their fellow citizens in the abiding principles of their regime. Whatever one might say of the long-term political importance of the *Bommai* decision, the pedagogical potential embodied in that case's eloquent essays on secularism are both difficult to miss and one of its great treasures. But that potential varies with the perceived moral authority of the educator, which in turn depends on the level of trust people have in his or her detachment from partisan ambition and engagement.[106] For example, Justice Verma's copious citations of *Bommai* teachings in the *Ayodhya Reference Case* decision are used to good effect as a device for instructing the public in the principles of secularism. However, that use may become clouded in an aura of suspi-

---

[105] Recall that in Israel the Supreme Court's activism was not constrained by the context of a complex revolutionary adjudicative setting. But that was attributable to the paradox of judicial review, in which the constraints imposed on the courts by the presence of parliamentary supremacy (and the absence of formal review powers in the judiciary) served to legitimate a more active role for the Court in construing the law.

[106] Cohen and Susser's comments on the role of courts in consociational polities are relevant here. There has been a lively scholarly debate over whether India conforms to the consociational model. (See Lijphart 1996, 90; and Brass 1991.) We need not resolve that debate here, since the point made by Cohen and Susser, that the perception of courts as politically disinterested institutions is especially vital in divided societies, applies to India regardless of the appropriate social science designation of the polity.

cion if it is associated (fairly or unfairly) with serious doubts about the justice's secular commitments (as could very well be the case in the altered chronology). A seemingly benign reference to the principle of *sarva dharma sambhava* could then easily be interpreted in a very different way—as a tendentious use of a respected maxim of political discourse for the purpose of advancing a barely concealed partisan agenda. The suspicion that the liberal principle of equal treatment was being used to pursue illiberal ends in a competitive struggle for the soul of the nation would surely be correlated with a squandering of *Bommai's* rich instructional potential. But for the other side, too, pursuing the goals of the original constitutional settlement in the newly unsettled environment of revolutionary complexity would reduce constitutive principles to political ideology and thereby undermine the educational mission of the Court. Under these circumstances, whichever side should emerge triumphant from this or that battle, the Indian people lose.

CONCLUSION

On June 1, 2001, a demonstration held in New York City protested the treatment of Hindus in Afghanistan under the Taliban regime. Joining the Hindus in condemning the Afghan government's oppressive policies was a group of Jews from Brooklyn. To many at the time, this gathering of Jews and Hindus must have seemed an unlikely alliance, but more specifically describing the participants quickly clarifies the significance of their common ground. The Jews were followers of the late Rabbi Meir Kahane, the Arab-hating Israeli politician whose militant movement had outlived its fiery leader's assassination. The Hindus were members of the Bajrang Dal, a vehemently anti-Muslim group whose loyalists in India had been prominent participants in the destruction of the Babri Masjid mosque in Ayodhya. (Their official Web site, HinduUnity.org, also goes by the name Soldiers of Hindutva.) On the day of the demonstration one of their leaders explained, "Whether you call them Palestinians, Afghans or Pakistanis, the root of the problem for Hindus and Jews is Islam."[107] In his home in Queens this leader displayed a large picture of Rabbi Kahane. "He was a great man. It almost appeared as if he was speaking for Hindus."[108]

Only something on the order of the Taliban could possibly prevent these groups from occupying the top position on a ranking of religiously

---

[107] *New York Times*, June 2, 2001. So strong, the newspaper article reported, was the anti-Muslim bond that some of the Hindus had marched earlier in the annual Salute to Israel Parade on Fifth Avenue. One of the Jewish organizers acknowledged that the relationship was a practical one that reflected "a common suffering at the hands of Muslims."

[108] Ibid.

based intolerance. Their hostility toward what each perceives to be an alien presence in their respective homelands—mostly Muslims in both cases—represents a challenge to secular rule in India and Israel. So vitriolic and incendiary are their standard messages that they regularly run the risk of having their Web site contracts cancelled as propagators of hate.[109] Each has pledged to help the other in the face of such a contingency (as has already happened on at least one occasion); after all, in the words of the Kahane group's director, "It is a core issue of free speech."[110] And so these fascistic organizations based in faraway lands have joined forces on American soil to alert the world to the horrors of religious fanaticism (personified in this instance by the Taliban), and also to remind their hosts of the importance of First Amendment freedoms!

The mutual attraction of these groups is mainly opportunistic; beyond agreeing on a common enemy, each professes to know little about the other's specific goals or situation. As with Veer Savarkar in the early days of Israeli and Indian independence, a sentimental attachment to the Zionist cause does not ground these recent counsels of support for Jews in the Middle East from Hindus on the subcontinent. Nor, it is safe to say, do the warm feelings held for the latter by the former indicate a considered appreciation for the virtues of Hindutva. One wonders if the appeal of the Zionist experiment to the New World enthusiasts of the Hindu *Rashtra* would be as great if they understood that their admirers from Brooklyn were pariahs in the Jewish homeland, outcasts whose ideas are seen by the vast majority of Israeli Jews as a pathological perversion of Zionism. Would they, in other words, find in the Israeli model a suitable example for emulation if they understood that its more representative spokespersons could never fairly be seen as "speaking for [those] Hindus" who espouse the views of the Bajrang Dal with respect to the treatment of non-Hindus?

---

[109] Here are recent examples from both Web sites in the aftermath of the September 11, 2001, attacks on New York City and Washington. The first is a "joke" from the Kahane site: "A son and his dad are taking a walk in New York on a beautiful spring day in 2021. They stroll down to where 'ground zero' was 20 years earlier. 'Son, this is where the World Trade Center used to be,' Dad says to his young son. The son replies, 'What was the World Trade Center?' Dad answers: 'This is where Arabs crashed the planes into the 2 World Trade Center office buildings.' The young son asks: 'Dad, what were the Arabs?' " The second statement comes from editorials on the Soldiers of Hindutva Web site. "The fact is that the highest incidences of violent crimes such as murder, rape, child molestation, dismemberment and armed robbery happen in Islamic countries. In Non-Islamic countries, wherever terrorist and subversive activities take place, one is sure to find the presence of Muslims." "The true fact is, Islam doesn't deserve a place at all in civilized human society. The sooner the satanic sect becomes extinct, the better it is for the world."

[110] *New York Times*, June 2, 2001.

But can it also be said that the appeal of Hindutva to the Brooklyn Jews would be similarly diminished if they discovered the actual standing of the Hindus from Queens among the mainstream of Hindutva supporters in India? Of course, framing this inquiry so ambiguously raises the critical question of whether groups like the Bajrang Dal represent the extreme end of the Hindutva spectrum or whether, like the Kach Party (which is banned from electoral participation in Israel) in relation to Zionist principles, it is more properly described as a perversion of the movement's historic aspirations. In an important sense, our hesitancy over how to respond appropriately to such a query betrays uncertainty over the future prospects of secularism in India.

Chapter Nine

CONCLUSION

Toward Secular Convergence

"IN INTERPRETING the provisions of this chapter a court of law shall promote the values which underlie an open and democratic society based on freedom and equality and shall, where applicable, have regard to public international law applicable to the protection of the rights entrenched in this chapter, and may have regard to comparable foreign case law." These words, taken from Section 35 of the new South African Constitution, are an invitation to judges in the postapartheid republic to seek outside help in the construction of a constitutional jurisprudence.[1] They suggest a model of constitutional development that is outward looking in two related senses: first, in its commitment to certain universal principles of democratic justice, and second, in its endorsement of comparative law as an appropriate source for the adjudication of cases. The text gives new meaning to the term *nonoriginalism*, which in its familiar understanding connotes a disinclination to be bound by the intentions of those who framed a legal document, but which here stands for the legitimation of foreign legal precedent as a basis for the growth of the law.

This constitutional language is noteworthy only for the explicitness of its acknowledgment of extraterritorial legal sources; the practice of searching beyond sovereign lines for legal guidance in constitutional cases is of course nothing new. Over the years, judiciaries have developed extensive histories of constitutional borrowing, usually without any official invitation to do so. All of these histories involve a mix of both acceptance and rejection of external case law. The drafting of South Africa's new Constitution deliberately traced the experience of other countries—especially Canada and Germany—and so it is perhaps unsurprising that provi-

---

[1] These words are taken from South Africa's interim Constitution. They have been replaced in the final Constitution by Section 39, which, in stating that a court "must consider international law," (39, 1,b) sharpens the mandate to consider public law.

sion was made for subsequent constitutional interpretation to seek guidance from these and other familiar sources of inspiration. While the pressure for indigenous legal development will always be present, its impact may be softened where the animating principles behind the emergence of a constitutional tradition are essentially emulative in nature.

The words of Section 35 also mark the globalization of liberal democratic institutions. It makes sense to view a system's openness to outside influence in relation to broader political trends—in this case the ascendance of liberal ideals (political and economic)—such that the transplantation of constitutional ideas and practices from one place to another projects a certain inevitability, much like what has occurred in recent years with the rapid adoption of market institutions by countries previously unfamiliar with the ways of capitalism.[2]

Unlike the South African case, the high courts in India and Israel have not been solicited by authoritative constitutional language to employ foreign case law in their legal rulings. However, both courts have, from their inception, welcomed precedents imported from abroad, particularly from the United States. From these precedents judges have sought guidance and legitimacy. But just as the American constitutional model has been only partially followed in India and Israel, American judicial decisions too have exerted a distinctly mixed pattern of influence over legal outcomes in these places. Different constitutional domains vary in degrees of judicial borrowing, a reflection of similarities and disparities in political circumstances surrounding particular issues. Certainly in the case of religion, the very different (yet occasionally overlapping) secular political contexts prevailing in the three countries have played a role in the acceptance and rejection of foreign precedents and legal perspectives as applicable sources for constitutional adjudication.

In the American Supreme Court, which historically has only rarely availed itself of comparative materials, debates have arisen recently over the wisdom and appropriateness of utilizing such sources. On one end of the Court, Justices Breyer and Souter have argued that the experience of other countries can provide valuable lessons for American judges, whereas on the other end, Justices Scalia and Rehnquist have voiced greater skepticism over the benefits of cross-national constitutional exploration. For example, in an important federalism case in 1997, Justice Scalia's response to Justice Breyer's suggestion that the Court follow the

---

[2] Here the Israeli and Indian examples may be instructive, for a distinctive feature of those polities is that their complex political dynamics point in two quite different directions: one toward the alignment of the political order with the constitutional commitments of Western liberal democracies, the other toward the restoration and development of a national homeland for a particular people (Israel), or the achievement of far-reaching social reconstruction in the face of entrenched religious opposition (India).

experience of other federal systems in assessing arrangements for the administration of national law left little doubt as to where he stood in these matters. "[S]uch comparative analysis [is] inappropriate to the task of interpreting a constitution, though it was of course relevant to the task of writing one."[3] For Scalia, "[O]ur federalism is not Europe's," an observation that presumably holds for other constitutional issues as well, including Church/State relations. Thus the sentiment expressed by the authors of a recent study of these relations in five countries, to the effect that "a comparative analysis of how other western pluralistic democracies resolve church-state tensions might shed light on this enduring issue in American politics,"[4] would doubtless strike Scalia as an unpromising constitutional avenue to pursue.

Indeed, one of the conclusions of that study is that with respect to free exercise rights, Germany and the Netherlands have a more "appropriate understanding of religious liberty" than does the United States.[5] It is "[a] more robust understanding of religious freedom [that] requires the state to take positive measures aimed at protecting and promoting the religious expression of *groups* or *communities*, since people live out their religious life within faith communities and associations."[6] Not surprisingly, the constitutional case that is singled out by the authors as particularly revealing of the misplaced emphasis in American First Amendment jurisprudence on faith as a private matter of individual conscience is *Employment Division v Smith*. That was the landmark case, decided in 1990, that abandoned the compelling state interest test for examining free exercise claims in challenges to laws of general applicability. Its author: Justice Antonin Scalia.

In this concluding chapter, I consider Scalia's opinion in this controversial case as a way of bringing together some of the broader themes of the book. Although the main focus throughout has been on the Indian experience, the comparative framework within which I have situated some of the threats and challenges to the secular principles of Indian constitutionalism requires that we take seriously the possibilities of critical engagement across political and cultural lines. In chapter 2 I suggested that models of secular constitutional development should not be viewed as rigidly deterministic, and while sociopolitical factors shaped the constitutional cultures within which issues such as the relationship of religion and the State get resolved, these cultures are open to adaptive possibilities

---

[3] *Printz* at 921. The case involved the "commandeering" provisions of the Brady Law's requirement for performing background checks on prospective gun buyers. Justices Souter and Rehnquist engaged in a similar debate in *Raines v Byrd*, the line-item veto case.

[4] Monsma and Soper 1997, ix.

[5] Ibid., 202.

[6] Ibid., 203.

that incorporate solutions which are, in whole or in part, identified with alternative models. It was suggested too that the internal tensions and contradictions within each of the context-based secular constitutions have the potential to produce significant convergence in the three nations' constitutional experiences. For example, a more consciously applied ameliorative perspective might result in American judges displaying greater solicitude for the plight of minority religions confronted by legal sanctions imposed by the legislative acts of an insensitive majority. Similarly, an Indian Supreme Court's reflexive inclination to accommodate the particular needs of different religious groups might be tempered by greater consideration for the assimilative needs of a radically diverse society. To revisit an earlier point, just as shaping a national identity is always, to some extent, a work in progress, so too is the place of religion within the constitutional order. Moreover, as Michael Walzer reminded us, the progression of this story sometimes involves figuring out which arrangements *there* can, with suitable modifications, be made useful *here*.[7] This is especially the case as the embrace of liberal democratic institutions assumes an increasingly international appearance, with the opportunities for cross-national borrowing, even when not formally prescribed in the manner of South Africa, increasing accordingly.

RECONSIDERING *SMITH*

Aside from the labeling error that resulted from a famous navigational miscalculation by Christopher Columbus, there is no obvious connection between the Indians of Oregon and the Indians of the subcontinent. Nevertheless, I want to argue that the adjudication of the dispute between two members of the Native American Church and the state of Oregon could have benefited from a familiarity with secular constitutional developments in India. Such familiarity is not *necessary* for a better resolution of the issues at hand, but it can help us to appreciate what a more satisfactory result would look like.

Employment Division, Oregon Department of Human Resources v Smith is arguably the most controversial free exercise decision ever handed down by the United States Supreme Court. "In effect," said Richard John Neuhaus, "the free exercise guarantee of the Religion Clause of the First Amendment has been declared null and void."[8] Neuhaus, normally a fervent supporter of the author of *Smith*'s majority opinion, went on to align himself with another commentator's view that "Antonin Scalia and *Smith* on religious freedom may have earned a place in the Court's

[7] Walzer 1997, 5.
[8] Neuhaus 1990, 64.

history alongside Roger Taney and *Dred Scott* on slavery."[9] Such heated expressions of outrage were not confined to the spiritual camp; thus the decision created an unusual oppositional coalition consisting of traditional civil libertarians and religious conservatives. The culmination of the political efforts of this strange alliance was the near-unanimous passage of the Religious Freedom Restoration Act, which sought to overturn the core of *Smith*. The Act's subsequent invalidation by the Supreme Court had more to do with a defense of the Court's institutional prerogatives than it did with a reaffirmation of the *Smith* holding.[10]

The case that generated all this controversy stemmed from the firing of two Native American Church members from their jobs in a private drug rehabilitation organization because they had ingested peyote during a religious ceremony. They subsequently were found ineligible for unemployment compensation, a denial that was then challenged as a violation of free exercise rights under the First Amendment. The consumption of peyote was a crime under Oregon law, which made no exception for the sacramental use of the drug. The right of the state to outlaw drug use was not at issue, only its failure to make an exception for a religiously based violation of the law. In the end, the Supreme Court held that an exemption was not mandated by the First Amendment, and that laws of general applicability that happened to place substantial burdens on religion were not presumptively unconstitutional. According to the Court, no longer would it be necessary in such cases for the State to demonstrate a compelling interest in the enforcement of these laws.[11]

As Stephen Macedo has pointed out, "Judgments about religiously based exceptions are likely to be highly contextualized matters."[12] This can be understood in various ways, but in reconsidering *Smith*, emphasizing context leads us back to our models of secular constitutional design. Seen from this perspective, Justice Scalia's opinion is notably expressive of the dominant assimilative strand in the American secular context. This

[9] Ibid., 68.

[10] The three dissenters in *City of Boerne v Flores* affirmed their profound misgivings with *Smith*, but only Justice Stevens, in a concurring opinion, defended the original judgment. Justice Kennedy's opinion for the Court was based on a reading of the scope of Congress's enforcement power under Section 5 of the Fourteenth Amendment.

[11] The intensity of the negative reaction to this doctrinal shift was heightened by the fact that neither of the parties to the case had requested of the Court that it revise its constitutional test. As Justice O'Connor pointedly remarked in *Boerne v Flores*, "In *Smith*, five members of this Court—without briefing or argument on the issue—interpreted the Free Exercise Clause to permit the government to prohibit, without justification, conduct mandated by an individual's religious beliefs, so long as the prohibition is generally applicable." *Boerne v Flores* at 546. This sentiment was echoed in the dissents of Justices Souter and Breyer.

[12] Macedo 2000, 211.

is signaled quite early in his opinion when he invoked the authority of *Reynolds v United States*, the notorious Mormon polygamy case from the nineteenth century. Just as the Court in that case rejected the claim that the application of criminal laws against polygamy required a constitutional exemption for those whose religion commanded the practice, so too, Scalia insisted, must the Court in *Smith* repudiate the same claim as applied to the illegal use of drugs for religious purposes. Quoting from *Reynolds*, he wrote, "To permit this would be to make the professed doctrines of religious belief superior to the law of the land, and in effect to permit every citizen to become a law unto himself."[13]

As I argued in chapter 3, this subordination of spiritual to temporal authority need not be viewed as hostility toward religion. Though perhaps less clear in the polygamy case, where specific animus toward Mormons was evident in the enforcement of the criminal laws, the broader view that finds in the uniform application of the law both a vindication of the regime-defining principle of natural equality and a safeguard against the threat of religious persecution demands to be taken seriously. The most thoughtful critic of this basically Lockean view, Michael McConnell, was also the most influential scholarly opponent of the *Smith* ruling. His critique of Justice Scalia's opinion went to the core of what was at stake in the constitutional debate. "The ideal of free exercise of religion [in contrast with the ideal of racial nondiscrimination] is that people of different religious convictions are different and that those differences are precious and must not be disturbed. The ideal of racial justice is assimilationist and integrationist. The ideal of free exercise is counter-assimilationist; it strives to allow individuals of different religious faiths to maintain their differences in the face of powerful pressures to conform."[14] From this perspective, Justice Scalia's refusal to provide constitutional redress for the prosecution of Smith's religiously inspired legal transgression in effect represented a capitulation to assimilationist pressure from secular forces within society.

Given McConnell's conviction that the existence of the free exercise right establishes the priority of divine authority over the democratically expressed will of the people, his critique of Scalia for having undermined the "counter-assimilationist" ideal of the First Amendment right makes perfect sense. Of course, in defense of Scalia one can say that it is precisely to advance the broader assimilationist objectives of American constitutionalism (which includes protection for religious liberty) that the presumption in favor of religiously based exemptions needs to be negated. Such reasoning would attach a more positive valence to the presence of

---

[13] Quoted in *Smith* at 879.
[14] McConnell 1990a, 1139.

"powerful pressures to conform," not because of any (at least conscious) hostility to religious pluralism, but because of the anticipated benefits flowing from the development of a liberal consensus on constitutional essentials. As outlined in chapter 6, the Indian Supreme Court's effort to employ similar reasoning to uphold the corrupt practices provision of the nation's main election law was, I suggested, less compelling than other arguments that might have been advanced in its support. These alternative arguments were more consonant with the ameliorative orientation of Indian secularism. Scalia's opinion, in contrast with the systemically awkward fit of Justice Verma's judgment, is quite comfortably situated within the main constitutional current of American secularism—but perhaps too much so.[15]

Indeed, what makes the *Smith* decision most vulnerable to attack is the apparent rigidity of its adherence to the dictates of assimilative secularism. That will no doubt appear as an odd assertion to make in light of the general argument of this book. After all, judicial conformity to the categorical orientation embedded in a particular model of secular constitutionalism would seem to be a good thing. Sometimes, as in the case of the Indian judges in the *Bommai* case whose ameliorative concerns were clearly understated, a principled consistency with the constitutional polity's secular aspirations may require some prudent obfuscation. Why, however, would we find fault with an opinion that boldly highlighted the underlying assumptions behind the approach to Church/State relations that best reflects the nation's circumstances?

One response—which we might call the *activist* answer—would call into question the desirability of judges simply accepting those circumstances rather than working aggressively to transform them. The example of Justice Barak in Israel comes readily to mind. Whether his efforts to move the Israelis away from the visionary model of secular constitutionalism will succeed remains to be seen, but his transformative agenda could serve to inspire judges in other countries. Justice Scalia, however, is unlikely to be such a judge. To be sure, some of his critics have seen his

---

[15] In the argument that follows I do not address myself to other weaknesses in the Court's opinion. McConnell and others have criticized Justice Scalia's ruling for the many alleged inadequacies in its use of text, history, and precedent. I share some of these misgivings, particularly in regard to the opinion's somewhat tortured application of precedents, but I have nothing to add to them here. It is worth noting that agreement in the outcome of the case did not necessarily connote admiration for Scalia's opinion. Consider, for example, William P. Marshall's rejoinder to McConnell: "The *Smith* opinion itself . . . cannot be readily defended. The decision, as written, is neither persuasive nor well-crafted. It exhibits only a shallow understanding of free exercise jurisprudence and its use of precedent borders on fiction. The opinion is also a paradigmatic example of judicial overreaching." Marshall 1991, 308–9.

Smith opinion as a blatant display of judicial activism that set the Court in a very different direction from where it had been headed in its free exercise jurisprudence.[16] But within the context of a comparative analysis of secularism, it is a quite conservative decision very much in harmony with the constitutive goals of the larger political system.

In contrast, my response does not dispute the wisdom of attempting to secure a strong measure of congruity between judicial doctrine and the facts on the ground. However, these facts are more complex than the Court suggested, thus raising the question whether a strictly categorical judicial approach to the free exercise issue does not represent an overly formalistic solution to (in this case) the polity's assimilative secular challenge. More specifically, in denying a presumption of constitutional validity to religiously motivated exemption claims, Justice Scalia instinctively, and correctly, orders spiritual and temporal affairs. As Christopher L. Eisgruber and Lawrence G. Sager have pointed out, "There is a substantial range of religiously motivated conduct—readily observable in contemporary national experience—that quite clearly must yield to conflicting secular laws."[17] Yet in affirming this reasonable principle, Justice Scalia's application of it to the case at hand also displays insufficient sensitivity to the conditions that foster assimilation into a common culture of political ideas. The extent of constitutional solicitude for religiously based illegal acts should not be determined through recourse to reflexive majoritarianism or misguided respect for the sanctity of spiritually guided motivations.

Looking at the opinion of the Court, we find three arguments bearing on the role of the judiciary in free exercise cases. Only the first was assented to—albeit with some reservations—in the concurring (O'Connor) and dissenting (Blackmun) opinions.

1. Theology: "[C]ourts must not presume to determine the place of a particular belief in a religion or the plausibility of a religious claim."[18] Ascertaining the

---

[16] Exactly where it had been headed is a matter of debate. Christopher L. Eisgruber and Lawrence G. Sager have argued that "[T]he pre-*Smith* accommodation jurisprudence as a whole was laced with confusion and contradiction." Eisgruber and Sager 1994a, 1307. For example, they claim that the Congress that passed the Religious Freedom Restoration Act was mistaken in its view of the prevailing doctrine before *Smith*. Thus, they maintain, the statute's "compelling state interest" language erroneously made it appear that that standard had in fact been applied consistently in free exercise exemption cases, whereas the reality was that the occasions where it had been invoked (basically in the unemployment compensation cases beginning with *Sherbert v Verner*) were the exception rather than the rule. If indeed their observation is a fair statement of the prior history, then it stands as a criticism of the many scholars and judges who have made similar assumptions regarding the earlier case law.

[17] Ibid., 1260.

[18] *Smith* at 887.

"centrality" of religious beliefs in evaluating the strength of an exemption claim is not, so the argument goes, legitimately within the judicial ken.[19]

2. Diversity: "[P]recisely because we value and protect . . . religious divergence, we cannot afford the luxury of deeming *presumptively invalid*, as applied to the religious objector, every regulation of conduct that does not protect an interest of the highest order."[20] To do otherwise in this cosmopolitan nation is, Justice Scalia insisted, to invite anarchy. (Both Justices O'Connor and Blackmun reacted strongly to the use of the word *luxury* in reference to a constitutionally protected right.)

3. Democracy: "[L]eaving accommodation to the political process will place at a relative disadvantage those religious practices that are not widely engaged in; but that unavoidable consequence of democratic government must be preferred to a system in which conscience is a law unto itself or in which judges weigh the social importance of all laws against the centrality of all religious beliefs."[21] Creating religious-practice exemptions may be desirable, but discerning the appropriate occasions for their provision is not for the courts to determine.

With reference to the facts of the case, these three arguments meant that (1) the sacramental use of peyote may very well be essential to the religious identity of members of the Native American Church, but the Court must studiously avoid reaching that conclusion for itself;[22] (2) while the accommodation of diverse religious practices by all faiths is a worthy goal for the polity, the asserted interest of the State in maintaining the integrity of its drug laws must not be second-guessed by the Court;

---

[19] As Harry F. Tepker Jr. has pointed out, the critique of a judicial test that weighs the centrality of a religious practice or doctrine as part of its application echoes objections that have often been raised against judicial balancing as a procedure for determining constitutional rights. Tepker 1991, 40. It is not clear how important these general jurisprudential concerns were in *Smith*, although it is worth noting that Justice O'Connor, never one to shy away from judicial balancing, also distanced herself from a "centrality" analysis. Similarly, Douglas Laycock, a leading student of the religion clauses, wrote that "If the Court is serious about getting federal judges out of the business of balancing, then a wholesale revolution in constitutional law is imminent." Laycock 1990, 31. While very critical of a "centrality" test, Laycock insists that balancing is essential for determining, as the Court must, the extent of a regulation's burden on religious exercise.

[20] Ibid. at 888.

[21] Ibid. at 890.

[22] As explained in Justice Blackmun's minority opinion, members of the Native American Church believe that the peyote plant embodies their deity, and eating it is an essential ritual of their religion. Blackmun pointed this out after agreeing with Justice O'Connor (and Justice Scalia) that courts should refrain from pursuing questions about the "centrality" of practices to a religion. But he quickly added, "[I] do not think this means that the courts must turn a blind eye to the severe impact of a State's restrictions on the adherents of a minority religion." Ibid. at 919.

(3) if there is to be a specific accommodation, that is, an exception to the enforcement of the drug law for sacramental use of peyote, it must occur as it has in other states, through appeal to the will of the majority as expressed in the state legislature.

The judicial role embodied in these three arguments and in their application in the Oregon case is clearly one that emphasizes a *passive* approach to free exercise adjudication. O'Connor criticizes this emphasis: "[T]he sounder approach—the approach more consistent with our role as judges to decide each case on its individual merits—is to . . . determine whether the burden on the specific plaintiffs before us is constitutionally significant and whether the particular criminal interest asserted by the State before us is compelling."[23] Her sharply crafted disagreement with her colleague's democratic argument (point 3) was attached to an increasingly familiar account of American history and political theory, in which "the harsh impact [of] majoritarian rule . . . on unpopular or emerging religious groups" was too prominent to be ignored.[24] What *could* be ignored was the centrality of particular beliefs and practices to a specific faith, for in this respect she agreed with Justice Scalia (and, as I noted in chapter 3, scholars such as Laurence Tribe and Richard Epstein) that matters of theological importance and disputation were not appropriate subjects for judicial resolution. But this too was a position shaped largely by the familiar, namely, her experience as an *American* public official, in which one *can* afford the luxury—in this case, of detachment from interpretive matters of sectarian belief—not so easily avoided by counterparts in other societies, especially India.

To be sure, an acquaintance with the Indian legal scene could easily strengthen the resolve of American judges to stay clear of theological issues and contestation. Thus the missteps of Indian judges in the *Shah Bano* and *Ayodhya Reference* cases serve as cautionary reminders of the problems that can follow from judicial invocation of an "essentials of religion" test. But there are also instances where, as in the polygamy cases, employing such a test possesses a plausible underlying logic, such that judges in religion cases might be well advised to exercise caution before removing it entirely from the quiver of their judicial arsenal.[25] As we have

---

[23] Ibid. at 899.

[24] See, for example, Smith 1997.

[25] I refer here to the Indian polygamy cases, but one can profitably speculate on whether the American polygamy cases would not have been better received had the judges deciding them opined on the centrality of multiple marriages to the Mormon religion. One possibility is that such an approach might have lessened the prejudicial tone of the rulings; the Court in *Reynolds* and *Beason* can easily be read as saying: Polygamy may be of the essence of Mormonism, but since it is such a barbarous, un-Christian practice, it must be banished from our national experience. The fact that the religion has thrived subsequent to polyga-

seen, in those instances where judges can be expected to consider the ameliorative mission of the secular constitution, curtailing religious practices
is, in effect, the price to be paid for upholding laws directed toward advancing the social welfare. What may mitigate the perception of this infringement as a purely heavy-handed utilitarian intervention (and thus a
failure, as Ronald Dworkin might put it, to take rights seriously) is the
often accompanying assessment of the centrality, or lack thereof, of the
restricted practice to the religion of the practitioner.[26] So if polygamy is
deemed not critical to what it means to be a Hindu, then a validation by
the Court of the State's restriction of the act arguably carries a lesser
threat to the Court's legitimacy than if no differentiation were made in
relation to the claims advanced on behalf of controversial religious beliefs
and practices. Of course, the Court must always weigh the countervailing
possibility that its power and prestige will be diminished when its authority to make such determinations is questioned. But given the Indian Constitution's unambiguous directive to the courts to extend a presumption
of constitutionality to welfare-oriented governmental acts that limit religious freedom, judges could feel emboldened, if not supremely confident,
of emerging unscathed from their occasional forays into the thicket of
theological debate. Add to this the unstructured quality of ecclesiastical
authority in Indian society, with its attendant cacophony of authoritative

---

my's legal demise testifies either to the extraordinary adaptive power of the religion or to
the fact that it was all along only incidental to one's affiliation with the faith. Indeed, in the
1964 case of *People v Woody*, the California Supreme Court focused on centrality to distinguish polygamy and peyote. "Polygamy, although a basic tenet in the theology of Mormonism, is not essential to the practice of the religion; peyote, on the other hand, is the *sine qua
non* of defendants' [Navaho] faith." To ban the sacramental use of peyote is to tear out "the
theological heart of Peyotism." *People v Woody*, 820, 818. But the reflection on Mormonism can be questioned. For example, Douglas Laycock reminds us that "The Mormons
eventually gave up polygamy, but only after a half a century of sometimes bloody conflict,
the legal dissolution of their church, and the seizure of all its property." Laycock 1991, 29.

[26] Dworkin's position is that if citizens possess a substantial, that is, moral, right, then
the government would be unjustified in overriding it, "even if they were persuaded that the
majority would be better off if [the right] were curtailed." Dworkin 1977, 191. But as Dworkin acknowledges, that is not to say the government is never justified in overriding such a
right. There are both weak forms of the right and very substantial public interests that may
alter how we assess a particular situation. Although Dworkin does not, as far as I know,
recommend to judges that they attempt to isolate those practices that are integral to the free
exercise of religion right, it seems as if such an effort may be necessary to fully realize the
logic of his basic argument about taking rights seriously. Incidentally, Dworkin's position
on the preferred status of religious exemptions bears on the core issue in *Smith*. "A government that is secular in principle cannot prefer a religious to a non-religious morality as such.
There are utilitarian arguments in favor of limiting the exception to religious or universal
grounds—an exemption so limited may be less expensive to administer, and may allow eas-
ier discrimination between sincere and insincere applicants. But these utilitarian reasons are
irrelevant, because they cannot count as grounds for limiting a right." Ibid., 201.

religious voices, and the expenditure of political capital from such adventures begins to look tolerable.

More tolerable, surely, than in the United States, where religion is not the great obstacle to social reform that it is in India, but where its more hierarchical organization does present a formidable obstacle to judicial theologizing. Nevertheless, the idea that the Court can responsibly adjudicate free-exercise exemption cases without ever having to consider the centrality question strains credulity.[27] The Indian experience shows why rulings based on such considerations are inherent in the process of balancing public and private interests, and also why the potential for overreaching should lead to a restrained view of the practice.[28] But that experience must be adapted to the contextually specific requirements of secularism in American constitutionalism. If in India judicial indifference to the substance of religious belief serves in some measure to legitimate an unjust status quo, in the United States it can undermine secularism's assimilative aspirations, which include an important ameliorative dimension. How so?

One of the Supreme Court's leading critics of *Smith*, Justice Souter, has based his critique of the ruling on a distinction between "formal neutrality" and "substantive neutrality."[29] It was, he claimed, an "unremarkable point," presumably because it added little to what had become a familiar theme for the many detractors of the decision: Free exercise embodied a substantive dimension that "require[d] government to accommodate religious differences by exempting religious practices from formally neutral laws."[30] The constitutional problem with the failure to provide an exemption lay in the fact that the enforcement of a law "neutral on its face" nevertheless unduly burdened a believer's free exercise right,

---

[27] Consider, for example, the problem that occurs when a religion discriminates on the basis of ascriptive criteria such as race, sex, or sexual orientation. Under Section 702 of Title VII of the Civil Rights Act, religions are exempted from the nondiscrimination requirement of the civil rights laws. So there is no presumption that when a church discriminates, say, in employment, it is acting illegally. It is not necessary to enter the debate as to whether this exemption is a good idea, or even whether it is a violation of the Fourteenth Amendment, to appreciate that when courts are asked to rule on the legality of an alleged discriminatory act, they must, in determining if the church qualifies for the exception, reflect on the centrality of discrimination to the beliefs of the implicated religion.

[28] Even a restrained view would be too extravagant for some critics of the practice. For example, Ira C. Lupu maintains that "[J]udicial resolution of theological controversy is both beyond judicial competence and out of constitutional bounds." It "runs the usual and grave risk of bias toward Western, monotheistic religions, which have a recognized center in worship of a Supreme Being." Lupu 1989, 959. This criticism must be taken seriously, but there may be a countervailing bias as well. Thus the relative thickness of non-Western religions, such as Hinduism, provides a recognized center in the existence of a way of life for affiliates whose lives are pervasively religious.

[29] *Church of the Lukumi Babalu Aye* 561–2.

[30] Ibid. at 562.

thereby producing an undeniable substantive deprivation. Conceptually, as Eisgruber and Sager have pointed out with respect to all the opinions in *Smith* (as well as to Congress and the president's Religious Freedom Restoration Act [RFRA] response), the deprivation—and also the reasons advanced for tolerating it—was considered within a "paradigm of privilege."[31] By this they meant that "[I]t is a matter of constitutional regret whenever government prevents or discourages persons from honoring their religious commitments," which is why, in order to prevent this from happening, "the principle of unimpaired flourishing" must be upheld.[32] That was the minority's position (and later, Justice Souter's), but the majority too conceived the salient issue to be the challenge of this principle to the rule of law.

Both sides, however, glossed over the more salient issue of equality. Souter's distinction would have been a little more remarkable had he used it to make a somewhat different point, that the main defect in the constitutional insistence on formal neutrality is that it leads to a denial of substantive equality for those whose affiliation with a minority religion renders them particularly vulnerable to the inattention or prejudice of the religious mainstream. Kathleen Sullivan has written that "[T]he big flaw in *Smith* [is that] it entrenches patterns of de facto discrimination against minority religions."[33] Justice O'Connor's opinion appeared to recognize this when she attacked the majority for, in effect, making "the price of an equal place in the civil community" contingent on abandoning the dictates of one's religion.[34] But the thrust of her argument was to establish that only governmental interests "of the highest order" can override the individual interest in living one's life in accordance with one's religious beliefs. It was an argument that, as Macedo has observed in connection with the RFRA response, "encourage[s] religious objections to generally applicable laws of all sorts, encourage[s] people to constantly regard the law from the point of view of their religious beliefs, and impair[s] the Constitution's transformative function."[35]

Indeed, this constitutional function is the essence of assimilative secularism. In pondering the complexities of the exemption problem, we

---

[31] Eisgruber and Sager 1994a, 1254.

[32] Ibid. The principle has been pressed by Douglas Laycock, who was instrumental in the preparation of RFRA. For him, formal neutrality prevents the realization of the substantive entitlement to exemptions required by the Free Exercise Clause. Laycock 1991, 16. "Exemptions should be routine and not exceptional." Ibid., 68.

[33] Sullivan 1992, 216. Or as one of Smith's attorneys put it in the oral argument before the Supreme Court, "[W]e are getting here to the heart of an ethnocentric view . . . of what constitutes religion in the United States." Quoted in Long 2000, 183.

[34] *Smith* at 897.

[35] Macedo 2000, 157.

should direct more attention to the connection between the norm of constitutional equality and the assimilative aspiration that is demanded by
the best interpretation of the religion clauses. "Because a liberal public
morality is always (more or less) in a state of coming-into-being, we
should accommodate dissenters when doing so helps draw them into the
public moral order; that is, when it helps transform a modus vivendi into
a deeper set of shared commitments. To the extent that we can make
mainstream public institutions more accessible to cultural and religious
outsiders, we may help integrate them into our shared institutions."[36] We
should, in other words, emphasize the ameliorative aspects of membership in the civic community of a diverse democracy, thereby accentuating
the benefits of having key minorities fully embrace the tenets that give
distinctive meaning to the polity. Improving the status of religious minorities relative to the cultural mainstream should enhance the possibilities
for a genuinely integrated political community in which the reality of citizenship is experienced equally, substantively as well as formally.[37]

In India, the ameliorative goal has developed within a social context in
which religion stands as a principal obstacle in the path of constitutionally
mandated societal reform. Accordingly, a prominent feature of Church/
State jurisprudence has been to frequently curtail free exercise rights in the
name of social justice. In the United States, ameliorative considerations do
not weigh nearly so heavily in constitutional cases involving religion, but
to the extent that they do at all, they pull in the opposite direction, toward
greater accommodation of free exercise claims. In some cases they support
the transformative agenda of American citizenship by contributing to the
removal of barriers to the outsider's identification with the ideas and ideals of the liberal political culture. The Fourteenth Amendment, which
protects citizenship rights, is, in its aims and in its relationship to the
conditions prevalent at the time of its drafting, the most ameliorative of
all American constitutional provisions. In Jane Rutherford's apt formulation, "Fourteenth Amendment equality principles and First Amendment
principles of religion are mutually reinforcing."[38] When applied to the
particulars in *Smith*, the reinforced norm of substantive equality requires
"equal opportunity to engage in sacramental practices."[39]

---

[36] Ibid., 205.

[37] Kenneth Karst has written eloquently on this theme. "[O]ur courts have a crucial role
in expanding the circle of belonging, as they translate the Fourteenth Amendment's guarantee of equal citizenship into substantive reality for people previously relegated to the status
of outsiders." Karst 1989, 3. With specific reference to religion, he writes that "[R]eligious
liberty is not to be conditioned on the individual's forfeiture of the status of equal citizenship." Ibid., 101.

[38] Rutherford 1996, 1074.

[39] Ibid., 1075.

In contrast, the third point in Justice Scalia's opinion for the Court recognizes only the principle of formal equality, requiring uniform treatment of all offenders who violate the prohibition against peyote use. The majority is to be treated identically with the members of the Native American Church; both, in essence, have a right to neutral and impartial enforcement of the State's drug laws. Strictly speaking, equal protection is guaranteed. However, the Indian experience reminds us to appreciate the looming difficulty in this arrangement. Some of the most serious challenges to secularism in India have involved instances where, rightly or wrongly, the jurisprudential invocation of formal equality has called into question people's good faith or good sense. The revival of Hindu nationalism is an extraordinarily complex phenomenon, but instrumental to its success to date has been the strategic commitment of its leaders and theoreticians to the precepts of majoritarian democracy. For some, this commitment also represents a principled effort to fulfill the constitutional promise of liberal equality; for many, however, it has provided political cover to pursue an illiberal agenda of Hindu religious and cultural domination. In the various constitutional confrontations considered in this study—over the adoption of a uniform civil code, over the dismissal of elected governments in three Indian states, over the interpretation and enforcement of the nation's main electoral law—we have seen how precarious the condition of religious minorities (especially Muslims) is when their interests are subsumed in a political discourse of formal equality. Judges who embrace this discourse are not necessarily dishonorable or intolerant; in most instances they are quite the opposite. But their decisions have often provided aid and comfort to those seeking assimilation of minority groups into the culture of the dominant majority.

Of course, in the United States, judges need not worry that they will become pawns in an elaborate campaign to redefine the essentials of national identity. Although the "tyranny of the majority" was a phrase applied originally to the American scene, it resonates more powerfully in connection with contemporary India. Still, for all the differences, the Indian example includes important lessons for American judges, perhaps most significant, that there is a fine line separating political from social assimilation. "Leaving accommodation to the political process" may do more than "place at a relative disadvantage those religious practices that are not widely engaged in"; it may have the more profound, if inadvertent, effect of submerging the way of life of a thickly constituted religious minority under the cultural sway of mainstream theology. Moreover, with regard to certain groups, notably Native Americans, the assimilative designs of the majority have been less a theoretical possibility than a historic reality. At the federal level this history has been recognized in the provisions of the American Indian Religious Freedom Act, which says: "[I]t shall be the policy of the United States to protect and preserve for American Indians their inherent right of freedom to believe, express, and exercise the traditional religions . . . including but not limited to access to sites, use and possession of sacred objects, and the freedom to worship through ceremonials and traditional rites."[40] The anomalous constitutional status of Native Americans (as the only minority whose formal rule-making authority to regulate many of their own affairs is specifically recognized in law) should send a clear message to judges of the unusual sensitivity required of them in adjudicating the free-exercise claims of tribal members. As Justice Blackmun wrote in his dissent in *Smith*, "[T]his Court must scrupulously apply its free exercise analysis to the religious claims of Native Americans, however unorthodox they may be."[41] In this vein, it should have focused on Congress's finding that certain substances, such as peyote, "have religious significance because they are sacred, they have power, they heal, they are necessary to the exercise of the rites of the religion, they are necessary to the cultural integrity of the tribe, and, therefore, *religious survival*."[42]

Assuming, then, that the Court's position on the subject of exemptions was at least in part intended to advance the assimilationist goals of the secular constitution, in the end its intransigence served to undermine this objective by shifting the focus from *political* assimilation to *social* assimilation. Al Smith, the respondent in the constitutional case, had, "[f]rom an early age . . . fiercely struggled against attempts to assimilate him into white society and fought to live his life the way he wanted."[43] Had the Court introduced ameliorative considerations into the constitutional equation, the line that separates the two kinds of assimilation might have been better maintained. Operationally this would have entailed considering the special circumstances attending the claim asserted by Smith—the centrality of the sacramental use of peyote to the practice of his religion, and the historic vulnerability of his faith (and tribal) community to perse-

---

[40] Pub. L. No. 95–341. In 1968 Congress passed the Indian Civil Rights Act, which extended many of the guarantees of the Bill of Rights and the Fourteenth Amendment to Americans of Indian descent. Some critics of the law within the Native American community, while conceding the altruistic motives behind the law's passage, saw it as just another chapter in the dismal history of cultural warfare perpetrated by the dominant culture on Native Americans. Interestingly, in deference to Indian sensibilities, Congress chose not to disturb the theocratic nature of much tribal authority by deleting guarantees against establishment of religion from the Act's list of protected rights. Such provision is consistent with a policy of exemptions, which by their very nature trigger Establishment Clause concerns.

[41] *Smith* at 921.

[42] Ibid. at 920–1 (emphasis added).

[43] Long 2000, 22.

cution by dominant forces within the wider culture.[44] Such solicitude should not be extended indiscriminately (in the manner of RFRA), but should be calibrated carefully to reflect the facts of each case. In doctrinal terms, the Court might therefore do well to follow Rodney Smolla's advice by adopting an intermediate scrutiny test that balances the "government's interest in the uniform adherence to laws of general applicability and the interest of individuals in receiving modest accommodation for the free exercise of religious beliefs."[45]

But what precisely is the constitutional basis for the accommodation? Here the Court should heed Eisgruber and Sager's observation that "What transforms religious accommodation from a mere policy concern to a constitutional issue is the vulnerability of religion to prejudice and persecution."[46] In their analysis, protection against discrimination, rather than privilege against all noncompelling governmental interests, should govern judicial determinations about exemptions. "[T]he latitude mainstream religions enjoy to consummate their sacraments argues for a failure of equal regard."[47] Thus a merely formal application of the equality principle deflects attention from the impact of a law on the free exercise of religion; insisting only on evidence of discriminatory intent provides insufficient safeguard against majoritarian indifference.

The argument in this form emphasizes victimization as the predicate for judicial action.[48] By factoring in calculations rooted in related concerns about assimilation and amelioration, the claim, while persuasive, is augmented by an affirmative, less defensive component. We might recall in this regard Justice Reddy's remark in *Bommai*, the case of the three elected Indian state governments that were (at least officially) dismissed for a "failure of constitutional machinery," specifically their alleged violations of secular principles. "Secularism is . . . more than a passive attitude of religious tolerance. It is a positive concept of equal treatment of all religions." For a majority of the justices this meant that the State was to be encouraged to *act* in furtherance of the basic features of the Constitu-

---

[44] In this regard consider what Carolyn N. Long has written about the Native American experience with peyotism: "As peyotism grew in popularity in Mexico and North America, efforts to suppress the religion became more prevalent. Christian missionaries and church leaders led the antipeyote campaign with the full support of federal Indian agents working in Indian Territory. Government and church officials opposed the religion because it hindered their efforts to assimilate Indians into the general population." Ibid., 11.

[45] Smolla 1998, 938.

[46] Eisgruber and Sager 1994a, 1248.

[47] Ibid., 1290.

[48] "From the recognition of victimization, and of vulnerability to future victimization, flows the constitutional objective of protection." Ibid., 1252.

tion, not simply to refrain from acting in ways that threaten fundamental rights. The principle of equal treatment needed to be loosened from its secure moorings in procedural justice and situated more proactively within the context of the Constitution's broader substantive objectives. In the Indian context, this meant an injunction to advance the ideal of a welfare State by conjoining secularism and egalitarianism. Under the rubric of the term *positive secularism*, government policies were held acceptable if their purpose was to eradicate social injustices attributable to religious practices, even if these policies targeted specific communities. In contrast, as we saw in chapter 4, the more *negative secularism* of American First Amendment jurisprudence produces (at least in theory) a much less active role for government, coupled with a strongly entrenched skepticism for the judicial targeting of religious communities in exemption cases.[49]

One would think, however, that it might be possible to infuse a greater positive element into American efforts, tempered to avoid unlimited flourishing that, in turn, diminishes the Constitution's transformative role in facilitating liberal assimilation. Would not such an infusion in fact be in the best interests of American secular constitutionalism? While a principal goal of free exercise jurisprudence is, and ought to be, protection *against* hostile action endangering vulnerable religious minorities, vital too is the support of public institutions *for* a civic community that rests solidly upon a broadly shared core of political ideas. If in India ameliorative considerations are a major chord in the harmonizing of religion and social reform, in the United States they can be played to good effect in a minor chord to help orchestrate the coherent integration of religious and political goals. So if the members of the Native American Church are insulated from Oregon's drug law, that protection also ameliorates their marginal status in society and may therefore, by the example set, strengthen the legitimacy of secular political beliefs that are central to the success of the American political experiment.[50] Michael McConnell's observation that "[T]he

---

[49] In practice American government, especially at the local level, has been active in granting exemptions to religious organizations. Increasingly states have instituted their own versions of RFRA, making it possible for "faith-based" groups to avoid compliance with, among other things, land-use regulations and health requirements. "We're in an era," explains Marci Hamilton, "when government is extraordinarily deferential to religious organizations. Legislators think that in this era there's a lot of political benefit in doing good things for religion, and saying no to religious requests is hard for them to do." Quoted in the *New York Times*, July 27, 2001. The *New York Times* article reporting this trend was entitled "Many States Ceding Regulations to Church Groups." What this government activism largely amounts to, then, is a calculated political decision to reduce the role of government in the enforcement of its general civil and criminal laws.

[50] Justice O'Connor wrote in her concurring opinion that "[T]he First Amendment was enacted precisely to protect the rights of those whose religious practices are not shared by

ideal of free exercise is counter-assimilationist" may now come to be seen as expressing at best a half-truth about the essence of the secular constitution. We would do well to ponder the implications of the other half.

REINVENTING THE WHEEL

> [W]e cannot start *de novo*, as if India had no history and
> as if people could change their nature merely by taking
> thought. Possibilities must be grounded in the nature of
> the actual. Civilisations must live on the lines of their
> own experience. Like individuals, even nations cannot
> borrow experience from others. They may furnish us
> with light, but our own history provides us with the
> conditions of action. The only revolutions that endure
> are those that are rooted in the past.[51]
> —S. Radhakrishnan

If Americans would be wise to introduce an ameliorative perspective into their reflections on Church and State, Indians too would benefit from a similar move, incorporating assimilationist reasoning into assessments of their own secular predicament. When Nehru wrote in *The Discovery of India* that countries such as his own were not as favorably situated as the United States in being able to solve their minority problems by "mak[ing] everyone conform to a certain type," he seemed at least open to the possibility that with an improvement in the Indian condition, the effort "to make every citizen 100%" Indian could proceed realistically. Even so, "with a longer and more complicated past," neither Nehru nor his compa-

---

the majority and may be viewed with hostility." *Smith* at 902. She then proceeded to deny, as she had in the case of *Lyng v Northwest Indian Cemetery Protective Assn.* (involving the building of a logging road through government-owned land long held sacred by Native Americans), the free exercise claim of a member of a Native American religious group. In both cases she found a governmental interest sufficiently compelling to withstand the individual's First Amendment challenge. Criticism of the opinion has focused on its failure to follow through on the promise of its noble sentiment about minority rights. Or as Eisgruber and Sager might say, O'Connor's ruling against an exemption for the sacramental use of peyote made her announcement of the principle of "unimpaired flourishing" ring rather hollow. Such a principle suggests a much more generous view of accommodation than what governed her ultimate decision. My argument is that the O'Connor position on the purpose of the religion clauses should be connected more to ameliorative/assimilationist considerations than to the principle of unimpaired flourishing. This would have the effect of lowering the state's threshold for demonstrating a sufficient interest in uniform enforcement, but also of elevating the broader systemic interest in accommodating groups that have a historic purchase on the Court's solicitude.

[51] Radhakrishnan 1995, 118.

triots could have been, on the eve of independence, sanguine about the prospects for an American-style solution to the dilemmas of diversity and disunity. But as Nehru also recognized, "Indian history is a . . . continuous adaptation of old ideas to a changing environment, of old patterns to new."[52] The idea of Indian unity is as old as Ashoka; how it will ultimately be attained in the world's largest democracy is still unclear, but undoubtedly religion will play a pivotal role.[53]

This being the case, the key question concerns the *kind* of assimilationist thinking that will shape the future of Indian secularism. Sunil Khilnani has noted that the "search for an internal principle of unity" has often fixated on the Hindu religion. But the search cannot end there, for the fragmentation evident in the caste system and in the "bewildering pluralism of Hindu beliefs" is an enduring alternative reality that demands further exploration.[54] To serve effectively as a unifying force, Hinduism had to be cleverly adapted to mute its inherent multiplicities, accentuating instead cultural commonalities and shared geography. Proponents of the faith's political reincarnation, Hindutva, have diligently sought to use the exclusivist ideology of ethnoreligious nationalism to create an Indian identity that automatically confers political and constitutional legitimacy upon people and practices of the country's religious majority. For those outside the fold, the promise of inclusion has been made contingent upon their assimilation into the unifying Brahminical culture that, in this view, must come to define the Hindu nation that is India. The struggle to establish the political primacy of this Hindu identity often assumes a violent form, as symbolized by Ayodhya, but it also pursues the path of the law, as illustrated most vividly in the *Hindutva Cases*. In essence, it is a struggle to instantiate a *visionary* model of Church/State relations, which would resemble in form the Israeli political paradigm, but which in practice could threaten the religious liberty that makes a constitution secular.

The opponents of this cultural assimilationist quest for unity have frequently found themselves defending their occasional support for the claims of minority communities, which exempts them from the offense of "communalism," the term of disdain they have attached to the followers of Hindutva. Their attempt to recapture the principled high ground is complicated by the fact that, by their actions over the years, they have indeed too often exposed themselves to the charge of hypocrisy, if not "pseudo-secularism." Moreover, to the extent that their defense of minor-

---

[52] Nehru 1959, 517.

[53] As noted in the introductory chapter, Ashoka was Nehru's favorite Indian leader, an "astonishing ruler," for whom the "dream of uniting the whole of India" was a consuming passion. Ibid., 132. Initially pursued through the sword, realizing the dream ultimately relied on Buddha's teachings.

[54] Khilnani 1997, 160.

ities has been genuinely principled and free from crass political calculation, it has not sustained a compelling argument that rivals in rhetorical
power the case for Indian unity made by the other side.

This failure is attributable in part to the tentativeness with which the
"anti-communalists" have pursued the ameliorative promise of the secular constitution. As we saw in chapter 4, incrementalism in the secular
pursuit of social justice makes sense within a complex social setting characterized by a deeply entrenched diversity of groups at various stages of
development. The norm of "principled distance" permits a measure of
differential treatment of these groups without conceding the Constitution's basic commitment to secular governance. In accordance with this
norm, for example, Muslim polygamy was legally tolerated at the same
time that the practice was legislatively proscribed for the majority community. Whatever the shortcomings of the Hindu Code Bill as an attempt
to reform religiously sanctioned regressive behavior, symbolically at least
it evinced a concern for the social conditions of Hindus, notably ignoring
the same conditions in the minority communities. Such neglect can be
benignly interpreted as a pragmatic, well-intentioned display of sensitivity
to the religious beliefs of vulnerable minorities, but it can very easily lapse
into a patronizing tolerance that cumulatively risks obscuring the logic of
ameliorative secularism. And in the process it most assuredly provides
potent ammunition for polemicists of cultural assimilation.

Countering them presents a formidable challenge. In particular, the burden of undoing deeply rooted social inequities is an inherently divisive
undertaking, and so the underlying premise of ameliorative secularism—
reducing inequality—does little (or so it would seem) to make the elusive
goal of Indian unity any less elusive. On the other hand, a fascinating
irony of the caste system and its historic persistence and pervasiveness in
India is that it has provided Indians with a profoundly significant shared
experience that, perversely, may in the end help to develop a positive sense
of national identity.[55] Overcoming the system's inequities potentially
serves the corollary interest in national integration. As Radhakrishnan

---

[55] How perverse is suggested by this comment by Tocqueville regarding the obstacles to
national unity represented in the phenomenon of caste. "There is a multitude of castes in
India. There is no nation, or rather, each of these castes forms a little nation of its own, that
has its own spirit, usages, laws, its own government. It is inside of caste that the national
spirit of the Hindus is enclosed. The motherland for them is caste. One could seek it elsewhere in vain, but in caste, it is alive." Tocqueville 1962, 447. As I suggested in chapter 3,
Tocqueville was not at all sanguine about the possibilities for transcending caste; hence for
him national unity was at best a dim prospect. As for the democratic prospect: "The very
fact that a caste-ridden society like India has embraced a democratic form of government
and practised it during forty years would have been hailed by Tocqueville, had he known
of it, as a signal victory of the providential trend towards equality which he has prophesied."
Bernard 1988, 404.

put it, "To develop a degree of organic wholeness and a sense of common obligation, the caste spirit must go."[56] Thus the constitutional project of social reconstruction, tied in large part to the commitment to secular governance, embodies a dual potential for advancing or retarding the long-sought objective of political consolidation.

The delicacy these matters demand defies doctrinaire (or even confident) resolution. As we have seen, the Hindu right has had some success exploiting the time-honored strategy of displacement of conflict, even if subordinating intracommunal fragmentation to the broad cultural appeal of Hindutva should turn out finally not to be a formula for enduring political prosperity.[57] The strategy has been particularly adept at capitalizing on the missteps of a political opposition that has, in its policy toward minorities, sometimes been insensitive to the appearance of pandering. The competing case for positive secularism must be made in a way that preserves the national focus on social reform while carefully balancing the fundamental interests in diversity and equal treatment, a balancing traceable to constitutional commitments to the maintenance and preservation of distinct cultures (e.g., Articles 29 and 30) and to the eventual adoption of uniform laws requiring compliance irrespective of religious affiliation (Article 44).[58] Cultural assimilation can only be effectively countered by political assimilation, specifically by emphasizing positive secularism as a central component of a shared political identity that respects India's various group identities and the State's ameliorative project.

We come full circle to the great symbol of Indian secularism—Ashoka's Wheel. As invoked at the Constituent Assembly by Nehru, Radhakrishnan, and others, it was meant to convey three related ideas about religion

---

[56] Radhakrishnan 1995, 133.

[57] It is possible to argue that the cultural politics of the Hindu right, while directed against minorities, is not inimical to the concerns of ameliorative secularism. After all, the BJP was the first mainstream political party to have a Dalit president. Also, the most anti-Brahminical of southern parties, the DMK (Dravida Monnetra Kazhagam), has allied itself with the BJP. Nevertheless, the BJP is essentially an upper-caste party, which has been forced by the necessities of operating within a fragmented political environment to adopt certain strategies to broaden its appeal. Thus ideologically it has attempted to integrate lower and middle sectors into a system that has maintained its Brahminical values. These political concessions have caused rifts in the party (e.g., in Gujarat and Uttar Pradesh) among purists and pragmatists. But the essential commitment of the party, which, to be sure, is relatively moderate in comparison with other parts of the *Sangh Parivar*, can fairly be described as being in tension with an egalitarian social agenda.

[58] As Susanne Hoeber Rudolph has noted, these constitutional provisions need not be viewed as contradictory. "They can be seen as points defining the perimeters within which Indian policy is elaborated. They constitute the defining end points of a legal narrative that seeks to satisfice alternative goals, to distribute value between opposites in ways that preserve both." Rudolph 1998, 16.

and politics in India: (1) that the spiritual and temporal domains were indissolubly bound together; (2) that the State had an obligation to remain impartial in its relations with the nation's various faiths; and (3) that the pursuit of a just social order was central to the vision of constitutional secularism. These notions are sometimes in tension with one another; for example, addressing egalitarian goals requires a modicum of differential treatment toward distinct communities. To keep the wheel running smoothly means adopting measures to reduce the level of friction from within, aligning the various components of the system so that they perform to maximum efficiency.

Indeed it could mean borrowing from the assimilative model to complement India's ameliorative orientation, mirroring what we imagined in our discussion of *Smith* and religiously based exemptions in the United States. Neither exclusive transformation nor exclusive conservation fulfills the promise of the secular liberal constitution; that is, a polity with transformative aspirations, whether assimilative or ameliorative, should strike a careful balance between communal sensibilities and secular objectives. Demanding reasonable respect for groups without endorsing unimpaired flourishing is a sensible general goal for both polities, although drawing specific lines in each instance will necessarily vary according to local requirements. We have seen that the American constitutional scheme, in recognizing the appeal and potential of religion in defining individual identity, guards against the threat this poses to the common political identity so critical to the achievement of constitutional aspirations. Or more succinctly, "The voting booth is the temple of American institutions."[59] Yet we have also seen that blindly worshipping at the altar of democracy can undermine pluralist interests vital to liberal constitutional values. Examples of these costs are being tallied in the unfolding of political developments in India, where provisionally, at least, the effects of majoritarian democracy have been notably and troublingly mixed in their impact on these values. Indeed, just how intricately perplexing these issues can become is evident in the counterintuitive words of the Hindu right's leading theoretician: "I am against a religious State; I am for the American way [in Church/State relations]."[60]

[59] Justice Brewer, as quoted in chapter 3.

[60] Arun Shourie, in an interview with the author, November 19, 1998, New Delhi. Shourie's remark was voiced in the context of an observation that was meant to distinguish his vision for India from that of the Israelis, for whom, as we have seen, he has great admiration. The main area of Shourie's disagreement with the Israelis pertains to their support for a regime of personal law. Indeed, it is a revealing disagreement. Thus the fact that religious nationalists in Israel are generally supportive of communally based law, whereas their counterparts in India are fervently attached to the idea of a uniform legal code, is suggestive of the very different political contexts within which secular issues are debated.

So the question, then, comes down to this: What advantage can Indians committed to the secular vision of their Constitution derive from the American approach that does not play into the hands of other Indians holding very different views? How can the benefits of political assimilation accrue to the first group without advancing the agenda of cultural assimilation espoused by the second?

The advantage lies in a deeply rifted polity's potential gain from the transformative possibilities of liberal political ideas. A society in which rigid social stratification dominates the legacy of the dominant religion would be wise to consider the workings of a system in which sectarian piety is constitutionally subordinated to the self-evident truth of human equality. To be sure, the thickness and pervasiveness of religious belief and practice in India mitigates against embracing this benign subordination as the organizing structure of its secular governance, but surely the moral resources of liberal equality would encourage a principled solidarity that is at once consistent with the polity's ameliorative ambitions and respectful of its pluralist heritage. In contrast with the United States, India's constitutional context requires greater solicitude for the claims of group autonomy; however, with the advance of secularly inspired progress in social reform, latent pressures for uniform treatment might be expected in time to mature into more enforceable legal obligations.

Understanding the demand for uniformity in relational or contingent terms, as connected to the progressive realization of ameliorative goals, should also help to parry the "liberal" challenge of the cultural assimilationists. Shourie's support for the "American way" is a classic example of jurisprudential borrowing without adequate regard for the complications associated with constitutional context. Conforming to a more exacting standard of Church/State separation clears a path to the high ground of principled jurisprudence, a sheltered perch from which charges of pseudo-secularism can be hurled with impunity upon the temporizing minions of Nehru's and Ambedkar's successors. In addition, a more separationist stance entails, in its most theoretically refined articulation, a commitment by the State to take minimal (if it were possible, no) cognizance of religion in its officially sponsored acts. Such formal indifference to religion conveniently impedes social reconstruction, rendering suspect the effort to single out regressive religious practices for special statutory and administrative attention. Thus, in line with the perceived procedural requirements of American-style First Amendment jurisprudence, caste and gender issues having a specific connection to particular faiths should be removed from the public agenda. Still permissible in this view would be religion-blind reform in accordance with a "one size fits all" arrangement. But under this formula, general standards of right conduct would undoubtedly be derived from politically dominant views in the religion of the majority, and so in the end this policy too would accommodate distinct ideological purposes on the Hindu right.

Of course, to deflect any intimation that the enthronement of a "religious State" is the specter behind publicly declared statements of principle, these standards have and will require artful casting in cultural terms, the alleged purpose of which is to preserve the unique essentials of a treasured way of life. Those wishing to thwart the culturally hegemonic designs that lie behind the liberal façade will need to expose this deployment of liberal doctrine as only a veneer, proving that a purely procedural approach abstracted from substantial social amelioration is seriously deficient as a secular solution in India. Critical to this demonstration is an honest and accurate explanation of the substantive commitment embodied in "the American way" (or other such formulations), one that makes clear that the essence of liberalism's political truth resides in the fact of our common humanity, and only derivatively from the forms through which constitutional democracy is processed.

But a narrowly rhetorical defense of natural equality will only go so far. It must accompany actions that promise realistic amelioration of social conditions rooted in a religiously sanctioned feudal past. Constitutional accommodation of such actions is necessary not only to achieve specific reforms but also to provide a legitimating backdrop for ideas that lie at the core of political assimilation and its unifying project. Radhakrishnan, the philosopher-statesman whose eloquent evocation of an ancient symbol to represent contemporary India's hopes for a more just society gave clarity to the secular intentions of many of the Constitution's framers, insisted that "[Our] new emphasis on the dignity and freedom of man demands a reshaping of the social order."[61] But policies alone, he suggested, were not sufficient. "Transform[ing] the mind of the people" is integral to the removal of "obstacles to social justice."[62] Indeed, securing "[t]he inviolable sanctity of the human soul, the freedom of the human spirit," was so critical as to be considered "the sole justification for the State."[63] This ennobling thought, which is very familiar to the tradition of Western political philosophy, is of course not unique to liber-

---

[61] Radhakrishnan 1995, 119.

[62] Ibid., 118.

[63] Ibid., 61. Radhakrishnan goes on to say: "We cannot all be welded into one man, though we can be merged into one crowd. We are born separately, and in our essential life we live alone. The State must protect the dharma of individuals and groups." Ibid. Importantly, then, the organization of society must be attentive to the dignity of the individual without ignoring the constitutive nature of groups, which possess their own dharma, that is to say, their own "forms and activities which shape and sustain human life." Ibid., 105.

alism or to the United States, even while its central role in American secular constitutional theory has distinguished the jurisprudence of Church/State relations. Much as Indians should endeavor to "live on the lines of their own experience," and therefore resist making this or any other jurisprudence a focus of reflexive emulation, one can hope that it will at least "furnish [them] with light," as they follow the Wheel of Law to its appointed destination.

BIBLIOGRAPHY

Abramov, Zelman. 1976. *Perpetual Dilemma: Religion in the Jewish State*. Rutherford: Fairleigh Dickinson University Press.

Ackerman, Bruce. 1991. *We the People: Foundations*. Cambridge: Harvard University Press.

Agnes, Flavia. 1999. *Law and Gender Equality: The Politics of Women's Rights in India*. New Delhi: Oxford University Press.

Ahmadi, A. M. 2000. "The Constitution—Its Tryst with Destiny: Flawed or Fulfilled?" Address delivered to the Conference on Fifty Years of Indian Republic, Toronto, Canada, April 1.

Aiyar, Mani Shankar. 1995. *Knickerwallahs, Silly-Billies & Other Curious Creatures*. New Delhi: UBS Publishers' Distributors Ltd.

Akhtar, Mohammad Jamil. 1997. *Babri Masjid: A Tale Untold*. New Delhi: Genuine Publication and Media Private.

Alexandrowicz, C. H. 1960. "The Secular State in India and the U.S." *Journal of the Indian Law Institute* 2.

Aloysius, G. 1994. "Trajectory of Hindutva." 29 *Economic and Political Weekly*, June 1.

Appleby, Scott. 2001. *Newsweek*. September 24.

Arendt, Hannah. 1963. *On Revolution*. New York: Viking Press.

Aristotle. 1962. *Politics*. New York: Oxford University Press.

Arzt, Donna E. 1991. "Religious Freedom in a Religious State: The Case of Israel in Comparative Constitutional Perspective." *Wisconsin International Law Journal* 9.

Audi, Robert. 1989. "The Separation of Church and State and the Obligations of Citizenship." 18 *Philosophy & Public Affairs* 259.

Austin, Granville. 1999. *Working a Democratic Constitution: The Indian Experience*. New Delhi: Oxford University Press.

———. 1966. *The Indian Constitution*. Oxford: Oxford University Press.

Avineri, Shlomo. 2000. "The Zionist Legacy and the Future of Israel." In *Zionism, Liberalism, and the Future of the Jewish State*. Ed. Steven J. Zipperstein and Ernest S. Frerichs. Providence: Dorot Foundation.

Avnon, Dan. 1998. "The Israeli Basic Laws' (Potentially) Fatal Flaw." 32 *Israel Law Review* 535.

The Ayodhya Reference: The Supreme Court Judgement and Commentaries. 1995. New Delhi: Voice of India.

Baar, Carl. 1990. "Social Action Litigation in India: The Operation and Limits of the World's Most Active Judiciary." *Policy Studies Journal* 19.

Baird, Robert D. 1969. "Human Rights Priorities and Indian Religious Thought." *Journal of Church and State* 11.

———. 1981. "Uniform Civil Code and the Secularization of Law." In *Religion in Modern India*. Ed. Robert D. Baird. New Delhi: Manohar.

Barak, Aharon. 1987. *Judicial Discretion*. New Haven: Yale University Press.

———. 1992–93. "The Constitutional Revolution: Protected Human Rights." 1 *Mishpat Umimshal*.

———. 1997. "The Constitutionalization of the Israeli Legal System as a Result of the Basic Laws and Its Effect on Procedural and Substantive Criminal Law." 31 *Israel Law Review* 3.

———. 1998. "The Role of the Supreme Court in a Democracy." 3 *Israel Studies* 6.

Barak-Erez, Daphne. 1995. "From an Unwritten to a Written Constitution: The Israeli Challenge in American Perspective." 26 *Columbia Human Rights Law Review* 309.

Barzun, Jacques. 2000. *From Dawn to Decadence: 500 Years of Western Cultural Life*. New York: HarperCollins.

Basu, Durga Das. 1998. *Introduction to the Constitution of India*. 18th ed. New Delhi: Prentice-Hall of India.

Bates, Stephen. 1993. *Battleground: One Mother's Crusade, The Religious Right, and the Struggle for Our Schools*. New York: Henry Holt.

Baxi, Upendra. 1985. *Courage, Craft and Contention: The Indian Supreme Court in the Eighties*. Bombay: N. M. Tripathi Private.

———. 1996. "*Hindutva* Verdict: Focus on Context." *Indian Express*, 8 March. Reprinted in *Religion and Law Review*.

Beg, Nasirullah. 1979. *Secular India and Minorities*. Lucknow: Madhur Printers.

Bellah, Robert N. 1975. *The Broken Covenant: American Civil Religion in Time of Trial*. Chicago: University of Chicago Press.

Ben-Gurion, David. 1954. *Rebirth and Destiny of Israel*. New York: Philosophical Library.

Berg, Larry L., Harlan Hahn, and John R. Schmidhauser. 1976. *Corruption in the American Political System*. Morristown: General Learning Press.

Berger, Peter L. 1967. *The Social Canopy: Elements of a Sociological Theory of Religion*. Garden City: Doubleday.

Berman, Harold J. 1983. "Religious Foundations of Law in the West: An Historical Perspective." *Journal of Law and Religion* 1.

Bernard, Jean-Alphonse. 1988. "Tocqueville: A Companion to an Indian Journey." 29 *Archives of European Sociology*.

Berns, Walter. 1970. *The First Amendment and the Future of American Democracy*. New York: Basic Books.

Bhagwati, P. N. 1985. "Judicial Activism and Public Interest Litigation." 23 *Columbia Journal of Transnational Law* 561.

Bhargava, Rajeev. 1998. "What is Secularism For?" In *Secularism and Its Critics*. Ed. Rajeev Bhargava. Delhi: Oxford University Press.

Birnbaum, Ervin. 1970. *The Politics of Compromise: State and Religion in Israel.* Rutherford: Fairleigh Dickinson University Press.

Black Jr., Charles L. 1969. *Structure and Relationship in Constitutional Law.* Baton Rouge: Louisiana State Press.

Bose, Sumantra. 1998. " 'Hindu Nationalism' and the Crisis of the Indian State: A Theoretical Perspective." In *Nationalism, Democracy and Development: State and Politics in India.* Ed. Sugata Bose and Ayesha Jalal. Delhi: Oxford University Press.

Bradley, Gerald V. 1989. "Church Autonomy in the Constitutional Order: The End of Church and State?" *Louisiana Law Review* 49.

Brandon, Mark E. 1998. *Free in the World: American Slavery and Constitutional Failure.* Princeton: Princeton University Press.

Brass, Paul. 1991. *Ethnicity and Nationalism: Theory and Comparison.* New Delhi: Sage.

Bruce, Steve, ed. 1992. *Religion and Modernization: Sociologists and Historians Debate the Secularization Thesis.* Oxford: Oxford University Press.

Burke, Thomas F. 1997. "The Concept of Corruption in Campaign Finance Law." 14 *Constitutional Commentary* 127.

Burt, Robert A. 1989. "Inventing Judicial Review: Israel and America." 10 *Cardozo Law Review* 2013.

Caldorola, Carlo. 1982. *Religions and Societies: Asia and the Middle East.* Berlin: Moutan Publishers.

Cardozo, Benjamin N. 1928. *The Paradoxes of Legal Science.* New York: Columbia University Press.

———. 1969. *The Nature of the Judicial Process.* New Haven: Yale University Press.

Carner, Mosco. 1947. "The Orchestral Music." In *The Music of Schubert.* Ed. Gerald Abraham. New York: W. W. Norton.

Carter, Stephen. 1993. *The Culture of Disbelief: How American Law and Politics Trivialize Religious Devotion.* New York: Harper Collins Publishers.

Cassels, Jamie. 1989. "Judicial Activism and Public Interest Litigation in India: Attempting the Impossible?" 37 *American Journal of Comparative Law* 495.

Chandhoke, Neera. 1999. *Beyond Secularism: The Rights of Religious Minorities.* New Delhi: Oxford University Press.

———. 2000. "The Tragedy of Ayodhya." In *Frontline* 17:13 (June 24–July 7).

Chatterjee, Abhas. 1995. *The Concept of Hindu Nation.* New Delhi: Voice of India.

Chatterjee, Margaret. 1997. *Studies in Modern Jewish and Hindu Thought.* New York: MacMillan.

Chatterji, P. C. 1984. *Secular Values for Secular India.* New Delhi: Pauls Press.

Chaudhuri, Nirad C. 1979. *Hinduism: A Religion to Live By.* Delhi: Oxford University Press.

Cohen, Asher, and Bernard Susser. 2000. *Israel and the Politics of Jewish Identity: The Secular-Religious Impasse.* Baltimore: Johns Hopkins University Press.

Cohen, Eric. 1989. "Citizenship, Nationality and Religion in Israel and Thailand." In *The Israeli State and Society: Boundaries and Frontiers.* Ed. Baruch Kimmerling. Albany: State University Press of New York.

Cohen-Almagor, Raphael. 1995. "Cultural Pluralism and the Israeli Nation-Building Ideology." *International Journal of Middle Eastern Studies* 27.

Cooley, Thomas M. 1893. "The Power to Amend the Federal Constitution." *Michigan Law Review* 2.

Constituent Assembly Debates. (1989). Official Reports. vol. 7 (December 4, 1948–January 8, 1949). Delhi: Lok Sabha Secretariat.

Cossman, Brenda, and Ratna Kapur. 1996. "Secularism: Bench-Marked by the Hindu Right." *Economic and Political Weekly.* vol. 38 (21 September).

Cox, Harvey. 1990. *The Secular City.* New York: MacMillan.

Cralle, Richard K., ed. 1855. *The Works of John C. Calhoun.* vol. 6. New York: D. Appleton.

Dahl, Robert A. 1970. *After the Revolution? Authority in a Good Society.* New Haven: Yale University Press.

Dasgupta, Swapan. 1995. "Delaying the Inevitable." In *The Ayodhya Reference: Supreme Court Judgement and Commentaries.* Ed. Arun Shourie. New Delhi: Voice of India.

De, Krishna Prasad. 1976. *Religious Freedom Under the Indian Constitution.* Columbia: South Asia Books.

Demarath III, N. J. 2001. *Crossing the Gods: World Religions and Worldly Politics.* New Brunswick: Rutgers University Press.

Demarath III, N. J., and Phillip E. Hammond. 1969. *Religion in Social Context.* New York: Random House.

Derrett, J. Duncan M. 1968. *Religion, Law and the State in India.* New York: Free Press.

Deveaux, Monique. 2000. *Cultural Pluralism and Dilemmas of Justice.* Ithaca: Cornell University Press.

Dhavan, Rajeev. 1987. "Religious Freedom in India." *American Journal of Comparative Law* 35.

———. 1994. "The Ayodhya Judgment: Encoding Secularism in the Law." 29 *Economic and Political Weekly,* 26 November.

Dobel, J. Patrick. 1978. "The Corruption of a State." 72 *American Political Science Review* 958.

Douglas, William O. 1956. *From Marshall to Mukherjee: Studies in American and Indian Constitutional Law.* Calcutta: Eastern Law House.

Dumont, Louis. 1970. *Homo Hierarchicus: An Essay on the Caste System.* Chicago: University of Chicago Press.

Dworkin, Ronald. 1977. *Taking Rights Seriously.* Cambridge: Harvard University Press.

———. 1986. *Law's Empire.* Cambridge: Harvard University Press.

Edelman, Martin. 1996. " 'Protecting' the Majority: Religious Freedom for Non-Orthodox Jews in Israel." In *Israel in the Nineties: Development and Conflict.* Ed. Frederick A. Lazin and Gregory S. Mahler. Gainesville: University Press of Florida.

Editorial Commentary. 1997. *Israel Law Review* 765.

Edwards, Paul S. 1996. "Defining Political Corruption: The Supreme Court's Role." 10 *BYU Journal of Public Law* 1.

Eisenstadt, S. N. 1992. *Jewish Civilization: The Jewish Historical Experience in a Comparative Perspective*. Albany: State University of New York Press.

Eisenstadt, S. N., ed. 1968. *The Protestant Ethic and Modernization: A Comparative View*. New York: Basic Books.

Eisgruber, Christopher L., and Lawrence G. Sager. 1994a. "Mediating Institutions: Beyond the Public/Private Distinction." 61 *University of Chicago Law Review* 1245.

———. 1994b. "The Vulnerability of Conscience: The Constitutional Basis for Protecting Religious Conduct." *University of Chicago Law Review* 61.

Elazar, Daniel J., and Janet Aviad. 1981. "Religion and Politics in Israel." In *Religion and Politics in the Middle East*. Ed. Michael Curtis. Boulder: Westview Press.

Eliash, Ben-Zion. 1983. "Ethnic Pluralism or Melting Pot: The Dilemma of Rabbinical Adjudication in Israeli Family Law." *Israel Law Review* 18.

Ely, John Hart. 1980. *Democracy and Distrust: A Theory of Judicial Review*. Cambridge: Harvard University Press.

England, Itzhak. 1987. "Law and Religion in Israel." *American Journal of Comparative Law* 35.

Epp, Charles R. 1998. *The Rights Revolution: Lawyers, Activists, and Supreme Courts in Comparative Perspective*. Chicago: University of Chicago Press.

Epstein, Richard A. 1990. "Religious Liberty in the Welfare State." *William and Mary Law Review* 31.

Euben, J. Peter. 1989. "Corruption." In *Political Innovation and Conceptual Change*. Ed. Terance Ball, James Farr, and Russell L. Hanson. Cambridge: Cambridge University Press.

Federal Farmer, no. 16. 1978 (originally published January 20, 1788). In *The Founders' Constitution*. vol. 1. Ed. Philip B. Kurland and Ralph Lerner. Chicago: University of Chicago Press.

Fehrenbacher, Don E. 1978. *The Dred Scott Case*. New York: Oxford University Press.

Fletcher, George. 1993. "Constitutional Identity." *Cardozo Law Review* 14.

Fowler, Robert Booth. 1989. *Unconventional Partners: Religion and Liberal Culture in the United States*. Grand Rapids: William E. Eerdmans.

Frontline. 2001. vol. 18, July 7–July 20.

Galanter, Marc. 1966. "The Religious Aspects of Caste: A Legal View." In *South Asian Politics and Religion*. Ed. Donald Eugene Smith. Princeton: Princeton University Press.

———. 1984. *Competing Inequalities: Law and the Backward Classes in India*. Berkeley: University of California Press.

———. 1989. *Law and Society in Modern India*. Delhi: Oxford University Press.

———. 1998. "Secularism East and West." In *Secularism and Its Critics*. Ed. Rajeev Bhargava. Delhi: Oxford University Press.

Galanter, Marc, and Jayanth Krishnan. 2000. "Personal Law and Human Rights in Comparative Perspective." *Israel Law Review* 34.

Gallup Jr., George, and Jim Castelli. 1989. *The People's Religion: American Faith in the 90's*. New York: MacMillan Publishing.

Galston, Miriam. 1994. "Rawlsian Dualism and the Autonomy of Political Thought." 94 *Columbia Law Review* 1842.

Gavison, Ruth. 1999. "The Role of Courts in Rifted Democracies." 33 *Israel Law Review* 216.

Glendon, Mary Ann. 1987. *Abortion and Divorce in Western Law*. Cambridge: Harvard University Press.

Glendon, Mary Ann, and Raul F. Yanes. 1991. "Structural Free Exercise." *Michigan Law Review* 90.

Glock, Charles Y., and Rodney Stark. 1965. *Religion and Society in Tension*. Chicago: Rand McNally.

Goldstein, Robert Justin. 2000. *Flag Burning and Free Speech: The Case of Texas v Johnson*. Lawrence: University of Kansas Press.

Government of India Press. 1967. *The Framing of India's Constitution: Select Documents*. New Delhi: Indian Institute of Public Administration.

———. 1993. *White Paper on Ayodhya*. New Delhi: GOI Press.

Greenawalt, Kent. 1988. *Religious Convictions and Political Choice*. Oxford: Oxford University Press.

Greenfeld, Liah. 1992. *Nationalism: Five Roads to Modernity*. Cambridge: Harvard University Press.

Grey, Thomas C. 1978. "Origins of the Unwritten Constitution: Fundamental Law in American Revolutionary Thought." 30 *Stanford Law Review*.

Gross, Aeyal. 1998. "The Politics of Rights in Israeli Constitutional Law." 3 *Israel Studies* 80.

Gutmann, Amy, and Dennis Thompson. 1996. *Democracy and Disagreement*. Cambridge: Harvard University Press.

Gutmann, Emanuel. 1981. "Religion and Its Role in National Integration in Israel." In *Religion and Politics in the Middle East*. Ed. Michael Curtis. Boulder: Westview Press.

Haksar, Vinit. 2001. *Rights, Communities, and Disobedience: Liberalism and Gandhi*. New Delhi: Oxford University Press.

Hamburger, Philip A. 1992. "A Constitutional Right of Religious Exemption: An Historical Perspective." *George Washington Law Review* 60.

———. 1993. "Equality and Diversity: The Eighteenth-Century Debate About Equal Protection and Equal Civil Rights." 1992 *The Supreme Court Review*. Chicago: University of Chicago Press.

Hansen, Klaus J. 1981. *Mormonism and the American Experience*. Chicago: University of Chicago Press.

Hansen, Thomas Blom. 1999. *The Saffron Wave: Democracy and Hindu Nationalism in Modern India*. Princeton: Princeton University Press.

Harel, Alon. 1996. "The Boundaries of Justifiable Tolerance: A Liberal Perspective." In *Tolerance: An Elusive Virtue*. Ed. David Heyd. Princeton: Princeton University Press.

———. 1999. "The Rule of Law in Israel: Philosophical Aspirations and Institutional Realities." In *Recrafting the Rule of Law*. Ed. David Dyzenhaus. Oxford: Hart Publishing.

Hareven, Alouph, ed. 1983. *Every Sixth Israeli: Relations Between the Jewish Majority and the Arab Minority in Israel.* Jerusalem: Van Leer Foundation.

Hartz, Louis. 1955. *The Liberal Tradition in America.* New York: Harcourt, Brace and World.

Heimsath, Charles H. 1964. *Indian Nationalism and Hindu Social Reform.* Princeton: Princeton University Press.

Herberg, Will. 1974 "America's Civil Religion." In *American Civil Religion.* Ed. Russell E. Richey and Donald G. Jones. New York: Harper and Row.

Hirschl, Ran. 1998. "Israel's 'Constitutional Revolution': The Legal Interpretation of Entrenched Civil Liberties in an Emerging Neo-Liberal Economic Order." 46 *American Journal of Comparative Law* 427.

Hofnung, Menachem. 1996. "The Unintended Consequences of Unplanned Constitutional Reform: Constitutional Politics in Israel." 44 *American Journal of Comparative Law* 585.

Huntington, Samuel P. 1981. *American Politics: The Promise of Disharmony.* Cambridge: Harvard University Press.

Hurd, Heidi. 1995. "The Levitation of Liberalism." 105 *Yale Law Journal* 795.

Iyer, V. R. Krishna. 1984. *Law and Religion.* New Delhi: Deep and Deep Publications.

Jacobsohn, Gary Jeffrey. 1977. *Pragmatism, Statesmanship, and the Supreme Court.* Ithaca: Cornell University Press.

———. 1993. *Apple of Gold: Constitutionalism in Israel and the United States.* Princeton: Princeton University Press.

———. 1996. "Three Models of Secular Constitutional Development: India, Israel, and the United States." 10 *Studies in American Political Development* 1.

Jaffa, Harry V. 1959. *Crisis of the House Divided: An Interpretation of the Issues in the Lincoln-Douglas Debates.* Garden City: Doubleday.

Jaffrelot, Christophe. 1995. *The Hindu Nationalist Movement in India.* New York: Columbia University Press.

Jain, Kiran, and P. C. Jain. 1998. *Chawla's Elections: Law and Practice.* New Delhi: Bahri Brothers.

Jaitley, Arun. 1995. "Judicial Backlash." In *The Ayodhya Reference: Supreme Court Judgement and Commentaries.* Ed. Arun Shourie. New Delhi: Voice of India.

Jhingta, Hans Raj. 1996. *Corrupt Practices in Elections: A Study Under the Representation of the People Act, 1951.* New Delhi: Deep and Deep Publications.

Johnson, Chalmers. 1966. *Revolutionary Change.* Boston: Little Brown and Company.

Juergensmeyer, Mark. 1993, *The New Cold War? Religious Nationalism Confronts the Secular State.* Berkeley: University of California Press.

Kapadia, K. M. 1966. *Marriage and Family in India.* Oxford: Oxford University Press.

Kapur, Ratna, and Brenda Kossman. 1995. "Communalizing Gender Engendering Community: Women, Legal Discourse and the Saffron Agenda." In *Women and the Hindu Right: A Collection of* Essays. Ed. Tanika Sarkar and Urvashi Butalia. New Delhi: Pauls Press.

Karst, Kenneth. 1989. *Belonging to America: Equal Citizenship and the Constitution*. New Haven: Yale University Press.

Karunakaran, K. P. 1965. *Religion and Political Awakening in India*. Delhi: Meenakshi Prakasham.

Kashyap, Subhash. 1993. *Delinking Religion and Politics*. New Delhi: Vimot Publishers.

Kathuria, Harbir Singh. 1990. *President's Rule in India: 1967–1989*. New Delhi: Uppal Publishing House.

Kessler, Sanford. 1994. *Tocqueville's Civil Religion: American Christianity and the Prospects for Freedom*. Albany: State University of New York Press.

Khilnani, Sunil. 1997. *The Idea of India*. New York: Farrar Straus Giroux.

Kishwar, Madhu. 1998. *Religion at the Service of Nationalism and Other Essays*. New Delhi: Oxford University Press.

Kohut, Andrew, John C. Green, Scott Keeter, and Robert C. Toth. 2000. *The Diminishing Divide: Religion's Changing Role in American Politics*. Washington: Brookings Institution Press.

Kosmin, Barry, and Seymour Lachman. 1993. *One Nation Under God: Religion in Contemporary American Society*. New York: Harmony Books.

Kretzmer, David. 1990. The Legal Status of the Arabs in Israel. Boulder: Westview Press.

Kuhn, Thomas. 1970. *The Structure of Scientific Revolutions*. Chicago: University of Chicago Press.

Kumar, Ravinder. 1987. "The Ideological and Structural Unity of Indian Civilization." In *Nation Building in India: Socio-Economic Factors*. Ed. R. C. Dutt. New Delhi: Lancer International.

Kymlicka, Will. 1989. *Liberalism, Community, and Culture*. Oxford: Oxford University Press.

———. 1995a. *Multicultural Citizenship: A Liberal Theory of Minority Rights*. Oxford: Oxford University Press.

Kymlicka, Will, ed. 1995b. *The Rights of Minority Cultures*. Oxford: Oxford University Press.

Laycock, Douglas. 1991. "The Remnants of Free Exercise." 1990 *The Supreme Court Review*. Chicago: University of Chicago Press.

Leibowitz, Yeshayahu. 1992. *Judaism, Human Values, and the Jewish State*. Cambridge: Harvard University Press.

Lerner, Ralph. 1968. "The Supreme Court as Republican Schoolmaster." 1967 *The Supreme Court Review*. Chicago: University of Chicago Press.

Levinson, Sanford, ed. 1995. *Responding to Imperfection: The Theory and Practice of Constitutional Amendment*. Princeton: Princeton University Press.

Levy, Leonard. 1986. *The Establishment Clause: Religion and the First Amendment*. New York: MacMillan.

Liebman, Charles S., and Eliezer Don-Yehiya. 1983. *Civil Religion in Israel: Traditional Judaism and Political Culture in the Jewish State*. Berkeley: University of California Press.

———. 1989. *Religion and Politics in Israel*. Bloomington: Indiana University Press.

Lieten, G. K. 1996. "Inclusive Views of Religion: A Rural Discourse in Uttar Pradesh." *Economic and Political Weekly*, 8 June.

Lijphart, Arend. 1996. "The Puzzle of Indian Democracy: A Consociational Interpretation." 90 *American Political Science Review.*

Lincoln, Abraham. 1953. *The Collected Works of Abraham Lincoln*, vol. 2. Ed. Roy Basler. New Brunswick: Rutgers University Press.

Lincoln, Bruce. 1985. "Notes Toward a Theory of Religion and Revolution." In *Religion, Rebellion, Revolution.* Ed. Bruce Lincoln. New York: St. Martin's Press.

Lipkin, Robert Justin. 1989. "The Anatomy of Constitutional Revolutions." 68 *Nebraska Law Review* 701.

Lipner, Julius. 1994. *Hindus: Their Religious Beliefs and Practices.* London: Routledge.

Lipset, Seymour Martin. 1990. *Continental Divide: The Values and Institutions of the United States and Canada.* New York: Routledge.

Locke, John. 1963. *A Letter Concerning Toleration.* The Hague: Martinus Nijhoff.

Lodge, Henry Cabot, ed. 1888. *The Federalist.* New York: G. P. Putnam's Sons.

Lok Sabha Debates. 1993. 10th series, vol. 23, no. 4, July 29.

Long, Carolyn N. 2000. *Religious Freedom and Indian Rights: The Case of Oregon v Smith.* Lawrence: University Press of Kansas.

Loomis, Charles P., and Zona K. Loomis, eds. 1969. *Socio-Economic Change and the Religious Factor in India: An Indian Symposium on Max Weber.* New Delhi: Affiliated East-West Press.

Lupu, Ira C. 1989. "Where Rights Begin: The Problem of Burdens on the Free Exercise of Religion." 102 *Harvard Law Review* 933.

Lustick, Ian. 1980. *Arabs in the Jewish State: Israel's Control of a National Minority.* Austin: University of Texas Press.

Macedo, Stephen. 2000. *Diversity and Distrust: Civic Education in a Multicultural Democracy.* Cambridge: Harvard University Press.

Madan, T. N. 1983. "The Historical Significance of Secularism in India." In *Secularization in Multi-Religious Societies.* Ed. S. C. Dube and V. N. Basilov. New Delhi: Concept Publishing Co.

———. 1984. "Judicial Activism: An Essential Part of the Judicial Function." 11 *India Bar Review* 246.

———. 1987. "Secularism in Its Place." *Journal of Asia Studies* 46.

———. 1997. *Modern Myths, Locked Minds: Secularism and Fundamentalism in India.* Delhi: Oxford University Press.

Maddigan, Michael M. 1993. "The Establishment Clause, Civil Religion and the Public Church," *California Law Review* 81.

Mahajan, Gurpreet. 1998. *Identities and Rights: Aspects of Liberal Democracy in India.* Delhi: Oxford University Press.

Mahmood, Tahir. 1995. *Uniform Civil Code: Fictions and Facts.* New Delhi: India and Islam Research Council.

———. 1996. "Supreme Court's *Hindutva* Judgments of 1995–96: Reflections in Retrospect," *Religion and Law Review.* vol. 5.

Malhotra, V. K. 1996. "Religion and Politics." *Hindustan Times*, 2 February. Reprinted in *Religion and Law Review*, 209. Ed. Tahir Mahmood.

Mandel, Michael. 1999. "Democracy and the New Constitutionalism in Israel." 33 *Israel Law Review* 259.

Mansfield Jr., Harvey C. 1987. "The Religious Issue and the Origin of Modern Constitutionalism." In *How Does the Constitution Protect Religious Freedom?* Ed. Robert A. Goldwin and Art Kaufman. Washington: American Enterprise Institute for Public Policy Research.

Mansfield, John H. 1984. "The Religion Clauses of the First Amendment and the Philosophy of the Constitution." *California Law Review* 72.

———. 1989. "Religious Speech Under Indian Law." In *Comparative Constitutional Law*. Ed. Mahendra P. Singh. Lucknow: Eastern Book.

Margalit, Avishai, and Joseph Raz. 1995. "National Self-Determination." In *The Rights of Minority Cultures*. Ed. Will Kymlica. Oxford: Oxford University Press.

Marshall, William P. 1991. "In Defense of *Smith* and Free Exercise Revisionism." 58 *University of Chicago Law Review* 308.

Marty, Martin. 1969. *The Modern Schism: Three Paths to the Secular.* New York: Harper and Row.

———. 1987. *Religion and Republic: The American Circumstance.* Boston: Beacon Press.

McCloskey, Robert G. 1994. *The American Supreme Court.* Chicago: University of Chicago Press.

McConnell, Michael W. 1986. "Accommodation of Religion." 1985 *The Supreme Court Review.* Chicago: University of Chicago Press.

———. 1990a. "Free Exercise Revisionism and the *Smith* Decision." 57 *University of Chicago Law Review* 1109.

———. 1990b. "The Origins and Historical Understanding of Free Exercise of Religion." *Harvard Law Review* 103.

———1992. "Accommodation of Religion: An Update and a Response to the Critics." *George Washington Law Review* 60.

Mead, Sidney E. 1975. *The Nation with the Soul of a Church.* New York: Harper and Row.

Melman, Yossi. 1992. *The New Israelis: An Intimate View of a Changing People.* New York: Birch Lane Press.

Merritt, Deborah Jones. 1988. "The Guarantee Clause and State Autonomy: Federalism for a Third Century." 88 *Columbia Law Review* 1.

Mirsky, Yehuda. 1986. "Civil Religion and the Establishment Clause." *Yale Law Journal* 95.

Mitra, Subrata. 1989. "The Limits of Accommodation: Nehru, Religion, and the State in India." *South Asia Research* 9.

Monsma, Stephen V., and J. Christopher Soper. 1997. *The Challenge of Pluralism: Church and State in Five Democracies.* Lanham: Rowman and Littlefield.

Montesquieu. 1966. *The Spirit of the Laws.* New York: Hafner Publishing.

Muralidharan, Sukumar. 2000. "Raising the Stakes." In *Frontline* 17:13 (June 24–July 7).

Murphy, Walter F. 1978. "The Art of Constitutional Interpretation: A Preliminary Showing." In *Essays on the Constitution of the United States*. Ed. M. Judd Harmon. Port Washington: Kennikat Press.

———. 1995. "Merlin's Memory: The Past and Future Imperfect of the Once and Future Polity." In *Responding to Imperfection: The Theory and Practice of Constitutional Amendment*. Ed. Sanford Levinson. Princeton: Princeton University Press.

Nahmod, Sheldon. 1991. "The Sacred Flag and the First Amendment." *Indiana Law Journal* 66.

Nandy, Ashis. 1988. "The Politics of Secularism and the Recovery of Religious Tolerance." *Alternatives* 13.

Nandy, Ashis, Shikva Trivedy, Shail Mayaram, and Achyut Yagnit. 1997. *Creating a Nationality: The Ramjanmabhumi Movement and Fear of the Self*. Delhi: Oxford University Press.

Narain, Harsh. 1990. *Myths of Composite Culture and Equality of Religions*. New Delhi: Voice of India.

Nauriya, Anil. 1996. "The Hindutva Judgments: A Warning Signal." 31 *Economic and Political Weekly* 1, 6 January.

Nehru, Jawaharlal. 1997. *The Discovery of India*. New York: Oxford University Press.

Neuhaus, Richard John. 1990. "Polygamy, Peyote, and the Public Peace." *First Things*, October.

Newbould, Brian. 1992. *Schubert and the Symphony: A New Perspective*. London: Toccata Press.

Noorani, A. G. 1995. "A Shocking Judgment with Selectivity in Quotation." *The Statesman*, 26–27 December. Reprinted in *Religion and Law Review*. vol. 5, 1996.

———. 1996. *Indian Affairs: The Constitutional Dimension*. Delhi: Konark Publishers.

———. 2000. "With a Partisan Motive." *Frontline*. 17:4 (19 February).

Nord, Warren A. 1995. *Religion & American Education*. Chapel Hill: University of North Carolina Press.

Nussbaum, Martha. 1997. "Religion and Women's Human Rights." In *Religion and Contemporary Liberalism*. Ed. Paul J. Weithman. Notre Dame: University of Notre Dame Press.

O'Sullivan, John. 1994. "America's Identity Crisis." *National Review*, November 21.

Paine, Thomas. 1985. *The Rights of Man*. New York: Penguin Books.

Panikkar, K. N. 1997. *Communal Threat, Secular Challenge*. Madras: Earthworm Books.

Parekh, Bhikhu. 1992. "The Poverty of Indian Political Theory." *History of Political Thought* 13.

Parliamentary Debates—Parliament of India. 1985. vol. 13, no. 3.

Patnaik, Arun, and K.S.R.V.S. Chalam. 1966. "The Ideology and Politics of Hindutva." In *Region, Religion, Caste, Gender and Culture in Contemporary India*. vol. 3. Ed. T. V. Sathyamurthy. Delhi: Oxford University Press.

Patton, Marcie J. 1995. "Constitutionalism and Political Culture in Turkey." In *Political Culture and Constitutionalism: A Comparative Approach*. Ed. Daniel P. Franklin and Michael J. Baun. Armonk: M. E. Sharpe.

Peled, Yoav. 1992. "Ethnic Democracy and the Legal Constitution of Citizenship: Arab Citizens of the Jewish State." *American Political Science Review* 86.

Perry, Michael. 1997. *Religion in Politics: Constitutional and Moral Perspectives*. Oxford: Oxford University Press.

Post, Robert. 1986. "The Social Foundations of Defamation Law." *California Law Review* 34.

Rabinovich, Itamar, and Jehuda Reinharz, eds. 1984. *Israel in the Middle East: Documents and Readings on Society, Politics and Foreign Relations, 1948-Present*. New York: Oxford University Press.

Radhakrishnan, S. 1995. *Religion and Society*. New Delhi: HarperCollins.

Rajan, Nalini. 1998. *Secularism, Democracy, Justice: Implications of Rawlsian Principles in India*. New Delhi: Sage.

Ram, P. R. 1996. "A Way of Life?" *Economic and Political Weekly*. 31:9 (21 March).

Randall, James G. 1963. *Constitutional Problems Under Lincoln*. Gloucester: Peter Smith.

Rao, B. Shiva, ed. 1966. *The Framing of India's Constitution: Selected Documents*—vol. 1. New Delhi: Indian Institute of Public Administration.

Rawls, John. 1993. *Political Liberalism*. New York: Columbia University Press.

Reddy, P. Ram. 1996. "Verdict Needs Reconsideration by Full Court." *The Hindu*, 20 February. Reprinted in *Religion and Law Review*. vol. 5.

Rekhi, V. S. 1993. "Religion, Politics and Law in Contemporary India: Judicial Doctrine in Critical Perspective." In *Religion and Law in Independent India*. Ed. Robert D. Baird. New Delhi: Manohar.

Rosenberg, Gerald. 1991. *The Hollow Hope: Can Courts Bring About Social Change?* Chicago: University of Chicago Press.

Rosenblum, Nancy L. 2000. "Pluralism, Integralism, and Political Theories of Accommodation." In *Obligations of Citizenship and Demands of Faith: Religious Accommodation in Pluralist Democracies*. Ed. Nancy L. Rosenblum. Princeton: Princeton University Press.

Rubinstein, Amnon. 1967. "Law and Religion in Israel." *Israel Law Review* 2.

Rudolph, Lloyd I., and Susanne Hoeber Rudolph. 1987. *In Pursuit of Lakshmi: The Political Economy of the Indian State*. Chicago: University of Chicago Press.

Rudolph, Susanne Hoeber. 1998. "Contesting Legal Pluralism in India: The Law and Politics of the Uniform Civil Code." Paper presented at the Annual Meeting of the American Political Science Association, Boston.

Rutherford, Jane. 1996. "Equality as the Primary Constitutional Value: The Case for Applying Employment Discrimination Laws to Religion." 81 *Cornell Law Review* 1049.

Saad, Lydia, and Leslie McAneny. 1994. "Most Americans Think Religion Losing Clout in the 1990s." *Gallup Monthly Poll*, April.

Sandel, Michael J. 1993. "Freedom of Conscience or Freedom of Choice?" In *Religious Liberty in the Supreme Court*. Ed. Terry Eastland. Washington: Ethics and Public Policy Center.

———. 1996. *Democracy's Discontent: America in Search of a Public Philosophy*. Cambridge: Harvard University Press.

Sarkar, Sumit. 1996. "Indian Nationalism and the Politics of Hindutva." In *Contesting the Nation: Religion, Community, and the Politics of Democracy in India*. Ed. David Ludden. Philadelphia: University of Pennsylvania Press.

Sathe, S. P. 1995. "Uniform Civil Code: Implications of Supreme Court Intervention." *Economic and Political Weekly*, 2 September.

Savarkar, V. D. 1967. *Historic Statements*. Bombay: G. P. Parchure.

———. 1969. *Hindutva*. Bombay: Veer Savarkar Prakashan.

Schattschneider, E. E. 1975. *The Semisovereign People: A Realist's View of Democracy in America*. Hinsdale: Dryden Press.

Schrecker, Paul. 1966. "Revolution as a Problem in the Philosophy of History." In *Nomos VIII: Revolution*. Ed. Carl J. Friedrich. New York: Atherton Press.

Secularism Alert. 1998. New Delhi: SAHMET.

Shapiro, Martin. 1989. "Corruption, Freedom and Equality in Campaign Financing." 18 *Hofstra Law Review* 385.

Sharot, Stephen. 1991. "Judaism and the Secularization Debate." *Sociological Analysis* 52.

Sheleff, Leon. 1995. "Human Rights, Western Values and Tribal Traditions: Between Recognition and Repugnancy, Between Monogamy and Polygamy." *Tel Aviv Studies in Law* 12.

Shklar, Judith N. 1990. *American Citizenship: The Quest for Inclusion*. Cambridge: Harvard University Press.

Shourie, Arun. 1995. "Steps Towards Secularism," in *The Ayodhya Reference: The Supreme Court Judgement and Commentaries*. Ed. Arun Shourie. New Delhi: Voice of India.

———. 1996. "The Hindutva Judgments: The Distance That Remain." *BJP Web Page*, 24 April.

———. 1997a. *A Secular Agenda*. New Delhi: HarperCollins.

———. 1997b. *Worshipping False Gods: Ambedkar and the Facts Which Have Been Erased*. New Delhi: ASA Publications.

Silberman, Charles. 1985. *A Certain People: American Jews and Their Lives Today*. New York: Summit Books.

Sircar, D. R. 1957. *Inscriptions of Ashoka*. Delhi: Publications Division.

Smart, Ninian. 1989. "India, Sri Lanka and Religion." In *Religion and Political Power*. Ed. Bustavo Benevides and M. W. Daly. Albany: State University of New York Press.

Smith, Anthony D. 1991. *National Identity*. Reno: University of Nevada Press.

Smith, Donald Eugene. 1963. *India as a Secular State*. Princeton: Princeton University Press.

———. 1970. *Religion and Political Development*. Boston: Little, Brown and Co.

Smith, Michael E. 1984. "The Special Place of Religion in the Constitution." 1983 *The Supreme Court Review*. Chicago: University of Chicago Press.

Smith, Rogers. 1988. "The 'American Creed' and American Identity: The Limits of Liberal Citizenship in the United States." *Western Political Quarterly* 41.

———. 1997. *Civic Ideals: Conflicting Visions of Citizenship in U.S. History.* New Haven: Yale University Press.

Smolla, Rodney A. 1998. "The Free Exercise of Religion After the Fall: The Case for Intermediate Scrutiny." 39 *William and Mary Law Review* 925.

Smooha, Sammy. 1978. *Israel: Pluralism and Conflict.* Berkeley: University of California Press.

———. 1993. "Part of the Problem or Part of the Solution: National Security and the Arab Minority." In *National Security and Democracy in Israel.* Ed. Avner Yaniv. Boulder: Lynne Rienner Publishers.

Sobel, Zvi, and Benjamin Beit-Hallahmi, eds. 1991. *Tradition, Innovation, Conflict: Jewishness and Judaism in Contemporary Israel.* Albany: State University of New York Press.

Sorabjee, Soli J. 1990. "Equality in the United States and India." In *Constitutionalism and Rights: The Influence of the United States Constitution Abroad.* Ed. Louis Henkin and Albert J. Rosenthal. New York: Columbia University Press.

———. 1995. "Appeal to Religion: Supreme Court's View." *Indian Express*, 18 December. Reprinted in *Religion and Politics.* Ed. Tahir Mahmood.

Spinner, Jeff. 1994. *The Boundaries of Citizenship: Race, Ethnicity, and Nationality in the Liberal State.* Baltimore: Johns Hopkins Press.

Srivastava, Dhirendva K. 1992. *Religious Freedom in India: A Historical and Constitutional Study.* New Delhi: Deep and Deep Publications.

Stern, Robert. 1993. *Changing India: Bourgeois Revolution on the Subcontinent.* Cambridge: Cambridge University Press.

Stolzenberg, Nomi Maya. 1993. " 'He Drew a Circle That Shut Me Out': Assimilation, Indoctrination, and the Paradox of a Liberal Education." *Harvard Law Review* 106.

———. 1997. "A Tale of Two Villages: (Or, Legal Realism Comes to Town)." In *Ethnicity and Group Rights.* Ed. Ian Shapiro and Will Kymlicka. New York: New York University Press.

Subhash, Manji. 1988. *Rights of Religious Minorities in India.* New Delhi: Patel Enterprises.

Sullivan, Kathleen M. 1992. "Religion and Liberal Democracy." In *The Bill of Rights in the Modern State.* Ed. Geoffrey R. Stone, Richard A. Epstein, and Cass R. Sunstein. Chicago: University of Chicago Press.

Sumner, Graham William. 1907. *Folkways.* Boston: Ginn and Co.

Sunstein, Cass R. 2001. *Designing Democracy: What Constitutions Do.* Oxford: Oxford University Press.

Sur, A. K. 1973. *Sex and Marriage in India: An Ethnohistorical Survey.* Bombay: Allied Publishers.

Tabory, Ephraim. 1981. "Hate and Religion: Religious Conflict Among Jews in Israel." *Journal of Church and State* 11.

Taylor, Charles, et al. 1992. *Multiculturalism and "The Politics of Recognition."* Princeton: Princeton University Press.

Tepker, Jr., Harry F. "Hallucinations of Neutrality in the Oregon Peyote Case." 16 *American Indian Law Review* 1.

Thakur, Ramesh. 1993. "Ayodhya and the Politics of India's Secularism." *Asian Survey* 33.

Thapur, Romila. 1997. *As'oka and the Decline of the Mauryas.* Delhi: Oxford University Press.

Tharoor, Shashi. 1997. *India: From Midnight to the Millennium.* New York: Arcade Publishing.

Thiemann, Ronald F. 1996. *Religion in Public Life: A Dilemma for Democracy.* Washington: Georgetown University Press.

Thompson, Dennis F. 1995. *Ethics in Congress: From Individual to Institutional Corruption.* Washington: Brookings Institution.

Tocqueville, Alexis de. 1945. *Democracy in America.* New York: Random House.

———. 1962. *Oeuvres Completes, vol. 3, Ecrits Et Discours Politiques.* Ed. J.-P. Mayer. Paris: Gallimard. Translated for the author by Lois Cooper.

Tribe, Laurence H. 1988. *American Constitutional Law.* Mineola: Foundation Press.

Tripathi, Keshari. 1974. *The Representation of the People Act, 1951.* Allahabad: Dardeval Publishing House.

Tushnet, Mark. 1999. "The Possibilities of Comparative Constitutional Law." *Yale Law Journal* 108.

Vanaik, Achin. 1997. *The Furies of Indian Communalism.* London: Verso.

Van DerVeer, Peter. 1994. *Religious Nationalism: Hindus and Muslims in India.* Berkeley: University of California Press.

Van Wagoner, Richard S. 1989. *Mormon Polygamy: A History.* Salt Lake City: Signature Books.

Varma, Pavan K. 1999. *The Great Indian Middle Class.* New Delhi: Penguin Books.

Varma, Vishwamath Prasad. 1964. *Modern Indian Political Thought.* Agra: Lakshmi Narain Agarwal.

Varshney, Ashutosh. 1993. "Contested Meanings: India's National Identity, Hindu Nationalism, and the Politics of Anxiety." *Daedalus* 122.

Venkatachalia, M. N. 2000. "There are Some Things of Eternal Verity." Interview in *Frontline* 17:4. February 19.

Verma, J. S. 1997. "Judicial Activism in an Asian Democracy." Address delivered at the 15th Lawasia Conference, Manila, Philippines, 27 August.

———. 1999. " 'Young' Ram of 75 Years." *Symbiosis Law Times*, February.

Verma, S. L. 1986. *Towards Theory of Positive Secularism.* Jaipur: Rawat Publications.

Vile, John R. 1995. "The Case Against Implicit Limits on the Constitutional Amending Process." In *Responding to Imperfection.* Ed. Sanford Levinson. Princeton: Princeton University Press.

Waldron, Jeremy. 1993. "Religious Contributions in Public Deliberation." 30 *San Diego Law Review* 817.

Walker, Graham. 1994. "The New Mixed Constitution: A Response to Liberal Debility and Constitutional Deadlock in Eastern Europe." *Polity* 26.

Wallace, Anthony F. C. 1956. "Revitalization Movements." 58 *American Anthropologist.*

Walzer, Michael. 1992. *What It Means to Be an American.* New York: Marsilio.

Walzer, Michael. 1994. *Thick and Thin: Moral Argument at Home and Abroad.* Notre Dame: Notre Dame Press.

——. 1997. *On Toleration.* New Haven: Yale University Press.

Way, Frank, and Barbara J. Burt. 1983. "Religious Marginality and the Free Exercise Clause." *American Political Science Review* 77.

Weber, Max. 1958. *The Religion of India: The Sociology of Hinduism and Buddhism.* Glencoe: Free Press.

Weiler, Gershon. 1988. *Jewish Theocracy.* Leiden: E. J. Brill.

Weiner, Myron. 1960. "The Politics of South Asia." In *The Politics of the Developing Areas.* Ed. Gabriel A. Almond and James S. Coleman. Princeton: Princeton University Press.

Weinrib, Lorraine Eisenstat. 1999. "Canada's Constitutional Revolution: From Legislative to Constitutional State." 33 *Israel Law Review* 13.

Weissbrod, Lilly. 1983. "Religion as National Identity in a Secular Society." *Review of Religious Research* 24.

Weithman, Paul J. 1997. "Religion and the Liberalism of Reasoned Respect." In *Religion and Contemporary Liberalism.* Ed. Paul J. Weithman. Notre Dame: University of Notre Dame Press.

Welch, Michael. 2000. *Flag Burning: Moral Panic and the Criminalization of Protest.* New York: Aldine De Gruyter.

White, Morton. 1978. *The Philosophy of the American Revolution.* New York: Oxford University Press.

Wiecek, William M. 1972. *The Guarantee Clause of the U.S. Constitution.* Ithaca: Cornell University Press.

Williams, David, and Susan Williams. 1991. "Volitionism and Religious Liberty." *Cornell University Law Review* 76.

Wirsing, Robert G., ed. 1981. *Protection of Ethnic Minorities.* New York: Pergemon Press.

Wolgast, Elizabeth H. 1994. "The Demands of Public Reason." 94 *Columbia Law Review* 1936.

Wunder, John. 1994. *"Retained by the People": A History of American Indians and the Bill of Rights.* Oxford: Oxford University Press.

Yalman, Nur. 1991. "On Secularism and Its Critics: Notes on Turkey, India and Iran." *Contributions to Indian Sociology* 25.

Yosifof v Attorney-General. 1962. In *Selected Judgments of the Supreme Court of Israel—vol. 1. 1948–53.* Ed. David Goitein. Jerusalem: The Ministry of Justice.

Cases

India

Appa. See *State of Bombay v Appa.*

Atheist Society of India v Government of A.P., AIR AP 320 (1992).

Ayodhya Reference Case. See *Dr. M. Ismail Faruqui and Others v Union of India and Others.*

Bommai. See *S. R. Bommai v Union of India.*

Comm. H.R.E. v Swamiar, AIR SC 282 (1954).

Dr. M. Ismail Faruqui and Others v Union of India and Others, 6 SCC 360 (1994).
Golak Nath v State of Punjab, A SC 1643 (1967).
Hindutva Cases. See *Prabhoo v Kunte*.
Indira Gandhi v Raj Narain, AIR SC 2299 (1975).
Indra Sawhney v Union of India, AIR 1993 SC 477 (1992).
Joshi. See *Manohar Joshi v Nitin B. Patel*.
Kesavananda v State of Kerala, A SC 1461 (FB) (1973).
Manohar Joshi v Nitin B. Patil, 8 SC 646, 677 (1995).
Minerva Mills Ltd. v Union of India, A SC 1789 (1980).
Mohd. Ahmed Khan v Shah Bano Begum, AIR SC 945 (1985).
Mohd. Aslam v Union of India and Others, WP (Civil) No. 135 (1996).
Prabhoo v Kunte, 1 Sup Ct 130 (1996).
Ramakant Mayekar v Celine D'Silva, Election Petition No. 21 of 1990 decided on 5th/6th August 1991 by S. N. Variava, J. of the Bombay High Court.
Ram Prasad v State of U.P., AIR Allahabad 411 (1957).
Ratilal v State of Bombay, AIR SC 388 (1954).
Saifuddin v State of Bombay, AIR SC 853 (1962).
Sarla Mudgal v Union of India, AIR SC 1531 (1995).
Shah Bano. See *Mohd. Ahmed Khan v Shah Bano Begum*.
Shrikekha Vidharthi v State of U.P., AIR SC 537 (1991).
S. R. Bommai v Union of India, 3 SC 1 (1994).
St. Xavier's College v State of Gujarat, AIR SC (1974).
State of Bombay v Appa, AIR Bombay 84 (1952).
State of Rajasthan v Union of India, 1 SCR 1 (1978).
Thackeray. See *Prahoo v Kunte*.
Yagnapurushdasji v Muldas, SCt J 502 (1966).
Yulitha Hyde v State, AIR Orissa 116 (1973).
Ziyauddin Burkharrudin Bukhari v Brigmohan Ramdass Mehra and Others, 2 SCC 17 (1976).

United States

Abington v Schempp, 374 US 203 (1963).
Abrams v United States, 250 US 616, 630 (1919).
Aguilar v Felton, 473 US 402 (1985).
Allegheny County v Greater Pittsburgh ACLU, 492 US 573 (1989).
Austin v Michigan Chamber of Commerce, 494 US 652 (1989).
Barnette. See *West Virginia v Barnette*.
Beason. See *Davis v Beason*.
Board of Education v Grumet, 114 SCt 2481 (1994).
Board of Education of the Kiryas Joel Village School District v Grumet, 512 US 687 (1994).
Boerne v Flores, 117 SCt 2157 (1997).
Bob Jones University v United States, 461 US 574 (1983).
Buckley v Valeo, 424 US 1 (1976).
Cantwell v Connecticut, 310 US 296 (1940).
Church of the Lukumi Babalu Aye v Hialeah, 508 US 520 (1993).

City of Boerne v Flores, 521 US 507 (1997).

Cleveland v United States, 329 US 14 (1946).

Coleman v Tennessee, 97 US 509 (1863).

Committee for Public Education v Nyquist, 413 US 756 (1973).

Davis v Beason, 133 US 333 (1890).

Employment Division, Oregon Department of Human Resources v Smith, 494 US 872 (1990).

Everson v Board of Education, 330 US 1 (1947).

Fay v New York, 332 US 261 (1946).

Federal Election Commission v NCPAC, 470 US 480 (1985).

Garcia v San Antonio Metropolitan Transit Authority, 469 US 528 (1985).

Gitlow v New York, 268 US 652 (1925).

Jacobellis v Ohio, 378 US 184, 197 (1964).

Kiryas Joel. See *Board of Education of the Kiryas Joel Village School District v Grumet.*

Late Corporation of the Church of Jesus Christ of Latter-Day Saints et al v United States, 136 US 1 (1890).

Lemon v Kurtzman, 403 US 602 (1971).

Luther v Borden, 48 US 1 (1849).

Lyng v Northwest Indian Cemetery Protective Assn., 485 US 439 (1988).

Lynch v Donnelly, 465 US 668 (1984.).

Marbury v Madison, 5 US (1 Cranch) 137 (1803).

McCollum v Board of Education, 33 US 203 (1948).

McGowan v Maryland, 366 US 420 (1961).

People v Woody, 61 Cal2d 716 (1964).

Plessy v Ferguson, 163 US 537 (1896).

Printz v United States, 521 US 98 (1997).

Raines v Byrd, 117 SCt 2312 (1997).

Reynolds v United States, 98 US 145 (1878).

Romer v Evans, 517 US 620 (1996).

Rosenberger v University of Virginia, 515 US 819 (1995).

Serbian Orthodox Diocese v Milivojevich, 426 US 696 (1976).

Sherbert v Verner, 374 US 398 (1963).

Smith. See *Employment Division, Oregon Department of Human Resources v Smith.*

Southern Pacific Co. v Jensen, 244 US 205 (1917).

Texas Monthly Inc. v Bullock, 489 US 1 (1989).

United States v Seeger, 380 US 163 (1965).

United States v Thind, 261 US 204 (1923).

Walz v Tax Commission of the City of New York, 397 US 664 (1970).

Watson v Jones, 80 US 679 (1871).

West Virginia v Barnette, 319 US 624 (1943).

Wisconsin v Yoder, 406 US 205 (1971).

Israel

Ben Shalom v Central Committee for the Elections of the Twelfth Knesset, 43(4) PD 221 (1988).

Bergman v Minister of Finance, 23(1) PD 693 (1969).
Gal. See United Mizrachi Bank plc v Migdal Cooperative Village.
Kol ha'am Co. Ltd. v Minister of Interior, 7 PD 871 (1953).
Neiman v Chairman of Central Elections Committee, 42 PD 4 177 (1988).
Ressler v Minister of Defense, 42(2) PD 441, 458 (1988).
Rogozinsky v State of Israel, 26(1) PD 129 (1972).
Rufeisen v Minister of Interior, 16 PD 2428 (1962).
Shakdiel v Minister of Religious Affairs, 42(2) PD 221 (1988).
Tamarin v State of Israel, 26(1) PD 197 (1972).
United Mizrachi Bank plc v Migdal Cooperative Village, 49(4) PD 221 (1995).
Yosifof v Attorney-General, 5 PD 481 (1951).
Zeev v Gubernik, 1 PD 85 (1948).

Australia

Adelaide Co. of Jehovah's Witnesses v The Commonwealth, 67 CLR 116 (1943).

INDEX

contextual secularism argument, 57. *See also* secularism

corrupt practices: application of to religiously framed campaign rhetoric, 172; conceptual expansion of, 172–76; connection between viewpoint neutrality and, 181–85; controversial resolution of, 15; court decisions on constitutionality of, 14; used to describe religiously inspired speech in electoral campaigns, 183; hypothetical responses of U.S. Supreme Court to American version of RPA and, 185–88; Indian elections overturned due to, 192–93; Indian law and approach of, 162–63; Indian religious speech freedom and, 14, 168–70, 172–73, 175–76; Indian Supreme Court judgments defining, 163–70; voided election of Manohar Joshi on grounds of, 194–97. *See also* free speech; RPA (Representation of the People Act) [India, 1951]

Cossman, Brenda, 208

culture: American Indian, and concepts of holy, 41; aristos and demos strata of, 254; distinguishing between political and constitutional, 23n.7; ethnorepublicanism of Israeli political, 78–79; Hinduism as "way of life" and, 35–36, 201–2, 206–9, 219; role of judiciary in free exercise cases and diverse, 273; secular understanding of composite, 261; as way of life, 28

Dahl, Robert, 240

Daniel, Brother, 47, 86

Davis v Beason (U.S.), 31–32, 59–65, 96

Declaration of Independence (Israel), 45, 46, 87n.104

Declaration of Independence (U.S.): incompatibility of slavery issue with, 135; natural rights included in, 141; secularism and language of rough draft of, 152n.80

deliberative theory of liberal democratic governance, 184

democracy: commitment of Hindu nationalism to majoritarian, 279; Israeli ethnic, 78–79; political unification/division as part of, 155; role of judiciary in free exercise cases and, 273; Tocqueville's defense of religion in, 39; "tyranny of the majority" and, 279; varieties of, 25–26. *See also* political liberalism

Derrett, J. Duncan M., 31, 97

Desai, Ashok, 197, 198, 206

Dharma: Ashokan understanding of, 7, 8; connection between caste system and, 7–8

Dhavan, Rajeev, 92, 100, 101, 192, 258

Directive Principles (India), 260

The Discovery of India (Nehru), 283

Don-Yehiya, Eliezer, 46

Douglas, Stephen, 142

Douglas, William O., 50, 71, 99, 100, 104

Dred Scott decision (U.S.), 142, 215n.85, 269

Dworkin, Ronald, 15, 191, 275

Eisenhower, Dwight, 67

Eisenstadt, S. N., 88, 89

Eisgruber, Christopher L., 69, 272, 277, 281

Election Commission (India), 174

Elon, Menachen, 76, 79, 87

Ely, John Hart, 194

Employment Division v Smith. See *Smith* case (U.S.)

encompassing group, 28–29

Epstein, Richard, 102, 274

equal civil rights: distinction between equal protection and, 73–74; to participation, 184; relationship between political identity and Israeli, 78–88; standards shaping religious liberty and, 73–74. *See also* citizenship

equal protection: "the anticaste principle" and, 91n.2; application to Israel, 74–88; assimilative secularism and constitutional, 277–78; comparison of U.S./Indian religious personal law and, 104–5; distinction between equal civil rights and, 73–74; Establishment Clause granting, 74; Israel's polygamy cases and, 81–84; Mormon polygamy cases and, 31–32, 59–65, 104–5, 270; *Romer v Evans* case over sexual orientation and, 109n.71; *Sarla Mudgal v Union of India* challenge to, 112–16. *See also* Article 44 (Indian Constitution); citizenship

"essentials of religion" test: in Indian Supreme Court, 97–101; problems following judicial invocation of, 274–76

establishment Church model, 27

Establishment Clause (First Amendment): assimilative aspiration embodied in, 74;